Social History of the
United States

Titles in ABC-CLIO's
Social History of the United States

Social History of the United States
The 1960s

Troy D. Paino

Series Editors
Daniel J. Walkowitz and Daniel E. Bender

A B C CLIO

Santa Barbara, California   Denver, Colorado   Oxford, England

Library of Congress Cataloging-in-Publication Data

Paino, Troy D. (Troy Dale)
  Social history of the United States : the 1960s / Troy D. Paino.
    p.   cm.—(Social history of the United States)
  Includes bibliographical references and index.
  ISBN 978-1-85109-915-3 (alk. paper) — ISBN 978-1-59884-127-5 (set)
  EISBN 978-1-85109-916-0 (ebook)
  1. United States—Social conditions—1960-1980.   I. Title.
  HN59.P35   2009
  306.0973'09046—dc22   2008006466

12 11 10 09   1 2 3 4 5

Senior Production Editor: Vicki Moran
Production Manager: Don Schmidt
Media Editor: Ellen Rasmussen
Media Resources Manager: Caroline Price
File Management Coordinator: Paula Gerard

This book is also available on the World Wide Web as an eBook.
Visit www.abc-clio.com for details.

ABC-CLIO, Inc.
130 Cremona Drive, P.O. Box 1911
Santa Barbara, California 93116–1911

This book is printed on acid-free paper ∞
Manufactured in the United States of America

Contents

Contents

Series Introduction

Ordinary people make history. They do so in ways that are different from the ways presidents, generals, business moguls, or celebrities make history; nevertheless, the history of ordinary people is just as profound, just as enduring. Immigration in the early decades of the 20th century was more than numbers and government policy; it was a collective experience of millions of men, women, and children whose political beliefs, vernacular cultural expression, discontent, and dreams transformed the United States. Likewise, during the Great Depression of the 1930s, President Franklin Delano Roosevelt advanced a broad spectrum of new social policies, but as historians have argued, ordinary Americans "made" the New Deal at the workplace, at the ballot box, on the picket lines, and on the city streets. They engaged in new types of consumer behavior, shifted political allegiances, and joined new, more aggressive trade unions. World War II and the Cold War were more than diplomatic maneuvering and military strategy; social upheavals changed the employment patterns, family relations, and daily life of ordinary people. More recently, the rise of the Christian Right in the last few decades is the expression of changing demographics and emerging social movements, not merely the efforts of a few distinct leaders.

These examples, which are drawn directly from the volumes in this series, highlight some of the essential themes of social history. Social history shifts the historical focus away from the famous and the political or economic elite to issues of everyday life. It explores the experiences ordinary Americans—native-born and immigrant, poor and rich, employed and unemployed, men and women, white and black—at home, at work, and at play. In the process, it focuses new attention on the significance of social movements, the behavior and meanings of consumerism, and the changing expression of popular culture.

In many ways, social history is not new. American historians early in the 20th century appreciated the importance of labor, immigration, religion, and urbanization in the study of society. However, early studies shared with political history the emphasis on leaders and major institutions and described a history that was mostly white and male—in other words, a history of those who held power. Several cultural shifts combined to transform how social history was understood and written in the last half of the 20th century: the democratization of higher education after World War II with the GI Bill and the expansion of public and land grant universities; the entry of women, children of immigrants, and racial minorities into the universities and the ranks of historians; and the social movements of the 1960s. Historians created new subjects for social history, casting it as "from the bottom." They realized that much was missing from familiar narratives that stressed the significance of "great men"—presidents, industrialists, and other usually white, usually male notables. Instead, women, working people, and ethnic and racial minorities have become integral parts of the American story along with work, leisure, and social movements.

The result has not simply been additive: ordinary people made history. The story of historical change is located in their lives and their struggles with and against others in power. Historians began to transform the central narrative of American history. They realized that—in the words of a popular 1930s folk cantata, "Ballad for Americans"—the "'etceteras' and the 'and so forths' that do the work" have a role in shaping their own lives, in transforming politics, and in recreating economics. Older themes of study, from industrialization to imperial expansion, from party politics to urbanization, were revisited through the inclusion of new actors, agents, and voices. These took their place alongside such new topics as social movements, popular culture, consumption, and community. But social history remains socially engaged scholarship; contemporary social issues continue to shape social historians' research and thinking. Historians in the 1970s and 1980s who focused on the experiences of working people, for instance, were challenged by the reality of deindustrialization. Likewise, historians in the 1990s who focused on popular culture and consumer behavior were influenced by the explosion of consumerism and new forms of cultural expression. Today's historians explore the antecedents to contemporary globalization as well as the roots of conservatism.

The transformation of the questions and agendas of each new era has made it apparent to historians that the boundaries of historical inquiry are not discrete. Social history, therefore, engages with other kinds of history. Social history reinterprets older narratives of politics and political economy and overlaps both areas. Social historians argue that politics is not restricted to ballot boxes or legislatures; politics is broad popular engagement with ideas about material wealth, social justice, moral values, and civil and human rights. Social historians, naturally, remain interested in changing political affiliations. They have, for example, examined the changing political allegiances of African Americans during the 1930s and the civil rights movement of the 1960s. So too have they examined the relationship of socialist and communist parties to working-class and immigrant communities. At the same time, social historians measure change by looking at such issues as family structure, popular culture, and consumer behavior.

For the social historian, the economy extends far beyond statistical data about production, gross domestic product, or employment. Rather, the economy is a lived experience. Wealthy or poor, Americans have negotiated the changing reality of economic life. Social historians ask questions about how different groups of Americans experienced and resisted major economic transformations and how they have grappled with economic uncertainty. The Great Depression of the 1930s, for example, left both urban workers and rural farmers perilously close to starvation. During the 1970s and 1980s, factories in the Rust Belt of the Midwest and Northeast shuttered or moved, and many Americans began laboring in new parts of the country and working new kinds of jobs, especially in the service sector. Americans have also grappled with the unequal distribution of wealth; some people advanced new ideas and engaged with emerging ideologies that challenged economic injustice, but others jealously guarded their privilege.

As social history has broadened its purview, it has transformed our sense of how historical change occurs. Social history changes our conception of chronology; change does not correspond to presidential election cycles. Social history also changes how we understand sources of power; power is constituted in and challenged by diverse peoples with different resources. Social historians, then, look at the long history of the 20th century in the United States and examine how the terrain has shifted under our feet, sometimes slowly and sometimes dramatically and abruptly. Social historians measure change in complex ways, including but also transcending demographic and geographic expansion and political transformation. How, for example, did the institution of the family change in the face of successive waves of immigration that often left spouses and children separated by national borders and oceans? Or during years of war with rising rates of women's wage and salary employment? Or following moralist reaction that celebrated imagined traditional values, and social movements that focused on issues of sexuality, birth control, homosexuality, and liberation? Historical change can also be measured by engagement with popular culture as Americans shifted their attention from vaudeville and pulp novels to radio, silent films, talkies, television, and finally the Internet and video games. The volumes in this series, divided by decades, trace all these changes.

To make sense of this complex and broadened field of inquiry, social historians often talk about how the categories by which we understand the past have been "invented," "contested," and "constructed." The nation has generally been divided along lines of race, class, gender, sexuality, and ethnicity. However, historians have also realized that analysts—whether in public or professional discourse—define these "categories of analysis" in different ways at different moments. Waves of immigration have reconfigured understandings of race and ethnicity, and more recent social movements have challenged the meanings of gender. Similarly, to be working class at the dawn of the age of industry in the 1900s meant something very different from being working class in the post-industrial landscape of the 1990s. How women or African Americans—to cite only two groups—understand their own identity can mean something different than how white men categorize them. Social historians, therefore, trace how Americans have always been divided about the direction of their lives and their nation, how they have consistently challenged and rethought social and cultural values and sought to renegotiate relationships of power, whether in the family, the workplace, the university, or the military. Actors do this armed with differing forms of power to authorize their view.

To examine these contestations, social historians have explored the way Americans articulated and defended numerous identities—as immigrants, citizens, workers, Christians, or feminists, for example. A post–World War II male chemical worker may have thought of himself as a worker and trade unionist at the factory, a veteran and a Democrat in his civic community, a husband and father at home, and as a white, middle-class homeowner. A female civil rights worker in the South in the 1960s may have seen herself as an African American when in the midst of a protest march or when refused service in a restaurant, as working class during a day job as a domestic worker or nurse, and as a woman when struggling to claim a leadership role in an activist organization.

Social historians have revisited older sources and mined rich new veins of information on the daily lives of ordinary people. Social historians engage with a host of materials—from government documents to census reports, from literature to oral histories, and from autobiographies to immigrant and foreign-language newspapers—to illuminate the lives, ideas, and activities of those who have been hidden from history. Social historians have also brought a broad "toolbox" of new methodologies to shed light on these sources. These methodologies are well represented in this series and illustrate the innovations of history from the bottom up. These volumes offer many tables and charts, which demonstrate the ways historians have made creative use of statistical analysis. Furthermore, the volumes are rich in illustrations as examples of the new ways that social historians "read" such images as cartoons or photographs.

The volumes in this series reflect the new subject matter, debates, and methodologies that have composed the writing of the United States' 20th-century social history. The volumes have unique features that make them particularly valuable for students and teachers; they are hybrids that combine the narrative advantages of the monograph with the specific focus of the encyclopedia. Each volume has been authored or co-authored by established social historians. Where the work has been collaborative, the authors have shared the writing and worked to sustain a narrative voice and conceptual flow in the volume. Authors have written the social history for the decade of their expertise and most have also taught its history. Each volume begins with a volume introduction by the author or authors that lays out the major themes of the decade and the big picture—how the social changes of the era transformed the lives of Americans. The author then synthesizes the best and most path-breaking new works in social history. In the case of the last three volumes, which cover the post-1970 era, scholarship remains in its relative infancy. In particular, these three volumes are major original efforts to both define the field and draw upon the considerable body of original research that has already been completed.

The ten volumes in the series divide the century by its decades. This is an avowedly neutral principle of organization that does not privilege economic, political, or cultural transformations; this allows readers to develop their own sense of a moment and their own sense of change. While it remains to be seen how the most recent decades will be taught and studied, in cases such as the 1920s, the 1930s, and the 1960s, this decadal organization replicates how historians frequently study and teach history. The Progressive Era (ca. 1890–1920) and postwar America (ca. 1945–1960) have less often been divided by decades. This highlights the neutrality of this division. In truth, all divisions are imposed: we speak of long decades or short centuries, and so forth. When historians teach the 1960s, they often reach back into the 1950s and ahead into the 1970s. The authors and editors of these volumes recognize that social processes, movements, ideas, and leaders do not rise and fall with the turn of the calendar; therefore, they have worked to knit the volumes together as a unit.

Readers can examine these texts individually or collectively. The texts can be used to provide information on significant events or individuals. They can provide an overview of a pivotal decade. At the same time, these texts are designed to allow readers to follow changing themes over time and to develop their own sense of chronology. The authors regularly spoke with one another and with the series editors to establish the major themes and subthemes in the social history of the century and to sustain story lines across the volumes. Each volume divides the material into six or seven chapters that discuss major themes such as labor or work; urban, suburban, and rural life; private life; politics; economy; culture; and social movements. Each chapter begins with an overview essay and then explores four to six major topics. The discrete essays at the heart of each volume give readers focus on a social movement, a social idea, a case study, a social institution, and so forth. Unlike traditional encyclopedias, however, the narrative coherence of the single-authored text permits authors to break the decade bubble with discussions on the background or effects of a social event.

There are several other features that distinguish this series.

- Many chapters include capsules on major debates in the social history of the era. Even as social historians strive to build on the best scholarship available, social history remains incomplete and contested; readers can benefit from studying this tension.

- The arguments in these volumes are supported by many tables and graphics. Social history has mobilized demographic evidence and—like its sister field, cultural history—has increasingly turned to visual evidence, both for the social history of media and culture and as evidence of social conditions. These materials are not presented simply as illustrations but as social evidence to be studied.

- Timelines at the head of every chapter highlight for readers all the major events and moments in the social history that follows.

- A series of biographical sketches at the end of every chapter highlights the lives of major figures more often overlooked in histories of the era. Readers can find ample biographical material on more prominent figures in other sources; here the authors have targeted lesser known but no less interesting and important subjects.

- Bibliographies include references to electronic sources and guide readers to material for further study.

- Three indices—one for each volume, one for the entire series, and one for all the people and events in the series—are provided in each volume. Readers can easily follow any of the major themes across the volumes.

Finally, we end with thanks for the supportive assistance of Ron Boehm and Kristin Gibson at ABC-CLIO, and especially to Dr. Alex Mikaberidze and Dr. Kim Kennedy White, who helped edit the manuscripts for the press. But of course, these volumes are the product of the extraordinary group of historians to whom we are particularly indebted:

The 1900s: Brian Greenberg and Linda S. Watts
The 1910s: Gordon Reavley
The 1920s: Linda S. Watts, Alice L. George, and Scott Beekman
The 1930s: Cecelia Bucki
The 1940s: Mark Ciabattari
The 1950s: John C. Stoner and Alice L. George
The 1960s: Troy D. Paino
The 1970s: Laurie Mercier
The 1980s: Peter C. Holloran and Andrew Hunt
The 1990s: Nancy Cohen

Daniel J. Walkowitz, Series Editor
Daniel E. Bender, Series Associate Editor

Volume Introduction

The social history of the 1960s is a story of grassroots movements that dramatically changed the social, cultural, and political landscape of the United States. As the civil rights movement marched toward its climax and the United States rapidly increased its involvement in the Vietnam War by mid-decade, Americans began taking to the streets and expressing their views in the public domain on a number of divisive issues. The 1960s witnessed the forces of social change aggressively challenge authority, tradition, and the status quo.

Although social change rarely occurs abruptly, the 1960s marked a decade when American society transformed into something quite different than it looked a decade earlier. Beginning with the idealism of the civil rights movement, the decade ended with the disillusionment of the Vietnam War. In between a variety of social movements began, gained momentum, and turned radical in an effort to change American values, politics, and economic order. These movements created a strong group consciousness among African Americans, students, women, homosexuals, the poor, and other minorities. The fight for civil rights and against the Vietnam War, poverty, environmental degradation, racism, sexism, and all forms of discrimination challenged the moral values of American society. These voices of social dissent caused a great strain on American institutions and caused a conservative backlash by decade's end. Not surprisingly, traditional values would not go down without a fight. By the dawn of the 1970s, faith in American liberalism, the belief that a pluralistic society would ultimately work its way toward social unity, seemed discredited.

Since the Supreme Court announced its decision in the case of *Brown v. Board of Education of Topeka* in 1954, African American activists had effectively mobilized and brought the plight of African Americans to the attention of the media and the world. The *Brown* decision was the culmination of decades of struggle in the courts by opponents of school segregation, particularly lawyers working for the National Association for the Advancement of Colored People (NAACP). In 1896, the Supreme Court announced its decision in *Plessy v. Ferguson* that communities could provide African Americans with separate facilities as long as those facilities were equal to those of whites. The *Brown* decision reversed *Plessy* by concluding that school segregation inflicted unacceptable psychological and social damage to African American children regardless of the relative quality of the separate schools. Writing for the majority on the court, Chief Justice Earl Warren wrote: "separate educational facilities are inherently unequal." The decision emboldened civil rights activists eager for allies in high places; the *Brown* decision indicated that they had one in the highest court in the land. For the next decade African Americans set out on a grassroots campaign of civil disobedience in an effort to desegregate the South and secure African American voting rights.

The successes of the civil rights movement early in the decade inspired the wave of social movements that followed. Nearing the 100-year anniversary of the Emancipation Proclamation signed by Abraham Lincoln, civil rights activists in 1961 eagerly awaited President John F. Kennedy's presidency. African Americans had grown impatient with the cautious approach of the Eisenhower administration. Many believed that John F. Kennedy would throw the weight of the Executive Branch behind their fight for equal rights. It did not take long for activists to realize that President Kennedy, worried about alienating southern Democratic voters and politicians, would also move slowly to end segregation. Instead of discouraging the movement, this realization helped mobilize activists and signaled the beginning of a more aggressive stage of the movement. Sit-ins, marches, voter registration campaigns, and commitment to nonviolent demonstrations in the face of aggressive and violent law enforcement helped bring international attention to the plight of African Americans and forced President Kennedy, President Lyndon B. Johnson, and Congress to act.

Despite the passage of the 1964 Civil Rights Act and the 1965 Voting Rights Act, young African Americans became disillusioned that federal legislation alone would not improve their economic and educational prospects. As a result, from 1965 to 1969 the movement became increasingly oppositional and violent. Race riots, Black Nationalism, and a call for "Black Power" signaled a departure from the reformist approach of Martin Luther King Jr. The assassinations of Malcolm X in 1965 and King in 1968 reinforced the view of young radicals like Stokely Carmichael, Huey Newton, Bobby Seale, and Angela Davis that the white power structure would not permit or tolerate African American equality. Instead, they thought African Americans' hopes rested in a true revolution where African Americans could determine their own destiny free of white influence. Rather than working within the existing political, social, and economic system, these revolutionaries militantly advocated for independence, power, and self-help. This more radical approach to social change mirrored the mounting revolutionary zeal of the late 1960s' antiwar movement.

The Vietnam War helped fan the flames of radicalism throughout American society. As poor African American men were drafted at disproportionately high rates and African American soldiers suffered much higher death rates than their white counterparts, Black Power activists cynically surmised that the military and government used the war as a way to kill the African American man and destroy African American communities. As a result, African American activists joined, in some cases reluctantly, the antiwar movement. Although the white middle-class students attracted to the ideology of the New Left felt a natural affinity with the civil rights movement, African Americans did not completely trust joining a movement where they would once again be in the minority. By the time King publicly declared his opposition to the war in 1967, reformers and radicals alike believed the Vietnam War reflected and reinforced the social and economic inequalities between African Americans and whites, leaving them no choice but to get involved in the cause to end the war.

The rise of the New Left on university campuses throughout the country in the early 1960s had laid the foundation for the antiwar movement. The formation of the Students for a Democratic Society and its *Port Huron Statement* most famously expressed the sentiments of the student movement that challenged the existing systems of authority and called for a participatory democracy where individuals had a direct say in the fundamentally important questions of the day. By the time President Johnson started sending thousands of U.S. troops to Vietnam in 1965, the student movement was primed to challenge the justification for the war. As U.S. involvement continued to expand over the next three years, these students joined forces with pacifists and religious groups such as the Women's International League for Peace and Freedom and other loosely affiliated organizations to oppose the means and aims of U.S. policy and actions in Vietnam.

After President Johnson approved Operation Rolling Thunder, the U.S. military operation that began a direct assault on North Vietnam in 1965, antiwar activists staged "teach-ins" to begin the process of consciousness-raising among students inspired by the "sit-ins" of the civil rights movement. Throughout 1965, activists conducted marches and protests to build support for their call for peace. As the war stretched on and American forces appeared to be stuck in a quagmire with diminishing hopes for ultimate success, more and more young people participated in these demonstrations and resisted the draft. Some of the most extreme acts of protest included immolations. As the United States' tactics to win the war became increasingly depraved, more political and social leaders got into the act and started questioning the Johnson administration's assumptions and methods of conducting the war. By the time of the Tet Offensive in 1968, it had become clear that the war would be the major issue of the 1968 presidential campaign. The growing chorus of opposition to the war ultimately drove President Johnson out of the race and forced other candidates to commit to a plan to end the war.

The antiwar movement of the 1960s became almost indistinguishable from a more general cultural revolution. The post–World War II baby boom generation created a distinct youth culture around music, sex, drugs, and protest against American mainstream society. The Vietnam War disillusioned a generation (often referred to as the "counterculture") poised to inherit an economy, society, and political system they saw as corrupt and dehumanizing. Dropping out of such a society became an attractive alternative for many young people facing the prospects of a military draft, a protracted war, and a soulless corporate economy.

The counterculture ran both parallel to and divergent from the grassroots political movements of the decade. Amid the growing social turmoil of the sixties, a conspicuous segment of America's middle-class white youth began to reject the dominant institutions and social values of their parents' generation. As historian David Chalmers has written, "they took delight in scandalizing its morality and in dreaming up new ways to do so" (Chalmers, 88). Like Tom Hayden's earlier call in the *Port Huron Statement* for student political dissent, the rise of the hippie between 1967 and 1969 signaled this generation's cultural dissent to dominant American society. Though its definition remained vague, the term *hippie* derived from the word "hipster" and applied to those young people of the sixties who rebelled against the conformity, materialism, and competitiveness of modern American society. In this way, the rise of the counterculture is explained both as a generational phenomenon, that is the reaction of the baby boom generation to the social mores of their parents' generation, and as an expression of social alienation and political revolt against the rationality, technology, and war of an industrial age. It was the excesses of the counterculture movement that caused an emotional and spirited political reaction from conservatives that, in addition to the faltering war in Vietnam, paved the way for Richard Nixon's presidential election in 1968.

The very public display by Yippies outside the 1968 Democratic National Convention in Chicago caused a backlash against antiwar protesters, the counterculture, and the Democratic Party. Yippies, slang for the Youth International Party, were a small group of political activists who used theatre of the absurd to make their point. In the wake of this display, a small majority of the electorate embraced Nixon, the Republican nominee, and his call for "law and order." Nixon and third-party candidate Gov. George Wallace of Alabama tapped into a growing hostility toward student protesters and social unrest. This rise of conservatism was a reaction not only to antiwar protests, but also to the civil rights movement and recent urban riots. The 1968 presidential election, between Nixon and Democratic Party nominee Hubert H. Humphrey of Minnesota, represented the growing polarization of American society over the Vietnam War and other divisive issues. Nixon appealed to a "Silent Majority" of working and middle-class Americans tired of antiwar and civil rights activists challenging authority and tradition. This conservative reaction essentially put an end to the liberalism of the Kennedy and Johnson administrations, which believed governmental programs could help solve some of the worst social problems.

Prior to the distraction of the Vietnam War, President Johnson's administration represented the apex of 1960s liberalism with its Great Society legislative agenda that relied on expanded governmental programs and agencies to attack a variety of social problems, including poverty. Michael Harrington's *The Other America* (1962) brought national attention to the systemic challenges facing the underclass of American society. By introducing his readers to the cycle of poverty, Harrington helped ignite both a political and social response to the problem. The problem was most acute in the geographical extremes: the inner cities and isolated rural areas. In the wake of postwar African American migration to northern cities, a large segment of the African American population found themselves confronting the loss of manufacturing jobs due to increased automation, business consolidation, and white flight to the suburbs. Feeling abandoned in decaying inner cities, African Americans took to the streets in several major American city riots between 1965 and 1967. Similarly, those living in the isolation of rural America like the Appalachian Mountains were dependent on the uncertainty of the business cycles of industries like coal mining. Being unskilled, undereducated, and cyclically unemployed led to feelings of hopelessness for hundreds of thousands of rural Americans. President Johnson's War on Poverty and Community Action Programs attempted to respond, but the Vietnam War drained these initiatives of both political and financial resources.

Taking President Johnson's call for maximum participation seriously, welfare rights activists formed organizations like the National Welfare Rights Organization, which advocated for an adequate income as a basic civil right. Demanding dignity for the poor, welfare rights activists believed the government owed every citizen a chance to participate fully in a market that increasingly determined the value of citizenship on the ability to consume. Unfortunately for the antipoverty movement, this position of money for nothing played into the hands of conservatives who exploited middle-class fears of welfare entitlement.

If the antiwar, counterculture, and antipoverty movements did not give conservatives enough to fear, they also had to confront the rise of the gay liberation and women's movements. The modern feminist movement began in the 1960s, fueled by the popularity of Betty Friedan's *The Feminine Mystique* (1963). A growing network of women activists began meeting in the early to mid-1960s at the state and national level to discuss the problem of sex discrimination, particularly in the workplace. This network served as the impetus for the formation of the National Organization of Women (NOW), the organizational base for the mainstream feminist movement for the remainder of the century. NOW concerned itself mostly with the public life of American women, but by the end of the decade a more radical women's movement emerged that focused on the private lives of women. Organizations like the New York Radical Women and the Red-stockings began challenging the traditional cultural definitions of women that assumed a dependency on men. Committed to starting a revolution, these radical women began to challenge everything about the male-dominated culture. In some cases, these challenges included the rejection of heterosexual relationships that some believed inherently placed women in a male-dependent state.

The rise of radical feminism coincided with the rise of the gay rights movement at the end of the decade. Although an underground homosexual social network and a few organizations existed to support the interests of this marginalized segment of society, the gay rights movement did not really come out of the closet, so to speak, until after the Stonewall riot of 1969. This act of police brutality at a gay club in New York City served to galvanize the movement behind a call for gay pride and gay liberation that found its voice in the proliferation of gay rights organizations in the 1970s.

The variety of social movements in the 1960s caused a balkanization of American society as people increasingly saw themselves as part of a special-interest group. Race, gender, sexuality, and age played a more prominent role in the political landscape. The reasons for this splintering of American society are many. One reason was that American society continued to become more diverse as the twentieth century progressed. Minority populations reached a critical mass and began organizing around interests unique to their status. Ethnic identity, for example, became another way for individuals to characterize their community, politics, and culture. Heretofore invisible to many, American Indians, Asian Americans, and particularly Mexican Americans began to organize and express their resistance to white dominant culture. Even Americans from European descent reconnected with their ethnic identity and made it a source of pride, political activism, and social engagement.

The liberalism of the 1960s alongside the rise of alternative cultures and oppositional social movements also contributed to the rise of the modern environmental movement. Although only the beginning of what became one of the most significant movements of the late twentieth century, opinions on the value and effects of science, technology, and industry on the environment became almost as intense as the battles over race, war, gender, and sexuality. Environmental scientists, conservationists, and preservationists opposed the unbridled enthusiasm for postwar technological and scientific progress that to them clearly interfered with the natural order of things. Living under the cloud of the Cold War and threat of nuclear annihilation reminded people that scientific innovation could sometimes lead to undesirable results. The publication of Rachel Carson's *Silent Spring* (1962), a chilling analysis of the effect of pesticides on the food chain, helped launch America's modern environmental movement, a reaction to this era of technology and consumerism. New scientific research also revealed the harmful effects of chlorofluorocarbons and other fossil fuel by-products on the ozone layer of the earth's atmosphere. By the end of the decade environmentalism had become a mass movement best represented by the success of the first Earth Day in 1970.

Despite the social unrest of the 1960s, at the end of the decade the vast majority of conservatives like the majority of Americans still supported the Vietnam War and a limited role of government in guaranteeing equal rights and opposed the mores and behaviors of the counterculture, radical feminists, and minority rights activists. As students, African Americans, women, gays, Chicanos, and Indians entered the public sphere to advocate for a more inclusive society, the seeds of the New Right were being planted as both population and cultural influence began to flow from the north and east to the south and west. By the end of the 1960s, the south and southwest had already begun to redefine the national culture. The battle over civil rights during the 1950s and 1960s drove the traditionally white Democratic south into the conservative wing of the Republican Party. George Wallace's third-party candidacy for president in 1968 symbolized this political, social, and cultural shift through his use of a populist rhetoric that made racial conservatism acceptable to both blue-collar Democrats and rural southerners.

Between the extremes of 1960s American society stood a lot of Americans with conflicted feelings about civil rights, the Vietnam War, corporate wealth and power, the role of government in eradicating poverty, the counterculture, the rise of identity politics, and scientific and technological advancements. While race, ethnicity, class, and gender sometimes influenced one's view on a particular topic, they were not always the determining factor. Age, religion, family, and geography also played a big role in one's view on a particular topic. People could ebb and flow between the polarities depending on what influence took priority on that issue and at that time.

Historian Mark Hamilton Lytle in *America's Uncivil Wars* (2006) argues that America's social, political, and economic elite of the 1950s, an almost exclusively white and male, Protestant, middle- and upper-middle-class, and socially and culturally conservative group, controlled business organizations, media, churches, colleges and universities, and government at both the local and national level. As this nation's aristocracy, this elite worked hard to preserve the country's traditions, ensure social cohesion, and arbitrate the critical issues of the day. Lytle contends that as American society became increasingly diverse as the twentieth century progressed, this elite could no longer represent the major elements of that society and lost its ability to arbitrate the critically important questions of the day. In Lytle's words, "the elite was inadequately inclusive to address the aspirations of a more socially diverse population" (Lytle, 6). African Americans, Latinos, gays, women, the poor, and other minority groups found the path into this elite blocked. The 1960s signaled the decade when these groups, following the example of the civil rights movement, hit a critical mass and began to work actively and publicly to pave the way for a more inclusive and diverse determination of social and cultural mores. The harder these groups worked for inclusion, however, the harder the old arbiters of tradition, social cohesion, and cultural mores attempted to preserve their power and authority through social institutions and Cold War consensus.

The social polarities and unrest of the 1960s revealed that the social, cultural, and political restlessness that existed beneath the placid surface of the 1950s had boiled to the top. As a result, the 1960s emerged as one of the most turbulent eras of the twentieth century. The buoyant optimism of the civil rights movement and America's postwar military prowess contributed to a bold and confident effort by the nation's political leaders and popular movements to tackle the major social and global problems of the day. By decade's end, however, this optimism had been replaced by a growing anxiety, cynicism, and even hostility over the social, economic, political, and military state of affairs. The hope of American liberalism was eclipsed by a growing frustration that a nation mired in an intractable war could not live up to its hopes and promises.

Through it all and despite the primitivism and communal utopianism of the counterculture, consumerism as a value and lifestyle persisted and expanded. As they did in the 1950s and continued to do in the 1970s, Americans in the 1960s embraced the notion that individual self-identity is derived from the consumption of goods and services. The New Left and counterculture rebels of the 1960s failed to appreciate the power and flexibility of modern capitalism that ultimately absorbed, produced, and sold for a profit the symbols of their values and ideas in the marketplace. For all of its social unrest, Americans at the end of the decade still believed in the economic and material solutions to social problems. For some, the 1960s was the decade in which shopping became Americans' secular religion with the invention of the suburban shopping mall. As the television became a staple of almost every household in America, the preoccupation with consumerism also invaded people's private lives like never before. The possession of homes, cars, appliances, clothes, vacations, and the like, not only became desirable, but an end in itself that defined self-identity and trumped spiritual fulfillment. In fact, some critics have gone so far as to say that the distinct but simultaneous rise of the counterculture and business culture produced a "carnival culture" in which "hip" sells. The convergence of the consumer culture with the counterculture essentially eliminated "high" culture from the public domain. With the triumph of the electronic media that catered to popular tastes and gratifications, mass culture dominated highbrow art. As 1960s cultural critic Marshall McLuhan pointed out in *Understanding Media* (1964), the medium became the message. What mattered was not the content, but rather the experience of seeing images. In this context, the 1960s could also be identified as a time when entertainment, an important part of the consumer culture, became a big part of Americans' lives. Sports, movies, television, and music began to dominate the public and private lives of most Americans.

In consumerism, Americans in the 1960s unintentionally discovered consensus. Granted, it was not the consensus that either side of the sixties' social and cultural wars had bargained for, but it was the one American capitalism produced. Both sides found plenty to dislike about the preeminence of consumerism in an electronic age, but both sides also discovered something to like. For the elites came the ultimate rejection of Marxist ideology by the New Left and threats of class warfare. More to the point, a lot of money was to be made by the production and steady consumption of goods and services. But the victory of American capitalism in the age of mass media also came at a cost for the social and cultural elites. It opened the door to those young baby boom activists in the New Left, counterculture, and women's and minority rights movements to influence the nation's social and cultural mores. In the end, the marketplace proved relatively receptive to the democratic impulses of the 1960s, creating a more inclusive and diverse American society. However, this inclusion did not mean equality as marginalized and underrepresented groups continued to fight for their economic and civil rights in a more contentious, less civil society.

References and Further Readings

Carson, Rachel. 1962. *Silent Spring*. Boston: Houghton Mifflin.

Chalmers, David. 1991. *And the Crooked Places Made Straight: The Struggle for Social Change in the 1960s*. 2nd ed. Baltimore: Johns Hopkins University Press.

Cohen, Lizabeth. 2003. *A Consumer's Republic*. New York: Alfred A. Knopf.

Fischer, Klaus P. 2006. *America in White, Black, and Gray: The Stormy 1960s*. New York: Continuum.

Friedan, Betty. 1963. *The Feminine Mystique*. New York: W. W. Norton.

Harrington, Michael. 1962. *The Other America*. New York: Touchstone.

Heath, Joseph, and Andrew Potter. 2004. *Nation of Rebels: Why Counterculture Became Consumer Culture*. New York: HarperCollins.

Lytle, Mark Hamilton. 2006. *America's Uncivil Wars: The Sixties Era from Elvis to the Fall of Richard Nixon*. New York: Oxford University Press.

McLuhan, Marshall. 1964. *Understanding Media: The Extension of Man*. New York: McGraw-Hill.

Issues of the 20th Century

The Civil Rights Movement

OVERVIEW

Buoyed by World War II–related advances, the symbolism of Jackie Robinson crossing the color line in 1947 to play Major League Baseball, and the Supreme Court's 1954 *Brown v. Board of Education of Topeka* decision that declared racial segregation of public schools unconstitutional, the civil rights movement found its stride in the mid-1950s. The clouds of protest had formed, offering the real hope of a revolution. Rosa Parks, a seamstress, in 1955 refused to give up her seat on a city bus to a white man and ignited a citywide boycott of the bus system in Montgomery, Alabama. For 381 days members of a united African American community formed car pools or walked to work, almost bankrupting the bus company and causing a severe loss in business to downtown stores. In November 1956 the Supreme Court ruled that bus segregation was unconstitutional, causing the city to finally relent. Significant for the effectiveness of its nonviolent direct protest, the Montgomery boycott also catapulted Martin Luther King Jr. to national prominence. In 1957, King and other southern African American clergy formed the Southern Christian Leadership Conference (SCLC) to join the National Association for the Advancement of Colored People (NAACP) and Congress of Racial Equality (CORE) as central advocacy groups for racial justice.

Trying to steer a course between calls for reform and resistance, President Dwight Eisenhower signed the 1957 Civil Rights Act into law. The product of a series of compromises, the mild bill authorized the Justice Department to seek injunctions against interference with the right to vote. The law ignored the issue of segregation and barely reduced the resistance by Southern election officials to African Americans voting or the acts of intimidation by white vigilante groups. Still, it was the first federal civil rights law since Reconstruction and offered African American activists a bit more hope for future progress.

But 1955 to 1959 also reminded African Americans that the obstacles to equality were formidable. For every victory African Americans achieved, white Southerners resisted with a vengeance. Whether with the murder of Emmett Till or the resistance to integration at Little Rock, Arkansas's Central High School, African Americans were reminded that equality would not be achieved without a cost. At the dawn of the 1960s, those involved in the civil rights movement shared feelings of hope, determination, impatience, frustration, and anger. These feelings fueled a more intense stage of the civil rights movement. This intensity brought the movement its greatest victories but also, by the end of the decade, its greatest disappointment and outrage.

The civil rights movement of the 1960s began on February 1, 1960, when four African American first-year students from North Carolina Agricultural and Technical College staged a sit-in at a Woolworth's "whites only" lunch counter in Greensboro. Refused service, the students returned the next day with more African American students and a few white ones. Well dressed and respectful, the students attracted crowds, both hostile and supportive, outside the store. Before long the daily sit-ins garnered national media attention and sparked similar protests throughout the South and sympathy demonstrations in the north. By the end of the year, thousands had taken part in this wave of spontaneous protests that inspired the formation of the Student Nonviolent Coordinating Committee (SNCC). The sit-ins and the formation of SNCC produced a broadening confrontation with Southern segregation and a growing involvement of young people in the nonviolent civil rights movement.

The influx of young activists energized the movement and strengthened existing organizations like Martin Luther King's SCLC and CORE. Bound together by their commitment to Christian nonviolence and a strong sense of African American community, these organizations worked together to bring the civil rights movement to the streets. Protests like the 1961 Freedom Riders, the 1963 confrontation with Police Commissioner "Bull" Connor in Birmingham, Alabama, followed by the March on Washington, and the 1964 Mississippi Freedom Summer brought international attention to the plight of African Americans, particularly those living in the segregated South, and helped pressure politicians to pass the Civil Rights Act of 1964 and Voting Rights Act of 1965.

From 1955 to 1965 the civil rights movement, employing boycotts, sit-ins, demonstrations, marches, and massive voting registrations made a serious dent in legal segregation and disfranchisement. By 1966, however, the civil rights movement was breaking up. Urban riots in the North signaled a troubling new phase in the struggle that went beyond the civil rights experience. In 1966 James Meredith, who had been the first African American admitted to the University of

Mississippi, was shot just inside Mississippi's state line during his solitary "victory over fear" march. Civil rights activists hurried to Mississippi to take Meredith's place. Young activists like Stokely Carmichael and Floyd McKissick, who just six years ago helped catapult the civil rights movement toward its greatest successes, now took direct aim at the movement's underlying principle of non-violence. In Greenwood, Mississippi, Carmichael made a call for "Black Power" and McKissick declared that nonviolence had outlived its usefulness. Frustration and powerlessness had caused young revolutionaries to consider violence in self-defense and call for a new race consciousness centered on African American history, art, student organizations, and pride. The rise of Black Power fractured the civil rights movement's cohesiveness and alienated the leaders of SCLC, NAACP, and the Urban League. By the end of the decade the rise of the Black Panther Party, Revolutionary Action Movement, and the Republic of New Africa signaled the decline of the mainstream civil rights movement amid the social and political unrest of the Vietnam War.

TIMELINE

1960   The beginning of lunch-counter sit-ins at Greensboro, North Carolina, at a Woolworth lunch counter.

Founding of the Student Nonviolent Coordinating Committee (SNCC), April 15–17.

President Dwight D. Eisenhower signs the Voting Rights Act of 1960 on May 6, which authorizes the appointment of "voting referees" who can register African Americans in areas where racial discrimination has been proven.

Elijah Muhammad, leader of the Black Muslims, on July 31 calls for the establishment of an all–African American state, which becomes a rallying cry for new supporters of Black Nationalism.

Amid the angry objections of white parents, four African American children enroll in two all-white schools in New Orleans on November 14, marking the first move toward desegregation in a southern major industrial center.

1961   James Farmer of the Congress on Racial Equality organizes freedom rides in the South in an attempt to desegregate interstate travel.

On September 1, ten African American children in Atlanta, Georgia, peacefully desegregate four high schools.

On December 12–16, Martin Luther King Jr. launches an all-out attack against segregation and discrimination in Albany, Georgia.

1962   On September 30, U.S. Supreme Court Justice Hugo Black orders the admission of James Meredith to the University of Mississippi. Meredith, the first African American admitted to the university, faces a tragic riot upon his arrival which ultimately requires a federalized National Guard to restore order to the campus.

1963   Martin Luther King Jr. leads civil rights protests in Albany, Georgia, and Birmingham, Alabama, forcing President John F. Kennedy to propose civil rights legislation.

On June 11, two African American students are admitted to the University of Alabama after an unsuccessful attempt by Gov. George Wallace to block their admittance.

A sniper in Jackson, Mississippi, assassinates Medgar Evers, the NAACP field secretary, on June 12. The accused assailant is later acquitted by a hung jury.

On August 28, approximately 250,000 participate in the March on Washington and listen to, among others, Martin Luther King Jr., who gives his "I Have a Dream" speech.

On September 15, four young African American girls die in the bombing of the Sixteenth Street Baptist Church in Birmingham, Alabama.

1964   Malcolm X announces his withdrawal from the Nation of Islam on March 12.

Sidney Poitier becomes the first African American to win an Academy Award for Best Actor.

The Council of Federated Organizations (COFO) organizes Freedom Summer, aimed to register African Americans in Mississippi to vote.

The Civil Rights Act of 1964 is passed.

From July 18 to August 30, a number of racial disturbances occur throughout the United States, beginning with a Harlem riot that follows the shooting of an African American teenager by a white police officer.

On August 4, the bodies of three civil rights workers, James E. Cheney, Michael Schwerner, and Andrew Goodman, are discovered in a shallow grave outside of Philadelphia, Mississippi.

Martin Luther King Jr. earns the Nobel Peace Prize.

1965   King organizes the civil rights march from Selma to Montgomery (Project Alabama) to campaign for a federal voting rights law.

The Voting Rights Act of 1965 is passed.

Malcolm X is assassinated on February 21 in New York City.

A riot breaks out in Watts, a section of Los Angeles, on August 11, 1965. As with the riot in Harlem and other cities the previous year, a clash between African Americans and white police officers triggers the disturbance, which lasts for ten days. Thirty-four are killed, almost 900 injured, over 3,500 arrested, and $225 million in property damage result from the riot.

1966   Floyd McKissick, a militant African American civil rights leader from North Carolina, replaces James Farmer as director of CORE.

On January 10, the Georgia state legislature denies Julian Bond a seat after his election because of his stance against the Vietnam War.

James Meredith is shot during his one-man "victory over fear" march.

Stokely Carmichael, recently named head of SNCC, calls for "Black Power" during a protest in Greenwood, Mississippi.

The University of Kentucky plays Texas Western University, which has an all–African American starting five on its team, in the National Collegiate Athletic Association (NCAA) national basketball championship basketball game.

CORE endorses the "Black Power" concept. SNCC later adopts the slogan, but King's SCLC and NAACP disassociate themselves from the concept.

Huey Newton and Bobby Seale found the Black Panther Party in Oakland, California.

1967   Adam Clayton Powell is ousted as chairman of the House Education and Labor Committee and denied his seat in the U.S. House of Representatives.

On April 4, Martin Luther King Jr. announces his opposition to the Vietnam War.

Race riots in Detroit, New York City, Cleveland, Chicago, Atlanta, Newark, and other American cities mark the worst summer of racial disturbances in American history.

H. Rap Brown, a militant African American youth, is named the new chairman of SNCC.

Thurgood Marshall is the first African American justice appointed to the U.S. Supreme Court.

1968   The Kerner Commission reports that "white racism" is the principal cause of the 1967 urban disturbances.

Martin Luther King Jr. is assassinated outside of a motel in Memphis, Tennessee, on April 4.

President Lyndon Johnson signs the Fair Housing Act, prohibiting racial discrimination in the sale and rental of most housing units in the country.

On May 11, Ralph David Abernathy, successor to Martin Luther King Jr., leads the Poor People's March.

Harry Edwards organizes the Olympic Project for Human Rights.

Tommie Smith and John Carlos lose medals for their raised-fist "Black Power" protest at the Mexico City Olympic Games.

Shirley Chisholm becomes the first African American woman elected to the U.S. House of Representatives.

1969   On March 10, James Earl Ray is sentenced to 99 years in prison for the assassination of Martin Luther King Jr.

On August 19, the FBI arrests Bobby Seale for the torture-murder of Alex Rackly, a man allegedly disloyal to the Black Panthers who was burned to death on May 19 in New Haven, Connecticut.

On December 4 and 5, Black Panther leaders Mark Clark and Fred Hampton are killed in a police raid in Chicago, Illinois.

GROWING IMPATIENCE

In the 1960 presidential election, fewer than one in four African Americans living in the South could vote. From all indications, the Civil Rights Act of 1957 had done little to ensure the African American vote due to local and state laws and customs. Worse yet, six years after *Brown v. Board of Education* and 13 years after Jackie Robinson broke the Major League Baseball color barrier, Jim Crow was still the law of the land in the South. The color line still separated public services and transportation, restaurants, and, most disappointingly, schools. African American children continued to attend underfunded and dilapidated schools that were almost always segregated. Reflecting on this incredibly slow progress and unfulfilled promises, African Americans began to question past tactics of leading civil rights organizations, particularly the NAACP. African American activists became convinced that real change could not take place by working through the existing legal and political structure. For real change to occur, the movement had to take direct action to challenge the underpinnings of a legal and political system that sustained and institutionalized a discriminatory society. Never giving up hope, these activists looked for strategies that expressed their sense of urgency and anger.

The "Sit-In" Protests

Custom, tradition, statute, and local ordinances combined to create a racially segregated society in the South. Whether by custom or ordinance, African Americans in southern and border states could not sit alongside whites in restaurants and at lunch counters. Joseph McNeill, an African American student at North Carolina Agricultural and Technical College, on the night of January 31, 1960, went to get a bite to eat at the bus terminal in Greensboro, North Carolina. Told they "don't serve Negroes here," McNeill went back to his dormitory to recount the incident to his roommate, Ezell Blair Jr., and fellow freshmen Franklin McCain and David Richmond. The four often sat up late at night discussing the plight of African Americans in the South, particularly Greensboro. Like other African Americans, they had grown tired of the snail's-pace progress of the civil rights movement. Greensboro, like other southern cities, had used subterfuge and delay tactics to evade the *Brown* ruling, and the indignity of being denied a meal at the Greensboro bus station triggered the desire to act in these four young men.

After a long discussion, McNeill suggested going to "whites only" restaurants to sit until served. The initial target would be the local Woolworth store's lunch counter. The next afternoon the four North Carolina A&T freshmen walked into the downtown Greensboro five-and-dime store, bought some school supplies, and took a seat at the lunch counter to order coffee and doughnuts. The waitress gave them the anticipated reply: "I'm sorry, we don't serve colored in here." Blair spoke up and questioned her assertion while holding up the receipts of their purchases. He pointed out that he and his friends had in fact already been served at a counter only two feet from where they sat. The manager came and tried politely to convince the four to leave, but the young men were determined.

On February 1, 1960, four young African American college students walked into the Woolworth Company, sat down at a whites-only lunch counter, and triggered the civil rights movement that spread across the nation. Shown here on February 2, 1960, are (left to right) Joseph McNeill, Franklin McCain, Billy Smith, and Clarence Henderson. (Library of Congress)

A crowd started to gather, with some calling the protesters "dirty niggers." The four would not move. They remained seated until the store closed and vowed to repeat their demand the next day. A movement had started.

On February 2, 23 North Carolina A&T students and four African American women from Bennett College sat with Blair, McCain, McNeill, and Richmond at the Woolworth lunch counter. The next day 63 students joined the protest. By Thursday scores of sympathizers, some white, packed the Woolworth store and diner. So many showed up that several left Woolworth's and began to sit-in at the lunch counter in the S. H. Kress store down the street. On Friday more than 300 African Americans participated in the protest. Local officials knew that something had to be done.

The protests continued throughout the winter and into the spring. When the students refused to compromise, Greensboro merchants and officials started arresting students on trespass charges. This enraged the African American community of Greensboro, provoking a massive boycott of targeted variety stores. After profits dropped by one-third, Greensboro's white leaders relented and agreed African Americans could be served coffee at local lunch counters. African American students in Greensboro had discovered a tactic that worked. By April there were sit-ins in seventy-eight Southern and border communities with approximately 2,000 students arrested. By the fall of 1961 an estimated 70,000 African

Americans and whites had actively participated in the massive wave of sit-ins. Students participating in sit-ins forced businesses in several southern cities to desegregate eating facilities and restrooms. These gains spawned a new wave of nonviolent direct action: "kneel-ins" in churches, "sleep-ins" in motel lobbies, "swim-ins" in pools, "wade-ins" on restricted beaches, "read-ins" at public libraries, "play-ins" in parks, and "watch-ins" in movie theaters. These demonstrations transformed the use of public accommodations in the border and upper Southern states, where by the end of 1961 nearly 200 cities had begun to desegregate.

The students involved in these acts of protest were in elementary school at the time of the *Brown* decision. The slow pace of change in the wake of that decision had made this generation impatient and unreceptive to calls for gradualism. The *Brown* decision and subsequent acts of protest by their parents' generation caused them to expect both desegregation and the end of disenfranchisement by the time they graduated from high school. By 1960, however, not only did very few African American children attend integrated schools, fewer than one in four of voting age in the South could register and vote. This generation of African Americans expected more progress. The postwar increase in opportunities for African Americans had fueled hope that they would live in an America of racial equality. The massive resistance in the South had caused the progress toward enfranchisement and integration to nearly stop. African American college students could see reminders of their second-class citizenry all around them. By 1960 their patience had run out. The right to eat at lunch counters was not the point; these students used the lunch counter as a symbol of Jim Crow and chose ordering a cup of coffee as the means to challenge all varieties of segregation and discrimination (Sitkoff, 70–82).

1960 African American Vote

On Wednesday, October 19, 1960, Martin Luther King was arrested with 52 other African Americans in Rich's Department Store in Atlanta for refusing to leave a table in its Magnolia Room restaurant. On the following Monday, all other "sit-ins" arrested in this episode were released; King alone was held in jail and, worse, sentenced on a technicality to four months' hard labor at the state penitentiary. Notre Dame law professor Harris Wofford, an aide to the Kennedy presidential campaign, advised John Kennedy to call King's spouse, Coretta Scott King, to express his concern and support. Kennedy reacted impulsively and called Mrs. King on October 25, while on the campaign trail in Chicago. Mrs. King informed a few of her closest friends, and word of the call quickly spread. The next day Robert Kennedy went a step further and called the judge, asking for King's release from jail.

The decision to make these calls was not without political risk. Support for King could cause Kennedy to lose the Deep South and the election. The challenge for the campaign was to get the word out about the call among African American voters while minimizing the danger of a backlash among white voters. Toward that end, the campaign printed a pamphlet that highlighted Kennedy's call to Mrs. King for mass distribution in the African American churches of the nation on the last Sunday before the presidential election. They ran no newspaper ads or did anything else likely to filter into the white press. They created a "dummy committee" of preachers to protect the Kennedy campaign from being identified as sponsors of the pamphlet. The pamphlet was titled "'No Comment' Nixon Versus a Candidate with a Heart, Senator Kennedy." Nearly two million copies of the pamphlet were distributed in approximately 10,000 churches on Sunday, November 6.

Nationally, Kennedy received 34,221,463 votes to Nixon's 34,108,582, for a popular margin of two-tenths of 1 percent. Kennedy won Illinois by fewer than 5,000 votes. As legions of analysts sifted the results, it did not take them long to discover that the most startling component of Kennedy's victory was his 40 percent margin among African American voters. In 1956, African Americans had voted Republican by roughly 60–40; in 1960, they voted Democratic by roughly 70–30. This 30 percent shift accounted for more than Kennedy's victory margins in a number of key states, including Michigan, New Jersey, Pennsylvania, Illinois, and the Carolinas. This swing in African American voters is even more dramatic when viewed in light of the fact that Kennedy started the election year as the Democratic contender least popular among African Americans. In addition, Nixon's civil rights record was generally considered creditable. In the summer, Nixon had insisted upon a strong civil rights plank in the most visible dispute at the Republican Convention, whereas Kennedy angered African Americans by selecting a southerner, Lyndon Johnson, as his running mate.

King's arrest, Kennedy's call to Mrs. King, and the pamphlet circulated throughout a network of African American churches emerged as the most convincing explanation for the surprising shift in the African American vote. Most people in the country did not learn of the saga until after the election, but as word leaked out, the press started attributing President Kennedy's call to Mrs. King and Robert Kennedy's call to the Georgia judge asking for King's release as major factors in Kennedy's election.

Creation of the Student Nonviolent Coordinating Committee

The spirit and success of the sit-in movement in 1960 and 1961 proved to be contagious. Emboldened by concessions obtained from businesses in southern and border states, students started demanding a larger role in the civil rights movement. As soon as the sit-in movement spread, Ella Baker, executive director of the SCLC, convinced the SCLC to donate $800 to support a conference for youth leaders. She believed the SCLC and NAACP could benefit from the new impatience and aggressiveness of the students and therefore sought a structure and a direction for the student movement that would keep it free from adult supervision, yet disciplined enough to keep it active and nonviolent.

The Youth Leadership Meeting convened on April 15, 1960, in Raleigh, North Carolina. Martin Luther King Jr. spoke at the meeting and made three specific recommendations to the students: create a continuing organization to coordinate the student struggle; initiate a nationwide campaign of "selective buying" to punish segregated variety-store chains; and recruit an army of volunteers who will go to jail instead of paying bail or fines. Above all else, King preached his philosophy of nonviolence to the students, exhorting them to hold dear the values of reconciliation. While many students embraced King's message, others emphasized the need for direct action and rebuked the NAACP and SCLC for their seemingly interminable patience and lack of aggression.

After lengthy discussions, the students voted not to affiliate with the SCLC or any other group but to be an independent enterprise named the Temporary Student Nonviolent Coordinating Committee. They elected Marion Barry of Nashville as their chairman and agreed to establish their headquarters in Atlanta, Georgia. They adopted a Statement of Purpose that echoed Dr. King's rhetoric: "We affirm the philosophical or religious ideal of nonviolence as the foundation of our purpose . . . and the manner of our action." In October 1960, a plenary conference meeting in the Atlanta University Center dropped "temporary" from its name and made the Student Nonviolent Coordinating Committee (SNCC) a permanent organization. Convinced that civil disobedience provided the fastest and most effective route to desegregation, African American youth insisted that the focus of the struggle be nonviolent direct action in the street, not NAACP-style legal skirmishes in the courtroom. Equipped with an organization, purpose, and method, African American students in the early sixties were filled with optimism, enthusiasm, and a belief they could not be defeated in their cause.

The Freedom Riders

Other long-established civil rights organizations, such as CORE, discovered newfound enthusiasm in the wake of the student sit-in movement. Civil rights leaders started to see the benefit of direct action and confrontational politics. On March 13, 1961, James Farmer, CORE's new national director, issued a call for volunteers to conduct Freedom Rides through the South to test racial discrimination in interstate-travel terminals. Federal law had prohibited segregation in vehicles engaged in interstate travel since 1946, but the law was seldom enforced. CORE decided that it was time to provoke southern authorities and induce the Justice Department into enforcing federal law.

CORE modeled the 1961 Freedom Ride on the 1947 Journey of Reconciliation organized by Bayard Rustin and George Houser of CORE and the Fellowship of Reconciliation. Aimed to inspire African Americans to exercise the freedom they had just won in the 1946 Supreme Court case *Morgan v. Virginia,* eight African Americans and eight whites took part in the Journey of Reconciliation. They traveled on train and bus through fifteen southern cities and staged socio-dramas, acting out the roles of bus drivers, policemen, segregationists, and pro-testers. The journey started on April 9, 1947, and ended on April 20 with few arrests and little violence. Few Americans even heard of the Journey of Reconciliation, but in the age of television Farmer had far greater ambitions for the 1961 Freedom Rides.

Like the Journey of Reconciliation, CORE's Freedom Ride would include in-terracial groups traveling throughout the South to challenge segregation and to demonstrate the extent to which the South disobeyed the law. The Freedom Rides would start in Washington, D.C., and test Jim Crow in terminal restaurants, waiting rooms, and restrooms. The Journey of Reconciliation concentrated on the upper South, but the Freedom Rides would go to the Deep South where the color line was much more engrained into the fabric of society. The Freedom Riders pledged to go to jail instead of paying fines or making bail. Farmer hoped for not only publicity, but also for the South to realize the expense of main-taining a segregated society. As Farmer said, "Fill up the jails, as Gandhi did in India, fill them to bursting if we had to" to make the maintenance of segrega-tion as expensive as possible (Sitkoff, 99–100).

On May 4, 1961, seven African Americans and six whites, split into two in-terracial groups, left Washington, D.C., on a Greyhound and a Trailways bus. The African American Freedom Riders primarily came from the ranks of the stu-dent sit-in movement, and the white riders came from socialist and peace orga-nizations. It did not take long for segregationists to take the bait and greet the riders with violence. At several locations the riders were brutally attacked by white mobs. In Anniston, Alabama, club-wielding Ku Klux Klansmen attacked one of the buses with stones and set it on fire. Governor John Patterson refused to intervene, claiming he could not protect a "bunch of rabble rousers." When the bus arrived in Birmingham, Alabama, segregationists waited all day to meet the riders, grabbing them as they left the bus, pulling them into alleys and cor-ridors and beating them with pipes. The Freedom Riders wanted to continue their protest, despite one being beaten unconscious and needing fifty-three stitches, but after the governor refused protection, no bus would transport them. The Freedom Riders reluctantly boarded a flight to New Orleans, thereby dis-banding the CORE-sponsored Freedom Ride on May 17.

SNCC leaders quickly conferred and agreed that the Freedom Ride must con-tinue. Veterans of the sit-in movement went to Birmingham and were quickly arrested and put in jail. The students went on a hunger strike, so Police Com-missioner Eugene T. "Bull" Connor drove them—against their wishes—to the

A bus carrying civil rights "Freedom Riders" is fire-bombed during a caravan to advocate black voting rights in 1961. The Freedom Riders were civil rights advocates, both black and white, who traveled to the South from the North on buses in 1961 as volunteers for the Congress of Racial Equality. (Library of Congress)

Tennessee-Alabama line. The students quickly got a car and drove back to Birmingham to the Greyhound bus station. Because no bus driver would drive the Freedom Riders, the protesters sat on bus-station benches and waited. Eighteen hours later a number of Freedom Riders boarded a Greyhound bus for Montgomery, Alabama. The two-hour ride went without incident. However, as the Freedom Riders disembarked the bus in Montgomery, white people poured out of the bus station and attacked the protesters. The mob grew to more than a thousand with no police in sight. The riders were subjected to severe beatings, with one Rider's leg broken and another's spinal cord injured, yet no one came to their rescue. Montgomery's police commissioner stated, "We have no intention of standing guard for a bunch of troublemakers coming into our city" (Sitkoff, 104–105).

The combination of mob violence, Alabama officials' callous indifference, and the Freedom Riders' courage made the event front-page news throughout the world. At the height of the Cold War, the Soviet Union used this incident as an example of American hypocrisy. The United States claimed to be a country of freedom and democracy in contrast to the Soviet Union's totalitarian regime, but the racial discrimination and segregation of the south contradicted these assertions. The entire episode put President Kennedy in an awkward position. Kennedy believed in integration and opposed Jim Crow, but he took a moderate position on civil rights so as not to alienate his party's political base in the South. Richard Nixon had received a majority of the white southern vote in 1960, and the Democratic margin in both the House and Senate had been cut. In order to push through his legislative agenda, President Kennedy believed he needed the southern Democrats. He despised the Freedom Riders' "in-your-face" protests but the violence and press coverage forced him to respond. The Southern segregationists had embarrassed President Kennedy and the country at a time when he was preoccupied with the United States' fight against communism and the nation's image abroad. President Kennedy asked Alabama officials to meet their responsibilities. Attorney General Robert Kennedy announced that the Justice Department would ensure that there would be no interference with peaceful interstate travel, and that a contingent of 350–400 U.S. marshals would be sent to Montgomery to protect the Freedom Riders. He also asked the Freedom Riders for a temporary cessation of the rides to provide a cooling-off period.

Despite more violence in Montgomery and Attorney General Kennedy's request, CORE, SCLC, SNCC, and the Nashville Christian Leadership Council established a Freedom Ride Coordinating Committee to continue the rides. Escorted by the National Guard, the Freedom Riders traveled from Alabama to Jackson, Mississippi, where 27 protesters were arrested and fined for entering an all-white cafeteria. Throughout the summer more protesters came to Jackson to violate the city's unconstitutional segregation ordinance. By the end of the summer, over 300 Riders had been arrested in Jackson. As the rides continued throughout the South during the summer of 1961, Attorney General Kennedy petitioned the Interstate Commerce Commission (ICC) to issue rules prohibiting racial discrimination in interstate facilities. On September 22 the ICC announced that by November 1 all interstate carriers and terminals had to display signs that declared all seating "is without regard to race, color, creed or national origin" (Sitkoff, 110).

The Reaction of the Ku Klux Klan

A significant number of conservative white southerners viewed the modern civil rights movement of the 1950s and 1960s as a death knell to their society and culture. As the civil rights movement gained momentum and released a wave of activism aimed at integrating southern society, white southern men turned to an almost 100-year organization originally created by a half-dozen young Confederate military veterans in 1866 near Pulaski, Tennessee. Initially organized as a secret social club to "have fun, make mischief, and play pranks on the public," as its first manual stated, it increasingly became focused on causing havoc for former slaves. Shrouded in secrecy, the club resembled other fraternal orga-nizations in the United States in the late 19th century, adopting rituals and

James Meredith and the
University of Mississippi

The challenge to segregation reached higher education when a federal court ordered the all-white University of Mississippi in 1962 to admit James Meredith, an African American applicant. Born June 25, 1933, Meredith served in the Air Force from 1951 to 1960. In the fall of 1962 Meredith risked his life when he successfully applied the laws of integration and became the first African American student at the University of Mississippi.

Mississippi's governor, Ross Barnett, following Arkansas governor Orval Faubus's response to the 1957 Little Rock Nine, ignored a federal court's decision and blocked Meredith's registration to the university. The Mississippi legislature went as far as to make Barnett the emergency university registrar, in a ruse to circumvent the court order binding the regular registrar from registering Meredith. Like President Eisenhower, President Kennedy had to order several hundred federal marshals to escort Meredith onto the Oxford, Mississippi, campus. After negotiations between Kennedy and Barnett, Meredith flew from Memphis to the Oxford airport where the field was lined with Army trucks, buses, jeeps, cars, and assorted government planes, plus piles of tents and riot equipment. Other supplies included dramatic items like giant searchlights.

Before Meredith's arrival on campus, 300 federal marshals were posted around the university's administration building, known as the Lyceum. While Meredith was safely installed in the dorm, a crowd of approximately 1,000, mostly students, gathered outside the Lyceum. While some shouted the rhythmic cheer, "Go to Cuba, nigger lovers, go to Cuba!" others lobbed pebbles, then rocks, at the lines of marshals standing outside. Senator George Yarbrough, a Mississippi state senator, stood inside the Lyceum with a proclamation signed by Governor Barnett which authorized him to take command of the highway patrol. Senator Yarbrough's intention was to order the patrolmen to withdraw from the scene, leaving the feds to defend themselves from the mob (Branch, *Parting the Waters,* 663).

After President Kennedy announced the integration of the University of Mississippi on national television, the mob of white segregationists formed on campus, shooting out streetlights, commandeering a bulldozer, and throwing rocks and bottles. Kennedy's television address aimed to placate the Mississippians angered by the federal court order. He praised the state of Mississippi, said he was only doing his duty in enforcing the court order, and offered no specific support for Meredith's mission. The riot went on all night, as the mob showed astonishing persistence. Rioters sent a bulldozer, then a car, crashing toward the Lyceum. Rioters wounded 160 of the marshals—28 by gunfire—and sent a stray bullet into the head of a local jukebox repairman, killing him. Two people died, the second a journalist from England, in the confrontation between troops and segregationists, while another 375 were wounded. Applauded by some for his willingness to use

Continued on next page

James Meredith and the University of Mississippi, Continued

federal authority to ensure the integration of the University of Mississippi and enforce a federal court order, Kennedy once again was forced to act in the face of white southern resistance to federal law. After troops restored order to the campus, new units totaling 23,000 soldiers, three times the population of Oxford, arrived on the campus to maintain order and protect Meredith as he attended classes. Mississippi officials joined the governor in blaming the riot entirely on "trigger-happy marshals" and other federal intruders.

In 1966 Meredith recounted his experience in the book, *Three Years in Mississippi.* Shortly after the publication of this book, Meredith organized the "Walk Against Fear," a march from Memphis to Jackson, Mississippi, to boldly challenge the physical violence African Americans faced in exercising their voting rights. Shot during the march, Meredith resumed the walk when he was physically capable, making it in time to join Martin Luther King Jr. and other prominent civil rights leaders in their triumphant entry into Jackson, Mississippi. Meredith later earned his LL.B., a graduate degree in the law, from Columbia University and, in a controversial move, served for a short time in 1989 on the staff of conservative senator Jesse Helms.

distinctive white robes with hoods to present a ghostly appearance. The Ku Klux Klan experienced a revival during the 1920s as a result of a growing myth created by D. W. Griffith's 1915 film *Birth of a Nation,* which held the Klan saved the South from the tyrannical rule of carpetbaggers, scalawags, Republicans, and African Americans. Based on the 1905 Thomas Dixon novel *The Clansman,* Griffith's film was an epic feature that revolutionized the movie industry and popularized the Klan through its portrayal of its members as chivalric heroes who saved the South from a black menace. This film caused a surge in Klan membership, particularly in the North where nativism was on the rise in response to the early 20th century wave of immigration. This reincarnation of the Klan targeted immigrants, Catholics, Jews, and African Americans.

Not surprisingly, white southerners turned again to the Klan to combat the effectiveness of the civil rights movement in the 1950s and '60s. The third incarnation of the Klan used the same tactics of the previous two: cross burnings, white hoods, and violent acts such as lynchings, kidnappings, stabbings, and beatings committed during the cover of night. The Klan used these tactics to intimidate civil rights activists in an effort to end the movement that threatened their way of life. Between 1956 and 1963, the Klan was responsible for over 125 bombings of churches, homes, and synagogues across the South. The most infamous bombing occurred in 1963 when the Klan bombed the Sixteenth Street

Baptist Church in Birmingham, Alabama, killing four young African American girls.

In general, the Klan appealed to blue-collar workers. Studies of Klan membership have revealed that the typical member was a skilled or unskilled worker in his thirties with a high school diploma. They viewed themselves as most affected by desegregation, losing economic, political, and social status as a result. The Klan during the 1960s had a peak membership of 50,000 (Singleton, 419–420).

Although responsible for such heinous acts as the kidnapping and killing of civil rights workers James Chaney, Andrew Goodman, and Michael Schwerner, the Klan during the 1960s never reached the power and influence it enjoyed during the 1860s or 1920s. Outraged by the Klan, President Lyndon Johnson eventually ordered the federal prosecution of Klan members for violating the civil rights of U.S. citizens (Ness, 1433–1438).

THE CIVIL RIGHTS MOVEMENT REACHES ITS ZENITH

The civil rights movement seemed to find its voice in the spring of 1963. The sit-ins and Freedom Rides of 1960 and 1961 put pressure on President Kennedy, but by 1963 growing impatience and a lack of progress turned into frustration, resentment, and discouragement. In order to make that final push toward a broad-sweeping civil rights and voting rights bills, civil rights activists knew they had to put even more political pressure on the Kennedy administration. To do that, Martin Luther King Jr. and others knew they had to force southern officials and politicians to overreact, gaining greater sympathy from the press and northern liberals. To incite a violent reaction, SCLC and SNCC returned to the Deep South.

1963 Albany, Georgia, Protests

Despite President Kennedy's willingness to use federal marshals and troops to force Governor Ross Barnett to comply with federal law, and Attorney General Kennedy's pressure on the ICC to integrate interstate carriers and depots, by the end of 1962 most civil rights activists believed the Kennedy administration lacked the necessary moral outrage to promote integration and voting rights for African Americans in the South. Leaders of the SCLC and SNCC knew that they would have to continue the confrontational protests of the sit-ins and Freedom Rides. Starting at the end of 1961, African Americans in Albany, Georgia, had marched, boycotted, and sat-in to win enfranchisement and full integration of public facilities to no avail. Though lasting for more than a year, the protests failed to accomplish anything. African Americans in Albany believed that their efforts were unsuccessful because Democratic Party politics caused the Kennedy administration to do nothing. The movement had also met a worthy adversary in Albany police chief Laurie Pritchett. He ordered his force to respond to the protesters' nonviolence in kind. Instead of physical abuse, police peacefully arrested African American protesters but kept their mistreatment to a minimum. When Kennedy never enforced the ICC ruling or applied pressure on Albany officials to end segregation, the protests in Albany fizzled.

1963 Birmingham, Alabama, Protests

Momentarily demoralized, King and other African American leaders reflected not only on the failed protests of Albany, but the success of the sit-ins and Freedom Rides. During a three-day strategy session in Savannah, Georgia, the SCLC decided to launch a massive demonstration that would provoke a confrontation with white segregationists. They chose to target Birmingham, Alabama, the most segregated big city in America. Although over 40 percent of Birmingham's population was African American, fewer than 10,000 of the 80,000 registered voters were African American. In many respects, the decision to target Birmingham was an audacious one. Not only firmly committed to the idea and reality of segregation and racial discrimination, Birmingham was considered one of the most dangerous cities for African Americans. White segregationists had conducted eighteen racial bombings and more than fifty cross burnings there between 1957 and 1963. In addition, Birmingham's police commissioner, Bull Connor, proudly assumed the role of vigilant defender of segregation and white supremacy. But these were the very reasons King and the SCLC targeted Birmingham; they wanted to trigger an overreaction by the authorities. Toward that end, King and his associates started planning in the spring of 1963 a top-secret plan they called "Project C," the "C" standing for confrontation.

Waiting to begin the demonstrations until after the April 2, 1963, mayoral runoff election, the campaign commenced with the issuance of a manifesto laying out the protesters' demands, which included an immediate end to racist employment practices and segregated public accommodations. In addition, SCLC insisted on the formation of a biracial committee to plan for further desegregation. After the manifesto, protestors started sit-ins at segregated downtown lunch counters. The second stage consisted of marches on city hall. Connor's police force arrested hundreds of African American marchers. Eager to get a response that would garner national attention, Birmingham officials complied by securing an injunction barring racial demonstrations. This provided King with the ammunition he needed. On Good Friday, April 12, King led some 50 hymn-singing volunteers on a march to city hall in violation of the injunction. An angry Police Commissioner Connor ordered their immediate arrest. Birmingham found itself in the national spotlight.

Civil rights demonstrators face fire hoses in Birmingham, Alabama, on May 4, 1963, during protests that became a focal point of the desegregation movement. (Bettmann/Corbis)

After his release, King launched the controversial third stage of Project C; controversial because it included using over 1,000 African American children to march from the Sixteenth Street Baptist Church to demonstrate and be arrested. African American children sang and chanted freedom slogans as they marched into town. As police approached, they knelt, prayed, and offered no resistance to Connor's forces. Critics from all sides took King to task for this tactic. Many felt it exploited the children, while others, like Malcolm X, thought it was cowardly: "Real men don't put their children on the firing line" (Sitkoff, 136). But King thought that young African Americans had more of a stake in this fight than anyone and would learn about the value of freedom and justice through sacrifice. King and other organizers of the protest also recognized that young African Americans had less to lose by sitting in jail. Their parents, on the other hand, had jobs they could lose. As more children gathered on May 3 at the Sixteenth Street Baptist Church to prepare to march, Bull Connor could no longer practice restraint. He ordered his forces to bar the exits of the church and charge Kelly Ingram Park in front of the church where some of the protesters had escaped. The police started beating demonstrators with nightsticks and used police dogs to help overpower some of the young protesters. When some adults came to the defense of the children, Connor ordered firemen to spray the crowd with high-powered hoses. The water came at such a force that it blasted African American protesters against the walls of buildings and down the streets. The hundreds of pounds of pressure tore the bark off of trees and the clothes off the backs of some of the children. All total, the police arrested more than 1,300 children during the two days of protests.

Project C ran into a third day and the police arrested an additional 200 demonstrators. King had accomplished his goal. Images of police with nightsticks and vicious dogs and firemen with high-powered hoses attacking the young protesters appeared on nightly newscasts and front pages of newspapers across the world. These images shocked, shamed, and raised the consciousness of Americans. The protests reached a peak on May 7 when a large number of students converged on downtown Birmingham in a raucous parade of protest. Connor ordered his forces to use an armored police tank to drive the students back into the ghetto. With hoses, clubs, dogs, and cattle prods, police attacked and the more resistant protesters reacted by throwing rocks and bricks. This violent confrontation forced city officials to come to the bargaining table to hammer out an agreement with SCLC. After three days of talks, the two sides came to an agreement that included the desegregation of lunch counters, restrooms, fitting rooms, and drinking fountains. It also included a concession by the industrial community of Birmingham to hire African Americans on a nondiscriminatory basis.

Unfortunately, the violence in Birmingham did not end with the agreement. Resentful of the concessions, segregationists and white supremacy groups set out on a campaign of terror that included bombing the Gaston Motel, local headquarters of the SCLC. Seeking vengeance, African Americans took to the streets and pelted arriving police and firemen with rocks and bottles. So incensed, the African Americans of Birmingham could no longer heed King's call for nonviolence and a police officer was stabbed, a white cabdriver attacked, and two grocery stores owned by whites set on fire. Eventually order was restored and the pact implemented. The highly publicized confrontation between African American protesters, particularly children, and Police Commissioner Connor's forces awakened white Americans to the plight of African Americans in the South and emboldened civil rights activists. After the success of Birmingham, the civil rights movement would no longer be satisfied with gradualism or small-scale protests.

Movement Pressures President to Act

In the wake of Birmingham, President Kennedy had to make a move on civil rights. Previously resistant to the cause, the images of Bull Connor's men attacking African American children in the streets of Birmingham spurred him toward a commitment to and identification with the civil rights movement. Concerned with the political fallout of Birmingham and fearful that extremists might take over the movement if he did not act, Kennedy began taking a stronger stand

MLK's Letter from the Birmingham Jail

While sitting in a Birmingham jail in 1963, Martin Luther King Jr. penned one of the most famous expressions of protest to oppression and discrimination in response to a request by several Alabama clergymen to open negotiations as opposed to provoking violence and to the Northern press. The *New York Times* also chastised King for the timing of the Birmingham protests. Optimistic about the city's new mayor, Albert Boutwell, the *Times* editorialized that his administration will serve as "a diminution, if not an end, to racial tensions that have grown alarmingly the last few days" (Branch, *Parting the Waters,* 737). But it was the response of local clergy that inspired King to react with his pen.

King read on page 2 of the April 13 *Birmingham News* that local white clergymen viewed the Birmingham demonstrations as "unwise and untimely." In the article the clergy pointed out "that such actions as incite hatred and violence, however technically peaceful those actions may be, have not contributed to the resolution of our local problems. We do not believe that these days of new hope are days when extreme measures are justified in Birmingham" (Branch, *Parting the Waters,* 738). In response to this rebuke, King composed around the margins of the newspaper an eloquent essay in defense of civil disobedience. He began by writing that as a Christian and American he had the duty to combat injustice wherever it existed. Writing to those who asked African Americans to wait or be patient, King declared he had never "engaged in a direct action movement that was 'well timed'":

> . . . When you have seen vicious mobs lynch your mothers and fathers at will and drown your sisters and brothers at whim; when you have seen hate-filled policemen curse, kick, brutalize, and even kill your black brothers and sisters with impunity; when you see that vast majority of your twenty million Negro brothers smothering in the air-tight cage of poverty in the midst of an affluent society . . . when you are harried by day and haunted by night by the fact that you are a Negro, living constantly at tiptoe stance never quite knowing what to expect next, and plagued with inner fears and outer resentments; when you are forever fighting a degenerating sense of "nobodiness"—then you will understand why we find it difficult to wait. (www.mlkonline.net)

He cited theologians like Thomas Aquinas, Paul Tillich, and Martin Buber to describe the moral responsibility of disobeying unjust laws, reminding his fellow ministers that Hitler's laws were technically "legal." He also warned that if they did not engage in nonviolent direct action, a generation of frustrated African Americans would turn to the emerging Black Nationalist ideologies of people like Malcolm X. Immediate civil disobedience was the only way to maintain the hope of integration and save a movement tired of delay, obstruction, and indifference. He concluded by writing:

Continued on next page

> ### MLK's Letter from the Birmingham Jail, Continued
>
> One day the South will know that when these disinherited children of God sat down at lunch counters they were in reality standing up for the best in the American dream and the most sacred values in our Judeo-Christian heritage, and thus carrying our whole nation back to great walls of democracy which were dug deep by the founding fathers in the formulation of the Constitution and the Declaration of Independence. (www.mlkonline.net)
>
> Like the early Christians, King made the jail the setting for spiritual judgment. Based on these Christian traditions, most Americans could appreciate the persecuted spirituality King now had to endure. In short, this was the early church reincarnate, with King rebuking those for their worldly attachments and fear of the state.

against segregationists like Alabama's Gov. George Wallace. When immediately following the Birmingham demonstrations Wallace announced his intention to block African American students from attending the University of Alabama, President Kennedy responded quickly and showed Wallace his resolve, forcing the governor to capitulate. After the first African American students registered for classes at the University of Alabama, President Kennedy went on national television to speak about his new commitment to desegregation and equal protection under the law. He joined the chorus of civil rights leaders who argued against gradualism when he said:

> Who among us would then be content with the counsels of patience and delay? One hundred years of delay have passed since President Lincoln freed the slaves, yet their heirs, their grandsons, are not fully free. They are not yet freed from the bonds of injustice; they are not yet freed from social and economic oppression. And this nation, for all its hopes and all its boasts, will not be fully free until all its citizens are free. (Sitkoff, 158)

In June of 1963, a month after the events of Birmingham, President Kennedy asked Congress to enact the most comprehensive civil rights law in history. The bill Kennedy proposed called for desegregating public accommodations, granting authority to the attorney general to initiate school desegregation suits, establishing a Community Relations Service to prevent racial conflict, and protecting African Americans from discriminatory hiring and employment practices. In the hands of Congress, liberals went even further by proposing the establishment of the Fair Employment Practices Commission and federal registrars to enroll African American voters. In the wake of Birmingham, the civil rights movement had gained momentum and support from the White House and the halls of Congress.

John F. Kennedy's Commitment to Civil Rights

Although he was initially viewed as a champion of equal rights and a reason for hope among civil rights activists, President Kennedy's first two and half years in office proved to be a disappointment to those in the movement. The initial hope derived from the Democratic platform at the 1960 convention, which included a pledge for strong federal action in the area of civil rights, Kennedy's own expression of support for effective civil rights legislation, and his politically savvy call to Coretta King while her husband sat imprisoned in a Georgia jail on a trumped-up charge in the fall of 1960. All of this pointed toward forceful and expedient action on civil rights by a Kennedy administration. It did not take long after his election for these hopes to be dashed.

Because of Kennedy's reluctance to spend his political capital to further the cause of civil rights, historians have debated the depth of Kennedy's commitment to the ideal of equality for African Americans. He did use his presidential powers to ensure the racial integration of public universities in Mississippi and Alabama, but otherwise he did not push for the sort of federal legislation he had talked about during his campaign due to the fear of alienating southern congressmen and senators who dominated congressional committees.

A generous view of Kennedy's passivity on this issue does not question his personal commitment to racial equality. This view holds that Kennedy waited for the right time to introduce civil rights legislation for politically sound reasons. To push too hard too soon would have done more harm than good, causing a political backlash that could have set the movement back decades. He did what he could, but he had to wait until the hearts and minds of Americans had changed enough to ensure success of such a broad-sweeping civil rights bill.

A less generous view of Kennedy's hesitancy to act questions the depth of his commitment. After all, when the civil rights movement caught fire in the 1950s, Senator Kennedy was not among its leading advocates. Prior to his becoming president, none of his friends or close associates was African American. Coming from the North, he had had little exposure to the violent racial bigotry in the South. Due to his privileged prep school and Ivy League upbringing, he was also not even well acquainted with the subtler but equally bitter racism in the North. In fact, while serving in the Senate Kennedy openly questioned how far the federal government should go in trying to combat segregation and discrimination. Historians with this view believe Kennedy's commitment to civil rights was long on profile but short on courage. Whenever possible, he avoided public fights on civil rights. Evidence to support this view includes his deference to southern senators in his appointment of white segregationist judges to the federal bench in the South. To these historians, Kennedy only acted in1963 because the civil rights movement and Bull Connor painted him into a corner and gave him no choice.

March on Washington

To rally support for Kennedy's civil rights bill and build on the momentum of the Birmingham protests, civil rights leaders in the summer of 1963 proposed a massive march on Washington, an idea first suggested in 1941 by the legendary leader of the Brotherhood of Sleeping Car Porters, A. Phillip Randolph. Organized by King and other prominent African American leaders, the 1963 planned march gained support from a broad coalition of organizations that included not only the primary civil rights groups, but also the National Council of Churches, the National Conference of Catholics for Interracial Justice, the American Jewish Congress, and the AFL-CIO.

Organizers of the march initially received a chilly response from the White House. President Kennedy feared that the march would not have its intended

Crowd gathered at the Lincoln Memorial to hear Martin Luther King Jr.'s famous "I Have a Dream" speech during the March on Washington, D.C., on August 28, 1963. (Library of Congress)

effect and would create an atmosphere of intimidation that would cause many legislators to vote against the bill. In fact, he thought the march would give some in Congress the out they were looking for. Even some moderate African American leaders agreed that if the march erupted into violence it could backfire and cause congressional resistance.

To quell the president's fears, the organizers shelved plans for acts of civil disobedience and settled for a mass rally. Marchers would peacefully parade from the Washington Monument to the Lincoln Memorial, where they would listen to performers and speakers. With these plans in place, President Kennedy at a July 17 press conference reversed his position, supported the march, and described the upcoming event as being "in the great tradition" of American demonstrations staged to demand a redress of grievances.

On August 28, 1963, approximately 250,000 African American and white demonstrators gathered at the Lincoln Memorial. Exceeding all expectations, the March on Washington became the largest demonstration in American history. On a hot and muggy summer day, the multitude listened respectfully and attentively to scores of speakers and artists such as Joan Baez; Peter, Paul and Mary; Bob Dylan; and Mahalia Jackson. The day culminated in the memorable speech by Martin Luther King Jr. that not only moved the crowd, but also became the eloquent justification for a century-old movement on the verge of experiencing its greatest cultural, political, and legal victory (Sitkoff, 162–164).

"Five score years ago, a great American in whose symbolic shadow we stand, signed the Emancipation Proclamation," King began. He proceeded to recount a 100-year history of racial discrimination and then declare: "So we have come here today to dramatize an appalling condition." He described the Declaration of Independence as a sacred obligation that proved to be a bad check for African Americans—"a check which has come back marked 'insufficient funds.'" He then shouted over the roars of the crowd that "we refuse to believe that the bank of justice is bankrupt. We refuse to believe that there are insufficient funds in the great vaults of opportunity of this nation." He gained momentum as he rhythmically spoke in an evangelical style that turned the demonstration into a massive church service:

> We can never be satisfied as long as our bodies, heavy with the fatigue of travel, cannot gain lodging in the motels of the highways and the hotels of the cities. We cannot be satisfied as long as the Negro's basic mobility is from a smaller ghetto to a larger one. We can never be satisfied as long as our children are stripped of their selfhood and robbed of their dignity by signs stating: "For Whites Only." We cannot be satisfied as long as the Negro in Mississippi cannot vote and the Negro in New York believes he has nothing for which to vote. No, no, we are not satisfied and we will not be satisfied until justice rolls down like the waters and righteousness like a mighty stream. Go back to Mississippi, go back to Alabama, go back to South Carolina, go back to Georgia, go back to Louisiana, go back to the slums and ghettos of our modern cities, knowing that somehow this situation can and will be changed.

With the crowd hanging on every word and exhorting him on, King's speech reached its stirring climax with a compelling description of his utopian vision for America:

> I have a dream that one day on the red hills of Georgia the sons of former slaves and the sons of former slaveowners will be able to sit down together at the table of brotherhood. I have a dream that one day even the state of Mississippi, a desert state sweltering with the heat of injustice and oppression, will be transformed into an oasis of freedom and justice. I have a dream that my four little children will one day live in a nation where they

will not be judged by the color of their skin but by the content of their character . . .

When we let freedom ring, when we let it ring from every village and every hamlet, from every state and every city, we will be able to speed up that day when all God's children, black men and white men, Jews and Gentiles, Protestants and Catholics, will be able to join hands and sing in the words of the old Negro spiritual, "Free at last! Free at last! Thank God almighty, we are free at last!"

King's speech and the massive peaceful demonstration made the civil rights movement acceptable to millions of white Americans. The March on Washington signaled the climax of the nonviolent stage of the civil rights movement and cemented King's position as leading spokesman for the African American cause. In 1964 King would win the Nobel Peace Prize for his leadership of the civil rights movement (Sitkoff, 159–164).

Civil Rights Act of 1964

After President Kennedy's assassination on November 22, 1963, Lyndon B. Johnson took the lead on getting the wide-sweeping civil rights bill through Congress. President Johnson had served in government since 1932 as a congressional aide, New Deal administrator, congressman, senator, Senate majority leader, and vice president. Through these experiences he had developed considerable political skills that helped him with the task at hand. As a southerner, President Johnson wanted to prove to the nation and Kennedy's skeptical staff that he was a true liberal and a supporter of racial equality. Despite a two-and-a-half-month filibuster by southern senators, Johnson successfully navigated the bill through Congress and signed the Civil Rights Act of 1964 into law on July 2, 1964.

Two days before July 4, Johnson introduced the legislation before him as a legacy of the American Revolution. "One hundred and eighty-eight years ago this week a small band of valiant men began a long struggle for freedom." He added that these men "knew that freedom would be secure only if each generation fought to renew and enlarge its meaning. From the minutemen at Concord to the soldiers in Vietnam, each generation has been equal to that trust." In that context, the Civil Rights Act of 1964 would make those "equal before God" also "equal in the polling booths, in the classrooms, in the factories, and in hotels, restaurants, movie theaters, and other places that provide service to the public" (Branch, *Pillar of Fire*, 388).

Seen as a landmark piece of legislation in the annals of American race relations, the law prohibited discrimination in employment on the basis of race, religion, sex, or national origin. In addition, the law barred discrimination in public accommodations, empowered the Justice Department to withhold federal funds from any segregated government-run program, and created the Equal

Employment Opportunity Commission (EEOC) to review complaints of discrimination. Though the Civil Rights Act resulted in the desegregation of public facilities throughout the South, including many public schools, the obstacles to African American voting rights persisted.

Freedom Summer

Although the protests of 1963 culminated in federal legislation prohibiting segregation, African American activists recognized that true equality could not be achieved without total enfranchisement. As a result, African American leaders and organizations turned their attention toward voting rights for African Americans living in the South. In fact, more radical activists viewed desegregation as largely an African American middle-class and urban issue that did little for the vast majority of poor African Americans living in the rural South. To them, enfranchisement was the critical issue because it held the key to empowering the dispossessed. Organizations like CORE looked to Mississippi, the poorest, most backward and illiterate, racist state in the South, to begin the fight for voting rights. African Americans made up 42 percent of Mississippi's population, but only one out of twenty African American adult Mississippians was registered to vote.

Bob Moses, a SNCC organizer from Harlem, reconvened the statewide interorganizational Council of Federated Organizations (COFO) to fight for African American voting rights. Moses chose David Dennis as his assistant program director; it was Dennis who came up with the idea for a Freedom Summer in 1964. African Americans and whites began to descend upon Mississippi to begin a massive voter-registration project. In response, state and local officials planned to harass and hamper the movement. The State Highway Patrol was expanded from 275 to 475 men, and many local police forces doubled their size in anticipation of the project. As summer approached, white violence against African Americans rose throughout Mississippi as members of white supremacy groups bombed and set fire to dozens of African American organization headquarters and churches. Unprovoked killings against African Americans and unpunished crimes against African Americans multiplied.

Despite working under the threat of violence, the Mississippi Summer Project persisted. Volunteers opened and operated nearly fifty "Freedom Schools" throughout the state and about the same number of community centers. They worked with local African Americans to establish bases for further political action by encouraging the emergence of new local leaders and helped educate Mississippi's African American community on how to bring about change. Just as important, Freedom Summer brought the attention of the nation on Mississippi racism. Assisted by the flagrant violence and brutality of white racists, the project became front-page news and helped foster a national consensus that the situation in Mississippi was intolerable and in need of immediate change.

Despite all the effort and attention, however, COFO could only register approximately 1,200 new African American voters.

Prevented from participating in the state's Democratic Party, COFO set up a new party and enrolled nearly 60,000 disenfranchised African Americans. The new Mississippi Freedom Democratic Party (MFDP) elected 44 delegates and 22 alternates to attend the 1964 Democratic National Convention in Atlantic City. The MFDP representatives went to Atlantic City to contest the seats traditionally held by white Mississippians on the grounds that the MFDP representatives belonged to the only freely chosen party in the state since African Americans were systematically denied access to the delegate selection process of the Mississippi Democratic Party. Fannie Lou Hamer made the seating of the MFDP representatives the central issue of the convention. Addressing the convention, Hamer described the struggles of trying to register African Americans to vote in Mississippi. She chronicled how her effort to exercise the most basic right of citizenship had caused her to lose her plantation job, get shot at, and to suffer a beating so severe that she could no longer walk.

Wanting to avoid a divisive floor fight, President Johnson looked for a compromise solution that a majority of the Southern delegation could accept. Convinced that African Americans had nowhere else to turn, and determined to avert a white southern secession to the Republican Party, President Johnson offered a place on the ticket to Hubert Humphrey, Minnesota senator and leading civil rights advocate, if he brokered a deal with the MFDP. Humphrey and his emissaries told the African American leaders to disassociate themselves from the SNCC workers who threatened disruptive direct action at the convention if the MFDP representatives were not seated. Not wanting to isolate the movement, Farmer and King reluctantly agreed with Bayard Rustin and Roy Wilkins to lobby for a resolution that gave two MFDP delegates the right to vote at the convention, did not seat any Mississippi regular delegates refusing to support the ticket, and promised not to seat delegations from states that disenfranchised African Americans at future conventions. With this resolution, the civil rights leaders gained more than Johnson wanted to offer, but it still did not satisfy those in the SNCC who felt it compromised their principles. Hamer backed away from the resolution and backed SNCC's opposition. Ultimately the MFDP voted to reject the compromise. President Johnson's attempt to manipulate African Americans at the 1964 convention further alienated SNCC from the mainstream of the movement, the federal government, and the Democratic Party. Because of MFDP's treatment at the convention, SNCC left the convention both demoralized and disillusioned.

Project Alabama

By the end of 1964, Martin Luther King and the SCLC focused all their attention on the goal of a strong voting-rights law. The lessons of Albany and Birmingham

The Chaney, Goodman, and Schwerner Murders

On June 15, 1964, about 300 of the more than 800 volunteers for the Mississippi Summer Project gathered at the Western College for Women in Oxford, Ohio. Bob Moses spoke and warned them of the dangers they were about to face, including the threat of dying for the cause. While in Oxford the volunteers learned the intricacies of voter registration and how to protect themselves against violence. Amid the training, Moses and other COFO workers learned that three SNCC volunteers investigating a church bombing in Neshoba County, Mississippi, had gone missing. They learned later that their car had been found badly burned just outside Philadelphia, Mississippi. Assuming the three had been murdered, the volunteers left for Mississippi.

Six weeks after the search for James Chaney, Andrew Goodman, and Michael Schwerner began, FBI agents uncovered their bodies in a newly constructed earthen damn just outside Philadelphia. Goodman and Schwerner were both shot once in the heart. Chaney, the sole African American, had suffered a severe beating before being shot twice in the body and once in the head. Six months later the FBI had obtained enough evidence to arrest 21 men, including the sheriff and deputy sheriff of Neshoba County. The Philadelphia chapter of the Ku Klux Klan had confronted the three freedom workers just outside of town after Deputy Sheriff Cecil Price apprehended them on a trumped-up charge of speeding. Waiting until after dark, Price drove the three men to a deserted road where three cars filled with Klansmen waited for them. They first pulled Schwerner from the car, taunted him, and shot him in the heart. They proceeded to kill Goodman in the same way. They then grabbed, beat, and shot Chaney. The Klansmen used a bulldozer to bury their bodies, and then they burned their car.

The murders cast a pall over the Mississippi Project. Although President Johnson sent dozens of FBI agents to Mississippi, their inability to find the missing three or protect the volunteers angered many COFO and SNCC workers. White terrorists continued to bomb African American homes and churches, assault COFO volunteers, and shoot some 30 civil rights workers. Local law enforcement also harassed volunteers by arresting several on phony charges. To make matters worse, President Johnson's emissary to Mississippi, former CIA director Allen Dulles, and FBI director J. Edgar Hoover blamed the violence in Mississippi on the civil rights activists and not the white terrorists. This caused many of the freedom workers in Mississippi to start carrying guns.

taught them how to use nonviolent demonstrations to provoke a reaction, gain national attention for their cause, and ultimately coerce a demanded end. With these lessons in mind, King plotted the strategy for Project Alabama to obtain the desired voting-rights law:

1. Nonviolent demonstrators will go into the streets to exercise their constitutional rights.
2. White racists will resist these demonstrations by unleashing violence against them.
3. Americans of conscience will demand federal intervention and legislation.
4. The administration will buckle under mass pressure and initiate measures of immediate intervention and remedial legislation.

Selma became the focal point of the Project Alabama campaign that aimed to have the federal government intervene to remove all barriers to African American voting.

King and SCLC were convinced that they could provoke the desired reaction in Selma. County sheriff James G. Clark made Selma notorious for its violent treatment of civil rights workers attempting to register voters in 1963. SCLC workers arriving in Selma were not disappointed when they encountered Sheriff Clark wearing a button that boldly read "Never!" Starting in early 1965 King led daily marches of hundreds of African Americans to the Dallas County Courthouse in an attempt to get their names on the voter lists. By the end of January, over 2,000 African Americans had been arrested. Still, King had not won the violent confrontation with Clark he had hoped for. Toward that end, King led a giant demonstration on February 1 that got himself and 770 other protesters arrested. The following day Clark arrested an additional 520 African Americans for parading without a permit, and on February 3 he arrested another 300. Throughout February the protests continued. As the month wore on, Clark became increasingly brutal. However, despite beatings and the killing of Jimmie Lee Jackson, a young African American participating in a voter demonstration in nearby Marion, the Selma demonstrations did not evoke the desired national indignation.

Stymied, King decided to organize a march from Selma to Montgomery on March 6 to present a petition of grievances to Gov. George Wallace. The governor issued an order prohibiting the demonstration, and King inexplicably canceled the march. Outraged, Hosea Williams, director of the SCLC field staff, gave in to pressure from SNCC militants and led 500 protesters down U.S. Highway 80 en route to Montgomery. As television news cameras rolled, the demonstrators marched in a long column singing freedom songs. As they approached the Edmund Pettus Bridge to exit Selma, approximately 100 of Sheriff Clark's men lined both sides of the bridge, and another 100 state troopers blocked the opposite end of the bridge. Unwilling to turn back, state troopers began to surge toward the African Americans while Clark's men attacked from the sides. Unprepared for this act of aggression, the marchers panicked and ran, fleeing the teargas, charging horsemen, and swinging nightsticks and chains. The troopers and deputies violently attacked protesters and bystanders, including women and children. In King's absence, the movement got the response and news coverage it desired. Finally the Alabama Project aroused indignation and put pressure on Washington to act.

Eager to seize the moment, King announced from Atlanta that he would come back to Selma to organize a second march on March 9 and to seek a federal injunction to prevent Governor Wallace and Alabama police from interfering. While considering the motion, a federal judge enjoined SCLC from marching, but King decided it was time to defy a federal court order. Under pressure from the White House, King made a secret compromise with federal officials to lead his followers to the Pettus Bridge, stop when halted by state troopers, pray, and then order the marchers to turn around. Nearly 1,000 African Americans and 500 sympathetic whites gathered for the march. The marchers encountered the state troopers when they reached the bridge. After granting King's request to pray, the state troopers broke ranks and moved to the sides of the highway. King then turned to his astonished followers and asked them to return to Brown Chapel where they had initially gathered.

Afterwards many militant African Americans voiced their disappointment and disillusionment with King. As the Alabama Project sat on the verge of disintegration, white violence rekindled demands for federal intervention. A gang of white terrorists attacked three white Unitarian ministers who had come to Selma to participate in the march. One of them, James J. Reeb of Boston, died two days after the beating. This sparked a pilgrimage of hundreds of protesters from across the country to Selma as tens of thousands of letters and telegrams poured into Washington demanding voting-rights legislation. On March 15, President Johnson gave a televised address to a joint session of Congress to request the passage of a voting-rights bill. Johnson told Congress and the nation that the "real hero of this struggle is the American Negro. His actions and protests, his courage to risk safety, and even to risk his life, have awakened the conscience of this nation."

After the speech, President Johnson asked the federal judge who issued the injunction to allow the march. He also called Governor Wallace to tell him that the marchers would be protected. On March 21, King spoke to more than 3,000 African American and white marchers gathered in front of Brown Chapel: "Don't you get weary, and it will lead us to the Promised Land. And Alabama will be a new Alabama, and America will be a new America." Protected by the National Guard, the demonstrators marched for 50 miles. Four days after the march had begun, they reached the outskirts of Montgomery where nearly 30,000 additional demonstrators joined them for the final three miles to the Alabama capitol where they staged a huge demonstration, triumphantly singing the "Battle Hymn of the Republic" (Sitkoff, 193–195).

The Voting Rights Act of 1965

After the Civil Rights Act became law, President Johnson turned to the problem of disenfranchisement. The events in Selma in March of 1965 lent greater urgency to this issue. With public pressure mounting after the news coverage of the violent attack on protesters by the state police, President Johnson seized the opportunity and promptly submitted a sweeping voting-rights bill to Congress. With public opinion overwhelmingly in favor of the bill, President Johnson went on national television and demanded its speedy passage. Lawmakers quickly fell in line and completed action on the bill in less than five months. The House of Representatives passed the voting rights conference report, 328–74, on August 3, 1965. The next day the Senate passed the exact bill, 72–18.

The president signed into law the Voting Rights Act of 1965 that authorized federal examiners to register qualified voters in counties where fewer than 50 percent of the voting-age population was registered, and suspended restrictions like the literacy tests that had been used to prevent African Americans from registering to vote. Together with the adoption in 1964 of the Twenty-fourth Amendment to the Constitution, which outlawed the federal poll tax, the Voting Rights Act allowed millions of African Americans to register and vote for the first time. The act particularly set its sights on the literacy test, historically the most notorious disenfranchising devise. In any state or county where fewer than 50 percent of the adults were registered to vote, it automatically suspended the operation of any "test" that was a prerequisite for voting.

Lawmakers also attempted to prevent southern officials from developing new techniques of discrimination. States and localities covered by the act would be required to obtain clearance from the attorney general of a three-judge district court in Washington, D.C., before implementing any new voting requirements or procedures. The effects of this law were extraordinary. In 1960 only 20 percent of eligible African Americans were registered; by 1964 the figure had risen to 39 percent, and by 1971 62 percent. After years of gradualism on civil rights, the president and Congress had finally taken the lead and used the deep reservoirs of federal power to promote equality.

THE CIVIL RIGHTS MOVEMENT
RADICALIZED, 1965–1969

The civil rights movement reached its 1960s' pinnacle with the passage of the Civil Rights Act of 1964 and Voting Rights Act of 1965. However, only five days after President Johnson signed the Voting Rights Act into law, the most destructive race riot in more than two decades broke out in Watts, Los Angeles' largest African American ghetto. The riot signaled the end to the era of nonviolence and

Texas Western v. Kentucky

A watershed-sporting event occurred amid the turbulence of the Vietnam War, urban riots, and rise of radical antiwar and civil rights activists. In the spring of 1966 the University of Kentucky Wildcats played the Texas Western University Miners for the National Collegiate Athletic Association (NCAA) men's basketball championship in the University of Maryland's Cole Field House. This in and of itself would have been an unremarkable event; however, the racial and cultural contrast in these two teams made for a poignantly symbolic moment in American history.

This game marked the first time an all-African American starting five (from Texas Western) competed against an all-white (University of Kentucky) team for a national title. Playing before an all-white audience with a Confederate flag amid the tightly packed rows of predominately Wildcat fans, the Miners put on a show of aggressive defense and team-oriented offense for the nation. African American basketball teams are commonplace today, but the Miners' racial makeup is remarkable when viewed in the context of their opponent, the surroundings, and the era in which they played the game. In 1966, even at the most liberal universities, basketball coaches observed strict racial quotas. At a time when the nation was still focused on the civil rights struggle, this game forced the country to confront the issue of race relations in a very public and celebrated way.

Legendary Wildcats coach Adolph Rupp, Kentucky, and the entire South had to face their future that night. Rupp, even when faced with the threat of losing federal funding for the school, had resisted the pleadings of his president to recruit his first African American player. Meanwhile, Texas Western administrators were concerned that coach Don Haskins played too many African Americans. Texas Western's starters ultimately upset Kentucky's all-white team, 72–65, but more significantly the game ushered in a new era of basketball and sports, particularly by signaling the official end to athletic segregation in the South. The most substantial increase in integration in the history of college sports occurred in the four years following the Miners' victory. The percentage of African Americans on college basketball teams jumped from 10 percent in 1962 to 34 percent by 1975. Suddenly, schools started seeking out African American athletes to play on their teams. These players carried with them not only the hopes of an integrated society, but also the hopes of athletic success for schools craving the monetary and political rewards of winning teams. All-white teams in the South and the unwritten rule about how many African Americans could play at a time in the North disappeared after this game. The next season, for the first time, there would be African American freshman basketball players in all Southern athletic conferences. Even the notoriously segregated Southeastern Conference started recruiting African American players. Rupp, however, held out until 1970 when he finally recruited his first and only African American player, Tom Payne, who played only one year for Kentucky (Fitzpatrick, 27).

Continued on next page

Texas Western v. Kentucky, Continued

Many regard the symbolic victory of Texas Western in 1966 as fleeting. In the immediate aftermath of the game, the polarizing combination of white backlash and African American militancy created a harsher and more pessimistic view of America's race relations. As colleges and universities increasingly coveted the talents of African American athletes, intercollegiate athletics increasingly became a microcosm for the racial problems plaguing the nation. In the name of athletic glory and monetary rewards, college administrators, coaches, and alumni began exploiting young African American players ill prepared for the academic rigors of college. While the debate over the ultimate significance of this game continues, it at the very least ushered in an era where issues of race were brought into mainstream America's living rooms because the games they watched on television graphically carried with them a racial component.

the rise of a more radical movement that did not believe in African American–white cooperation.

In many respects the beginning of the end for the nonviolent era of the civil rights movement predates the Watts riot. A militant civil rights faction that belonged to a longstanding African American radical tradition existed behind the scenes during the height of the 1950s and '60s nonviolent protests. From 1962 to 1964 an increasing number of young African Americans, particularly those working for SNCC, became unconvinced in the effectiveness of gradualism. Observing the mounting frustration among young African Americans, James Baldwin predicted widespread racial unrest that would erupt into violence in his 1963 *The Fire Next Time*. Some of these radical activists, like Gloria Richardson of the Cambridge Movement, were the first to combine the campaign for racial equality with the demand for economic justice. Richardson and others started becoming confrontational and unequivocal in their demands for an immediate end to segregation and job discrimination.

Tapping into this growing militancy, the Reverend Albert Cleage organized the Northern Negro Grass Roots Leadership Conference in November 1963 after the NAACP excluded African American nationalist supporters of Malcolm X and the Freedom Now Party from the Northern Negro Leadership Conference in Detroit. At this meeting Richardson and others expressed their support for Malcolm X's call for armed self-defense by African Americans taking a stand for their civil rights. Richardson and Lawrence Landry later organized ACT (not an acronym) in early 1964 to support the principle that African Americans should do whatever is necessary to be free. In 1964, *Ebony* magazine described how these African American activists were "preparing for war with local police, the

Stokely Carmichael, head of the Student Nonviolent Coordinating Committee, speaks against the draft at the University of California at Berkeley on October 29, 1966. (AP Photo)

national guard and federal troops" by literally stockpiling weapons (*Ebony,* July 1964). These early warnings, however, did little to prepare people for what happened in Watts in 1965.

In some ways, the nonviolent component of the civil rights movement became a victim of its own success. After the passage of the Civil Rights Act of 1964 and Voting Rights Act of 1965, African Americans residing in the abject poverty of the ghetto began to question the integrationist version of the American Dream preached by civil rights leaders like Martin Luther King Jr. Amid growing distrust of white domination, young African American leaders like SNCC leader Stokely Carmichael started calling for African American self-reliance and racial pride under the banner of "Black Power." In 1966, SNCC turned its back on the goal of racial integration and embraced the separatist ideology espoused by Malcolm X.

Carmichael is credited with initiating the Black Power movement during the historic march against fear across the state of Mississippi in June 1966. James Meredith had started the march, but just a few days after the march began Meredith was shot by a sniper and hospitalized. Leaders of the major civil rights organizations, including Carmichael and SNCC, decided to continue the march in Meredith's absence. Meredith recovered from his wounds and rejoined the march in time to enter Jackson, Mississippi, triumphantly and address a mass rally from the steps of the Mississippi State Capitol building. When the marchers arrived in Greenwood, Mississippi, on June 16, Carmichael was arrested for attempting to defy a police order. After being released on bail, Carmichael spoke to a crowd gathered in the hot Mississippi sun. He started slowly but his voice rose as his speech built toward a dramatic crescendo. Filled with emotion, Carmichael cried out: "This is the twenty-seventh time I have been arrested. I ain't going to jail no more. What we gonna start saying now is black power." In return, the crowd yelled back: "Black Power!" A new slogan and stage of the civil rights movement was born (Carson, 209–210).

While some in the Greenwood crowd sensed that this was a turning point in the civil rights movement, most could not articulate the meaning of "Black Power" with any precision. However, many would later agree with Carmichael's assessment that Black Power was "a call for black people in this country to unite, to recognize their heritage, to build a sense of community." Carmichael insisted that "the concept of Black Power rests on a fundamental premise: Before a group can enter the open society, it must first close ranks" (Toure and Hamilton, 44).

The Nation of Islam

Active since before World War II, the Nation of Islam found a resurgence amid the growing popularity of its most popular adherent, Malcolm X, during the 1960s. The Nation of Islam originated in 1931 when a man named Elijah Poole (1897–1975) was visited by a mysterious figure, Wallace D. Fard. Poole's meeting with Fard convinced him that African Americans were descended from Muslims, lost in America, and destined for redemption through Islam. At the same time, Poole believed the white race to be the misguided creation of an evil experiment. In 1931 Poole changed his name to Elijah Muhammad and began proselytizing and winning converts to his belief system.

Most of the followers of Elijah Muhammad came from the underclass of American society. Many of these recruits became members of the Nation of Islam while serving time in prison. The Nation of Islam emphasized Black Pride, dignity, self-determination, and the language of victimization. It trained both men and women in separate roles, emphasizing a woman's duties as mother, wife, and homemaker. Black Muslims rejected forced assimilation and integration. Many, like Malcolm Little (Malcolm X), changed their names as a symbol of their rejection of the identity imposed upon them and their family by slave owners.

In order to facilitate the creation of a community centered around Muhammad's teachings and concept of Islam, the Nation of Islam published the newspaper *Muhammad Speaks,* issued statements over radio stations, and established two universities of Islam, one in Detroit and another in Chicago. These schools were used to promote the concept of Africa's glorious past. Elijah Muhammad also formed the Fruit of Islam, a paramilitary organization, to defend his community of believers against white violence.

The Malcolm X Factor

A once-obscure Black Nationalist group, the Nation of Islam gained prominence in the 1960s for teaching African Americans to take responsibility for their own lives, to be disciplined, to live by strict codes of behavior, and to reject any dependence on whites. The most famous Black Muslim, as whites often referred to them, was Malcolm Little, a former drug addict and pimp who had spent time in jail and reformed his life after joining the Nation of Islam. He adopted the name Malcolm X to denote his lost African surname.

Malcolm X converted to the Nation of Islam while serving time in the same prison Elijah Muhammad was sentenced to for draft dodging during World War II. Malcolm X then took the Nation of Islam teachings and integrated them into his own concepts of Black Nationalism. Malcolm X's intelligence, oratorical skills, charisma, and uncompromising opposition to all forms of racism and oppression made him a favorite particularly among young African Americans. While he did not advocate violence as many of his critics claimed, he did insist that African Americans had the right to defend themselves, violently if necessary, from those who attacked them. King's nonviolence is often juxtaposed against Malcolm's presumed support for violence, but at the heart of Malcolm's message was the call for African Americans to pursue their liberation "by any means necessary." For Malcolm this left violence as an option, but he did not suggest it as a preferred mode of action to bring about change. In a 1965 speech he said, "I don't advocate violence, but if a man steps on my toes, I'll step on his" (Payne, "You Duh Man!" 193).

As a Black Muslim, Malcolm X preached the party line about "white devils," but after he left the Nation of Islam in 1964 because of a power struggle with Elijah Muhammad, he denied there were fundamental differences among people based on race. After a pilgrimage to Mecca, the holiest site of traditional Islam, and a tour of Africa, Malcolm X embraced the struggle of all colonized peoples and moved away from a simple antiwhite ideology and toward an internationalist vision of the future. "I believe, as the Koran teaches, that a man should not be judged by the color of his skin but rather by his conscious behavior, by his actions, by his attitude toward others and his actions towards others." (Payne, "You Duh Man!" 193).

On February 21, 1965, Malcolm X was assassinated while giving a speech at the Audubon Ballroom in Harlem. Three members of the Nation of Islam were later convicted of the murder. Immediately following his death, the *New York Times* dismissed Malcolm X's life as "pitifully wasted" because of his "ruthless and fanatical belief in violence" and declared the world indifferent to his murder (*New York Times*, February 22, 1965, p. 20; *New York Times*, February 28, 1965, p. 74). For a brief time, it appeared that Malcolm X would quickly fade from the public's memory. Doubleday canceled the printing of Malcolm X's autobiography, cowritten by Alex Haley, but Grove Press picked up its rights and published it in October 1965. Published just after the Watts riots of August, it became one of the decade's most influential books, inspiring the Black Power movement and turning Malcolm into an icon for the cause. *The Autobiography of Malcolm X* presented a life that did not flinch from martyrdom, magnifying the allure of an unfinished myth.

Race Riots, 1965–1967

On August 11, 1965, white police officers pulled over a man in a car in Watts on suspicion of drunk driving. As the typical crowd of onlookers gathered around the arrest scene, the mother of the suspected drunk driver scuffled with the patrolmen. When the onlookers began to jeer the police, the police brandished rifles and called for reinforcements. The African American onlookers became increasingly defiant and started to pelt newly arriving officers with rocks and bottles. By 10:00 p.m. the angry crowd had become a rampaging mob, over-turning cars and smashing shop windows. By midnight, looters took to the streets as thousands of African Americans vented their repressed anger with white authority throughout the night. Calm returned at dawn, but the crowds reassembled the next evening. More than 5,000 rioters took to the streets, break-ing windows, turning over cars, setting fires, and looting in protest against the brutality of the Los Angeles Police Department (LAPD). Some attacked whites and sniped at responding police and firemen. By Friday afternoon, the LAPD officials called for help from National Guard troops who rushed into Watts to restore or-der. Instead of order, the presence of the National Guard seemed to exacerbate the problem. By Saturday the number of rioters had multiplied. Over 14,000 Guardsmen and 1,500 police officers struggled to restrain and subdue the more than 50,000 African American rioters. Chaos ensued for three more days. When the six-day melee ended, 34 four had been killed, approximately 900 injured, almost 4,000 arrested, and roughly $30 million worth of property damaged.

Watts triggered a series of riots across the nation in the ensuing years. The summer of 1966 witnessed a large number of race riots and racial disturbances. Tired of suffering from police brutality, the indignity of white racism, oppres-sive poverty, insufferable living conditions, and little hope for a better future, African Americans living in ghettos in cities all over the country went on a ram-page. Images of African American mobs taking to the streets, breaking windows, smashing cars, trashing stores, and throwing bottles and bricks at police regu-larly ran on the evening news. In response to the apparently out-of-control violence, National Guard troops patrolled the streets of Chicago, Cleveland, Dayton, Milwaukee, and San Francisco, where rioters damaged $5 million worth of property.

The violence reached an apex during the summer of 1967. President John-son's National Advisory Commission on Civil Disorders recorded nearly 150 racial outbreaks during that summer, with nearly one-third of those considered "major or serious." Violence spread throughout the ghettos of Boston, Buffalo, Cincinnati, New Haven, Providence, Wilmington, Cambridge, and scores of other cities. Not surprisingly, Newark, New Jersey, experienced the bloodiest race riot. Newark had the nation's highest rates of African American joblessness, condemned housing, crime, cases of tuberculosis, and maternal mortality. The racial divide could not have been any larger as the majority African American population lived in abject poverty in a city controlled by a corrupt all-white administration. The Newark riot began on July 12, 1967, after the rumor that an African American taxi driver had been arrested and beaten to death at the hands of white police spread throughout the African American community. By the second evening of rioting, police used live ammunition to quell the rioters, killing five African Americans. The riot lasted three more days with the National Guard killing 20 more African Americans, wounding approximately 1,200, and arresting another 1,300. Property damage was estimated at $10 million.

A similar riot also broke out in Detroit during the summer of 1967. Unlike Newark, Detroit had a progressive mayor supported by the African American community and aggressively attending to the problems of the African American ghetto. With many African American city officeholders and millions of federal dollars pumped into Detroit's antipoverty and urban-renewal programs, the city seemed like an unlikely place for a massive race riot. Moreover, a booming auto industry offered Detroit African Americans economic opportunities African Americans in other cities could only dream of. However, police–African American relations replicated those of Watts and Newark. Recurring occurrences of police brutality created much resentment toward the Detroit Police Department. On July 23, the mass arrest of African Americans at a nightclub selling liquor after the legal closing time set off six days and nights of riots. Fires destroyed 1,300 buildings, leaving 5,000 African Americans homeless and jobless. Fires and looting caused a total property loss of approximately $250 million. Untrained and scared National Guardsmen opened fire on many of the rioters, killing most of the 43 killed during the uprising. In total, the 1967 race riots accounted for at least 90 deaths, over 4,000 casualties, and almost 1,700 arrests.

The National Advisory Commission on Civil Disorders blamed the riots on poverty, unemployment, slum housing, and segregated schools in the nation's cities. As a result, the commission recommended the creation of two million new jobs in America's ghettos, an end to de facto segregation, the construction of six million new units of public housing, and a national welfare system that would supplement the income of the poor. Conservatives attacked these conclusions, arguing that criminals, out-of-control youths, agitators, and a permissive society that had indulged African Americans' antisocial tendencies caused the civil unrest of the 1960s. The race riots from 1965 to 1967 became examples to many for the need of law and order that Richard Nixon, Republican Party nominee, preached on the 1968 presidential campaign trail.

SNCC and CORE's Call for Black Power

By mid-1965 both CORE and SNCC took a decisive turn away from the goals of integration, interracialism, and nonviolence. CORE's election of Floyd McKissick as its national director and SNCC's selection of Stokely Carmichael as its leader symbolized the shift of these two organizations toward a more radical agenda. The growing chasm between the old guard civil rights leaders and the new guard represented by McKissick and Carmichael was demonstrated at the "Meredith March Against Fear" in 1966.

On June 5, 1966, James Meredith, who had integrated the University of Mississippi in 1962, set out to march 225 miles from Memphis to Jackson. He did this to try to instill courage in southern African Americans afraid to vote, but on the second day of the walk a white man along Highway 51 jumped out of the bushes, shot, and wounded Meredith. Eager to capitalize on the shooting, the major civil rights organization decided to continue the march. Although some moderate civil rights leaders like Roy Wilkins and Whitney Young refused to participate because of the revolutionary zeal of Carmichael and McKissick, King decided to join the march as a moderating influence. On the first day, however, it became clear that King would have little effect on the young radicals. Carmichael shouted at a rally that "the Negro is going to take what he deserves from the white man" and "white blood will flow." Following his arrest in Greenwood, Mississippi, for erecting a tent on the grounds of an African American high school contrary to state troopers' orders, Carmichael shouted to a large crowd of protesters: "We been saying freedom for six years and we ain't got nothin'. What we gonna start saying now is Black Power!" Carmichael continued by rhythmically chanting: "We . . . want . . . Black . . . Power!" Eventually the entire crowd joined Carmichael in unison. Carmichael egged the crowd on by yelling back to the crowd: "What do you want?" The crowd replied: "Black Power!" Despite King's effort to insist upon an integrationist message, several at the march clearly embraced Carmichael's more resistant and impatient approach. From that moment, "Black Power" became a catch phrase for the more revolutionary and oppositional faction of the movement (Sitkoff, 213).

Carmichael believed that the initial step in any liberation movement was to cultivate a group consciousness centered on the need for immediate action. "The first stage is waking up our people," he said. "We have to wake them up to the impending danger. So we yell, Gun! Shoot! Burn! Kill! Destroy! They're committing genocide! Until the masses of our people are awake." Picking up on the ideology of Malcolm X, Carmichael and other Black Power spokespersons viewed African American retaliatory violence as a justifiable response in order to survive the continued acts of brutality against them. Carmichael said, "nothing more quickly repels someone bent on destroying you than the unequivocal message: 'O.K., fool, make your move, and run the same risk I run—of dying'" (Van Deburg, 19).

Derided by African Americans and whites alike, Black Power did galvanize many whom the civil rights movement had not mobilized into concerted action. It spawned several new associations and community organizations, a stronger faith in self-reliance, and attention to the needs of the lower classes. Black Power engendered feelings of pride, a psychological precondition for equality. It made black beautiful, causing many to throw away skin bleaches and hair straighteners. African Americans celebrated their racial characteristics and joyously affirmed their lifestyles, music, food, dialect, and culture. As James Brown sang: "Say it loud—I'm black and I'm proud." Those a part of the Black Power movement grew out their Afros and awakened interest in the neglected history and culture of Africa. The movement spawned several writers and scholars of African American history and culture, helping to establish Black studies programs at several universities. In short, Black Power helped African Americans to discard the disabling self-hatred inculcated by white culture.

The incendiary rhetoric of Black Power leaders like Carmichael also did much to fracture the civil rights movement and alienate sympathetic whites. Under Carmichael's leadership, the SNCC refused to work within the larger civil rights movement, expelled its white staff members, and denounced all white supporters and financial backers. Not surprisingly, by 1967 the organization was bankrupt and of marginal influence. Carmichael incessantly talked to the media about "killing," "offing," or "executing" "honkies" and "pigs." Ultimately Carmichael estranged himself completely from the mainstream civil rights movement by identifying himself with the paramilitary group known as the Black Panthers.

The Black Panthers

Founded by Huey Newton and Bobby Seale, the Black Panthers probably more than any other group represented the radical and more militant faction of the civil rights movement in the late 1960s. Established in Oakland, California, in 1966, the Black Panther Party promised to defend African American rights even if it required violence. Black Panthers proudly presented themselves as a rogue paramilitary organization whose members marched in lines and wore weapons openly and proudly. Although seldom practitioners of violence, they deliberately created an image of militant African Americans willing to fight for justice. The Black Panthers coined the expression, "all power to the people," to convey their belief that the exercise of power was a basic human need. They did not seek power over people, but the power to control their own destinies.

In the late 1960s, no revolutionary nationalist group received more publicity than the Black Panthers. Given all the attention they received, it is remarkable that the Panthers never had more than 100 core members around the Oakland area. However, their flare for the dramatic always seemed to attract television cameras and the organization ultimately spawned chapters in some 35 cities in

Members of the Black Panthers march in Manhattan to protest the murder trial of Huey Newton on July 22, 1968. (Bettmann/Corbis)

19 states and the District of Columbia by the end of the decade. They dressed, spoke, and behaved in a manner designed to provoke a reaction. The original Panther uniform was a black leather jacket, beret, powder-blue shirt with scarf or turtleneck shirt. Several wore dark sunglasses to add to their intimidating presence. Always armed, they presented themselves as disciplined, well trained, and fully committed to the goal of liberation. Because of their presence, strong rhetoric, and weaponry, white America and J. Edgar Hoover's FBI saw the Panthers as the number one threat to the internal security of the nation.

Beyond their intent to intimidate white America and authority, the Black Panther Party stood for community control and African American self-help. Toward this end the Panthers organized socialistic programs aimed at educating the masses to the politics of revolution. The primary vehicle they used to do this was a "survival program" to help organize and sustain black America until the revolution could be launched. Individual chapters of the survival program provided an array of social services like breakfasts for children, free shoes and clothing, legal assistance, medical care, and screening for sickle cell anemia. They also operated liberation schools where African American youths were taught about revolution and liberation and the importance of African American cohesion and self-reliance. The Panthers also promoted voter registration not only to increase the African American vote, but also as a way to place more African

American and poor people on juries. The survival programs were not meant as a definitive answer to the problem of African American oppression; rather, they were only aimed at keeping African Americans from perishing from a lack of care and sustenance.

The Black Panther Party embraced the African American cultural nationalism espoused by the likes of Maulana Karenga, leader of the Los Angeles–based U.S. organization. Karenga argued for the necessity of cultural awareness among African Americans that centered on the revival of African traditions—real or invented—of dress, language, religion, and familial arrangements as well as the rejection of white supremacy. Ultimately the Black Panther Party separated itself from Karenga's call for cultural nationalism and African American capitalism. The Panthers continued to assert that cultural pride was a necessary phase of African American people's political development, but it did not guarantee liberation, nor did African American skin necessarily identify one as an automatic ally. Eventually the Panthers severed all ties with Karenga after U.S. members killed two prominent Panthers, John Huggins and "Bunchy" Carter, in a UCLA campus shootout.

Were the Black Panthers a Negative or Positive Influence on the Civil Rights Movement?

Although the Black Panthers' initial 10-point program made reasonable demands such as decent housing, education, employment, and an end to police brutality in African American communities, it also included the need for African Americans to determine their own destiny and secure self-defense "by whatever means necessary." Their implied violent tactics, celebration of communism and Mao Zedong's *Little Red Book,* stance against the Vietnam War, and sympathies for other oppressed populations, particularly those in third world countries, caused an extreme and hostile reaction by white America. However, it also caused an angry reaction by those working within the mainstream civil rights movement. To them, such militant language, symbolism, and tactics diminished the political support African Americans received from white liberals.

Historians such as Robert J. Norell believe that the Black Panthers and the Black Power movement did much to undermine the post-1965 reform efforts of the civil rights movement. Author of *The House I Live In: Race in the American Century,* Norell believes, "the black-power effort was romanticized at the time, and it has been romanticized very consistently ever since." Other historians like Claude A. Clegg III, author of *An Original Man: The Life and Times of Elijah Muhammad,* argue that the civil rights movement had already lost momentum before Black Power and the Black Panthers arrived onto the scene. "Civil rights had achieved what it set out to achieve—franchise, the end of statutory racial discrimination. It was a triumphant. However, some of the more difficult questions,

Tommie Smith and John Carlos at the 1968 Olympics

Harry Edwards, a young sociology professor at San Jose State University, organized the Olympic Project for Human Rights in order to bring attention to racial injustice in the United States. Edwards, a former basketball and track athlete at San Jose State, gained national attention in 1967 when he led African American students in a highly publicized protest movement at San Jose State, which culminated in the cancellation of the season-opening football game against University of Texas at El Paso. His 1968 Olympic Project for Human Rights called for a boycott of the 1968 Olympic Games in Mexico City. Edwards assembled a group of African American athletes who threatened to boycott the games unless certain demands were met, including the restoration of Muhammad Ali's heavyweight boxing title (see the next chapter), exclusion of South Africa from participation, and the ouster of Avery Brundage as president of the International Olympic Committee (IOC). The athletes ultimately decided to participate in the games, choosing instead to show forms of protest to highlight racial discrimination in the United States and around the world.

Among those athletes joining Edward's Olympic Project for Human Rights were sprinters Tommie Smith and John Carlos. Smith ran track for San Jose State and became acquainted with Edwards while a student there. Smith went to the 1968 Olympics as one of the world's premier sprinters. In 1966 he set four world records in the 200 meter and 220-yard sprints. The next year he captured the world record in the 400 meter and the 440-yard events. Carlos once ran for East Texas State University, but transferred to San Jose State after experiencing racial discrimination. Slightly less accomplished and not as outspoken as Smith, Carlos had an impressive record in his own right. In 1969 he was Amateur Athletic Union and National Collegiate Athletic Association champion in the 200 meter and 220-yard sprints and tied the world records in the 60-yard and 100-yard dashes.

Despite their track accomplishments before and after the 1968 Olympic Games, both will forever be remembered for their protest after the 200-meter finals in Mexico City. After Smith won the gold medal and Carlos won the bronze medal in the race, they took the podium alongside silver medalist Peter Norman of Australia. To protest the treatment of African Americans in the United States, Smith and Carlos refused to stand with their hands over their hearts as the American flag was raised. Instead, each wore one black glove and raised their clinched fists and bowed their heads during the national anthem. This became one of the most enduring symbols of the 1960s and the Black Power movement of the late 1960s. As punishment, Smith and Carlos were suspended from the U.S. team and expelled from the Olympic Village.

such as economic equity, basic attitudes, and the empowerment of the inner cities, remained." The noted Afro-American studies scholar William L. Van Deburg said of the Panthers, "My position is that cultural and psychological change is the most important legacy of black power. It was the Panthers' major contribution to what black personhood could be" (Joseph, *The Chronicle of Higher Education,* March 2, 2007, A12–17).

The Black Arts Movement

Inspired by African American artists such as Langston Hughes, Zora Neale Hurston, Ralph Ellison, James Baldwin, and Richard Wright, the Black Arts Movement began in 1964. One day after the assassination of Malcolm X on February 22, 1965, poet and playwright Amiri Baraka (formerly LeRoi Jones) announced the establishment of the Harlem Black Arts Repertory Theater/School (BARTS), which marked a turning point in African American culture, emphasizing African American consciousness, self-determination, and segregation from the white racist American culture. Directly correlating with the rise of Black Power, BARTS helped spread the Black Arts Movement by promoting and developing African American artists via conventions, festivals, and cultural centers throughout the United States. The first national Black Arts conventions were held in Detroit in 1966 and 1967. Black Arts festivals began in Harlem (1965) and Newark (1967). The Black Arts Movement is directly responsible for the establishment of over 800 African American theaters and cultural centers throughout the United States. In 1968 Larry Neal and Amiri Baraka edited *Black Fire,* a thick volume of poetry, essays, and drama, which drew national attention to the renaissance of African American artists. This renaissance included the paintings of Vincent Smith; the photography of Billy Abernathy; the drama of Amiri Baraka; the novels of Alice Walker, Ishmael Reed, and Toni Morrison; the acting of Danny Glover, Lou Gossett Jr., and Al Freeman; the music of Nina Simone; and the poetry of Nikki Geovanni.

All-African People's Revolutionary Party

Stokely Carmichael became an admirer of Kwame Nkrumah, the first president of the newly independent nation of Ghana and proponent of a unified sub-Saharan African state. Carmichael left the United States in 1969 to join Nkrumah, who was living in exile in Guinea. Carmichael changed his name to Kwame Toure in honor of Nkrumah and Guinea's President Ahmed Sekou Toure. While there, Toure founded the All-African People's Revolutionary Party (A-APRP) with the goal of creating a unified and liberated Africa under a socialist government. He believed that the liberation and empowerment of Africans and people of African descent, including African Americans, could only be achieved through the establishment of this African state. Though the party never became very large, Toure worked tirelessly traveling around the world in support for the cause of Pan-Africanism. Until his death in 1998 Toure continued to make Guinea his home but periodically returned to the United States in order to attract new members to the A-APRP. While somewhat successful, the organization never attracted enough members or attention to influence American politics.

Women's Role in the Civil Rights and Black Power Movements

During the last two decades historians have focused more attention on the contributions of women to the civil rights and Black Power movements of the 1960s. Though their contributions and leadership were often ignored or diminished, women like Septima Clark, Fannie Lou Hamer, Annie Devine, and Victoria Gray played major roles in utilizing local organizations to mobilize working-class African American southerners. Clark, a teacher from Charleston, South Carolina, developed adult education programs that provided literacy training for African American southerners to prepare them to register to vote. Ultimately taken over by SCLC and directed by Clark, the Citizenship School program formed the basis for the "Voter Education Project," which was responsible for the registration of thousands of southern African American voters.

Fannie Lou Hamer, Annie Devine, and Victoria Gray were among the founders of the Mississippi Freedom Democratic Party in 1964 to challenge the all-white Democratic Party in the state. All three carried out grassroots organizing for the party among the African American working classes in numerous cities and towns. They were so successful at grassroots organization because of their ability to use formal church networks in rallying civil rights activism.

When the civil rights movement made its transition to the more militant demands of Black Power, African American women participated and assumed leadership roles in organizations previously characterized as male-dominated. Women activists involved in the Black Power movement were highly visible, outspoken, and militant in their pursuit of African American equality. They sometimes placed themselves in dangerous positions and questioned nonviolence as the most appropriate strategy to bring about social change. However, in a movement full of contradictions regarding proper gender roles, the talents and contributions of these women often went underutilized and unrecognized. The lead prophet of the Black Power movement, Malcolm X, often expressed patriarchal attitudes and values, and one of the distinctive tenets of the Black Power movement was the belief in African American male dominance.

Yet women like Ruby Doris Smith and Angela Davis assumed prominent roles in this militant stage of the civil rights movement. Smith, a longtime member of

SNCC and participant in the 1961 Freedom Rides, ultimately turned her back on the hopes of integration and embraced African American separatism. Interestingly, immediately following Black Power's historic introduction, in an interview with *Ebony* magazine Smith said that African American men should be the leaders of the civil rights movement. However, until enough African American men got involved, she claimed, African American women would have to carry much of the burden. Smith's comments reflect the difficulty women like her had in juggling their traditional family responsibilities with their leadership commitments. It also reflects that in the mid- to late 1960s race loyalty trumped gender issues in the minds of most African American women civil rights activists.

Davis, an iconic symbol of Black Power, often confronted resistance from African American men. While organizing a rally in San Diego, Davis complained that male members of SNCC and later the Black Panthers criticized her for doing a "man's job." To them, a woman was supposed to inspire her man and educate his children, not lead. Davis thought this male attitude was particularly ironic given that "much of what I was doing had fallen to me by default." Davis confronted this attitude in a 1968 Los Angeles SNCC staff meeting when men started complaining that women were taking over the organization, "calling it a matriarchal coup d' etat." The men pointed to many myths about African American women in their complaint: They were too domineering, they wanted to control everything, they wanted to rob the men of their manhood. As a result, the men reasoned, African American women assuming leadership roles within the organization "were aiding and abetting the enemy, who wanted to see black men weak and unable to hold their own" (Giddings, 316).

This growing sexism within the Black Power movement made life very difficult for these strong and committed African American women. Their leadership was being criticized and chastised from both outside and inside the movement. Not only had African American women played a major role in the modern civil rights movement, but strength and self-reliance had been a part of the African American female persona since slavery. To now be told that they had stepped out of bounds and that the struggle for equal rights could not succeed until they returned to their proper places was both insulting and infuriating. Some historians have argued that the Black Panthers' politics of gender ultimately affected its ability to function as an effective political organization. However, when the Black Panthers severed ties to Karenga's U.S. organization, Bobby Seale publicly stated that one reason for the split was the inherent male chauvinism of cultural nationalism: "Cultural nationalists like Karenga, are male chauvinists. . . . What they do is oppress the black woman. Their black racism leads them to theories of male domination" (White, 80). Huey P. Newton later went so far as to call for a coalition between the Panthers and the Women's Liberation and Gay Liberation movements. Newton also expressed in his 1967 essay, "Fear and Doubt," that the African American man "feels that he is something less than a man. . . . He is ineffectual both in and out of the home. He cannot provide for, or protect his family" (Newton, 81). So in many ways he embraced the patriarchal norms of the larger society that the man should be the breadwinner and the woman should stay at home and raise the children. Understandably because they themselves were products of the dominant culture, the Panthers decried the class and gender biases of the larger white society, but also reaffirmed many of those same shortcomings.

1968 White Backlash

The 1968 presidential election symbolized the white backlash against the previous decade's civil rights movement and emergence of Black Power. The Republican presidential nominee, Richard Nixon, campaigned against open housing and busing for racial balance. He also promised to slow efforts at school integration and to appoint conservative justices to the federal courts. Nixon embraced a strategy to appeal to traditional white Democratic voters, particularly in the South, who had grown tired of the civil rights movement. Alabama governor George Wallace entered the presidential race under the banner of the American Independent Party to appeal to the growing sentiment that the cause of civil rights and African American equality had gone too far. Wallace made the fear and resentment of African Americans the central message of his campaign. Despite the tremendous obstacles in running a successful third-party campaign in a U.S. presidential election, he garnered 9.9 million votes, almost 14 percent of the turnout.

Immediately following his victory, President Nixon began pandering to the Wallace constituency to ensure his reelection in 1972. Referred to as Nixon's "Southern Strategy," he conceded the African American and white liberal vote to go after white Southerners, suburbanites, and ethnic workers troubled by the prospects of racial equality. Toward that end, his administration urged Congress to impose a moratorium on court-ordered busing, nominated conservative "strict constructionist" federal judges, particularly to the Supreme Court, and pleaded with the Supreme Court to postpone the desegregation of Mississippi schools. The administration also lobbied Congress to defeat the fair-housing enforcement program and the extension of the Voting Rights Act of 1965. It also cut funding for the Offices for Civil Rights in the Justice and Health, Education, and Welfare departments, vetoed bills and impounded funds designed to assist African Americans, and fired government officials who sought to implement integration guidelines. The chairman of the EEOC and the U.S. Commission on Civil Rights and head of the Small Business Administration's program for minorities resigned in protest. Unfortunately for African Americans, Nixon's southern strategy worked as he won every state except Massachusetts and the District of Columbia in the 1972 election.

EFFECTS OF THE VIETNAM WAR ON THE CIVIL RIGHTS MOVEMENT

The radicalization of the civil rights movement by the likes of SNCC, CORE, and the Black Panthers Party correlated with the escalation of the Vietnam War (see the next chapter). As President Johnson began increasing the number of American troops serving and fighting in Vietnam in 1965, most Americans viewed opposition to the government's foreign policies as disloyal. Martin Luther King Jr. immediately called for an end to the war, but after a severe backlash from influential and wealthy white liberals, he backed off and went along with other moderates within the movement to keep the issue of civil rights divorced from foreign policy.

Because of the cost of the Vietnam War, President Johnson admitted that he could not do all he would like to do to advance racial justice and wage his war against poverty at home. As a result, the radical wing of the civil rights movement split from King and the other moderates in vehemently opposing the war. By 1966 SNCC and CORE joined other antiwar groups in aggressively protesting President Johnson's Vietnam policies. As the war progressed, King decided he could no longer keep quiet. He concluded that to do so would make a mockery of his life's work of promoting love and nonviolence. As a result, in 1967 he came out to give his "declaration of independence from the Vietnam War." King concluded that the war and racial injustice were inextricably linked. After the passage of the Civil Rights Act of 1964 and Voting Rights Act of 1965, King sought to forge an interracial alliance of the poor and oppressed. As the war lingered and escalated, he became convinced that it was robbing the nation of valuable resources necessary to create new jobs and to eradicate poverty, particularly in the nation's cities. Despite intense pressure from the Johnson administration, King continued to speak out, insisting that the United States was spending $500,000 to kill each enemy soldier but only $35 a year to assist each impoverished American.

As 1967 progressed, King threw himself completely behind the antiwar efforts, burning all bridges to the administration. He assumed the leadership of the massive Spring Mobilization Against the War, urged Americans to become conscientious objectors, and declared the United States "the greatest purveyor of violence in the world today" (Sitkoff, 219). As a result of King's stand, he became alienated from many of his traditional allies. President Johnson covertly tried to destroy his influence, white liberals and moderate and conservative African Americans like Roy Wilkins and Jackie Robinson denounced him for going too far in his remonstrance. At the same time, young radicals believed King's opposition to the war was too little, too late. Ironically, King's finest hour in passionately and eloquently speaking out against the war signaled his waning influence on the civil rights movement.

Poor People's March in Washington, D.C., on June 18, 1968. (Library of Congress)

Going into 1968 King looked to regroup by organizing a Poor People's March on Washington. He envisioned an interracial coalition of the dispossessed marching on Washington in greater numbers than his famous 1963 March on Washington for racial justice. In March 1968, King interrupted his efforts to organize the Poor People's Campaign to go to Memphis to rally support for the mostly African American sanitation workers of the city striking for union recognition and better wages. He attempted to organize a protest march in Memphis, but it quickly degenerated into chaos and violence. The police responded by dispersing the crowd with gunfire and tear gas. Despondent over his apparent ineffectiveness, King committed to staying in Memphis to show that it was still possible to hold a nonviolent demonstration.

On April 3, King gave an address where he mentioned recent threats on his life. "I don't mind," he said.

> Like anybody, I would like to live a long life, Longevity has its place. But I'm not concerned about that now. I just want to do God's will. And He's allowed me to go up to the mountain. And I've looked over and I've seen the Promised Land! I may not get there with you, but I want you to know tonight that we as a people will get to the Promised Land. (Sitkoff, 220–221).

The next evening King was assassinated while on the balcony at the Lorraine Motel.

Civil Unrest in the Wake of King's Assassination

Many historians and civil rights activists believe that the civil rights movement died with King. After all, King embodied the spirit and belief in nonviolent protest that characterized the civil rights movement from 1954 to 1965. His principled leadership and eloquence inspired African Americans and whites alike to struggle against racism and the systems and structures that reinforced African American oppression. Respect for King kept white liberals engaged and energized in the struggle; with his death the middle ground between moderates and the radical faction of the movement washed away. No other African American leader commanded enough respect and influence to appeal to both races while not completely alienating the young revolutionaries attracted to the more strident politics of the Black Panthers and Stokely Carmichael.

In the wake of King's death, no person could step forward to galvanize the movement and instill a common vision for an entire people. Ralph Abernathy tried to continue King's Poor People's March on Washington, but with very poor results. The nation barely noticed the march that ultimately disintegrated into a morass of disunity and criminality. In King's absence, mainstream America's growing resentment against the fiery urban riots and confrontational politics of the young African American radicals went unchecked. Young African American activists' association with the antiwar movement, the counterculture, and student rebellions justified old prejudices and new antagonisms. White liberals abandoned the cause in reaction to the Black Power movement, and the white working class in the North became nervous over the consequences of racial equality. Like in the South, the white working class started to fear the loss of jobs and the intrusion of African Americans into their neighborhoods and schools. Politicians like Ronald Reagan in California in the 1966 gubernatorial race made hay by playing to these fears. Candidates running on "law and order" and "get tough with blacks" campaigns won elections in almost every city that had experienced a riot.

The African American Soldier

The draft classification system during the Vietnam War favored middle- and upper-class white males, so poor African American men were drafted at disproportionately high rates. Rather than fight in a controversial war, many white, middle-class men of draft age chose college, designated professions, and the reserves as acceptable alternatives to regular military service. The reliance on an inequitable draft during the Johnson and Nixon administrations demonstrated to those involved in the civil rights movement the power the dominant white culture had over African American men. Because of general economic inequality between African Americans and whites and the discriminatory implementation of draft laws, the class bias of the draft imposed a special burden on African

United States Army soldiers fire at a suspected Viet Cong position during a search-and-destroy mission. The draft and Project 100,000, which aggressively recruited underprivileged youths, hit the African American community particularly hard. Martin Luther King Jr., who believed that disproportionate numbers of African Americans were being sent to Vietnam, described the conflict as "a white man's war, a black man's fight." (National Archives)

American men. Most of the numerous ways that middle-class white Americans could legally evade the draft were not realistically accessible to African American men. Approximately 12 percent of draft-age men were African American; yet they were drafted at rates that exceeded that number. In 1963, for example, African American men accounted for 18.5 percent of those drafted. In 1967 that percentage dropped to 16.3, but considering the fact that only 29 percent of draft-age African American males were eligible to serve because of inadequate academic skills and poor health, it is clear that African American men had to disproportionately carry the burden of fighting the war (Graham, 18–19).

Already confronting a significant draft risk, the poor became even more vulnerable when the Department of Defense launched Project 100,000. In August 1966, Robert McNamara presented this program as a chance for the military to help previously rejected young men escape poverty. McNamara argued that these men could attain marketable skills that would transfer to the private sector after their military service. This seemed like an ideal way for the Johnson administration to converge its flagging "War on Poverty" (see "The Antipoverty Crusade" chapter) with its resource-draining military campaign in Vietnam. They argued that the military could become an indispensable employer of jobless men. This argument did not sell among the growing cries for Black Power. Reflecting on the motive of Project 100,000, Stokely Carmichael cynically surmised, "that the [white] man is moving to get rid of African American people in the ghettoes" ("Negroes Expected").

In 1966, the Department of Defense released casualty figures that gained the attention of the African American community. In 1965 and 1966, the African American army death rate approached 21 percent (Binkin and Eitelberg, 76). Responding to complaints by civil rights leaders, the Department of Defense began to reduce the number of African American soldiers serving on the front lines, resulting in a significant reduction in these fatality rates. Their high death rates revealed that most African American men served in the army or marines—the services that endured the heaviest casualties—either because of their draftee status or their lack of technical training. These facts led Carmichael to go on NBC's *Meet the Press* and refer to the African American GI as a "mercenary." "When this country says to a black youth in the ghetto and to black youths in the rural South that their only chance for a decent living is to join the Army, and they throw in all sorts of rationalizations about how you can get skills. . . . It is saying to that black man that his only chance for a decent life is to become a hired killer because that's the sole function of an Army" ("Excerpts from Interview," 36). Cleveland Sellers of SNCC went even further by charging that the draft amounted to "a plan to commit calculated genocide" (Roberts, 7). Harlem's congressman, Adam Clayton Powell, compared the draft to "Hitler's twin system of eugenics and education. . . . First we provide an inferior education for black students. . . . Next we give them a series of tests that many will flunk because of an inferior education. Then, we pack these academic failures off to Vietnam to be killed" (Semble, 4).

Ali's Draft Resistance

Muhammad Ali's 1967 refusal to serve in the military and ensuing four-year legal battle with the Department of Justice sparked a national debate over the responsibilities of citizenship, inequities of the draft, and the state of race relations (see the next chapter). Ali's draft refusal was important to African American GIs because it suggested that they could define their manhood with militant antiwar politics rather than the hegemonic warrior role. After receiving his draft notice, Ali famously said, "I am a member of the Black Muslims, and we don't go to war unless they're declared by Allah himself. I don't have no personal quarrel with those Vietcongs" ("Clay Plans to Apologize," 17).

While many within the African American community regretted Ali's decision to resist the draft, many African American leaders rallied to his defense. King praised Ali for resisting the draft, and Carmichael denounced the government for drafting Ali in the first place: "It's about time we're going to tell him [the white man], hell no, we won't go" ("Dr. King Accuses Johnson"). An organization of African American sports activists, the Olympic Project for Human Rights, called upon powerful boxing commissions to restore Ali's heavyweight title. In 1968, African American civil rights activists from CORE, the National Black Anti-Draft Union, and other organizations assembled outside Madison Square Garden to protest the title fight between Buster Mathis and Joe Frazier arranged to replace the exiled heavyweight champion. Ali's draft resistance represented an emergence of a committed antiwar movement within the African American community.

Reaction to Ali's resistance by African American soldiers was mixed. Some African American soldiers prided themselves in their military service and the military's relative commitment to racial equality and opportunity. Other young African American soldiers saw Ali as a model of a new African American man who was not intimidated by government coercion. Ali became a symbol of a new era of African American consciousness and redefinition of African American manhood.

Black Power in the Military

After experiencing discrimination within the military, several African American soldiers looked to the Black Power movement for explanations of their oppression and for strategies of liberation. The influence of Black Power ideology caused black soldiers to emphasize their racial identity over military allegiance. African American soldiers often congregated informally in their tents to participate in "soul sessions" in which they socialized together and discussed racial issues. They also established more formal organizations that emphasized cultural awareness: The Malcolm X Association, Unsatisfied Black Soldiers, Better Blacks United, and De Mau Mau. African American GIs used these organizations and Black Power rhetoric to interpret their oppression and redefine their masculinity according to the values of their brotherhood.

This process of socialization formed around these informal and formal associations included a series of interactive gestures that created a strong sense of racial pride and unity within the brotherhood. The slapping of hands, finger snapping, and chest bumping amounted to ritual greetings referred to as "the dap," the Vietnamese word for "beautiful." Men from different regions and different branches of the military shared their own variations of the dap, but when they encountered a stranger they would become acquainted by teaching one another their specific variations of the handshake. African American soldiers also signified African American masculinity by growing out their Afros. By embracing their long, bushy hair and glorifying their African American bodies, African American soldiers rejected white aesthetics. A few conservative commanding officers attempted to humiliate radical GIs by ordering their Afros cut in public, but African American soldiers often risked jail sentences in order to display their racial identity through their hairstyle. In addition, African American soldiers wore black sunglasses, black armbands, black shirts, and black gloves to showcase their African American masculinity.

African American soldiers also started rallying around black, red, and green flags. Black represented their African and black American culture, red represented the blood African Americans had shed throughout history, and green symbolized youth and new ideas. Many African American soldiers even started to adopt the mercenary and genocide theories of outspoken activists like Stokely Carmichael and Adam Clayton Powell. For African American soldiers these theories explained their high casualty rates and marginal status in the military. Denied rank and privilege, African American soldiers embraced racial solidarity as a source of power and masculinity, and rumors of Vietnam as a race war only reinforced their unity (Graham, 90–119).

Conclusion: Legacy of the 1960s Civil Rights Movement

The 1960s brought revolutionary and permanent changes in American race relations. The decade witnessed the end of Jim Crow segregation and federal legislation that ensured the protection of African Americans' most basic civil rights, including the right to vote. The enfranchisement of southern African Americans ended political control of the Democratic Party in the south and allowed African American candidates to enter the political arena. Even white candidates who once had been segregationists now courted the African American vote.

Much of these gains in civil rights, however, took place during the first half of the decade when African American activists like Martin Luther King were willing to work within the constraints of a post–World War II consensus in a faith that continued economic growth, combined with finely tuned government programs, could solve most social problems, including civil rights. By 1965, fissures in this liberal consensus started to appear. As President Lyndon Johnson fought to expand his Great Society (see "The Antipoverty Crusade" chapter) and the United States' involvement in Vietnam (see the following chapter), it became apparent that while many Americans supported legislation that banned segregation and provided African Americans with basic political rights, they balked at more ambitious proposals for redressing economic inequality.

The African American struggle for civil, political, and economic equality ultimately revealed that the liberal consensus was an illusion. From 1965 on, the movement grew increasingly radical as African Americans pressed for not only civil rights, but for economic and political rights as well. By 1966, King's civil rights movement was overshadowed by the more militant calls of Black Nationalists demanding an end to black economic oppression. The urban riots from 1965 to 1968 underscored the deep racial divide that still tore at the fabric of America. The end of the decade saw the civil rights movement disintegrate, unable to end the more entrenched forms of segregation and discrimination. African Americans, particularly those living in the central cities, continued to make up a disproportionate number of the American poor, unemployed, and undereducated.

BIOGRAPHIES

Baldwin, James, 1924–1987

Writer

Born in New York City, Baldwin experienced a religious conversion at the age of 14 and became a preacher at the Fireside Pentecostal Assembly in Harlem. Baldwin also wrote poetry at a young age and soon found himself torn between his public church and private artistic lives. At age sixteen he began a homosexual relationship with a Harlem racketeer that caused him to feel like a hypocrite. At age 18 he left the church and broke off his relationship with the racketeer. In 1944 the author Richard Wright helped him win the Eugene F. Saxon Fellowship to work on his first novel, *In My Father's House,* which he struggled to publish. Ultimately tired of his faltering writing career and America's racism, Baldwin bought a one-way ticket to Paris in 1948, where he met writers such as Jean-Paul Sartre, Jean Genet, and Saul Bellow. He wrote arguably his best novel, *Go Tell It on the Mountain,* while in the Swiss Alps in 1951. Largely autobiographical, the novel was well received and nominated for the National Book Award in 1954. After the publication of his second novel, *Giovanni's Room* (1956) and his first collection of essays, *Notes of a Native Son* (1955), Baldwin's writing career was in full swing. He would periodically return to the United States throughout the 1950s and '60s, meeting Martin Luther King Jr. in 1961 and becoming very involved in the civil rights movement. By 1963 he was featured on the cover of *Time* magazine as a major spokesman for the movement after the publication of his most influential work, *The Fire Next Time.* In this book, Baldwin examines the racial tensions that existed in the United States. Because of the success and notoriety of this book, Baldwin was responsible for giving the movement its literary voice. Some critics believe Baldwin lost that voice after the death of King and transformation of the civil rights movement from integrationist to separatist. He spent most of his last two decades in France, and his work became more detached from the problems of American life. In his collection of essays, *No Name in the Street* (1972), Baldwin laments the movement's failures.

Bond, Julian, 1940–

SNCC Founder

Born Horace Julian Bond in Nashville, Tennessee, Bond, while a student at Morehouse College, helped found the Committee on Appeal for Human Rights (COAHR), which advocated for equal employment rights for African Americans in Atlanta, Georgia. COAHR took out advertisements in Atlanta's newspapers taking the city to task for employing African Americans only in low-paying menial positions and organized sit-ins at public buildings, lunch counters, and restaurants. Bond served as a reporter and managing editor for COAHR's newspaper, *Atlanta Inquirer.* Bond's work with the paper helped diversify the civil rights movement's methods and helped him hone his media skills. He dropped out of Morehouse during his senior year to become communications director for the Student Nonviolent Coordinating Committee (SNCC). He worked for SNCC until 1965 when he ran for and won a seat in the Georgia legislature. Soon after his victory he was quoted as supporting a SNCC statement that condemned the Vietnam War. As a result, the legislature accused him of giving "aid and comfort to the enemies of Georgia" and voted 184–12 not to seat him. Two years and two elections later, both of which Bond won, the U.S. Supreme Court overturned the legislature's action. In 1968, Bond led a rival delegation to the Democratic National Convention; one that he claimed better reflected Georgia's racial demographics. When he successfully won a place at the convention for his delegation, Bond gained great fame and national political support.

Angela Davis, 1944–

Activist

Born into a middle-class family in Birmingham, Alabama, Angela Davis grew up subjected to the violence, racism, and segregation of the Deep South. While pursuing a graduate degree in California, Davis joined the Black Power movement and became active in both the Student Nonviolent Coordinating Committee (SNCC) and the Black Panther Party. In 1968, she joined the African American cell of the Communist Party in Los Angeles. After Davis was hired as a professor at the University of California, Los Angeles, state officials tried to remove her from her duties because of her radical political affiliations. Davis had to defend herself against state repression, police harassment, and Federal Bureau of Investigation enquiries. Her battle with state and federal agencies made national headlines and turned Davis into a celebrity and symbol for the Black Power movement. The FBI put Davis on its most-wanted list after a gun registered in her name was used in a violent attempt to take over a California courtroom in 1970. Two people were killed, including the judge, in the crossfire between the defendant's seventeen-year-old brother George Jackson, who was using the gun registered in Davis's name, and San Quentin guards. Although Davis was not involved in the incident, she was arrested and charged with kidnapping, murder, and conspiracy. The subsequent trial in 1971 drew even more media attention and caused Davis to become a lightning rod for issues of race, class, and gender. Davis was acquitted of all charges.

Fannie Lou Hamer, a Mississippi field hand for most of her life, became a prominent advocate of civil rights. As Mississippi's Democratic Party refused African American members, Hamer helped form the Mississippi Freedom Democratic Party (MFDP) whose members attempted to unseat the regular party delegation at the Democratic National Convention in 1964. (Library of Congress)

Fannie Lou Hamer, 1917–1977

Activist

The twentieth child of sharecropper parents, Fannie Lou grew up in extreme poverty in the Mississippi Delta. After dropping out of school at the age of 12 to work in the cotton fields alongside her older siblings, she married Perry "Pap" Hamer in 1944 and moved to Ruleville, Mississippi. In 1962 she began attending meetings sponsored by the Student Nonviolent Coordinating Committee (SNCC) aimed to educate African American people of their rights and register them to vote. That year Hamer took a bus to Indianola, Mississippi, with other African Americans in an attempt to register to vote. Most were turned away, but Hamer was given a complex literacy test that required applicants to copy and interpret passages of the Mississippi state constitution. Hamer failed the test and returned home only to be informed by her landlord that if she continued to try to register to vote she and her family would be evicted from his property. Hamer gathered her family and moved immediately. She continued to face harassment including open gunfire, but she remained determined and said of the experience, "They kicked me off the plantation, they set me free" (Gates and West, 250). Hamer began working for SNCC and the Council of Federated Organizations (COFO), studied and passed the literacy test in December 1962, and diligently helped other African Americans to register to vote. She was arrested and beaten in Winona, Mississippi, in 1963 while attending citizenship classes, but her hardships and determination made her a symbol of the civil rights movement. In 1964 she became the voice of the Mississippi Freedom Democratic Party (MFDP), an outgrowth of 1964's Freedom Summer, and ran as the MFDP candidate for the U.S. Senate. Hamer also went to the Democratic Party's nominating convention in Atlantic City, New Jersey, to protest against systematic exclusion of African American representation from the state party's 1964 delegation. Her protest led to a compromise that seated only two MFDP delegates but pressured the Democratic Party to vote that in the future segregated delegations would not be seated. In 1967, Hamer played an important role in founding and leading the National Welfare Rights Organization with George Wiley.

Esther Cooper Jackson, 1917–

Activist

Raised in an activist family, Cooper earned a master's degree in sociology from Fisk University where she joined the Communist Party and became a leader of the recently formed Southern Negro Youth Congress (SNYC). As a leader of SNYC, she tapped into the locally based networks of African American organizations such as churches, women's clubs, and the NAACP. As the executive secretary of the national Committee for Defense of Negro Leadership, Jackson spent much of her time during the 1950s defending her husband, James Jackson, against charges of subversion issued by the House Un-American Activities Committee. She helped found and then edit *Freedomways* magazine that served as an important voice for the civil rights movement from 1961 until 1985.

John Lewis, 1940–

Congressman

Born in Troy, Alabama, the son of a sharecropper, Lewis became involved in the civil rights movement in 1958 right after graduating from high school. Inspired by his Christian beliefs and Martin Luther King Jr., Lewis led sit-ins in Nashville, Tennessee, two months before the famous 1960 Greensboro, North Carolina, sit-ins. He dropped out of Fisk University in 1963 to work full-time for the civil rights movement. He returned to Fisk to earn his degree in 1967. Lewis assumed a leadership role within the Student Nonviolent Coordinating Committee (SNCC) and became a part of what became known as the Big Six civil rights leadership group that included King from the Southern Christian Leadership Conference, Roy Wilkins of the

Civil rights leader John Lewis at a meeting of the American Society of Newspaper Editors on April 16, 1964. (Library of Congress)

NAACP, Whitney Young of the Urban League, James Farmer of CORE, and Dorothy Height of the National Council of Negro Women. Lewis was scheduled as a speaker at the 1963 March on Washington, but leaders from these other groups feared his prepared remarks were too radical and asked him to tone them down; he reluctantly agreed. SNCC's turn toward a more radical agenda in the mid-1960s led to Lewis's ouster as SNCC chairman in 1966. Lewis continued to work for the next three decades with several organizations involved with community organizing and civil rights. Elected to Atlanta's city council in 1981, Lewis was elected to the U.S. Congress in 1986.

Bobby Seale, 1936–

Black Panther

Raised in Texas and Oakland, California, Seale attended Merritt Community College in Oakland after a stint in the Air Force. Inspired by the success of the civil rights movement in the South, he led a successful struggle for a black studies curriculum while a student at Merritt. After college he became the youth program director at the North Oakland War on Poverty Center. While working at the center in 1966 he founded the Black Panther Party along with Huey P. Newton. The party organized armed patrols to protect citizens from police brutality. The California state legislature introduced a bill outlawing these activities in 1967, prompting Seale to lead an armed protest at the capital in Sacramento, publicly introducing the Black Panther Party to the rest of the world. In August 1968, Seale spoke at the Democratic National Convention in Chicago and was later arrested for inciting a riot. During the subsequent trial he was bound and gagged by orders of the judge when he tried to assert his right to defend himself. All charges were eventually dropped. Seale became an even greater symbol of resistance when a year later he was arrested on charges of conspiracy to murder a Federal Bureau of Investigation informant. Ultimately acquitted, Seale ran for mayor of Oakland in 1973. Although he was unsuccessful, his ability to force the white incumbent into a runoff election paved the way for the city's first African American mayor, Lionel Wilson, in 1977.

REFERENCES AND FURTHER READINGS

Abernathy, Ralph David. 1989. *And the Walls Came Tumbling Down*. New York: HarperPerennial.

Austin, Curtis. 2006. *Up Against the Wall: Violence in the Making and Unmaking of the Black Panther Party*. Fayetteville: University of Arkansas Press.

Baldwin, James. 1963. *The Fire Next Time*. New York: Vintage International.

Bass, Paul, and Douglas W. Rae. 2006. *Murder in the Model City: The Black Panthers, Yale, and the Redemption of a Killer.* New York: Basic Books.

Binkin, Martin, and Mark J. Eitelberg. 1982. *Blacks and the Military.* Washington, DC: Brookings Institution.

Branch, Taylor. 2006. *At Canaan's Edge: America in the King Years, 1965–68.* New York: Simon and Schuster.

Branch, Taylor. 1988. *Parting the Waters: America in the King Years, 1954–63.* New York: Simon and Schuster.

Branch, Taylor. 1998. *Pillar of Fire: America in the King Years, 1963–65.* New York: Simon and Schuster.

Burner, Eric. 1994. *And Gently He Shall Lead Them: Robert Parris Moses and Civil Rights in Mississippi.* New York: New York University Press.

Button, James W. 1978. *Black Violence: Political Impact of the 1960s Riots.* Princeton, NJ: Princeton University Press.

Carson, Clayborne. 1981. *In Struggle: SNCC and the Black Awakening of the 1960s.* Cambridge: Harvard University Press.

Chafe, William H. 1980. *Civilities and Civil Rights: Greensboro, North Carolina, and the Black Struggle for Freedom.* New York: Oxford University Press.

Chestnut, J. L., Jr. 1990. *Black in Selma: The Uncommon Life of J. L. Chestnut, Jr.* New York: Farrar, Straus and Giroux.

"Clay Plans to Apologize in Chicago for Remarks about Draft Classification." 1966. *New York Times* (February 22): 17.

Clegg III, Claude A. 1997. *An Original Man: The Life and Times of Elijah Muhammad.* New York: St. Martin's Press.

Collier-Thomas, Bettye, and V. P. Franklin, eds. 2001. *Sisters in the Struggle: African American Women in the Civil Rights–Black Power Movement.* New York: New York University Press.

Crawford, Vickie, et al. 1990. *Women in the Civil Rights Movement: Trailblazers and Torchbearers, 1941–65.* Bloomington: Indiana University Press.

Doyle, William. 2001. *American Insurrection: The Battle of Oxford, Mississippi, 1962.* New York: Doubleday.

"Dr. King Accuses Johnson on War." 1967. *New York Times* (May 1).

"Excerpts from Interview with Six Civil Rights Leaders on Racial Problems in U.S." 1966. *New York Times* (August 22): 36.

Fitzpatrick, Frank. 1999. *And the Walls Came Tumbling Down: Kentucky, Texas Western, and the Game That Changed American Sports.* New York: Simon and Schuster.

Gates, Henry Louis, Jr., and Evelyn Brooks Higginbothan, eds. 2004. *African American Lives*. New York: Oxford University Press.

Gates, Henry Louis, Jr., and Cornell West. 2000. *The African-American Century: How Black Americans Have Shaped Our Country*. New York: The Free Press.

Giddings, Paula. 1984. *When and Where I Enter: The Impact of Black Women on Race and Sex in America*. New York: Bantam Books.

Graham, Herman, III. 2003. *The Brothers' Vietnam War: Black Power, Manhood, and the Military Experience*. Gainesville: University Press of Florida.

Joseph, Peniel E. 2006. "Black Power's Powerful Legacy." *The Chronicle of Higher Education* (July 21): B6–B8.

King Martin Luther Jr. "Letter from Birmingham Jail, 1963" www.mlkonline.net.

Martin, Waldo E., Jr., and Patricia Sullivan, eds. 2000. *Civil Rights in the United States*. Vols. 1 and 2. New York: Macmillan Reference.

Matthews, Tracye A. 2001. "No One Ever Asks What a Man's Role in the Revolution Is: Gender Politics and Leadership in the Black Panther Party, 1966–71." Collier-Thomas, Bettye and V. P. Franklin, eds., *Sisters in the Struggle: African American Women in the Civil Rights-Black Power Movement*. New York: New York University Press.

McAdam, Doug. 1988. *Freedom Summer*. New York: Oxford University Press.

Meier, August, and Elliot Rudwick. 1973. *CORE: A Study in the Civil Rights Movement, 1942–1968*. New York: Oxford University Press.

Meredith, James. 1966. *Three Years in Mississippi*. Bloomington: Indiana University Press.

"Negroes Expected to Make Up to 30 Percent of Draft 'Salvage.'" 1966. *New York Times* (August 25): 1, 6.

Ness, Immanuel. 2004. *Encyclopedia of American Social Movements*. Vols. 1–4. Armonk, NY: M. E. Sharpe.

Newton, Huey P. 1972. *To Die for the People: The Writings of Huey Newton*. New York: Vintage Books.

Norrell, Robert J. 2005. *The House I Live In: Race in the American Century*. New York: Oxford University Press.

Paper, Lewis J. 1975. *John F. Kennedy: The Promise and the Performance*. New York: Da Capo Press.

Payne, Charles. 1995. *I've Got the Light of Freedom: The Organizing Tradition and the Mississippi Freedom Struggle*. Berkeley: University of California Press.

Payne, Charles. 2001. "You Duh Man! African Americans in the Twentieth Century." *Perspectives on Modern America: Making Sense of the Twentieth Century*. New York: Oxford University Press.

Pearson, Hugh. 1994. *The Shadow of the Panther: Huey Newton and the Price of Black Power in America*. Reading, MA: Addison-Wesley.

Perry, Bruce. 1991. *Malcolm: The Life of a Man Who Changed Black America*. New York: Station Hill.

Roberts, Gene. 1967. "Rights Leader Refuses to Be Inducted into Army." *New York Times* (May 2): 7.

Robnett, Belinda. 1997. *How Long? How Long? African-American Women in the Struggle for Civil Rights*. New York: Oxford University Press.

Semble, Robert B., Jr. 1966. "Powell Charges Draft Test Bias." *New York Times* (May 11): 4.

Singleton, Carl, ed. 1999. *The Sixties in America*. Vol. 2. Pasadena, CA: Salem Press.

Sitkoff, Harvard. 1981. *The Struggle for Black Equality, 1954–1980*. New York: Hill and Wang.

Toure, Kwame (Stokely Carmichael), and Charles V. Hamilton. 1992. *Black Power: The Politics of Liberation in America*. New York: Vintage Books.

Van Deburg, William L. 1992. *New Day in Babylon: The Black Power Movement and American Culture*. Chicago: University of Chicago Press.

Weisbrot, Robert. 1990. *Freedom Bound: A History of America's Civil Rights Movement*. New York: W. W. Norton.

White, E. Frances. 1990. "Africa on My Mind: Gender, Counter Discourse, and African-American Nationalism." *Journal of Women's History* 2, no. 1 (Spring): 80.

X, Malcolm, with Alex Haley. 1966. *The Autobiography of Malcolm X*. New York: Ballantine Books.

The Student and
the Antiwar Movement

OVERVIEW

Even though the U.S. military involvement in Vietnam predates the 1960s, as John F. Kennedy began focusing more and more attention onto Indochina in the ongoing fight against the spread of communism the Cold War peace movement remained relatively quiet with regard to the government's Vietnam policy. In fact, the first organized demonstrations against American involvement in Vietnam did not occur until the summer of 1963. News of the South Vietnamese government's shooting of nine Buddhists who were protesting the discriminatory practices of Roman Catholic president Ngo Dinh Diem, specifically his banning of the Buddhist flag and his raids on Buddhist pagodas, triggered very mild protests by pacifists in Philadelphia, New York, and Washington, D.C. For the most part, the issue of U.S. involvement in Vietnam remained far from the center of the nation's attention during the summer of 1963. The continuing civil rights struggle seemed a greater threat to the nation's domestic future than U.S. intervention into the affairs of Southeast Asia.

Nevertheless, the rise of the New Left on university campuses across the country in the early sixties served as a precursor to the antiwar movement that would eventually shake the United States and its foreign policies to the core. Although the militancy of the post-1965 antiwar movement made the establishment of the New Left earlier in the decade seem tame by comparison, the rise of organizations like the Students for a Democratic Society (SDS) laid the intellectual foundation for a movement that would later actively and even violently

challenge governmental authority. Almost quaint by comparison to the radicalism of the antiwar and Black Power movements of the late sixties, the rise of the
New Left at the beginning of the decade called for a democratic renewal based
on the tradition of civic republicanism that linked the ideas of Aristotle to John
Dewey. After the adoption of the *Port Huron Statement* in 1962, SDS spearheaded a movement that called for a new experiment in democratic idealism.
This movement grew out of young people's concern about the major problems
that plagued American society in the early sixties: poverty, racism, the arms race,
and the apparent limits on social change through electoral politics.

The emergence of the New Left and organizations like SDS provided the ideological and organizational base to mobilize against a war that came to symbolize the corruption of the codependent relationship among government, the
military, and corporate America. Events of 1963 and 1964 planted the seeds for
the full-scale antiwar movement of the late 1960s. Slowly but surely, disturbing
information about U.S. policy in Vietnam began trickling down to pacifist, religious, civil rights, disarmament, Old Left, and New Left organizations. To facilitate the spread of this information, in October of 1963 the Friends Committee
on National Legislation began the Vietnam Information Center (VIC) in Washington. In 1964 the VIC began a "Write to the President Drive" to plead for withdrawal. On April 7, 1964, 250 members of the Women's International League for
Peace and Freedom went to Washington to lobby against the U.S. involvement
in Vietnam. They argued against the brutality of the war that included the use
of napalm and made a plea for an immediate and honorable withdrawal of U.S.
forces in Vietnam. On July 3, 1964, the same day President Lyndon B. Johnson
signed the Civil Rights Act of 1964, David Dellinger, writer for *Liberation* magazine, a publication that discussed social issues from a leftist perspective, organized a demonstration against the Vietnam War in Lafayette Square across from
the White House. Present were some of the early public leaders of the antiwar
movement: Dellinger, A. J. Muste, folksinger Joan Baez, and Rabbi Abraham
Feinberg. More specifically, the demonstration publicized the "Declaration of
Conscience" written by a group of activists associated with *Liberation* magazine.
This declaration, among other things, proclaimed a "conscientious refusal to
cooperate with the United States government in the prosecution of the war in
Vietnam" ("Declaration of Conscience").

Most Americans were not aware of these early signs of an antiwar movement.
Until the summer of 1964, most Americans did not pay attention to U.S. foreign
policy as it related to Southeast Asia. However, the conflict in Vietnam occupied
U.S. presidential administrations from Harry Truman until Gerald Ford. For more
than a decade U.S. troops fought in Vietnam, making it the nation's longest war.
In the spring of 1965 Americans started paying attention as the Johnson administration took the war to the Vietcong with sustained bombing raids on North
Vietnam. In response, pacifists and student activists started an oppositional
campaign that in many ways defined a generation. As both the number of troops

deployed and casualties mounted, the antiwar movement intensified and caused two presidents to resort to unethical and illegal tactics to limit its effectiveness.

The antiwar movement reached its apex at the end of the 1960s without achieving total victory. The Vietnam War lingered on into the 1970s, but the antiwar movement caused the Johnson and Nixon administrations to alter their plans in a way that may have saved thousands of American and Vietnamese lives.

TIMELINE

1962	Organizing convention of the Students for a Democratic Society (SDS) is held at Port Huron, Michigan, on June 11–15.
1963	South Vietnamese president Ngo Dinh Diem is assassinated on November 1.
1964	U.S. destroyer *Maddox* is involved in incident with North Vietnamese torpedo boats on August 1.
	U.S. destroyers *Maddox* and *C. Turner Joy* report they are under attack by North Vietnamese gunboats on August 4.
	Gulf of Tonkin Resolution that empowers the president to respond militarily to North Vietnamese armed aggression passes both the U.S. Senate and the House of Representatives on August 7.
	Free Speech Movement begins at the University of California at Berkeley.
1965	U.S. military begins Operation Rolling Thunder, a series of bombing raids on North Vietnam on March 2.
	Alice Herz immolates herself in protest of U.S. involvement in the Vietnam War.
	The first "teach-in" is held at the University of Michigan on March 24.
	SDS organizes a march on Washington to protest the Vietnam War on April 17.
	Nationwide "teach-in" organized by the Inter-University Committee for a Public Hearing is held on the campuses of 122 universities on May 15–16.
	"Vietnam Day" held at the University of California at Berkeley on May 21–22.

National Security Advisor McGeorge Bundy debates the U.S. military's presence in Vietnam with University of Chicago professor Hans Morgenthau on national television on June 21.

First International Days of Protest organized by the Berkeley Vietnam Committee is held on October 15–16.

Norman Morrison immolates himself in front of the Pentagon on November 2 in protest of the Vietnam War.

Roger LaPorte immolates himself on November 9 in protest of the Vietnam War.

1966   Senate Foreign Relations Committee Chair Sen. J. William Fulbright initiates hearings on the Vietnam War on January 28.

Second International Days of Protest are held on March 25–26.

The Selective Service System qualification exams are introduced in May.

The Cleveland Area Peace Action Council (CAPAC) organizes the First Cleveland Conference to discuss tactics to protest the Vietnam War.

President Lyndon B. Johnson approves deployment of 431,000 U.S. troops in Vietnam in June.

"Fort Hood Three" refuse Vietnam deployment in June.

The United States begins bombing petroleum, oil, and lubricant (POL) storage depots around the Haiphong-Hanoi region in June.

CAPAC sponsors Second Cleveland Conference in September.

CAPAC sponsors Third Cleveland Conference in November.

1967   Harrison E. Salisbury's January *New York Times* article chronicling the effects of U.S. bombing around Hanoi is published.

Martha Gelhorn's January *Ladies Home Journal* article describing the effects of napalm on children in Vietnam is published.

A. J. Muste, considered by many to be the father of the antiwar movement, dies on February 11.

Petition signed by 5,000 scientists protesting the use of chemical and biological weapons is submitted to the White House on February 13.

Students "sit-in" at the University of Wisconsin—Madison to prevent Dow Chemical, makers of napalm, from interviewing recruits on February 21.

Martin Luther King Jr. gives an antiwar speech at Riverside Church in New York City at an event sponsored by the Clergy and Laymen Concerned about Vietnam on April 4.

Muhammad Ali refuses induction on April 28.

On October 21 50,000 antiwar activists participate in the National Mobilization Committee's march on Washington to protest the Vietnam War.

Sen. Eugene McCarthy, Minnesota Democrat, announces his candidacy for the presidency of the United States on November 30 and becomes the antiwar candidate.

1968   The Fifth Avenue Peace Parade Committee stages a rally on the United Nations in New York City on February 24.

Senator McCarthy almost beats President Johnson in the March 11 New Hampshire primary.

Sen. Robert Kennedy, New York Democrat, announces his candidacy for president on March 16.

My Lai massacre on March 16.

U.S. House of Representatives calls for a congressional review of U.S. Vietnam policy on March 18.

President Johnson goes on national television on March 31 to announce his withdrawal from the presidential race.

Martin Luther King Jr. is assassinated in Memphis, Tennessee, on April 4.

Columbia University students take over several university buildings in protest of Vietnam War on April 23.

On April 27, 100,000 activists participate in the National Mobilization Committee's antiwar demonstration in New York City.

Robert Kennedy is assassinated in Los Angeles during a campaign stop on June 5.

The violent confrontation between Chicago police and antiwar demonstrators outside the Democratic National Convention is broadcast on national television in August.

Republican Richard Nixon narrowly defeats Democrat Hubert Humphrey in November presidential election.

1969   Nixon secretly begins bombing Cambodia in March.

The Chicago Eight are indicted on conspiracy charges in March.

Nixon withdraws 25,000 troops from Vietnam and announces his policy of "Vietnamization" in June.

The radical Weathermen split from SDS in June.

Weathermen begin their Days of Rage in Chicago on October 9.

The First Vietnam Moratorium Day is held on October 15.

Nixon delivers his "Silent Majority" speech on November 3.

The March Against Death is held in Washington, D.C., on November 13.

The Second Vietnam Moratorium Day is held on November 15.

INTO THE QUAGMIRE

John F. Kennedy entered the White House in 1961 every much the cold warrior as his predecessors, Harry Truman and Dwight Eisenhower. To Kennedy and others, the fate of the free world seemed to hang in the balance as he assumed the presidency. If the United States faltered in defending freedom, Kennedy reasoned, "The whole world . . . would inevitably begin to move toward the Communist bloc" (Brown, 217). Kennedy quickly assembled a domestic and foreign policy team of advisors that believed the United States not only must contain the spread of communism, it must also "move forward to meet communism, rather than waiting for it to come to us and then reacting to it" (Farlie, 72).

Vietnam stands as the most tragic legacy of Kennedy's global activism. In the eyes of Kennedy and his advisors, South Vietnam was a test case of America's determination to uphold its commitments in the fight against communism and of its capacity to meet the new challenges posed by guerrilla warfare in the emerging nations. By the end of January 1961, Kennedy approved an additional $42 million in aid to support an expansion of the South Vietnamese Army against the risk of a large-scale offensive by the Communist Vietcong insurgency. Kennedy did not dramatically expand military commitments in Vietnam during the spring of 1961, but he did send additional "advisors" and 400 Special Forces troops to train the South Vietnamese in counterinsurgency techniques. The United States also sent clandestine teams of South Vietnamese across the seventeenth parallel into North Vietnam to attack enemy supply lines, sabotage military and civilian targets, and agitate the Hanoi regime. At the same time, the CIA initiated its "secret war" in Laos to destroy operations along the Ho Chi Minh Trail that served to supply Vietcong forces within South Vietnam.

During the summer of 1961 the Soviet Union's Nikita Khrushchev affirmed the Soviet commitment to wars of liberation, causing some of Kennedy's advisors to urge an all-out effort in Vietnam. By late 1961, Kennedy had become convinced that he must prove his toughness to Khrushchev. The issue to Kennedy was not whether Ngo Dinh Diem, the unpopular president of South Vietnam, was a good ruler, but whether the United States could continue to accept with impunity Communist aggression in South Vietnam. Kennedy agreed to increase the volume of American assistance and the number of advisers in the hope that this would be enough to retard the military and political deterioration in South Vietnam. He claimed that North Vietnam's aggression in South Vietnam justified this response. Secretly Kennedy and his advisors recognized that Diem's repressive and inefficient government constituted a big obstacle to defeating the insurgency, but the State Department could not identify a South Vietnamese politician who could step in and effectively take the reins from Diem. So Kennedy decided to try to work with Diem by offering a gradually expanded amount of aid.

From 1961 to 1962 American military assistance to South Vietnam more than doubled. "Project Beefup" drastically expanded the United States' role in Vietnam by sending major items like armored personnel carriers and more than 300 military aircraft. In addition, the number of American "advisers" increased from 3,205 in 1961 to 9,000 by the end of 1962. Kennedy also authorized the use of defoliants to deny the Vietcong cover and to secure major roads and, on a limited basis, the use of herbicides to destroy Vietcong food supplies. Though this influx of American equipment and personnel provided an initial boost to South Vietnam's counterinsurgency efforts, by late 1962 the Vietcong had regained the momentum. Their success in mobilizing the peasants meant they could boast an estimated 300,000 members and a passive following of more than one million South Vietnamese. As a result, it was becoming increasingly difficult for anyone to distinguish between Vietcong and innocent civilians. Diem's forces, constantly under attack, often did not take the time to make the distinction, gunning down civilians, including women and children. This gave the Vietcong a powerful propaganda tool. The destruction of villages with napalm and defoliants turned villagers against the government, but American and South Vietnamese military officials claimed these techniques were necessary to combat the Vietcong's ground operations.

In late 1962 the American press corps in Saigon started filing the first reports that challenged the administration's assertions of the counterinsurgency's effectiveness. Reporters claimed the war was being lost and described Diem's government as corrupt, repressive, and unpopular. Blaming Diem for the counterinsurgency's effectiveness, reporters for the first time claimed that the U.S. government was deliberately deceiving the American people. Critical newspaper reports also started chronicling the loss of American lives in Vietnam. Alarmed by these reports, President Kennedy attempted unsuccessfully to get the *New York Times* to recall journalist David Halberstam, one of the administration's harshest critics.

CBS News anchor Walter Cronkite (left) and President John F. Kennedy tape a television interview on the lawn of the president's Hyannis Port, Massachusetts, summer home on September 2, 1963. (Library of Congress)

The Protest of the Buddhist Priests

An upheaval among Buddhists in the major cities of South Vietnam in May 1963 signaled even deeper problems for the Diem regime and the already faltering American policy of containment. The affair began when crowds gathered in Hue to protest orders forbidding the display of flags on Buddha's birthday were fired upon by South Vietnamese troops. This incident sparked new and vigorous protests. Buddhist leaders accused the government of persecution and demanded religious freedom. Diem blamed the entire incident on the Vietcong. Angered by his denials, Buddhist priests organized a hunger strike, and large crowds gathered for public demonstrations in Hue and Saigon. The uprising became more intense when a Buddhist monk immolated himself in front of a large crowd in downtown Saigon. The politically savvy Buddhist leadership had tipped the foreign press to the event, and an American photographer captured the poignant image of the monk engulfed in flames. Soon the photo appeared in newspapers and on television screens around the world.

   The immolation of the elderly monk incited not only a rebellion in South Vietnam against Diem's ineffective and repressive regime, but also public consternation in the United States over Kennedy's Vietnam policy. The Kennedy administration feared that the Buddhist uprising in South Vietnam might undercut American support for the war and further endanger a counterinsurgency program that many already suspected was failing. The demonstrations and immolations continued; in all, seven monks burned themselves to death. Diem's contempt for the protestors and Buddhist monks was no help. Some within the administration began to view the Buddhist crisis as representative of fundamental defects in Diem's regime and concluded that a change in leadership was necessary.

In late August, American-trained South Vietnamese Special Forces carried out massive raids in various cities, ransacking the pagodas and arresting more than 1,400 Buddhists. Although it was unclear whether Diem ordered the raids, his refusal to disavow the initiative convinced the Kennedy administration that he had become too much of a burden. Within days after the raid on the pagodas, a group of South Vietnamese Army generals opened secret contacts with the United States. These contacts developed into plans for a military coup.

Shortly after the coup, President Kennedy was assassinated on November 22, 1963. His successor, President Johnson, did not waver from Kennedy's ardent anticommunism and fear of Southeast Asia's vulnerability to communism.

The Gulf of Tonkin Incident and Johnson's Offensive Strategy

An incident off the coast of North Vietnam during the summer of 1964 helped President Lyndon B. Johnson win congressional support for his military plans in Southeast Asia, while his subsequent military reprisals against North Vietnam naval bases immediately following this incident galvanized the American public behind the president's plans.

American naval forces conducted surveillance missions in the Gulf of Tonkin off the coast of North Vietnam to aid South Vietnamese amphibious attacks. When North Vietnam resisted these attacks, President Johnson told the nation that North Vietnamese torpedo boats engaged in unprovoked attacks on American destroyers in international waters. Johnson had already decided to retain President Kennedy's foreign policy advisors and declared his intention to not let Southeast Asia fall to communism. Kennedy's administration had spent much of its time propping up the unpopular Diem regime in South Vietnam. However, after Diem retaliated against the Buddhist priests protesting religious persecution by ordering his military to raid temples in 1963, Kennedy decided Diem would have to be removed. Ambassador Henry Cabot Lodge Jr. informed military leaders in Saigon that the United States would support a military coup, and on November 1, 1963, Diem was driven from office and assassinated by officers of the South Vietnamese Army. Diem's ouster unintentionally set the stage for the Americanization of the Vietnam War. The United States had now directly involved itself in establishing a government and sustaining a military that had little support within South Vietnam.

After Kennedy's assassination on November 22, 1963, President Johnson quickly discovered that Diem's removal from office did not improve the popularity or legitimacy of the Saigon government. In response, Secretary of Defense Robert McNamara and other advisors argued that only a full-scale deployment of U.S. forces could prevent the defeat of South Vietnam against the Communist revolutionary movement known as the National Liberation Front. The incident in the Gulf of Tonkin in the summer of 1964 gave Johnson the cover to go before Congress and ask for the authority to order such a deployment.

While engaged in electronic espionage off the coast of North Vietnam on the morning of August 1, the destroyer *Maddox* encountered a group of North Vietnamese torpedo boats. Assuming the *Maddox* had been supporting covert attacks by South Vietnamese gunboats, North Vietnam closed in on the destroyer. In a brief engagement, the *Maddox* opened fire and the North Vietnamese patrol boats launched torpedoes. The Navy then ordered another destroyer, the *C. Turner Joy,* to join the *Maddox* in the Gulf of Tonkin. On the night of August 4, while patrolling near the North Vietnam coast, the *C. Turner Joy* and the *Maddox* reported they were under attack. While North Vietnamese gunboats were operating in the area, in the aftermath of the incident no conclusive evidence ever proved that an attack occurred.

Despite serious questions about the nature and even existence of the alleged attacks, the Johnson administration used the incident to garner congressional authorization to escalate the war in Vietnam. On August 7, the Gulf of Tonkin Resolution, authorizing President Johnson to "take all necessary measures to repel any armed attack against the forces of the United States and to prevent further aggression," passed by 88 to 2 in the Senate and 416 to 0 in the House. One of the two senators who opposed the resolution, Sen. Wayne Morse of Oregon, argued that it amounted to a "declaration of war" and made the case that the United States, not North Vietnam, was the "provocateur" in South Vietnam. Morse continued with this prescient remark: "It is dangerous to give to any President an unchecked power, after the passage of a joint resolution, to make war. Consider the procedural complications that could develop if Congress decided that the President was making serious mistakes in the conduct of a personal war—for it would be a Presidential war at that point" (Zaroulis and Sullivan, 23).

In response to these concerns, President Johnson promised during the 1964 presidential campaign that he would not send American boys nine or ten thousand miles away from home to do what Asian boys could do for themselves. Yet with the election over and congressional support in hand, the Johnson administration began direct bombing campaigns against North Vietnam and the deployment of ground troops. Amid the climax of the civil rights movement, President Johnson's Great Society initiatives, and relative economic stability, most Americans paid little attention to the developments in Southeast Asia. Early indications, however, revealed that the American people supported President Johnson's aggressive military attacks against the enemy. Only weeks before the Gulf of Tonkin incident, 58 percent of the voters polled by Louis Harris expressed their disapproval of Johnson's handling of the Vietnam conflict. Suddenly, after the attacks, resolution, and reprisals, 85 percent of voters polled said they supported the president's efforts (Hammond 1988, 101).

Operation Rolling Thunder

The first phase of escalation began on March 2, 1965, with Operation Rolling Thunder, a long series of bombing raids on North Vietnam intended to cripple the economy and put the United States in a favorable negotiating position. The bombing particularly targeted the Ho Chi Minh Trail, an elaborate network of paths, bridges, and shelters used by supporters of the National Liberation Front to get from North Vietnam to South Vietnam by way of Laos and Cambodia. The brainchild of National Security Advisor McGeorge Bundy, Operation Rolling Thunder was a protracted, intense, and immense bombing campaign. From 1965 to 1968 the U.S. military dropped more than a million tons of bombs on North Vietnam at a cost that exceeded $1.7 billion. From 1965 until 1973 the United States dropped three times as many bombs on North Vietnam as had fallen on all of Europe, Asia, and Africa during World War II.

President Johnson committed to Bundy's plan after a February 6 attack by the Vietcong on U.S. Army barracks in Pleiku and a nearby helicopter base, killing nine Americans and destroying five aircraft. Bundy convinced Johnson that they must immediately initiate a policy of sustained reprisal against North Vietnam. Like the Gulf of Tonkin incident, the raid in Pleiku was the pretext and not the cause of the massive attacks on North Vietnam. President Johnson's advisors had become convinced that such an attack was necessary to prevent South Vietnam from falling. It was simply a matter of finding the right opportunity to justify measures to which the administration was already committed. Operation Rolling Thunder signaled a dramatic shift in the war; instead of limited reprisal strikes, the United States had committed itself to a sustained and regular bombing campaign that now served as an argument for further escalation should that become necessary. Indeed, after Rolling Thunder began, there was almost immediate pressure to expand it. The use of napalm was authorized to ensure greater destructiveness, and pilots were given the authority to strike alternative targets without prior authorization if the original targets were inaccessible.

The expanded air war also provided the pretext for the introduction of the first U.S. ground forces in Vietnam. Official U.S. ground troops started arriving on the shores of Danang, South Vietnam's second-largest city, one week after the start of Operation Rolling Thunder. By the summer of 1965 these troops launched search-and-destroy missions to uncover and kill Vietcong forces. Fearful of losing

Secretary of State Dean Rusk (left), President Lyndon B. Johnson (center), and Secretary of Defense Robert McNamara (right) meet on February 9, 1968, at the height of the Vietnam War. (National Archives)

congressional support for expanding military involvement, the Johnson administration kept its new offensive strategy a secret. From 1965 to 1968 the war in Vietnam increasingly became an American war fought for American aims. By 1966 more than 380,000 American troops were deployed in Vietnam. This dramatic shift in U.S. policy ignited a swift response by a quickly expanding antiwar movement.

The American news media immediately began to scrutinize the State and Defense departments press briefings on these attacks. A lot of attention centered on the number of civilian casualties resulting from the military assault. The North Vietnamese began to report high civilian casualties, recognizing that this might turn the American people against the war. In 1966 Hanoi Radio began to report that American jets had escalated the war by attacking Hanoi's suburbs and residential areas. Although the U.S. military denied these reports, western travelers in Hanoi confirmed that residential areas were suffering severe damage from these attacks. This caused several media outlets to question the administration's veracity on the state of the war. The *Chicago Tribune*, for example, pointed out that the Communists appeared to have been "more truthful than the Washington news managers, who resorted to a series of denials and evasions and only confessed the facts after they had been found out" ("Managed News Again").

The apparent coverup of actual events tainted the Johnson administration's image and reliability as it related to the war, giving ammunition to those who opposed it.

The Vietnam Generation

Fifty-three million Americans came of age during the Vietnam War. Roughly half of this number were women and therefore immune from the draft. Only 6,000 women saw military service in Vietnam, none in combat. Almost 27 million men came of draft age between August 4, 1964, when the Gulf of Tonkin Resolution marked the formal entry of the United States into the war, and March 28, 1973, when the last American soldiers left Vietnam. Of that number, only 2 million served in Vietnam. Over 51,000 died and another 270,000 were wounded, 21,000 of whom suffered a permanent disability.

While some young men coming of age during the Vietnam War had grown accustomed to the existence of the draft and even looked forward to military service, others saw the draft as an unpleasant but acceptable fact of life. In 1966 a survey of high-school sophomores found that only 7 percent mentioned the draft or Vietnam as one of "the problems young men your age worry about most." However, when the same individuals were asked the same question after they graduated in 1969, 75 percent mentioned the draft and Vietnam as a major problem to worry about (Baskir and Strauss, 4–5).

Although only 6 percent of all young men were called to fight, the draft cast a shadow over the entire generation. In practice, the draft did not act in an arbitrary and omnipotent way, but as an instrument of Darwinian social policy where those with connections and money could rig the system and escape service. Through an elaborate structure of deferments, exemptions, legal technicalities, and noncombat military alternatives, the draft rewarded those who had the power to manipulate the system. For this generation, unlike the World War II generation, military service in Vietnam was not a source of pride or national honor. Instead, most viewed it as a penalty reserved for those poor souls unfortunate enough to not have the means to avoid service. Many students defended their deferments with a large dose of arrogance: "There are certain people who can do more good in a lifetime in politics or academics or medicine than by getting killed in a trench," said one Rhodes scholar (Baskir and Strauss, 7).

According to a Notre Dame survey, approximately 15 million of the draft-age men who did not see combat took proactive steps to manipulate the system. Class did not always determine one's ability to avoid service. Those living in the inner city could escape by never registering for the draft. High-school dropouts could marry and have children. However, the greatest number of ways to escape service were reserved for those young men of privilege. Through status

Table 2.1. Likelihood of Vietnam-era Service

	Military Service	Vietnam Service	Combat Service
Low-income	40%	19%	15%
Middle-income	30%	12%	7%
High-income	24%	9%	7%
High-school dropouts	42%	18%	14%
High-school graduates	45%	21%	17%
College graduates	23%	12%	9%

Source: Baskir and Strauss, 1978, 9.

deferments, physical exemptions, or safe enlistments, young men of means could stay far away from Vietnam (Baskir and Strauss, 7–8).

Not surprisingly, the draft and the means of avoidance created racial inequities that became a major scandal by the end of the decade. At the end of World War II, African Americans comprised 12 percent of all combat troops; by the beginning of the Vietnam War, their share had grown to 31 percent. As a result, the Defense Department undertook a concerted effort to reduce the minorities' share of the fighting. The share of African American soldiers went down to 16 percent in 1966 and 13 percent in 1968. By 1970 the figure for all services had dipped below 9 percent. Over the course of the war, however, minorities did more than their fair share of the dying. Yet the most serious inequities were social and economic. Poorly educated, low-income blacks and whites together bore a disproportionate share of the war's burden. The earlier referenced Notre Dame survey found that men from disadvantaged backgrounds were about twice as likely as their better-off peers to serve in the military, go to Vietnam, and see combat. In 1965–1966, only 2 percent of all draftees had a college degree (Baskir and Strauss, 8–9).

In addition to the legal manipulations of the system, an increasing number of young men opted to resist or desert. Vietnam-era draft resisters and deserters totaled more than 1 million. Roughly 570,000 of them committed draft violations that could have resulted in five-year prison sentences. Only about 25,000 of these were ever indicted, and fewer than 9,000 convicted. Just over a third of those convicted spent any time in jail. Most served less than a year of their sentence (Baskir and Strauss, 11–12).

THE BEGINNING OF AN ANTIWAR MOVEMENT

The seeds of the antiwar movement were planted in the New Left in the early 1960s. The rise of new American radicals occurred primarily on university campuses. Sublimely convinced of their power to make history and change the world, these radicals committed themselves to a variety of experiments in organizing citizens and establishing their own small communities of freedom. Through a deliberately open-minded process of collective decision-making, they formulated a flexible strategy for social change that briefly proved surprisingly effective.

The New Left of the early 1960s owed much of its political ideology to the civic republicanism of Aristotle and John Dewey. Robert Alan Haber, a resident radical from Ann Arbor, Michigan, in many ways began a movement that ultimately attracted hundreds of thousands of converts throughout the sixties. A perpetual student at the University of Michigan, Haber methodically presented his political views among a small cadre of impressionable classmates. At the end of the Eisenhower administration and at the dawn of the sixties, Haber argued that there was cause for hope for advocates of radical social change. The driving force for this change would not be the proletariat, as socialists believed, but university students. After a decade of apathy, Haber witnessed a change in students arriving at the University of Michigan. Once students were exposed to the injustices of racism and an unequal distribution of wealth, he predicted, they would organize to fight militarism, racism, and poverty.

The New Left of the 1960s ignited a dramatic renewal of the democratic spirit in America that challenged existing systems of authority. Those who joined this movement and came of age in the sixties no longer felt the same compulsion to obey those whom they had previously considered superior to themselves because of age, rank, education, or class. Some viewed these developments as hopeful signs for a more egalitarian society; others deplored these developments as an excess of democracy that undermined the legitimate aspects of authority. In either case, the rise of the New Left and the organization of SDS created a political, social, and cultural milieu among American university students primed to challenge American military aggression in Southeast Asia.

Students for a Democratic Society

The University of Michigan became a hotbed for student activism as a result of Haber's charismatic and passionate call for radical social change. Instead of looking to the proletariat to initiate this revolution, as most socialists had done for over a hundred years, Haber believed college students could act as the driving force for reform. After more than a decade of apathy among college students, those who enrolled at the end of the 1950s were stirred by the racial injustices exposed by the civil rights movement. Haber argued that students needed an organization to illuminate the connections among issues like the arms race, poverty, racial injustice, and student discontent. Democracy became the concept that could bring the poor, African Americans, and students together under a common cause because all three groups felt that they lacked a voice in the larger society.

After becoming an active socialist in 1958, Haber joined the Student League for Industrial Society (SLID) to help promote his vision. The novelist Upton Sinclair had helped to found SLID's precursor, the Intercollegiate Socialist Society, in 1905. Clarence Darrow and Jack London were also among the original sponsors of an organization designed to promote socialism to American college students. Unlike its rival, the Young People's Socialist League (YPSL), SLID used the rhetoric of democracy instead of socialism, evoking a more honored American political tradition. In 1960 Haber and African American and white college students from across the country gathered in Ann Arbor for a human rights convention that served as the introduction of a new organization: Students for a Democratic Society (SDS). At this convention Haber was named the SDS field secretary to serve as the new organization's ambassador to campuses across the country. Haber later became the first president of SDS.

Tom Hayden, a student at the University of Michigan, helped breathe life into the fledgling student organization in 1962 by authoring most of what became known as the *Port Huron Statement,* a document that made the connection between national excesses abroad and antidemocratic practices at home while committing SDS to the creation of a "New Left" in American politics. While never particularly large in numbers, SDS provided a foundation for the antiwar movement on campuses across the country throughout the 1960s.

Free Speech Movement

In the fall of 1963 and spring of 1964, the San Francisco area generally and the University of California at Berkeley in particular were rocked with civil rights demonstrations against employers who engaged in discriminatory hiring practices. A large number of Berkeley students participated in these protests and roughly 500 were arrested, causing some state legislators to demand that the university discipline and control its students. On September 14, 1964, Katherine Towle, the dean of students, at the request of Vice Chancellor Alex Sheriffs, wrote a letter to student political groups to inform them that university policy restricted the use of the campus's Bancroft Plaza for the solicitation of support for off-campus social and political action. In response, eighteen student groups from across the political spectrum asked the dean to reverse the new policy. Calling themselves the United Front, the student groups defied the policy and continued to recruit students for their various causes. After a confrontation with Chancellor Clark Kerr, the fragmented United Front disbanded and was replaced by the Free Speech Movement.

The Free Speech Movement (FSM) consisted of an executive committee of about fifty students and a steering committee of around twelve students. After failed negotiations with the university administration, the FSM decided to escalate the conflict by putting tables up in the plaza and around campus to recruit.

The Port Huron Statement

On June 12, 1962, 59 mostly young activists gathered at Port Huron, Michigan, and drafted the manifesto, *The Port Huron Statement,* helping to ignite a decade of dissent among college-age young people. Gathered primarily to write a vision for the relatively new SDS, the conference quickly turned into a heated debate between Michael Harrington, a veteran socialist, and Tom Hayden, a 22-year-old activist from the University of Michigan. By the morning of June 16, however, the group came together to overwhelmingly ratify *The Port Huron Statement.*

The statement became a pivotal document, elevating SDS to national prominence after its publication. It also helped to popularize the concept of "participatory democracy" and galvanize the New Left on university campuses. Later in the decade thousands of young people put the concept of participatory democracy to the test by dropping out of society to live in communes and small collectives. Participatory democracy constituted a social system "governed by two central aims: That the individual share in those social decisions determining the quality and direction of his life; that society be organized to encourage independence in men and provide the media for their common participation." *The Port Huron Statement's* preamble began, "We are people of this generation, bred in at least modest comfort, housed now in universities, looking uncomfortably to the world we inherit." Throughout its subsequent 63 pages it spouted ideas that would define the student and antiwar movement and counterculture of the sixties: utopianism, participatory democracy, individualism, and the importance of community. It also explicitly made the connection between the university and radicalism by declaring, "social relevance, the accessibility of knowledge, and internal openness— these together make the university a potential base and agency in a movement of social change."

Historian James Miller wrote that *The Port Huron Statement* captured "the New Left at its most thoughtful and plainspoken; it shows clear debts to native traditions of progressive reform and pragmatism; and, in a powerful provocative way, it weaves together a cogent critique of American society with a romantic yearning for new personal values" (Miller, 14).

The sticking point between the FSM and the administration was the prohibition of using the campus to organize illegal off-campus action. On November 23, 1964, the FSM temporarily occupied the administration building. A week later four key FSM activists who had organized FSM demonstrations received a letter from the administration notifying them that they had violated university regulations. In response, 2,000 student activists seized the administration building on December 2. After a spirited rally, featuring folk singer Joan Baez, Gov. Pat Brown ordered the police to clear the building. All told, 773 students were arrested.

Students sleep and play guitar at a sit-in at the University of California at Berkeley, Sproul Hall, December 2, 1964. (UPI/Corbis-Bettmann)

Chancellor Kerr canceled classes the following Monday to meet with a new committee of department chairs. Kerr later read terms he hoped would resolve the conflict with the students, including amnesty for violations of old school rules. The next day, to the delight of the FSM, the Academic Senate voted for no restrictions on the content of speech or advocacy. When new campus regulations were drafted in the spring of 1965, the university ignored the content of speech in favor of stringent time, place, and manner rules. Later that semester, nine students were arrested for displaying and saying the word "fuck" on Bancroft Plaza. The nine were later convicted in municipal court. The FSM of 1964–1965 was the beginning of what came to be called the "six-year war" on the Berkeley campus and helped ignite student activism across the country.

The Teach-In

Voices protested against the United States' Vietnam policies during the Kennedy administration, but those voices did not become a choir until Operation Rolling Thunder. Three weeks later the first "teach-in" on Vietnam took place. A take on the civil rights movement's "sit-in," the term "teach-in" connoted nonviolent protest. Classes at colleges and universities were canceled so that a daylong analysis of the Vietnam War could occur instead. Teach-ins were part protest, part festival, and part educational symposium.

Appropriately, the first teach-in was held at the University of Michigan at Ann Arbor on March 24, 1965. Forty-nine faculty members organized the event and 3,000 students participated in an all-night event that included a torchlight parade, folk singing, and a series of lectures and seminars on Vietnam. Twice during the night the hall where the teach-in took place had to be evacuated because of bomb threats; the participants had to stand outside in below zero weather as the lecturers continued their talks.

In the following weeks colleges and universities across the country got into the act. On campuses such as the University of California–Berkeley, University of Chicago, Columbia University, University of Pennsylvania, New York University,

University of Wisconsin–Madison, Harvard, Kent State, Marist, teach-ins were held throughout the spring of 1965.

The first wave of teach-ins culminated on the weekend of May 15–16, 1965, when 122 campuses connected to a radio hookup participated in a nationwide discussion on U.S. policy in Vietnam. Organized by the Inter-University Committee for a Public Hearing on Vietnam, a group spawned by the spring teach-ins across the country, this national teach-in reached more than 100,000 students and an incalculable number of home listeners. The most anticipated participant and defender of the administration's policies, National Security Advisor McGeorge Bundy never showed because he went on a secret mission to the Dominican Republic where President Johnson, in an attempt to thwart a revolution, had deployed U.S. troops.

At the end of May 1965, as many as 30,000 protesters gathered at the University of California at Berkeley to attend that spring's final teach-in. Like the previous week in Washington at the nationwide teach-in, scheduled pro-administration spokesmen withdrew at the last minute, leaving the event entirely in the hands of antiadministration speakers. One of the organizers of the event, graduate student Jerry Rubin, would become a notorious figure in the radical wing of the antiwar movement in the years to come. The event attracted national figures like Dr. Benjamin Spock, comedian Dick Gregory, and author Norman Mailer and was considered a great success both in terms of the quality of the speeches given and the size of the crowds that gathered to listen. Most important, this event established Berkeley's Vietnam Day Committee, the group responsible for much of the organization of the West Coast antiwar movement.

Johnson's "Truth Team"

The extent of these sober protests got the Johnson administration's attention. Johnson sent out a so-called truth team headed by Thomas F. Conlon of the Agency for International Development to visit campuses in the Midwest to counter the influence of the teach-ins. Conlon's presence on campuses did little to dissuade the protesters; in fact, he acted as a lightning rod that helped galvanize the nascent student antiwar movement.

In June 1965, the month following the nationwide teach-in, McGeorge Bundy attempted to make up for his absence at both the national and Berkeley teach-ins by facing a panel of six faculty and students at Harvard to answer questions about the administration's Vietnam policy. Bundy used Harvard as a warmup for a more national stage. A week after the Harvard event, Bundy went on CBS with Hans Morgenthau of the University of Chicago to debate the Administration's policy. Moderated by Eric Sevareid, the broadcast resembled more a question-and-answer session than an actual debate. Bundy reiterated the administration's commitment to South Vietnam, and that it reserved the right to escalate the war.

Bundy also pointed out that Morgenthau had been wrong when he claimed Laos would not fall to communism. Morgenthau retorted that because he had been wrong about Laos did not mean he was wrong about Vietnam. Morgenthau went on to make the case that the United States had to figure out a way to get out of Vietnam with honor. In other words, he softened the "out now!" cries of the student antiwar protestors by staking out a position that Johnson had to employ some "face-saving devices" before withdrawal in order to protect the power and prestige of the United States. Many professors like Morgenthau who were involved in the teach-ins recognized that the extreme position of immediate withdrawal had little appeal to the vast majority of Americans, who might not like the Vietnam War but could not accept the humiliation of appearing defeated.

The First Antiwar March on Washington

In addition to these events aimed at educating the American public on the dangerous foreign policies of the Johnson administration, more traditional protests against the war started to heat up in response to the massive troop deployment and bombings in Vietnam. SDS sponsored the first nationwide demonstration against the war on April 17, 1965, when more than 20,000 protesters marched on Washington.

After a series of speeches by activists and songs by artists such as Joan Baez and Judy Collins, the protesters moved their way down the Mall toward the Capitol with a petition for Congress that called for an immediate end to the war in Vietnam. A few hundred students engaged in a brief sit-in after nobody greeted them at the Capitol. While some of the students wanted a peaceful protest, others shouted that they should charge into the building. This tension between those who wanted peaceful, legal demonstrations in order to expand the movement and those who urged more radical tactics persisted throughout the antiwar movement. On this day, the more restrained approach won the day as the protesters handed the petition to a police officer at the Capitol doors and peacefully went away.

The First International Days of Protest

Amid these "debates" over the Johnson's administration's escalation of U.S. involvement in Vietnam, the Berkeley Vietnam Day Committee began planning the First International Days of Protest, to be held October 15–16, 1965, in conjunction with protests around the world. On October 15 approximately 10,000 protesters set out on a peace march in Berkeley to stage a teach-in on a vacant lot across from the Oakland Army Base. The Oakland police turned back the crowd, and the protesters ultimately returned to campus to hold their teach-in. In New York, 20,000–25,000 paraded down Fifth Avenue. Despite the taunting by unsympathetic spectators, and red paint, tomatoes, and eggs being thrown at them, the protestors achieved their goal of making a compelling visual statement against the war. For example, the Bread and Puppet Theater paraded oversized dummies through the streets including a bloodied Uncle Sam and two seven-foot ghosts carrying a bandaged child on a stretcher.

Similar rallies occurred in London, Stockholm, Brussels, Copenhagen, and Tokyo. Approximately 100,000 protesters participated in demonstrations in fifty cities across the United States. At one such demonstration David J. Miller, a 22-year-old Catholic Worker, stood outside the Army Induction Center in Manhattan and burned his draft card. This simple act had serious implications in light of the new law that made draft card destruction a felony. An article in the September *Catholic Worker* by Tom Cornell had claimed that the new law signaled the increasing effectiveness of the antiwar movement.

American Immolations

Miller's draft-card burning signaled the protesters' increasingly resistant stance. But Miller's act paled in comparison to immolation. On November 2, 1965, Norman R. Morrison, a 32-year-old Quaker and pacifist, walked to the Pentagon, doused himself with kerosene, and set himself on fire in front of the windows of Secretary of Defense Robert S. McNamara. Morrison's act emulated the Buddhist monks who had immolated themselves in protest of President Ngo Dinh Diem's regime. Anne Morrison, Norman's widow, said he gave his life "to express concern over the great loss of life and human suffering caused by the war in Vietnam. . . . He felt that all citizens must speak their true convictions about our country's actions." In a note he left his wife, Morrison wrote, "Know that I love thee but must act for the children of the priest's village" (*Baltimore Sun,* November 3, 1965). Morrison's suicide shocked the nation and Secretary of Defense McNamara, who later admitted that he was horrified by this outcry against the killing that was destroying the lives of so many American youths and Vietnamese.

Morrison was not the first Quaker to set himself on fire in protest of the Vietnam War; Alice Herz had done the same thing in Detroit immediately following the United States' initial bombing of North Vietnam. Exactly a week after Morrison's death, another young man, Roger A. LaPorte, a 21-year-old member of the Catholic Worker movement, knelt in front of the United Nations in the cross-legged position of the Buddhist monks, doused himself with gasoline, and set himself on fire. He died the following day, but first he explained he did this "as a religious action" in protest against the war (Zaroulis and Sullivan, 1–5).

ESCALATION OF THE WAR
AND ANTIWAR MOVEMENT, 1965–1968

Despite these increasingly passionate and desperate acts protesting the war, the Johnson administration proceeded undeterred. Relying on military tactics developed during World War II, the Air Force and Navy continued to advance the expectation that overwhelming airpower would destroy the enemy's warmaking capacity. The civilian leadership in the Johnson administration accepted the military's arguments because the bombing of North Vietnam sacrificed fewer American lives and was consequently more palatable to Americans back home. In short, it seemed to offer a quick and easy solution to a complex problem despite the lack of results. The United States continued to gradually increase its bombings from 1965 until 1967. Sorties against North Vietnam increased from 25,000 in 1965 to 79,000 in 1966 and 108,000 in 1967; the tonnage of bombs dropped increased from 63,000 to 136,000 to 226,000 (Littauer and Uphoff, 39–43).

Initially the bombings targeted military bases, supply depots, and infiltration routes in the southern part of North Vietnam, but in 1966 the air strikes increasingly aimed at the more northern industrial centers and transportation systems. The bombings did take their toll on North Vietnam's industrial and agricultural productivity and inflicted an estimated $600 million worth of damage on a nation struggling to develop a modern economy. The administration asserted that these bombings produced minimal civilian casualties, but the CIA estimated that in 1967 total casualties ran as high as 2,800 per month and that these estimates were heavily weighted with civilians. Secretary of Defense McNamara privately conceded that civilian casualties were as high as 1,000 per month during intensive bombings (Littauer and Uphoff, 39–43).

Despite the intensity of these air raids, they did not produce the desired results. In fact, the United States had destroyed many major targets by 1967 with no demonstrable effect on the war. North Vietnam demonstrated great ingenuity in responding to the bombings. Civilians were evacuated from the cities and dispersed across the countryside while industries and storage facilities were scattered and concealed both in caves and underground. An estimated 90,000 North Vietnamese, many of them women and children, worked to keep transportation routes open by living underground and using 30,000 miles of tunnels to keep supplies and ammunition flowing. Piles of gravel were kept along major roadways so the "Youth Shock Brigades" could fill craters within hours of a bombing. Concrete and steel bridges were hastily replaced with pontoon bridges made of bamboo stalks, and truck drivers covered their vehicles with palm fronds and banana leaves and traveled at night without the use of headlights. To make matters worse for the U.S. military, losses in military equipment, raw materials, and vehicles were replenished by increased aid from the Soviet Union and China (Van Dyke).

The United States paid a great price for these air raids. The direct cost of the air war, including operations of the aircraft, munitions, and replacement of planes lost, was estimated at more than $1.7 billion in 1965 and 1966. From 1965 to 1968 the United States lost 950 aircraft at a cost of roughly $6 billion. Opposition to the war at home increasingly focused on these bombings, which many believed were both inefficient and immoral (Herring, 145–148).

Search and Destroy

The United States quickly learned that the war would not be won solely from the air. Gen. William Westmoreland, commander of the U.S. forces in Vietnam, demanded and received a dramatic increase in ground forces to conduct "search and destroy" missions against the Vietcong and North Vietnamese army units. This surge in military tactics stirred the antiwar movement and invited increased media scrutiny about the nature of this war.

In June 1966 President Johnson approved a force level of 431,000 to be reached by mid-1967. By the end of 1967 Westmoreland had developed a request to increase that number to 542,000. In a war without front lines and territorial objectives, Westmoreland relied on a "body count" to measure progress. Those in charge of units were pressured by the chain of command to keep track of the number of "kills." Because of the pressure to produce favorable figures, Westmoreland's body counts were inherently unreliable because little effort was made to distinguish between dead Vietcong and dead noncombatants. To win favor with the authorities, units would count any dead body as Vietcong. Even if it is assumed that the military padded the figures by as much as 30 percent, however, it became clear that Westmoreland's tactic of taking the war to the Vietcong was inflicting huge losses. Official estimates placed the number of deaths at 220,000 by late 1967.

Members of the press question General William Westmoreland and U.S. Ambassador Maxwell Taylor (speaking into the microphone). News stories from the battlefield often received the most accurate reporting when journalists and military commanders cooperated. However, for many soldiers and commanders fighting in the Vietnam War, print and broadcast journalists were as much the "enemy" as the Communist forces. (National Archives)

Based on these numbers, the military command insisted that the United States was winning the war. Despite the impressive body-count figures, it was clear to many observers by mid-1967 that there was little hope of a quick military victory (Herring, 153–154).

In addition to the bombings and search-and-destroy missions, the U.S. military engaged in a particularly cruel campaign of extensive defoliation and military bombardment that destroyed the Vietnam countryside and agricultural production for years to come. Frustrated by the Vietcong's ability to respond to air attacks and employ civilians to hide and transport supplies, soldiers, and ammunition, the U.S. military adopted a relocation strategy that aimed to uproot villagers from their homes to refugee camps or cities. Once the homes were vacated, the military proceeded to destroy the villages and countryside. More than 100 million pounds of chemicals such as Agent Orange were sprayed over millions of acres of forests, destroying an estimated one-half of South Vietnam's timberlands, in an attempt to eliminate possible Vietcong sanctuaries. American planes also sprayed napalm, a jellied gasoline, to flush the enemy out from hiding.

The more the State and Defense departments denied the extent of the collateral damage of these attacks, the more the American media looked into the recurring allegations that these operations were slaughtering innocent civilians. The fact that the Military Assistance Command, Vietnam (MACV), the official military news management agency, did not acknowledge the use of napalm, defoliation, and sophisticated armaments such as cluster bombs despite everyone in South Vietnam knowing better, increasingly made it look like the United States was engaged in a covert war of terror. The more the military tried to control the press, the harder it became for the Johnson administration to maintain public support for the war. By 1966, attempts to control the press began to unravel (Hammond, *Reporting Vietnam,* 76–94).

Senator Fulbright's Senate Foreign Relations Committee Hearings

As the number of troops deployed in Vietnam increased and the bombings continued, President Johnson's Vietnam policies started to come under greater scrutiny. While Sen. Wayne Morse of Oregon continued to be the most outspoken congressman in opposition to President Johnson's policies, the antiwar movement gained credibility and momentum in early 1966 when the highly respected senator, friend of President Johnson, and chairman of the Senate Foreign Relations Committee, J. William Fulbright of Arkansas expressed his regret over supporting the Gulf of Tonkin Resolution. He then announced that the Senate Foreign Relations Committee would hold broad and investigative hearings on U.S. involvement in Vietnam. Millions of Americans watched the three-week-long hearings on ABC and NBC (CBS chose to air sitcom reruns instead).

The two principal administration witnesses, Secretary of State Dean Rusk and Gen. Maxwell Taylor, came across as resolute and pragmatic in their testimonies. Both Rusk and Taylor offered a simplistic, straightforward explanation of why the United States had to fight this war. In short, the United States was there to defend one country, South Vietnam, against the aggression of another country, North Vietnam. Unlike Rusk and Taylor, George F. Kennan and Lt. Gen. James M. Gavin testified there was no justification for the United States' initial involvement in Vietnam, especially weighed against other interests and commitments around the globe. Kennan and Gavin believed that any escalation in the bombing would increase the likelihood of China's involvement. Rusk countered that "if we do not meet those responsibilities, we shall find a Red China much more voracious and much more dangerous, if they should discover that this technique of aggression is successful." Kennan, however, made a point that seemed to resonate with Senator Fulbright and other members of the committee when he predicted that victory in South Vietnam would exact a "cost of a degree of damage to civilian life and of civilian suffering, generally, for which I would not like to see this country responsible" (*The Vietnam Hearings,* 52–222).

The 1966 Fulbright hearings offered millions of Americans the opportunity to hear for the first time respected diplomatic and military experts lay out reasons to oppose the war. They watched Kennan, distinguished senior statesman and the author of the "containment" doctrine that initially justified America's strong anticommunist stance after World War II, assert that the United States had no just cause to be in Vietnam. The antiwar movement for the first time had allies in high places. No longer would it be so easy to label war protesters unpatriotic or illegitimate.

The American people and media responded to the hearings along ideological lines. Antiwar activists and journalists who questioned the justification and execution of the war praised the inquiry. However, those who tended to support the administration policy were less satisfied with the hearings. For its part, the Johnson administration believed that the hearings did little to turn the American public against the war and consequently viewed them as a success (Hammond, 78–79). Fulbright found the public responses to the hearings "encouraging." The hearings marked the beginning of an extended public relations battle between doves in Congress and hawks in the Johnson administration. Immediately following the hearings in 1966, it was still unclear which side was winning the battle (Berman, 57–58).

The Struggles of the National Coordinating Committee to End the War in Vietnam

Despite the Fulbright hearings, the antiwar movement languished for much of 1966. One of the primary vehicles for the movement, the National Coordinating

Committee to End the War in Vietnam (NCC), disbanded after a split between the Old and New Left over whether to unequivocally demand the immediate withdrawal of U.S. forces from Vietnam. Suffering from disorganization and lack of leadership, antiwar protests were sporadic and haphazard. The most significant event occurred on March 25–26 at the Second International Days of Protest, the last project organized by the moribund NCC. Hundreds of thousands of antiwar activists participated in rallies, parades, and demonstrations around the world. In New York City, the largest U.S. demonstration, over 20,000 protested against the war. Representatives from approximately 150 groups associated with the antiwar movement marched down Fifth Avenue from Ninety-first to Seventy-second Street. A. J. Muste, a legendary figure in the peace and civil rights movements of the 1950s and 1960s and leader of the Fifth Avenue Peace Parade Committee, spoke at Central Park and declared the occasion a testament to the "power and unity" of the antiwar movement. Others in attendance were not as optimistic that the continuation of parades, demonstrations, and speeches would have any appreciable effect on the administration's policies. In fact, from all indication, they made President Johnson and his advisors more determined to execute the war in Vietnam on their own terms.

Although the movement lacked clear direction, the Johnson administration's defense of Vietnam took a hit when McGeorge Bundy, the author of the "policy of sustained reprisal," left the White House to become president of the Ford Foundation. Bundy embodied the policies that had escalated the United States' involvement in Southeast Asia since the Kennedy administration. His policy of "sustained reprisal" justified Operation Rolling Thunder, and his commitment to that policy seemed to infuse the administration with the patience and determination necessary to stay the course in Vietnam. Now Johnson and his small team of national security advisors were left to continue the fight without the assistance of possibly the most committed and articulate advocate for the war. The administration had one less defender of policies that were coming under increasing attack by Senator Fulbright and others.

The Cleveland Conferences

For the most part the antiwar movement lacked cohesion and clear direction in 1966. It benefited more from acts by the military and administration than internal organization and leadership. For example, the administration's decision to bomb petroleum, oil, and lubricant (POL) storage depots in the densely populated Haiphong-Hanoi area during the summer of 1966 shocked the world and enraged and energized opponents of the war at home.

With a sense of urgency to make the movement more effective, one of the founders of the teach-in movement, Prof. Sidney Peck of Case Western Reserve University, decided to hold a series of meetings sponsored by the Cleveland Area

Peace Action Council (CAPAC) to help organize and provide direction for the fractured antiwar movement. Known as the Cleveland Conferences, CAPAC invited representatives from 13 different organizations to discuss tactics. The Cleveland Conferences of 1966 adopted Muste's call for nonexclusion; embracing all, as Peck put it, "who are in any way, for whatever reasons, opposed to the war" (Zaroulis and Sullivan, 93). Three Cleveland Conferences in 1966 created a new national movement void of the usual acrimony and political maneuverings. In his eighties, Muste believed that a working coalition had now been created that could mount a significant attack against the Johnson administration and the war in Vietnam.

Draft Resistance

A young draft-eligible man from Big Lake, Minnesota, Barry Bondhus, introduced a new form of civil disobedience to the antiwar movement's arsenal in the spring of 1966. He broke into his local draft board and destroyed hundreds of 1-A draft records by covering them with two large buckets of human feces produced by him, his father, and 11 brothers who were all opposed to the war and the draft. Big Lake One, as the Bondhus action came to be known, ignited draft-board raids across the country that reached near-epidemic proportions by 1969 and was often referred to as "the movement that started the Movement."

In the past, young men used draft deferments for college, graduate school, teaching, and parenthood to avoid the draft until they reached the cut-off age of 26. Responding to criticism of racial and class bias inherent in the system, the Selective Service System introduced qualification exams in May of 1966. The use of this exam set off another wave of protests. The Selective Service System gave these tests to high school seniors, college undergraduates, and graduate students, intending to use the tests to determine future student deferments if monthly draft calls exceeded 30,000 per month. Harlem's Representative Adam Clayton Powell Jr. saw the move as a racist ploy to send African Americans to Vietnam in disproportionately large numbers. In response, 400 students at the University of Chicago seized and held the school's administration building for three days. In one act of protest, SDS activists prepared and distributed a "counter-draft" exam in an antiwar movement recruitment effort. The SDS exam was given to over 500,000 young men on May 14, 1966. In response to growing concerns, the Selective Service System quickly abandoned the exam, but it served to give fuel to the growing movement against the draft.

Those wanting to avoid the draft now had three choices: Enlist in the National Guard or the reserves, become a conscientious objector, or ignore any induction notices entirely and risk prosecution for draft evasion. Some left the country for Canada or Sweden to wait out the war. Young people on college campuses voiced their objection to the draft by participating in draft-card burnings, closing down

The Fort Hood Three

The movement also experienced a public relations boon when three privates in the Army stationed at Fort Hood, Texas, refused to serve in Vietnam. Muste's Fifth Avenue Peace Parade Committee introduced the Fort Hood Three at a press conference and used them and their families as a focal point for protests throughout the summer of 1966. The three soldiers, Dennis Mora, James Johnson, and David Samas, read a statement before television cameras that declared their opposition to the war they considered "immoral, illegal, and unjust." They went on to say that they had been told "that many times we may face a Vietnamese woman or child and that we will have to kill them. We will never go there—to do that. . . . We oppose this criminal waste of American lives and resources" (Halstead, 177–178).

The antiwar movement gained its strength from unlikely sources like the Bondhus family in Minnesota and the Fort Hood Three. The three ultimately suffered a court-martial and two-year prison sentence for their stand. Yet after the POL bombings and the publicity of the Fort Hood Three, polls still showed that the majority of the American public approved of Johnson's war policies. Leaders of the antiwar movement knew that they had to do more to convince the American people and the Johnson administration that the Vietnam War must end.

induction centers, and breaking into Selective Service offices to destroy or mutilate files.

Muhammad Ali, the Conscientious Objector

Muhammad Ali, heavyweight champion of the world, became the most famous draft resister when he refused his induction on April 28, 1967. Born Cassius Clay, Ali quickly rose to fame when he upset Sonny Liston for the heavyweight title in Miami on February 25, 1964. Known as the "Louisville Lip" for his verbose showmanship, Clay, who recently joined the Nation of Islam, a little-known Muslim sect that preached racial segregation and black autonomy, changed his name after the Liston fight to Cassius X—like all Black Muslims he had dropped his "slave name." The Honorable Elijah Muhammad, leader of the Nation of Islam, later awarded him a new name: Muhammad Ali, "worthy of all praise most high."

Ali's conversion created quite a stir. Some went as far as to call Ali a traitor. After returning from Africa, Ali announced, "I'm not no American, I'm a black man (Lipsyte and Levine, 246). Many journalists wrote that he was "ungrateful" to a country that had made him rich and famous. Others claimed that the Black Muslims had "brainwashed" him. Former champion and challenger to Ali's throne

Muhammad Ali, formerly Cassius Clay, and Howard Cosell on "Speaking of Everything with Howard Cosell" on WABC radio in 1965. Cosell was one of a handful of journalists who agreed to recognize Clay's name change. (Library of Congress/ World-Telegram photo by Bill Mitchell)

Floyd Patterson said, "the image of a Black Muslim as the world heavyweight champion disgraces the sport and the nation. Cassius Clay must be beaten and the Black Muslims' scourge removed from boxing" (Lipsyte and Levine, 252). Ali's November 22, 1965, fight against Patterson was billed as a Holy War, the good crusading Christian integrationist versus the evil Muslim separatist. Ali won, punishing Patterson for twelve rounds while taunting him: "No contest, get me a contender" (Lipsyte and Levine, 254).

As the war in Vietnam escalated and Fulbright's Senate Foreign Relations Committee 1966 hearings revealed deep divisions over the administration's policies, a reporter asked Ali, "Well, what do you think about the Vietcong?" Ali responded, "I ain't got nothing against them Vietcong." Conservative reporters once again went on the attack. Columnist Red Smith wrote: "Squealing over the possibility that the military may call him up, Cassius makes himself as sorry a spectacle as those unwashed punks who picket and demonstrate against the war." Others, like Howard Cosell, defended Ali's constitutional right to free expression. Buckling under pressure from the federal government, state boxing commissions would no longer license Ali's fights; his next four title defenses were against foreign fighters in Toronto, London, and Frankfurt.

Ali, classified by the draft board in Louisville as 1A and therefore likely to get drafted, applied for a conscientious-objector deferment, but was denied. By late 1966 the federal government, possibly sensing a showdown with the Selective Service board, allowed Ali back in the United States to box. Ali's decision to not fight in the war made him a symbol of resistance. In the spring of 1967 a newsman from Chicago asked him, "What about just playing the game like other big-time athletes? You wouldn't be sent to the front lines. You could give exhibitions and teach physical fitness." Ali responded: "What can you give me, America, for turning down my religion? You want me to do what the white man says and go fight a war against some people I don't know nothing about, get some freedom for some other people when my own can't get theirs here?"

On April 28, 1967, Ali refused to take one step forward, thus fulfilling legal technicalities that made his case eligible for a civil trial before a federal judge. Ali declared, "I don't have to be what you want me to be, I'm free to be who I want." Ali's act of courage gave strength to antiwar protesters and others who held passionate political convictions. Boxing commissioners responded to Ali's refusal to be drafted by either withdrawing their recognition of him as champion or refusing to license him to fight in their states. Ali was convicted of draft evasion despite his claim of conscientious objection. As his case made its way to the Supreme Court, there was a growing feeling that his conviction would be overturned on constitutional grounds. Eventually Georgia succumbed to the pressure of black politicians and allowed Ali to fight Jerry Quarry on October 26, 1970. Five months later he lost a memorable fight against Joe Frazier in Madison Square Garden. Ali during the prime of his career had not fought a serious opponent for three and a half years. Ali would redeem that loss to Frazier in two equally memorable rematches.

On June 28, 1971, the U.S. Supreme Court handed down a five to four decision overturning Ali's conviction. By this time Ali had emerged as a much more popular symbol. His loss to Frazier and willingness to stand up against the government at great personal cost transformed him from the Louisville Lip into a charismatic athlete of conscience (Lipsyte and Levine, 240–275).

The Media's War Coverage

On December 14 the United States renewed its bombing of the Hanoi area. These attacks kicked off another round of protests against the war. More notably, in December of 1966 a *New York Times* Pulitzer Prize–winning journalist, Harrison E. Salisbury, had after months of effort received his visa to visit North Vietnam. Salisbury's eyewitness reporting of the December bombings revealed that the administration had intentionally misled the American people about the so-called surgical precision of the attacks. Salisbury reported that the bombs killed civilians and destroyed churches, schools, homes, and factories in Hanoi and other North Vietnamese cities. For the first time, the American people had first-hand evidence to doubt the government's honesty with regard to the execution of this war. By 1967 the media became more involved in investigating and reporting the nature of the war in Vietnam. These reports provided increasing evidence to support the claims of antiwar protesters and ultimately put President Johnson on the defensive.

In response to revelations about the administration's dishonesty, 2,500 members of Women Strike for Peace charged the Pentagon in an effort to see those responsible for sending their sons to Vietnam. The protesters carried enlarged photos of napalmed Vietnamese children. Eventually Secretary McNamara allowed the protesters into the Pentagon, but he refused to personally meet with them. Instead he ordered an aide to receive their demands. Sen. Jacob Javits, a Republican from New York, met with several of the women protesters, but he was booed when he denied that the United States used toxic gas in Vietnam. Javits's meeting with Women Strike for Peace showed the growing concern over the use of chemical and biological weapons in the prosecution of this war.

Protests Against Chemical Weapons

Five thousand prominent scientists signed a petition presented to the White House on February 13, 1967, asking the president to initiate a study of government policy on chemical and biological warfare and to stop the use of Agent Orange in Vietnam immediately. Before the end of February students at the University of Wisconsin participated in a sit-in at the office of recruiters for the Dow Chemical Company, the only company that produced and supplied napalm B, a petroleum jelly that sticks to whatever it splatters on and burns at 1000 degrees Fahrenheit. The military dropped 120-gallon containers of napalm, usually in Vietcong trenches and entrances to protective tunnels, where it sucked out all the oxygen, causing the occupants to either suffocate or burn to death. Survivors of napalm attacks, many of them children, were hideously scarred for life. Horrific pictures of children burning from napalm became a powerful tool used by the antiwar movement, particularly by Women Strike for Peace.

Picking up on the cause, Martha Gellhorn wrote an article in 1967 titled "Suffer the Little Children . . ." for the *Ladies' Home Journal*. She interviewed a New Jersey woman who had adopted three Vietnamese children and the article detailed the effects of napalm on its victims, particularly children: "The chemical reaction of this napalm does melt the flesh, and the flesh runs right down their faces onto their chests and it sits there and grows there. . . . These children can't turn their heads, they were so thick with flesh." Physicians had organized the Committee of Responsibility for Treatment in the U.S. of War-Burned Vietnamese

Vietnam War protestors, including Coretta Scott King and Dr. Benjamin Spock, crowd the White House gates on May 17, 1967. (Lyndon Baines Johnson Library and Museum)

Children, but the State Department refused to allow any Vietnamese children into the country. Finally, in October 1967, after 500 physicians and twenty hospitals had volunteered their services and facilities, three children were brought to San Francisco for treatment, a mild response given the magnitude of the problem.

As the media shined its light on the horrific effects of American military tactics, campus protests against the war spread across the country. Many believed Dow Chemical embodied the evils of this war. In the fall on over sixty university campuses, including Wisconsin, Illinois, Michigan, Minnesota, Harvard, Columbia, and several branches of the University of California, students engaged in sit-ins and other obstructionist techniques to prevent Dow from interviewing prospective employees. SDS organized most of the demonstrations, which signaled SDS's move away from nonviolent demonstrations, provoking police in some cases to overreact with riot squads, dogs, and tear gas. At the University of Wisconsin, Madison police dressed in riot gear charged a building where thousands of student protestors were preventing interviews. The police cleared the building, but students emerged bloodied and battered. The crowd outside became upset and started throwing rocks and bricks at the police. The police responded with mace, dogs, and a riot squad that ultimately dispersed the crowd.

Martin Luther King Jr. and a Declaration of Independence from the Vietnam War

The antiwar movement gained momentum when in the winter and spring of 1967 the eloquent leader of the civil rights movement, Martin Luther King Jr., began speaking out forcefully against the Vietnam War. His impassioned speech took place at an event sponsored by the Clergy and Laymen Concerned about Vietnam on April 4, 1967, in New York City. There he told an overflow audience of approximately 3,000 that "the war in Vietnam is but a symptom of a far deeper malady within the American spirit, and if we ignore this sobering reality we will find ourselves organizing clergy—and laymen—concerned committees for the next generation. We will be marching and attending rallies without end unless there is a significant and profound change in American life and policy." He went on to say that "if we were to get on the right side of the world revolution, we as a nation must undergo a radical revolution of values. When machines and computers, profit and property rights are considered more important than people, the giant triplets of racism, materialism, and militarism are incapable of being conquered." He concluded his speech by invoking those images that had aroused such anger from opponents of this war:

> This business of burning human beings with napalm, of filling our nation's homes with orphans and widows, of injecting poisonous drugs of hate into the veins of peoples normally humane, of sending men home from dark and bloody battlefields physically handicapped and psychologically deranged, cannot be reconciled with wisdom, justice, and love. A nation that continues year after year to spend more money on military defense than on programs of social uplift is approaching spiritual death. (www.mlkonline.net)

King's emergence as a leader of the antiwar movement certainly helped the cause of longtime activists, especially within the African American community. Many civil rights activists were already concerned that a disproportionately large number of African Americans were drafted, wounded, and killed in the war. Consequently leaders in SCLC and CORE praised King's speech and his bold stand against the war. However, some within the civil rights movement feared his position would alienate Johnson's supporters. After all, President Johnson ultimately championed and signed into law both the Civil Rights Act of 1964 and the Voting Rights Act of 1965. Therefore, many African American civil rights leaders distanced themselves from King in the aftermath of his speech. Jackie Robinson criticized King publicly and Roy Wilkins criticized him privately at a NAACP board meeting just a week after the speech. At that meeting, the board voted not to unite the civil rights and antiwar movements. Whitney Young Jr., the executive director of the National Urban League, echoed the NAACP by stating that the support for civil rights programs and the question of the Vietnam War should remain separate. (Muste, *Declaration of Independence from the War in Vietnam.*)

Angry students organized a strike in protest and a hastily organized student-faculty committee was appointed to address the tension on campus. The committee decided to temporarily ban Dow from campus and suspend 13 students. Three professors ultimately lost their jobs for joining the strike. Despite these and other protests against Dow, the military continued to use napalm. However, the protest raised public awareness of the particularly brutal nature of this war.

THE VIETNAM WAR AND THE 1968 PRESIDENTIAL ELECTION

Going into the fall of 1967 it had become clear that the two major party candidates for the 1968 presidential election would be Lyndon Johnson and Richard Nixon. Everyone, of course, knew the president's stand on the war, and Nixon, the presumptive favorite for the Republican Party's nomination, refused to debate the Vietnam issue; he would only say that he had a plan for peace. This caused activists to scramble for an antiwar candidate to challenge Johnson and/or Nixon. In late October of 1967 they found their man in Eugene McCarthy, the senior senator from Minnesota. In his announcement speech on November 30, McCarthy took a page from Reverend King by linking the issue of the war to broader social and economic issues: the war on poverty, the reduction of foreign aid, war-related inflation, and the need to restore faith in the "processes of American politics and of American government" (Zaroulis and Sullivan, 127).

As the antiwar movement gained momentum during 1967, President Johnson fought back. Like he did with the Vietcong, Johnson tried to link the antiwar movement to Moscow, Peking, and Hanoi. He made these claims despite CIA intelligence that concluded there was no significant evidence to show Communist control of or influence on the U.S. peace movement. In September 1967 Johnson gave a speech in San Antonio, Texas, claiming that the fighting in Vietnam was staving off World War III. But the evidence was mounting against Johnson's policies and one of the chief architects of the Vietnam War, Secretary of Defense Robert McNamara, started to express his growing concerns with the policies he had helped set in motion. In June 1967 McNamara ordered a secret, massive study of the war which four years later would become known as the Pentagon Papers. In August he testified before a closed Senate Preparedness Investigations Subcommittee that the massive aerial bombardment of North Vietnam was not having its desired effect. He testified that there was "no reason to believe that North Vietnam can be bombed to the negotiating table." McNamara tried to reverse the administration's policies to no avail, and by mid-November he had been replaced by Clark Clifford (Oberdorfer, 113–114).

On Veterans Day, Johnson toured eight military installations in Vietnam to exhort the troops and continue his plan to win the propaganda war at home.

President Lyndon B. Johnson greets American troops in Vietnam in 1966. (National Archives)

Vice President Hubert Humphrey while in Vietnam declared on NBC's *Today Show,* "We are beginning to win this struggle." Walt W. Rostow, one of Johnson's most trusted advisors, used his Psychological Strategy Committee to leak positive war-related information to newspapers. General Westmoreland went to the National Press Club to report progress and declare that we had "reached an important point when the end begins to come into view." For the first time the general put a timeline on U.S. withdrawal by predicting within two years the South Vietnamese would be fighting their own war. This campaign to sway public opinion on the war reached a receptive American audience that desperately wanted to believe what its government was reporting (Zaroulis and Sullivan, 145).

The faith the American people placed in its government, however, would not be able to withstand the events of 1968. Though rising battlefield casualties and the antiwar movement had eroded support for the war, President Johnson entered 1968 still confident in the prospects of his re-election campaign. As 1967 came to an end, it seemed that he had every reason to be optimistic. In September 1967 U.S. officials helped elect Nguyen Van Thieu president of South Vietnam. The administration hoped that Thieu's regime would broaden support for the war at home, legitimize the South Vietnamese government in the eyes of the American public, and advance the military struggle against the communists.

The Tet Offensive

These hopes were dashed on January 30, 1968, when the Vietcong conducted a massive, well-orchestrated attack on strategic and urban areas in South Vietnam. Known as the Tet Offensive, the assault coincided with the Vietnamese holiday of Tet, the celebration of the lunar New Year. The Vietcong hit 36 of the 44 provincial capitals and five of six major South Vietnamese cities, including Saigon, where they assaulted the U.S. embassy. Planned since the previous fall, the attack demonstrated that the U.S. and South Vietnamese militaries underestimated their opponent.

Strictly speaking, the Tet Offensive was a failure for the Vietcong because it did not bring about the collapse of the South Vietnamese government. It did, however, successfully destroy the morale of the American military. The offensive convinced many within the administration that the war could not be won. General Westmoreland asked for 206,000 additional troops, but Johnson refused to take the politically explosive step of calling up the reserves.

Covered extensively by the media, the Tet Offensive made the administration and military's optimistic reports and predictions look foolish. Journalists previously reluctant to depart from Washington's conventional wisdom suddenly viewed the war as hopeless. The foremost television newsman at the time, Walter Cronkite of CBS, went to Vietnam in the midst of the Tet Offensive to see for himself how things were going. He came back to New York and produced a half-hour CBS News special, *Report from Vietnam by Walter Cronkite*. He somberly concluded the show by saying, "It seems now more certain than ever that the bloody experience of Vietnam is to end in a stalemate" (Cronkite, "Report on Vietnam"). He went on to predict that North Vietnam had the means to match the United States' escalation of the war, and "with each escalation, the world comes close to the brink of cosmic disaster. . . . It is increasingly clear to this reporter that the only rational way out then will be to negotiate, not as victors but as an honorable people who lived up to their pledge to defend democracy, and did the best they could" (Cronkite, "Report on Vietnam"). This television broadcast, visually reaching millions of Americans, probably did more than any other news of the war to attract new recruits to the peace movement. A Gallup poll conducted just before the Tet Offensive found that 56 percent of Americans supported the war. Three months after the offensive, those supporting the Johnson administration's war policies had fallen to 41 percent.

Clean for Gene

The growing opposition to the war immediately impacted the 1968 presidential campaign. In the aftermath of the Tet Offensive, antiwar activists converged on New Hampshire, site of the first primary election, to campaign for Eugene McCarthy. A core of student activists from a hundred campuses went "clean for

Gene" by cutting their hair and putting away their blue jeans and tie-dyed shirts to avoid alienating voters. Identified early as the antiwar candidate, McCarthy's support rose quickly after Tet, especially on the university campuses and within the liberal community. President Johnson won the New Hampshire primary, but McCarthy received over 42 percent of the vote. In fact, Johnson only received 230 more votes than McCarthy. McCarthy's strong showing against an incumbent president reflected the country's profound dissatisfaction with the direction of the war, even among those who supported it.

McCarthy later battled Sen. Robert Kennedy in a series of primaries, but lost to Vice President Hubert H. Humphrey, also from Minnesota, in a combative battle for delegates at the Democratic National Convention in Chicago. On the day that McCarthy lost the nomination, the delegates to the Democratic convention voted down a Vietnam peace plan, sparking a massive antiwar demonstration in downtown Chicago. Some believe his late, unenthusiastic endorsement of Humphrey contributed to the vice president's defeat in the general election.

Viewed as quixotic, cynical, and aloof, McCarthy after his defeat resigned from the Foreign Relations Committee, declined a bid for reelection in 1970, and made half-hearted attempts to run for president in 1972, 1976, and 1988. In 1980 he endorsed Republican Ronald Reagan, and in 1982 he ran for his old Senate seat in Minnesota but lost in the Democratic primary. A former teacher, economist, columnist, poet, and author of several books, McCarthy passed away in 2005.

Kennedy Enters, Johnson Exits

Sensing the president's vulnerability after Tet and his embarrassing showing in the New Hampshire primary, Sen. Robert Kennedy of New York decided to enter the presidential race. The Tet Offensive prompted Kennedy to deliver his strongest speech yet against Johnson's war policies, claiming the offensive had shattered the illusion on which such policies were based. In the wake of the Tet Offensive Johnson's approval rating dropped from 48 percent to 36 percent. Recognizing the erosion of his political support, President Johnson stunned the American people when on March 31, 1968, at the end of an uneventful televised address, he announced he would no longer seek re-election and would devote the remaining months in office to seeking peace in Vietnam.

The Tet Offensive set off a turbulent year in America. On April 4 James Earl Ray assassinated Martin Luther King Jr. on a motel balcony in Memphis, Tennessee. As word of King's death spread, riots broke out in 125 cities across the nation (see previous chapter). The antiwar movement had lost its most eloquent spokesman. but his death did little to slow the movement's momentum.

As the presidential race moved into the summer, McCarthy and Kennedy engaged in an intense battle for the Democratic nomination. After entering the

Columbia University Uprising

On April 23, 1968, the Columbia University chapter of SDS called a rally at "the sundial"—a gathering place for students in the center of campus. The intent of the rally was to protest a disciplinary meeting where six students, including Mark Rudd, the president of the Columbia chapter of SDS, had been summoned after they participated in a protest against the university's connection to the Institute for Defense Analysis, a Pentagon-sponsored organization that advised the government on defense strategy in exchange for funding. After the students refused to attend the meeting, the Columbia administration placed them on disciplinary probation. As Rudd tried to lead a crowd of several hundred students into Low Library, where the university's administration offices were, things got out of hand. Unable to gain entrance into the building, the demonstration began to spread. Rudd led the students to a smaller building, Hamilton Hall, and took a hostage, Henry Coleman, acting dean of Columbia College. During the next two days, students successfully entered Low Library and occupied the offices of Grayson Kirk, Columbia's president; they also occupied Fayerweather, Avery, and Mathematics halls.

The police overreacted to the Columbia occupation. In the early morning hours of April 30, 1,000 police charged the buildings, wielding nightsticks and clearing students at the entrances. Students were clubbed and dragged out of the buildings. Over 700 students were arrested, and nearly 150 were injured, prompting roughly 100 charges of police brutality.

Administrators suspended classes for three days; when they resumed, thousands of students went on strike. The Columbia demonstration signaled a violent turn for campus protests. Protesters destroyed considerable property, including academic research, and New York police resorted to violence to regain control of the campus. Students took hostages and threatened bodily harm to university officials, and antiwar activists like Tom Hayden called on other campuses to replicate the extreme Columbia demonstration. In attendance at the Columbia uprising, Hayden wrote in *Ramparts* magazine, "Columbia opened a new tactical stage in the resistance movement which began last fall: from the overnight occupation of buildings to permanent occupation; from mill-ins to the creation of revolutionary committees; from symbolic disobedience to barricaded resistance. . . . Students at Columbia discovered that barricades are only the beginning of what they call 'bringing the war home'" (Hayden in Teodori, 346–347).

race in mid-March, Kennedy defeated McCarthy in all but one primary (Oregon). On June 5 at a celebration for Kennedy's narrow primary victory in California, he was killed by Sirhan Sirhan, a young Palestinian who opposed his pro-Israel stance. To antiwar activists McCarthy now seemed their only chance to avoid another four years of a prowar presidency. Kennedy's assassination shattered the dreams of many who hoped for social change through the political system. During his brief campaign Kennedy had energized traditional liberals, including blue-collar workers and African Americans. Many Democrats did not view the more cerebral McCarthy as a viable candidate in the general election, so Sen. George McGovern of South Dakota entered the race to try to keep the Kennedy coalition together. Meanwhile, Vice President Humphrey started lining up pledges from traditional Democratic constituencies, and it appeared the Democratic Party would nominate someone closely associated with Johnson's war policies. Antiwar activists scrambled to make a statement at the Democratic National Convention to be held in Chicago in August.

1968 Democratic National Convention

As with the rest of the country, the Vietnam War divided the Democratic Party. Sensing Vice President Humphrey's nomination, antiwar activists desperately wanted to make an oppositional statement. Protesters from across the broad spectrum of the antiwar movement converged on Chicago. The atmosphere surrounding the convention was tense. On August 22, just four days before the Democratic Convention, Jerome Johnson, a seventeen-year-old Native American from Sioux Falls, South Dakota, was shot and killed by Chicago police. Police claimed Johnson shot at them first, but many activists coming to Chicago questioned that account. To make matters worse, Jerome Johnson was allegedly a "Yippie," young protesters eager to play the role of absurd comics. This created a volatile situation between the police and activists, between Mayor Richard Daley and those outside the convention hall intent on creating as much chaos as possible.

Abbie Hoffman and Jerry Rubin were the ringleaders of the Yippies (the Youth International Party), a group comprised of antiwar protesters, musicians, Beat poets, freelance hippie activists, and comedians. Decedents of beatniks, Yippies viewed America as a boring, sexually repressed place where anxious men waged war against the poor, powerless, and unconventional. Instead of engaging in the overly earnest protests that characterized the antiwar movement, Yippies preferred orchestrating humorous events aimed at garnering as much publicity as possible. The Yippies came to Chicago to make a statement and have a little fun on a grand stage with a national television audience. With theatrics geared toward that audience, the Yippies called for the end of the war, the legalization of marijuana, and the abolition of money. To mock the self-important ruling elite and further divert attention away from more serious protesters, the Yippies nominated a live pig named Pigasus for president.

Daley guaranteed law and order by preparing a large security force that included all 12,000 city police, 6,000 National Guardsmen, and 7,500 Army troops. The mayor also warned the press not to stir up trouble during the convention. Daley's show of force had a chilling effect on the planned protests; no more than 10,000 attended the protests during the four-day convention. Primed for an altercation, police and protesters engaged in minor skirmishes for much of the convention. The night of the nominations, however, police used mace, tear gas, and clubs to disperse a relatively orderly protest outside the convention hall. While protesters chanted, "The whole world is watching," the television networks ran film of the riot during the nominating speeches. Some of the police turned on photographers and TV cameramen in an attempt to destroy any images or recordings of the riot, actions described from the stage of the convention by Sen. Abraham Ribicoff of Connecticut as "Gestapo tactics." The country watched in horror as America seemed to be coming apart before their eyes.

Much to the chagrin of the antiwar movement, the American people overwhelmingly sided with Richard Daley and the police in this altercation. In the riot's aftermath, polls found that Americans approved of these acts of aggression by a 2–1 margin. For many voters, images of the Chicago riot cemented the impression that the Democrats were the party of disorder. Vice President Humphrey ultimately won the nomination, but he had an uphill climb in the general election.

For the antiwar movement the scene outside the Chicago Amphitheatre destroyed the dream that the war could be stopped from within the system. For many within the movement it also meant that nonviolent protest would not work against such a pernicious system. And for those observers of the Chicago riot, the antiwar movement would forever be linked to violence. The fact that much of the violence came from the police was irrelevant. As the polls indicated, Americans believed that the protesters were at fault for what happened. Televised for everyone to see, the police riot of the 1968 Democratic Convention polarized the American people even further. The civil war in Vietnam was causing a civil war at home.

Nixon's Victory

Things looked bad for the antiwar movement heading into the election. Richard Nixon demonized the protesters, calling for law and order in the land, and Hubert Humphrey represented a continuation of President Johnson's policy. In mid-October of 1968, however, antiwar activists could gain some satisfaction from McGeorge Bundy's public announcement that he had changed his mind about the United States' presence in Vietnam. One of the architects of the war's escalation, Bundy now said the United States should withdraw. He came to the conclusion that continued escalation of the war would simply not work and that continuation on the present course was unacceptable. He then laid out a plan that called for a steady and systematic reduction of American troops in Vietnam. Bundy's plan anticipated Richard Nixon's Vietnamization policy.

Nixon narrowly won the election, 43.4 percent to 43 percent. Despite the Democratic debacle, Humphrey made a late surge on the back of Eugene Mc-Carthy's late endorsement and President Johnson's October 31 announcement that bombing of North Vietnam had ceased and that peace talks would begin. Nixon countered by intimating that he had a plan for ending the war, but in fact no such plan existed. The antiwar movement would soon have a new target: Richard Nixon. Initially Nixon sought to end the war by expanding its scope as a way to pressure the North Vietnamese to negotiate. It did not take long, however, for Nixon to realize the American people would not support this approach.

Governor George Wallace and the Silent Majority

The turbulent events of 1968 convinced a lot of observers that American society was in the throes of revolutionary change. The 1968 election revealed that the response of most Americans to the turmoil was conservative. The most visible sign of the conservative backlash against the civil rights, antiwar, and countercultural movements of the sixties was the surprising success of George Wallace's presidential candidacy. As governor of Alabama Wallace had established himself as one of the nation's leading spokesmen for the defense of segregation. In 1964 he had run in a few Democratic presidential primaries and had done fairly well, even in some states outside of the South. In 1968 he became a third-party candidate for president on a platform of conservative causes. Although he never threatened to win the election, at times during the race he polled at over 20 percent.

Tapping into the conservative sentiment that Wallace's campaign expressed, Nixon effectively mobilized the "silent majority" by recognizing that many Americans had grown tired of hearing about their obligations to the poor, minorities, and criminals. As a result, he successfully ran on a law and order and "peace with honor" theme.

NIXON'S WAR

Nixon tried to persuade the North Vietnamese to go along with a mutual troop withdrawal from South Vietnam, but the offer was refused. In March of 1969 Nixon tried to apply more pressure by ordering secret bombing raids on the neighboring country of Cambodia, through which the North Vietnamese transported supplies and reinforcements. On May 9 the *New York Times* published William Beecher's account of the bombings, causing the White House to respond aggressively. Convinced that word of the secret bombings leaked from within the White House, Nixon ordered the wiretapping of several National Security

Advisor staffers, the military aide to Secretary of Defense Melvin Laird, and ultimately four newspapermen. Nixon claimed that he kept the Cambodia bombing secret so as not to arouse the antiwar movement.

He had reason to be concerned. Cambodia was a neutral country, and Congress had not given the president authority to wage war against it. If word of his illegal act got out, certainly it would spark outrage. Within months of taking office, Nixon employed methods, known as his "dirty tricks," that came to characterize his administration's method of operation: spying, secrecy, and deception. He used those same methods to wage war against the antiwar movement at home. Surveillance of the antiwar movement was nothing new, but Nixon took it to a new level. Nixon literally sent thousands of FBI, CIA, and U.S. Army agents into the field to keep an eye on peace activists. These agents served as informers and provocateurs charged with derailing protests against the administration's policies. Ultimately ineffective in destroying the antiwar movement, the willingness to engage in these "dirty tricks" set the stage for Watergate and Nixon's ultimate self-destruction.

When the intensified bombing on Cambodia failed, Nixon and his national security advisor, Henry Kissinger, advanced a policy of "Vietnamization" that would initiate a gradual withdrawal of U.S. troops. On June 8, 1969, Nixon announced that 25,000 troops would be withdrawn and replaced by South Vietnamese forces. Antiwar activists believed Vietnamization did little to end the war; as Ellsworth Bunker, ambassador to South Vietnam, noted, it was just a matter of changing "the color of the bodies." While roughly 200 American soldiers died each week in Vietnam during the summer of 1969, the American public supported Nixon's vague plan to extricate the United States from Southeast Asia. Most Americans by this time had become weary of nightly scenes of carnage broadcast on television amid the backdrop of the contentious domestic political landscape. Yet many Americans still did not completely trust their new president and his plans (Lee and Haynsworth, 13).

The Weathermen

As the organizational structure of SDS crumbled amid ideological disagreements in June 1969, a radical faction of the group formed the "Weathermen" to take its place. Their name came from a line in Bob Dylan's "Subterranean Homesick Blues": "You don't need a weatherman to know which way the wind blows." The Weathermen embraced the ideology of Black Panther leader Huey Newton (see previous chapter) who said, "In order to get rid of the gun it is necessary to pick up the gun." Their style was paramilitary, and their strategy was wanton violence. Professing their admiration for Che Guevara and preparing themselves for guerrilla warfare, the Weathermen hoped to become outlaws.

Demonstrators protest the trial of the Chicago Eight. The Chicago Eight, antiwar activists arrested for protests during the Democratic National Convention held in Chicago in 1968, drew attention to their cause during a lengthy and often bizarre trial. (Library of Congress)

On October 9, 1969, a few hundred Weathermen gathered in Chicago with the avowed intention to "bring the war home." Called the "days of rage," the radicalized activists embarked upon street demonstrations marked by random vandalism and running battles with the police. Ultimately the Weathermen's most prominent leaders, Mark Rudd and Bernadine Dohrn, went underground and launched a terrorist campaign of sporadic bombings for several years. The only casualties of these attacks were three Weathermen who accidentally blew themselves up while constructing bombs in a Greenwich Village townhouse.

These former SDS leaders created a cell of committed revolutionaries who had grown disdainful of the mass of students they had once felt called to educate. They captured the rhetoric and puritanical zeal of the Old Left, but without a deep appreciation for the difficult struggles of the workers and outcasts. Frustrated and angry, they devolved into anarchy and lost most of their followers. As a result, their inclination toward wanton violence and hapless self-destruction played directly into the hands of their enemies.

The Chicago Eight

In March 1969, Tom Hayden, Rennie Davis, Dave Dellinger, Abbie Hoffman, Jerry Rubin, Bobby Seale, John Froines, and Lee Weiner were indicted on charges of conspiracy to incite a riot in Chicago during the Democratic National Convention. Nixon was determined to defeat the antiwar movement, and the indictment against the "Chicago Eight" was a part of this larger campaign. In certain circles, the indictments turned the defendants into celebrities on par with rock stars.

The conspiracy trial began in Chicago in September 1969 for what were now the Chicago Seven (Bobby Seale's case had been severed from the group). Once optimistic in his call for social reform, Hayden and the other defendants had grown increasingly oppositional as the sixties and the Vietnam War progressed. Openly defiant as the trial began, the defendants became even more hostile and isolated as the trial wore on. Hayden, author of the *Port Huron Statement,* leader of the sixties student protest movement, once known as an intellectual intent on lead-ing a movement of respectful dissent, appeared at the trial more an oppositional activist who used apocalyptic rhetoric. At the apex of his fame, Hayden bewildered many of his erstwhile liberal allies with calls for a revolution to start "a new soci-ety in the streets . . . with its own natural laws, structures, language and sym-bols" (Miller, 308–309). With the spectacle of the Democratic National Convention, the Columbia University uprising, and now the trials of the Chicago Eight, it seemed that the student-led antiwar movement had set out on a new, more radical course. With calls for "direct action" and "life and death conflicts" with the establishment, student leaders committed themselves to an all-or-nothing mission. The revolu-tionary zeal of the Chicago Eight, Weathermen, and other student activists alien-ated many inside and outside the antiwar movement, ultimately detracting from the cause.

On February 20, 1970, Hayden was sentenced to five years in prison for his role in the Chicago demonstrations. Throughout the trial the judge, Julius J. Hoff-man, demonstrated unbridled hostility and contempt for the defendants. Hayden remained free while he appealed his conviction. In the fall of 1972, a federal ap-peals court, commenting that "the demeanor of the judge and prosecutors would require reversal if other errors did not," overturned Hayden's conviction. By then, the charismatic leader of the student movement had no movement to lead (Miller, 260–313).

The Moratorium

In contrast to the Weathermen's approach, a more moderate group of student activists made plans for a more gradualist approach that they believed had the potential for radical results. These activists formed the Vietnam Moratorium Committee to initiate a nationwide movement that would bring all normal uni-

Peace activists organize at their headquarters in preparation for the Moratorium to End the War in Vietnam. Held on October 15, 1969, the rally at the Washington Monument was the largest nationwide protest to date against U.S. involvement in Vietnam. (Library of Congress)

versity activity to a halt on October 15 while students undertook a door-to-door campaign to raise the consciousness of Americans. The intent was to escalate the protest month by month as long as the war persisted. Vietnam Moratorium Day was peaceably observed by millions of Americans in thousands of communities across the nation. Except for very isolated incidents, no violence broke out; instead, in town after town, there were silent vigils, readings of fallen soldiers' names, candlelight processions, church services, and large public gatherings to hear politicians, ministers, and leaders of the antiwar movement speak. What started as a student protest ended in an opportunity for young people and adults alike to gather and peacefully express their opposition to the war. In Washington, D.C., a candlelight procession of 30,000 passed the White House while they softly sang, "Give Peace a Chance."

Basking in the success of the first Moratorium Day, the Vietnam Moratorium Committee planned the next demonstration for November 15. The Nixon administration meanwhile planned its counterattack. Vice President Spiro Agnew assumed the role of attack dog against the antiwar movement. Agnew characterized antiwar protesters as an "effete corps of impudent snobs who characterize themselves as intellectuals" and "nattering nabobs of negativism." As the

November 15 demonstration drew nearer, Agnew described it as "a carnival in the streets" by a "strident minority." Some within the administration went as far as asserting that Communists organized, or at least inspired, the moratorium. In anticipation of the protest, Nixon gave his famous "silent majority" speech on November 3. Arguably one of the most divisive speeches ever given by a sitting president, Nixon identified the country's real enemy as "a minority" who are trying to impose their will on the majority "by mounting demonstrations in the streets" and threatening the nation's "future as a free society." He called for his fellow Americans, "the great silent majority," to stand up against these demonstrators and support him in his efforts to impose law and order in the streets of America (Zaroulis and Sullivan, 264–273).

Young Americans for Freedom

Not all young people during the 1960s opposed the war. The Young Americans for Freedom, for example, gave strong support to U.S. military intervention in Vietnam, along with advocacy for free-market economics, states' rights, and limited government. The Young Americans for Freedom was a militant conservative youth group founded in 1960 with the help of William F. Buckley Jr., editor of the *National Review* and host of the television show *Firing Line*.

At its inception, the group issued what became known as the Sharon Statement, which put an emphasis on the individual's use of his God-given free will, and that political freedom must be accompanied by economic freedom. Young Americans for Freedom also believed in the importance of U.S. sovereignty and defeating communism. Members actively campaigned for Barry Goldwater during his ill-fated 1964 presidential election and organized counterdemonstrations in response to the SDS antiwar demonstrations.

The Young Americans for Freedom played a significant role in moving the Republican Party to the right of the political spectrum. Despite its relatively small membership, the Young Americans had a profound influence on the long-term American political landscape. The organization remained active in Republican politics well into the 1980s, offering strong support to Ronald Reagan and the conservative movement.

The March Against Death

The antiwar movement was not deterred. Norma Becker, cofounder of the Fifth Avenue Peace Parade Committee, had worked tirelessly to organize a November 13th March Against Death. An estimated gathering of at least 45,000 marched across the Arlington Memorial Bridge, down Pennsylvania Avenue, and to the Capitol where they placed name placards of fallen soldiers in 40 waiting caskets. Hour by hour they silently came, marching through two nights and into Saturday morning, through wind, rain, and thunderstorms. Each marcher paused opposite the main entrance of the White House to say aloud the name of the dead soldier on his or her placard. The caskets were then carried in a mass march to the Washington Monument.

The March Against Death was a prelude to what government officials estimated as a 250,000-person demonstration on November 15. Others estimated the number closer to 500,000 as some 4,000 buses transported demonstrators from across the country. By noon two-thirds of the 41 acres surrounding the Washington Monument were covered with people. Unlike the October 15 demonstration and the March Against Death, the November 15 protest had the feel of a festival where rock and folk musicians played before a congenial mass audience. Artists like John Denver; Pete Seeger; Arlo Guthrie; and Peter, Paul and Mary sang protest songs to the delight of the crowd. As Dr. Benjamin Spock spoke into a microphone, asking President Nixon if he was listening, Seeger led a hand-clasped crowd in singing, "Give Peace a Chance."

While the organizers of these fall 1969 demonstrations were pleased with their success, they had no way of knowing their impact on the Nixon administration. As it turned out, Nixon and Kissinger contemplated escalating the war, including the possible use of nuclear weapons. The antiwar sentiment expressed by these massive demonstrations created a political climate that made it impossible for them to move forward with this plan. Instead, Nixon continued to attack the antiwar movement at home, using the FBI to investigate movement leaders in an attempt to link them to the Communist Party. While these efforts found some success in discrediting and isolating the movement's leaders, there is no question that the antiwar movement experienced some of its greatest successes in the fall of 1969. Two huge, peaceful demonstrations had rescued its public image from the Chicago Democratic National Convention of the previous year and put the Nixon administration on the defensive.

The My Lai Massacre

To make matters worse for the administration, news of the My Lai massacre hit the newspapers in a *New York Times* article by Seymour Hirsch published November 13, 1969, the same day as the March Against Death. The massacre had occurred on March 16, 1968, coincidentally the day Robert Kennedy announced his candidacy for president. On patrol in Quang Ngai Province, soldiers from the American Division under the command of Lt. William Calley entered the hamlet of My Lai, looking for Vietcong guerillas. Finding the villagers uncooperative, the soldiers murdered 347 Vietnamese civilians with grenades, bayonets, guns, and fire, and then tossed the bodies into a shallow ditch. Word of this atrocity ignited more public outrage and more questions about the justification and nature of this war.

After a long and much-publicized trial during the summer of 1971, a military court found Lieutenant Calley guilty of at least 22 murders in the My Lai incident of 1968 and sentenced him to life imprisonment. The trial, verdict, and sentence once again brought public attention to the brutality that had attended the war, setting off a bitter debate on the question of responsibility for alleged war crimes. Ultimately Calley served only days at Fort Leavenworth before being transferred to Fort Benning. There he served under house arrest until President Nixon issued him a pardon. He was released in 1974.

Conclusion:
The Antiwar Movement's Decline

Even with all the bad news coming from Indochina and the success of the 1969 demonstrations, the antiwar movement could not bring about the end of the war. By 1971 the intensity of the antiwar movement had subsided. Student strikes continued through 1972 but never at the scale of the 1969 Moratorium days. Antiwar groups like SDS, hindered by police harassment and FBI and CIA infiltration, fractured and dissolved. Nixon's Vietnamization policy also took the steam out of the movement. When Nixon took office, more than 543,000 American soldiers were stationed in Vietnam; by the end of 1970, only 334,000 remained. By the end of 1972, only 24,200 soldiers continued to serve in Vietnam. Despite the war's expansion into Cambodia and Laos, Nixon's promise to continue troop reduction, stop the draft, and institute an all-volunteer army deprived the antiwar movement of important issues. Most important, the antiwar movement suffered because it was delivering a message, regardless of its truth, that most Americans did not want to hear.

Biographies

Bettina Aptheker, 1944–

Activist

Bettina Aptheker was born in Brooklyn, New York, the daughter of the well-known Communist theoretician Herbert Aptheker. She moved from New York to attend the University of California at Berkeley in 1962 and joined seven other activists to organize the Free Speech Movement (FSM) in the fall of 1964. Aptheker proposed that the FSM be patterned after the Communist Party organization of Popular Front movements during the 1930s. Aptheker then helped form a new group, the Free Student Union (FSU), to organize students like a labor union. Within a month of its creation, the FSU sold roughly 3,200 memberships at 25 cents apiece. The FSU advocated co-op housing, a co-op book-store, student parking, a student voice in faculty hiring and tenure decisions, and autonomous student government. Aptheker continued to be an active member of the radical New Left throughout the 1960s. Unlike other women, Aptheker refused to take a back seat to men and remained a vocal leader of the student movement. She remained a strident Marxist, became close friends with Angela Davis, and taught African American and Women's Studies at the University of California at Santa Cruz (Rorabaugh, 23–24, 45, 132).

David Dellinger, 1915–2004

Pacifist

One of the founders of *Liberation* magazine, David Dellinger was a strong voice for pacifism throughout much of the 20th century. By the late sixties, he had become one of the national leaders of the antiwar movement. He visited Ho Chi Minh in North Vietnam and felt a bond of Christian identification with the Communist leader, later writing in his memoirs that he imagined himself and Ho Chi Minh as "members of the same Beloved Community" (Berman, 79). One of the Chicago Seven tried and convicted on charges of conspiracy and intention to incite a riot at the 1968 National Democratic Convention, Dellinger had his conviction overturned by an appellate court.

Robert Allen Haber, 1935–

First SDS President

Born in 1935, Haber was named for Robert La Follette, the senator from Wisconsin and prominent Progressive. His father, William, was a first-generation immigrant of Rumanian Jewish ancestry who had studied at the University of Wisconsin in the 1920s. William Haber was a renowned economist and labor arbitrator who supported Franklin Roosevelt and the New Deal, becoming one of the architects of the Social Security system. In 1936, he accepted a position at the University of Michigan, where he taught until he retired. Robert inherited his interest in politics from his father and developed into Ann Arbor's resident radical by the late 1950s. He called for radical social change, joined the Student League for Industrial Democracy, and later helped organize the Students for a Democratic Society, becoming its first president and spokesperson in the early 1960s.

Mark Rudd, June 2, 1947–

Weatherman

The son of a real estate agent and lieutenant in the Army Reserves, Rudd developed organizational skills and a political consciousness while a student at

Columbia University. He became involved with the Students for a Democratic Society and organized the Columbia sit-in of 1967. He later became disillusioned with SDS and helped form the small band of radicals known as the Weatherman Underground Organization. Increasingly frustrated by his inability to change the political culture of the United States, Rudd came to believe that militant confrontation offered the only hope for substantive change. Rudd is credited with much of the inflammatory rhetoric of the group and is blamed for its overt machismo and confrontational tactics that ultimately strained gender relations within the Weatherman organization. He went underground for seven years, ultimately turning himself in on October 13, 1977. Rudd eventually became a professor of mathematics at a community college in New Mexico.

Mario Savio, 1942–1996

Free Speech Advocate

Mario Savio, leader of the Free Speech Movement, speaks during a demonstration at the University of California, Berkeley, on December 2, 1964. The movement marked the first massive countercultural protest by college students. (Hulton Archive/Getty Images)

In 1963 Mario Savio transferred to the University of California at Berkeley from Queens College, New York. He developed into the charismatic leader of the United Front and later the Free Speech Movement (FSM) during the 1964–1965 academic year. Savio served on the FSM's steering committee and acted as the organizations chief spokesperson. Eventually Savio and fellow student Jack Weinberg, two of the more radical members of the FSM, became the de facto leaders of the movement, alienating many of the more conservative and even liberal students from the organization. Savio continued to agitate the university's administration by violating rules against solicitation for unlawful off-campus activities. Eventually Savio and Weinberg received a six-week suspension from classes. Savio and other FSM leaders later organized a seizure of the university's administration building that resulted in the arrest of 773 students. Immediately after that highly publicized demonstration, Savio gave an emotional speech on the importance of free speech on December 7, 1964, to thousands of students gathered in front of Berkeley's administration building. The next day the Academic Senate voted against any restrictions on the content of speech and advocacy. Savio and the FSM had won an important victory and helped ignite student activism on college campuses throughout the country. He eventually dropped out of school, worked menial jobs for 20 years, and then returned to San Francisco State University to earn his bachelor and master's degrees in physics in the 1980s. He died at the age of 53 from a heart attack. At the time, he taught mathematics and philosophy at Somona State University. After his death, the University of California at Berkeley officially named the steps at the Sproul Plaza the "Mario Savio Steps."

Paul Soglin, 1945–

Activist, Alderman, Mayor

Paul Soglin became involved in the antiwar movement at the University of Wisconsin at Madison in the fall of 1967. Paul's father, Albert, taught math in the Chicago public schools but was suspended without pay for two years when he refused to sign a state loyalty pledge required of government employees. Paul's mother, Rose, became active in the movement for nuclear disarmament. In fact, Rose named her son Paul in honor of Paul Robeson, the black singer, actor and civil rights activist who was a hero of the American left. By Paul's second semester at the University of Wisconsin, he had become the secretary of the local branch of the Student Nonviolent Coordinating Committee. Paul became active in the antiwar movement as a result of the protests against Dow Chemical recruiters on the campus in Madison. He filed a suit in federal court to prevent the university from usurping the free speech rights of the protesters and helped lead the student seizure of the university's Commerce Building on October 17, 1967, in an effort to prevent Dow recruiters on campus. This seizure led to a violent and bloody confrontation with local police that is dramatically retold in David Maraniss's *They Marched Into Sunlight*. Police beat Soglin on his back and legs with billy clubs. Soglin became a Madison alderman in 1968 and mayor of Madison in 1973. He served as mayor from 1973 to 1979 and again from 1989 to 1997. He ran again in 2003, this time regarded as the conservative candidate, and lost.

REFERENCES AND FURTHER READINGS

Anderson, Terry. 1994. *The Movement and the Sixties*. New York: Oxford University Press.

Baskir, Lawrence, and William A. Strauss. 1978. *Chance and Circumstance: The Draft, the War, and the Vietnam Generation*. New York: Alfred A. Knopf.

Berman, William C. 1988. *William Fulbright and the Vietnam War: The Dissent of a Political Realist*. Kent, OH: Kent State University Press.

Breines, Wimi. 1982. *Community and Organization in the New Left, 1962–1968*. South Hadley, MA: Praeger.

Brown, Sevrom. 1969. *The Faces of Power: Constancy and Change in United States Foreign Policy from Truman to Johnson*. New York: Columbia University Press.

Cronkite, Walter. 1968. "Report from Vietnam," CBS News (February 27). Full text of report at http://www.alvernia.edu in the *Sibley history text cite*.

Crozier, Michel, Samuel P. Huntington, and Joji Watanuke. 1975. *The Crisis of Democracy; Report on the Governability of Democracies to the Trilateral Commission*. New York: New York University Press.

DeBenedetti, Charles, and Charles Chatfield. 1990. *An American Ordeal: The Antiwar Movement of the Vietnam Era*. Syracuse, NY: Syracuse University Press.

"Declaration of Conscience." 1965. *Catholic Worker* (February).

Farber, David. 1988. *Chicago '68*. Chicago: University of Chicago Press.

Farlie, Henry. 1973. *The Kennedy Promise: The Politics of Expectation*. Garden City, NY: Doubleday.

Gellhorn, Martha. 1966. "Suffer the Little Children." *Ladies Home Journal*.

Gitlin, Todd. 1987. *The Sixties: Years of Hope, Days of Rage*. New York: Bantam Books.

Halstead, Fred. 1978. *Out Now! A Participant's Account of the American Movement Against the Vietnam War*. New York: Monad Press.

Hammond, William M. 1988. *The Military and the Media, 1962–1968*. Washington, DC: Center for Military History.

Hammond, William M. 1998. *Reporting Vietnam: Media and Military at War*. Lawrence: University Press of Kansas.

Hauser, Thomas. 1991. *Muhammad Ali, His Life and Times*. New York: Simon and Schuster.

Herring, George C. 1979. *America's Longest War: The United States and Vietnam, 1950–1975*. New York: Wiley.

King Martin Luther Jr. "Beyond Vietnam, April 4, 1967," www.mlkonline.net.

Lee, J. Edward, and H. C. Haynsworth. 2002. *Nixon, Ford, and the Abandonment of South Vietnam*. Jefferson, NC: McFarland.

Lipsyte, Robert, and Peter Levine. 1995. *Idols of the Game: A Sporting History of the American Century*. Atlanta: Turner Publishing, Inc.

Littauer, Raphael, and Norman Uphoff, eds. 1972. *The Air in Indochina*. Boston: Beacon Press.

"Managed News Again." 1966. *Chicago Tribune* (December 28).

Matusow, Allen J. 1984. *The Unraveling of America*. New York: Harper and Row.

Miller, James. 1987. *Democracy Is in the Streets: From Port Huron to the Siege of Chicago*. New York: Simon and Schuster.

Muste, A. J. "Declaration of Independency from the War in Vietnam," in *A. J. Muste Memorial Institute Essay Services,* War Resisters League.

Oberdorfer, Don. 1972. *Tet!* Garden City, NY: Doubleday.

Rorabaugh, W. J. 1989. *Berkeley at War, the 1960s*. New York: Oxford University Press.

Sale, Kirkpatrick. 1973. *SDS*. New York: Random House.

Schulzinger, Robert D. 1997. *A Time for War: The United States and Vietnam, 1945–1975*. New York: Oxford University Press.

Teodori, Massimo. 1969. *The New Left: A Documentary History*. Indianapolis: Bobbs-Merrill.

Van Dyke, Jon M. 1972. *North Vietnam's Strategy for Survival*. Palto Alto, CA: Pacific Books.

The Vietnam Hearings. 1966. New York: Random House.

Zaroulis, Nancy, and Gerald Sullivan. 1984. *Who Spoke Up? American Protest Against the War in Vietnam, 1963–1975*. Garden City, NY: Doubleday.

The Antipoverty Crusade

OVERVIEW

The welfare rights movement in the 1960s occurred at the intersection of politics and grassroots activism. The civil rights movement of the late 1950s and early 1960s brought the plight of poor people, particular poor African American people, to the attention of the American public and politicians. In turn, presidents, politicians, and policymakers passed laws and created government agencies to offer economic opportunity to the poorest Americans. President John F. Kennedy was among the first politicians to exploit this issue while vying for the 1960 Democratic Party presidential nomination during a campaign stop in West Virginia. His effective use of the unemployment problem in that state brought widespread attention to the issue of poverty amid America's postwar affluence.

By the mid-1960s it was hard to distinguish between the civil rights movement and the War on Poverty. After the postwar migration to northern cities, the erosion of manufacturing jobs in the wake of increased automation and business consolidation, and the residential segregation accelerated by white migration to the suburbs, African Americans in the 1960s found themselves relegated to life in the decaying inner cities. In 1962 Michael Harrington's *The Other America* raised Americans' consciousness about those groups facing the biggest economic challenges: minorities, the uneducated and unskilled, and the long-term unemployed. Harrington introduced the nation to the cycle of poverty.

Picking up on President Kennedy's and Harrington's work, President Johnson declared an unconditional "War on Poverty" in his 1964 State of the Union address. With the Economic Opportunity Act of 1964 and the creation of the Office of Economic Opportunity (OEO), a federal agency was armed to wage this war. The Johnson administration and the OEO developed a comprehensive antipoverty program that included initiatives such as Community Action, Model Cities, Job Corps, Head Start, and Volunteers in Service to America (VISTA).

At the foundation of these initiatives stood the principle of "maximum participation of the poor." Building upon lessons learned from the civil rights movement, activists for the poor took the concept of maximum participation to heart and began to get involved in influencing, organizing, and running antipoverty programs. Just as important, they became forceful advocates for the rights of the poor. Their activism ultimately began to challenge the power relationships between races and classes, causing much of the middle-class political support for such programs to evaporate by the end of the decade.

The organization of the National Welfare Rights Organization (NWRO) in 1966 probably best typifies the rise and fall of this social movement. At the center of the welfare rights efforts lay a grassroots social movement composed of thousands of welfare recipients and other poor people. At the 1966 meeting of local activists which led to the formation of the NWRO, participants agreed upon four goals: adequate income, justice, dignity, and democracy. The overarching goal was to establish a minimum standard of living as a human and citizenship right. Many activists viewed welfare rights as an extension of the civil and political rights gained through agitation in both the South and the North in the 1950s and 1960s.

Antipoverty activists took the principle of maximum participation a step further than the Johnson administration had intended. This movement claimed adequate income a right for every citizen of the United States. As NWRO Executive Director George Wiley and New York City welfare rights leader Beulah Sanders testified before the Joint Economic Committee of Congress in 1968: "We believe that the way to do something about poverty is to give people money they need to meet the basic necessities of life at least at a minimum level for health, decency and dignity." They did not just want jobs; they wanted "adequate income for those who cannot work" (Kornbluh, 68).

Activists also sought to make legal, political, and economic institutions work for them as well as for the wealthy. Legal Service attorneys funded through the OEO initiated antipoverty litigation in several localities. One of the primary ways in which Legal Service attorneys assisted welfare rights efforts was by representing clients in "fair hearings." Administrative in nature, fair hearings allowed welfare recipients the chance to appeal aid denials or the inadequacy of awarded welfare grants. Fair hearings became central to welfare rights strategies for changing governmental policy from below.

The poor and those advocating on behalf of the poor demanded dignity from a system that often treated those living below the poverty line as parasites. To them, "dignity" included full participation for poor people in the market, including participation as consumers. As Juliet Greenlaw, an Aid for Families with Dependent Children (AFDC) recipient and NWRO representative, said at a 1968 Democratic Platform hearing:

> Welfare gives us enough for food and rent and second-hand clothes for us and our children, and in some states, not even enough for food. But food and rent is not all of life. Why wouldn't we be able to buy perfume once in a while—or a ring—or even a watch? Every woman wants and needs some of these things—particularly when we see all other women having them. . . . Our children drop out of school because they don't have decent clothes, let alone the things that other children take for granted—enough school supplies, money for a class trip, a graduation suit or dress. (Kornbluh, 74)

Welfare rights activists demanded full participation in the political decisions that affected their lives. As Sanders told the President's Commission on Income Maintenance in 1969: "Everyone has their own plan on what to do with welfare recipients. Well, the only thing you can really do is get up off your Seventeenth Century attitudes, give poor people enough money to live decently, and let us decide how to live our lives." Building from the empowering experiences of the civil rights movement, these activists demanded the ability to form their own communities and organizations, which would act autonomously to determine their own fate (Kornbluh, 65–78).

Made possible by President Johnson's War on Poverty, welfare rights activists took the concept of maximum participation literally. Their declaration that an adequate income was their human right, however, played into the hands of conservatives alarmed by the excesses of the politics and culture of the Left in the late 1960s. The white middle class would not accept the concept of money for nothing. President Nixon and other politicians on the right exploited these expressions of entitlement from welfare recipients during his successful 1968 presidential campaign. The financial drain of the Vietnam War and Nixon's New Federalism and Family Assistance Plan (FAP) signaled the beginning of the end for the welfare rights movement. Despite guaranteeing a minimum income for all families, the inclusion of a strong work incentive component in the law meant a rejection of NWRO's initial goals. From this time forward, welfare recipients have had to fight the stigma of being on the public dole, and the perception that they are an unnecessary drain on the nation's resources.

TIMELINE

1960   John F. Kennedy makes a campaign stop in West Virginia to exploit the state's problem of unemployment to win the state's primary election.

1961   The Area Redevelopment Administration Act is passed.

1962   Michael Harrington's *The Other America* is published.

                The Manpower Development and Training Act is passed.

1964   Lyndon B. Johnson makes his "War on Poverty" State of the Union address.

                The Economic Opportunity Act is passed.

                Sargent Shriver is named director of the Office of Economic Opportunity.

                The Citizens Crusade Against Poverty is organized.

                The Job Corps and Volunteers in Service to America are created.

1965   Head Start Program begins.

                The Office of Economic Opportunity funds the Child Development Group of Mississippi.

                People in the Watts section of Los Angeles riot.

                President Johnson convenes the Task Force on Urban Problems.

                Appalachian Volunteers receive Office of Economic Opportunity funding.

                Daniel Patrick Moynihan publishes *The Negro Family* report.

1966   The Office of Economic Opportunity funds the Mississippi Action for Progress.

                The Children Crusade to Washington takes place.

                Demonstration Cities and Metropolitan Development Act (Model Cities) is passed.

                The Appalachian Group to Save the Land and People is organized.

                The federally funded Legal Services program begins.

                The National Welfare Rights Organization is created.

                The National Farm Workers Association is organized.

1967   Riots break out in Newark, New Jersey.

                The first National Conference on Black Power is held in Newark.

                March for Understanding takes place in Newark.

Riots start in Detroit.

The Kerner Report is issued from the National Advisory Commission on Civil Disorders.

Appalachian volunteer Joseph Mulloy is arrested for sedition.

1968   Robert Kennedy makes campaign stop in California to support striking migrant farm workers.

1969   Nixon introduces the Family Assistance Plan.

THE POVERTY PROBLEM REVEALED

Although middle-class organizations, African American ministers and radical groups like the Congress of Racial Equality (CORE) and the Student Nonviolent Coordinating Committee (SNCC), whose leadership came mostly from college students, intellectuals, and professionals, led the civil rights movement, its success relied on the participation of hundreds of thousands of mostly poor African Americans living in the South and North.

In the immediate aftermath of World War II, poor African Americans were impacted by the zealous anticommunism of the Cold War era. Political purges in the unions, arts, sciences, and professions along with the "Attorney General's list" of subversive organizations and the 1947 Taft-Hartley Act requiring all union officials sign an annual oath that they were not members of the Communist Party, created a political climate that made advocacy for the poor, workers, and minorities dangerous. Even after the *Brown v. Board of Education* decision of 1954 and the Montgomery bus boycott of 1955, segregationist elites throughout the South formed White Citizens Councils aimed at intimidating African Americans from supporting the civil rights movement. But the 1960 sit-in at a Woolworth's lunch counter in Greensboro, North Carolina, ignited a wave of sit-ins at stores, theaters, churches, and public swimming pools throughout the South, drawing many poor African Americans into the civil rights movement. From the sit-ins came a heightened emphasis on direct action, spawning new organizations such as SNCC.

Militant young African American and white college students joined SNCC and began interacting with hundreds of thousands of poor southern African Americans in antisegregation, community organizing, and voter-registration drives in the early 1960s. The student New Left organization, Students for a Democratic Society (SDS), began working with SNCC to create the Economic Research and Action Project (ERAP), which launched community-organizing projects among the urban poor of northern cities in 1964. ERAP heavily influenced the Johnson administration's War on Poverty.

A volunteer with the Southern Regional Council's voter registration drive urges two African Americans in Mississippi to register ahead of the 1964 elections. (National Archives)

After the civil rights movement won victories against segregation and disenfranchisement, the movement emerged as primarily a fight for the poor. Martin Luther King Jr., for example, increasingly focused on poverty and employment. He had connected the problem of segregation and poverty before the Civil Rights Act of 1964, making "Jobs and Freedom" the official slogan of the 1963 March on Washington. After the passage of the Voting Rights Act of 1965, King devoted all of his energies to building a poor people's movement that included a broad coalition of poor whites, African Americans, Latinos, Native Americans, Asian Americans, and others. It was in this vein that King went to Memphis in April 1968 to support a strike of African American sanitation workers.

The Northern Migration

Notions of poverty in the 1960s were shaped in part by the massive migration of roughly nine million mostly poor people out of the south and into the north between 1910 and 1960. Even though slightly more than half of these migrants were white, the most dramatic shift occurred in the geographic and political-cultural locus of the United States' African American population. In 1910, 90 percent of all African Americans lived in the south, but by 1960 the population was evenly divided between the south and the urban north. For African Americans, northward migration represented a continuation in their historic quest for freedom and economic opportunity. White migrants, particularly from Appalachia, also left the south where coal-mining machines replaced workers and where lumber barons and strip-miners pushed farmers off their eroded land for economic opportunity in midwestern and northeastern industrial cities.

For African American migrants, northern workplaces often seemed to recapitulate historic southern patterns of racial prejudice. In the Midwest, countless southern African Americans watched poorly educated whites from Kentucky or Tennessee exploit skin color to secure jobs. African American job-seekers had to show a stubborn determination to secure even the most menial job; promotions were almost completely out of the question. Yet the move northward offered African Americans a new arena for struggle, one centered on jobs. In this struggle African Americans partnered with white workers to form a powerful, biracial labor movement in the 1940s and 1950s for the first time in American history. As a result, African American workers in the auto, steel, railroad, and meatpacking industries earned wages that often exceeded their wildest dreams. To them, labor activism was part of a larger mission, one intimately connected with their new home in the Democratic Party that at least temporarily viewed labor unions and broad-based civil rights organizations as logical allies.

Southern white migrants from Appalachia prospered early, and steadily, compared to their African American counterparts, primarily because they gained easier access to semiskilled jobs, and they had the freedom to move around within urban areas. By the 1940s and 1950s, when the greatest migrations out of the south took place, changes in the northern economy fundamentally altered the status of unskilled workers. Automation and firm consolidation began to erode the jobs as early as the mid-1950s. At this time big labor started to draw back its support for civil rights. The decline of heavy manufacturing left African American workers vulnerable, regardless of union affiliation.

The combination of lost jobs and residential segregation solidified African Americans' status as second-class citizens in northern cities. Beginning in the 1950s, whites fled the inner cities, reversing generations of population growth and leaving African Americans increasingly concentrated in areas with declining tax revenues. As whites fled to the suburbs and working-class fringes, they took jobs with them. New businesses had few incentives to locate within decaying inner cities. Chicago, Detroit, and Cleveland ranked high among all the cities losing employment opportunities from the late 1950s on, creating an explosive condition in the inner-city African American ghettoes. During the Kennedy administration the numbers of those receiving federally supported Aid to Families with Dependent Children (AFDC) grew sharply as the urban poor suffered from suburbanization, urban renewal projects, declining public transportation and schools, and the export of jobs to Taft-Hartley "right to work" states.

The Appalachian Poor and the 1960 Presidential Election

Looking for traction in his fledgling bid for president in 1960, John F. Kennedy hit upon an issue that resonated with voters while campaigning in West Virginia. Needing a victory in the West Virginia primary, Kennedy toured the state in late April with a message that appealed to the more than 100,000 unemployed West Virginians. Referring to the boarded-up windows of out-of-work miners as "Eisenhower curtains," Kennedy attacked the Republicans indifference to the plight of the miners and unemployed. He derided Vice President Nixon's view that the economic condition of the United States could not be better:

> Let them tell that to the 4 million people who are out of work, to the 3 million Americans who must work part time. . . . As long as there are 15 million American homes in the United States substandard, as long as there are 5 million American homes in the cities of the United States which lack plumbing of any kind, as long as 17 million Americans live on inadequate assistance when they get older, then I think we have unfinished business in this country. (Schlesinger, 1005–1006)

Kennedy used the issue of joblessness to great effect in West Virginia. His ultimate victory in that primary forced his chief opponent, Hubert Humphrey from Minnesota, out of the race. During the general election campaign in the fall of 1960 Kennedy returned to West Virginia to once again attack "Republican indifference and neglect" (*New York Times,* September 19, p. 1). This time he offered a five-point program intended to solve the problem of chronic unemployment. Kennedy promised that if elected president he would commit his administration to a policy of full employment and send to Congress a specific program to carry this pledge out. He offered the following:

1. Developing of public resources in the fields of power, transportation, and natural resources;

2. Stimulating private investment by eliminating the artificial Republican restrictions on the money supply;

3. Developing new schools, increasing teachers' pay, and promoting the advance of science and technology;

4. Addressing the problem of machines replacing workers by working with industry and labor to develop a strategy for putting displaced workers back to work.

The Other America

Michael Harrington's 1962 book, *The Other America,* caused Americans to redis-
cover the problem of poverty. Harrington described the poor as "those who, for
reasons beyond their control, cannot help themselves" (Harrington, 162). Harrington's book did not become a bestseller right away, but it challenged assumptions about America's post–World War II affluence. Harrington pointed out that
despite all the rosy assumptions about the "liberal consensus," more than one-
fifth of the nation lived in a condition of deeply entrenched poverty. While the
number of Americans suffering from poverty had fallen in the decade following
the war (from 28 to 21 percent), there had been only a 1 percent reduction since
1957.

Harrington exposed the misery of the "new" particularly deprived poor that
included 40 to 50 million people:

> The other America does not contain the adventurous seeking a new life and
> land. It is populated by failures, by those driven from the land and bewil-
> dered by the city, by old people suddenly confronted with the torments of
> loneliness and poverty, and by minorities facing a wall of prejudice. (Har-
> rington, 10)

President Kennedy read *The Other America* and asked his advisors to study the
problem of poverty. Kennedy had observed the face of economic suffering during
his 1960 campaign in West Virginia, but after reading Harrington's exposé he became more committed to attacking the problem. President Lyndon Johnson inherited the staff work and directed it forward at full speed. When President Johnson
ultimately declared a "War on Poverty," Harrington's book soared to the top of the
bestseller list. For the first time in three decades, poverty was front-page news.

Harrington's book successfully raised the consciousness of policymakers and
Americans on the plight of the poor. Central to Harrington's analysis was a description of those groups that faced the strongest barriers to vertical migration:
minority groups discriminated against because of race or color; the uneducated
and unskilled; and the long-term unemployed. He explained that as the composition of low-income groups becomes more static, the cycle of poverty becomes
increasingly difficult to break. As groups become accustomed to a low-income
status, expectations and aspirations fade, and they become isolated from the
more affluent populations. In essence, they live in an economic underworld largely
ignored by mainstream America. A journalist by trade, Harrington wrote in a style
that captivated a large reading audience. In describing what sociologists and
economists sometimes refer to as "insular poverty," Harrington dramatically described a "culture of poverty" that defined these groups' existence.

5. Giving special federal assistance to particularly hard hit areas like West Virginia.

Making good on his promise, President Kennedy signed the Area Redevelopment Administration bill into law in 1961. This bill targeted areas of high chronic unemployment like Appalachia with $375 million in federal funding to stimulate economic activity and build needed public facilities. Most of the funds were to be devoted to long-term loans; the balance was to be distributed to the communities in the form of grants. By the end of 1963, the agency had committed a little over $200 million which purportedly created 20,000 new jobs. More important, Kennedy's exploitation of this issue brought attention to the problem of poverty amid the apparent abundance of a postwar America.

Kennedy's focus on the white poor in Appalachia also served the purpose of expanding his political coalition during the 1960 campaign and his presidency. Concerned about being too closely associated with the civil rights movement, Kennedy reached out to poor whites in part to counteract white southerners' defection to the Republican Party. His stop in West Virginia helped him keep his southern Democratic base intact while simultaneously reaching out to African American voters.

The Poor Helping Themselves

In 1962 Congress passed the Manpower Development and Training Act (MDTA). Sold as a way to help people help themselves and thereby get off welfare, Congress enthusiastically saw this as a way to end the cycle of poverty for millions of Americans. Federal expenditures on job training increased from $200 million to $1.4 billion from 1964 to 1970. The Job Corps, the Neighborhood Youth Corps, the MDTA, and Jobs in the Business Sector (JOBS) all sought to make the poor more employable. By 1973 the MDTA program had enrolled 2.2 million people at a cost in federal money of $3.2 billion (Patterson, 123).

In 1964, President Johnson built on President Kennedy's MDTA by creating Job Corps. Modeled in many respects on the New Deal's Civilian Conservation Corps, Job Corps would teach young men (women were initially excluded) new skills at rural and urban residential centers. Removing these men from family and neighborhoods reflected the suspicion of policymakers that environmental factors fed the cycle of poverty. By 1966 it became apparent that the primary focus of the War on Poverty had shifted to job-training programs. Forty-six percent of OEO's budget during the 1967 fiscal year was devoted to job creation or training programs. If unemployment was viewed as the primary cause of poverty, then efforts to deal with this problem presumably would produce the greatest effects. Secretary of Labor Willard Wirtz asserted that the cost of on-the-job training was recovered in two years in savings from welfare expenditures (Zarefsky, 97).

President Lyndon B. Johnson visits with Job Corps students at the Camp Gary Job Corps Center in San Marcos, Texas, on November 8, 1965. (Lyndon Baines Johnson Museum and Library)

Support for the Job Corps wavered as the success rates of its participants failed to meet expectations and the dropout rate rose. The challenges facing 1960s' job-training programs demonstrated how difficult it would be to eradicate poverty. For one, the Job Corps trained most of its recruits for service jobs, the sector of the economy that offered the lowest wages and fewest job opportunities at the time. In addition, the Job Corps worked with the hardcore unemployed. Its recruits suffered not only from a history of poverty but lacked the education and intellectual skills necessary to make them readily employable. Nearly a third of the enrollees could not read a simple sentence; 60 percent came from broken homes; 40 percent came from families on welfare; half could not read or do arithmetic at the fifth-grade level (Andrew, 74).

The Job Corps also suffered from the eruption of violence at several Job Corps centers. Critics claimed that this violence contributed to a high withdrawal rate and deterred prospective enrollees. The high dropout rate, regardless of its cause, meant that funds were being spent on persons who did not remain in the corps long enough to benefit from the experience. The high cost of training was also seen as a defect in the program. Job Corps training centers were in some cases so badly managed that the cost of training an enrollee was greater than the cost of a Harvard education (Zarefsky, 98).

No promise of a job for trainees presented the most fundamental problem to the federal government job-training programs in the sixties. Critics argued that the best cure for joblessness was an expanding economy. They claimed that a general stimulation of the economy would do more to combat unemployment than job-training programs. Supporters of the programs maintained that the unemployable and the hardcore poor possessed limited skills to find work in an increasingly complex industrial system. If any hope existed for these people, they argued, job-training programs needed to continue.

After riots in several Job Corps centers and numerous instances of financial mismanagement, Congress granted governors the power to veto Job Corps and volunteer projects in their states. From 1965 until 1968 governors in 10 states vetoed 30 OEO grants.

VISTA

Volunteers in Service to America (VISTA) was the domestic version of the Peace Corps, first proposed by President John F. Kennedy in 1963 but defeated by conservatives in Congress. VISTA made it into the act establishing the OEO only after governors were given the right to veto VISTA projects in their states.

Though underfunded, VISTA workers started training in late 1964. Their initial education focused on psychology, sociology, economics, and the culture of poverty. After six weeks of training and education, VISTA workers, mostly middle class, young, and well educated, served in one of six poverty tracts defined by geography, ethnicity, and economic problems. They taught the poor English and office skills, established food cooperatives, advised people on their legal problems, assisted with hostile landlords, served as liaisons between public schools and parents, organized youth clubs, and built bus shelters for rural school children.

Imbued with the same idealism as the Peace Corps, VISTA attracted a large number of recruits. During its first three years roughly 70,000 people submitted applications to serve. But the relatively small $3-million initial congressional appropriation kept the program small. Although VISTA intended to utilize 4,000 volunteers, by the end of the first year it had managed to recruit and train only about 1,100. Due to funding limitations, VISTA ultimately could only accept about 20 percent of the applications received. The young idealists serving as VISTA workers became active in community-improvement efforts. They led rent strikes and helped organize labor actions against employers. Sometimes labeled as "radicals" and "Marxists" by local politicians, some VISTA workers lost their posts due to their community activism.

The War on Poverty

President Lyndon Johnson, more than his predecessor, acknowledged that the social ills of racism, inadequate schools, and substandard healthcare could not be addressed without a more general and unconditional War on Poverty. President Johnson announced in his first State of the Union address on January 7, 1964, that "this administration today, here and now, declares unconditional war on poverty in America." Often accused of expanding the New Deal social-welfare programs of Franklin D. Roosevelt, Johnson's declaration more accurately reflected the optimism of the postwar era than the desperation of the Depression era. Franklin Roosevelt, faced with the ravages of the Depression, had urged the nation toward the much more modest goal of economic recovery. President Johnson rallied the nation around the loftier goal of ending poverty altogether.

Conservatives often point to this address as the beginning of excessive government spending on entitlement programs and the acceptance of a permanent

President Lyndon B. Johnson listens to Tom Fletcher describe conditions in his town of Inez, Kentucky, after declaring the nation's War On Poverty on April 24, 1964. (Bettmann/Corbis)

welfare state in America. Ironically the budget President Johnson announced that day called for a one-half of 1 percent (roughly $500 million) reduction in federal spending and a significant tax cut for most Americans. Among the Johnson administration's proposals were an expansion of the redevelopment programs for depressed areas initiated by President Kennedy, increased use of food stamps, the creation of a domestic National Service Corps similar to the Peace Corps, special school aid funds for needy areas, medical care for the aged, extension of the minimum wage, and expanded housing programs. At the same time, President Johnson, almost sounding like an advocate for supply-side economics, asserted, "We must release $11 billion of tax reduction into the private spending stream to create new jobs and new markets in every area of this land. . . . The new budget clearly allows it. Our taxpayers surely deserve it. Our economy strongly demands it. We need a tax cut now to keep this country moving" (*New York Times,* January 8, 1964, p. 1).

Even before his declaration of war against poverty, Johnson had established the Office of Economic Opportunity (OEO) in 1964 and appointed President Kennedy's brother-in-law, Sargent Shriver, its leader. In 1965, the Johnson administration created a series of new programs whose purpose was to provide education, healthcare, housing subsidies, and job training to the poor. The OEO attempted to coordinate these programs by allowing local communities to get involved in the organization and implementation of the services. As a result, community-based antipoverty organizations began to spring up in cities throughout the country.

Johnson's establishment of the OEO and his War on Poverty reflected the growing public awareness of the plight of the poor amid the apparent prosperity of the postwar years. As the apex of the civil rights movement neared, Johnson followed the lead of social activists and put the problem of poverty at the top of his domestic agenda.

WIDENING PARTICIPATION IN PROSPERITY, A FOCUS ON THE YOUNG

President Kennedy's Council of Economic Advisors explained in 1963 that a dramatic program designed to aid the poor made both political and economic sense. Politically it would reach out to poor whites, perceived as an important move in light of Kennedy's recent support of an expansive civil rights law. Economically it would be a good investment. The Council of Economic Advisors stated in January 1964, "We pay twice for poverty: once in the production lost in wasted human potential, again in the resources diverted to coping with poverty's social by-products. Humanity compels our action, but it is sound economics as well." President Johnson, embracing the suggestions of the Council, declared in March 1964, "Our fight against poverty will be an investment in the most valuable of our resources—the skills and strengths of our people. And in the future, as in the past, this investment will return its cost many-fold to our entire economy" (Patterson, 130).

The Council of Economic Advisors' optimism about eradicating poverty reflected the post–World War II liberal consensus. Despite the economic sluggishness of the late 1950s, continuing economic growth was assumed. In fact, the council originally named its proposals "Widening Participation in Prosperity." The council believed that the "conquest of poverty" was well within their reach. Approximately $11 billion would bring all poor families up to a decent standard of living, they surmised. This was less than one-fifth of the annual defense budget and less than 2 percent of the Gross National Product.

Those within the Kennedy and Johnson administrations pushing an anti-poverty program were not interested in creating a welfare state. Instead, they saw this program as creating opportunity for the poor, which is why they called the new federal agency created to wage this war on poverty the Office of Economic Opportunity (OEO). As a result, much of the focus of this program would be on the young. Walter Heller, chairman of the Council of Economic Advisors, constantly cited evidence that showed the correlation between low educational levels and poverty. He advised Johnson to "emphasize that the major focus on the attack on poverty is on youth: to prevent entry into poverty." The best way to do this, he later asserted, is through expanding educational opportunity (Patterson, 132).

The development of a comprehensive antipoverty program also reflected the postwar faith in social science. While presidential advisors recognized that welfare had to remain a central part of the program, they also believed that creating opportunity and eliminating poverty required social, political, cultural, and economic structural reform. Community action became an important concept in the initiation of that reform. Community Action projects were described as anti-poverty efforts that developed employment opportunities, improved human performance, motivation, and productivity, or bettered the conditions under which people lived, learned, and worked. The Economic Opportunity Act that President Johnson signed into law on August 20, 1964, directed local communities to designate public or private nonprofit agencies to apply for federal grants. These agencies would use this money to invest in their communities with programs aimed to lift the poor out of poverty. They also served as the organizational base for the 1960s' grassroots effort to eradicate poverty (Patterson, 130–133).

Head Start

Head Start was the national program aimed to offer educational opportunities to underprivileged children. Head Start's focus on children and education made

Lady Bird Johnson, wife of President Lyndon B. Johnson, visits with children in a Head Start classroom at Kemper School in Washington, D.C., on March 19, 1968. The goal of the Head Start preschool program is to increase school readiness for young children from low-income families. (Lyndon Baines Johnson Museum and Library)

it one of the more popular War on Poverty initiatives and it remains in existence to this day. Grounded on several virtually unchallenged liberal assumptions of the day, Head Start placed its faith in nurture over nature. Success in school and life largely depended on experience, not heredity, and for poor children the culture of poverty was the critical molding experience. Most important, Head Start drew on the research of several experts who emphasized the importance of the earliest childhood years in stimulating mental capacity.

Sargent Shriver set the program in motion when in January 1965 he asked Dr. Robert Cooke, head of the department of pediatrics at Johns Hopkins, to form an advisory council of educators, doctors, economists, and psychologists to help plan an early childhood intervention project for the Office of Economic Opportunity. The product of that advisory council's quick work, Head Start was officially launched on February 19, 1965, at a White House ceremony presided over by First Lady Lady Bird Johnson. Like other early War on Poverty programs, Head Start was rushed into operation. More ambitious than his advisory council, Shriver moved forward with a large preschool program during the summer of 1965 with a target enrollment of 100,000 children.

The advisory council established criteria for funding community Head Start projects and made plans for in-service teacher training programs. With its heart-warming mission, Head Start attracted 200,000 volunteers to work as local Head Start aides in the summer of 1965. In a matter of weeks, local groups from all over the country applied for Head Start funding. By July the OEO had committed about $82 million to fund local Head Start programs around the country. Head Start aimed not only at improving the school performance of disadvantaged children, but it also intended to improve children's health, get parents more involved in their children's education, encourage community control over antipoverty programs, and create career opportunities in education for the poor.

During the summer of 1965 more than half a million four- and five-year-old preschool children in 2,500 rural and urban communities enrolled in eight-week Head Start programs. Through ad hoc organizations or civic groups, local activists and volunteers ran many of the programs in school districts. A disproportionate number of Head Start's beneficiaries were African American children of urban ghettos and southern rural areas. The children who participated were those who scored lowest in achievement as measured by standardized tests.

The Child Development Group of Mississippi

In May 1965 the OEO bypassed an uncooperative Mississippi state government and gave $1.5 million to the Child Development Group of Mississippi (CDGM), a group organized by the Delta Ministry, an arm of the liberal National Council of Churches of Christ headquartered in Mt. Beulah Center. The grant would be administered by Mary Holmes Junior College. Most CDGM leaders were civil rights activists who had participated in the previous year's Mississippi Freedom Summer project. Led by Tom Levin, a radical New York psychoanalyst, CDGM saw this as an opportunity not only to improve poor children's educational performance, but also to get poor African Americans politically engaged.

During the summer operation, CDGM successfully brought a more liberal and egalitarian culture into rural African American Mississippi. At eighty centers throughout the state, children were introduced to art, music, dance, and theater. Using puzzles, toys, and lively social interaction, Head Start workers got children involved in a variety of intellectually stimulating activities. They also served milk and hot meals, collected medical profiles, immunized children against childhood diseases, and helped poor parents take advantage of free local health services.

CDGM also created hundreds of paid jobs for grossly underemployed Mississippians, particularly African American women, as nursery-school teachers, aides, janitors, and cooks. From the outset the organizers of these Head Start centers in Mississippi embraced the principle that the poor of the Mississippi Delta who were the primary beneficiaries of the initiative should also help staff and run the program and play central roles in its planning and implementation. OEO officials in Washington enthusiastically endorsed this idea because it represented a perfect embodiment of one of the central tenets of the new antipoverty program—"maximum feasible participation of the poor."

The initial CDGM plan was rather limited in scope: a three-month summer Head Start program, affecting about 3,200 eligible three- to five-year-olds, mostly from the Delta. Because of the unique participatory role of the parents in the program, the African American community responded to this new educational venture with great enthusiasm. Between May and mid-June 1965 the clamor for places in the program doubled enrollments over what was initially projected. For the first time many of the parents working as teachers, teachers' aides, maintenance workers, and administrative assistants earned real salaries or substantial hourly wages. As a result, the economic impact of CDGM on the African American community in the Mississippi Delta was as important in inspiring hope and a new vision for the future as the educational opportunities being provided for their children. CDGM wanted to help create a way in which these oppressed people could, for the first time, begin to share power in society through methods they devised and which were deeply meaningful to their daily lives, especially the lives of their children.

CDGM faced challenges from the beginning, including from middle-class African Americans accustomed to working with the existing white power structure that sought to maintain its relative power within the African American community. But the most intense challenge, not surprisingly, came from the whites of Mississippi. Because CDGM insisted on desegregated instruction centers, these programs offended Mississippi's segregationists. CDGM staffers also provoked the white establishment in Mississippi. Levin and others saw Head Start as an opportunity to start a government-supported social reformation. Polly Greenburg, OEO's southwest regional analyst for Head Start, said that many CDGM staffers considered the project's importance not to be "its nursery school activities, but rather its long range political significance" (Unger, 193). Segregationists opposed CDGM's effort to encourage African American empowerment and racial integration and seized on its fiscal sloppiness to attack its work.

Despite these challenges, the OEO renewed funding of CDGM in February 1966 with a multimillion-dollar budget increase, allowing expansion from a three- to a nine-month program. This funding represented a significant victory for Mississippi's poor African American community over the white power structure of the state. Unfortunately this victory was fleeting. Mississippi senator John Stennis, head of the Senate Appropriations Committee, accused CDGM with mishandling federal grant money. Stennis threatened to hold up an emergency appropriation to support the Vietnam War effort if something was not done to clean up CDGM. CDGM had to respond to a list of demands that included relocating its headquarters and removing Levin as the director. In October 1966, over the protests of several civil rights activists, Shriver shifted OEO support from CDGM to Mississippi Action for Progress (MAP), a hastily thrown together group headed by more moderate figures from both races.

With the help of its many defenders within the liberal establishment, the OEO eventually restored partial funding to CDGM. Those from the Field Foundation, a major national philanthropic organization, initially stepped in to provide temporary funding to CDGM while activists lobbied the administration to restore the funding. By late November 1966 they secured the support of Vice President Hubert Humphrey, who advanced two arguments within the administration. First, he warned that denying CDGM funds would imperil the administration's standing with crucial groups in the liberal coalition that consistently supported Johnson's domestic programs. Second, restoring some of CDGM's funding would not hurt Democratic prospects in Mississippi since, in terms of presidential politics, the state would probably vote Republican for the foreseeable future. As a result, OEO restored funding to CDGM Head Start centers with over $5 million. Thereafter MAP and CDGM fought over funding and where each would locate their programs within the state.

The new funding came with more federal strings attached, which meant less educational innovation and increasing bureaucratic regulation. Inevitably the Head Start program lost some of its early luster of educational and social uniqueness. By 1968, CDGM found itself beset by internal conflicts exacerbated by the constant external pressure applied by those bound and determined to see it fail.

In many ways the saga of the CDGM revealed the internal tensions of President Johnson's War on Poverty. If one took seriously the principle of "maximum feasible participation of the poor," as the organizers and participants of CDGM clearly did, then changes in power relations were bound to occur. More times than not, those in control devoted their resources and connections to prevent such a change.

Children Crusade to Washington

In order to put pressure on Congress and the OEO to restore funding to the various Head Start programs in Mississippi, CDGM organized a Children Crusade to Washington in February 1966. Fifty children and twenty-three adults traveled in two chartered buses to Washington, D.C., to conduct a teaching demonstration in the halls of Congress. CDGM invited its best teachers to come and to each bring five or six children whose families they knew well, with signed parental releases.

The group arranged to conduct the demonstration in Rep. Adam Clayton Powell's Hearing Room. Representative Powell (D-NY) was chairman of the House Education and Labor Committee, which oversaw the antipoverty program. CDGM sent out press releases and arranged for the best possible press and television coverage. While members of the House Education and Labor Committee looked on, the young Mississippians unloaded crayons, toys, drawing paper, and even a live mouse in a cage and proceeded to demonstrate a Head

Start preschool class. Theodore M. Berry, director of the federal Community Action programs, told the Mississippi delegation that CDGM would receive a pared-down $3-million grant, nearly half of what was once promised. CDGM was not satisfied. Polly Greenburg noted that the $8 million it cost to build one bomber was enough to fund their entire program. "We felt our children's futures were being traded for bombers to kill Vietnamese children." After further negotiations, the delegation left Washington with a promise of $5.6 million (Greenburg, 453).

MAXIMUM FEASIBLE PARTICIPATION

The earliest advocates for mobilizing the poor to work toward an end to poverty were officials and social scientists working on President Kennedy's Committee on Juvenile Delinquency. They believed that ending poverty depended on avoiding entanglement in what Robert Kennedy called "the Federal government's system of vested interest," meaning the professional social workers, bureaucrats in existing federal agencies, and city machines. Theorists like Lloyd Ohlin believed that winning the War on Poverty depended on community action that aimed at creating new opportunities for broad and comprehensive changes in the life of the poor. Early proponents of community action, however, differed on how it would actually work. Some, like Ohlin, wished to involve the poor in community action and were prepared to confront City Hall if necessary, but only if experts were in place to provide organization and leadership. Others, like Leonard Cottrell, expressed distrust for experts and placed their faith in individual initiative and self-reliance. A disciple of Saul Alinsky, a veteran radical and community organizer, Cottrell believed that poor people needed independence. Dependency on experts would erode self-realization and self-responsibility, necessary ingredients for escaping a culture of poverty. Yet others, like Columbia University's Richard Cloward, believed direct action and conflict were necessary for progress. Cloward and other radicals believed that to feel empowered the poor must directly challenge City Hall and win (Patterson, 133).

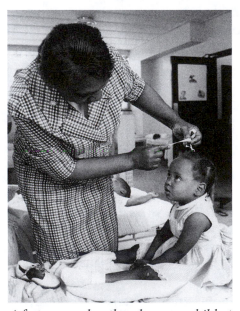

A foster grandmother dresses a child at McMahon Memorial Shelter in New York City, May 1967. "Foster Grandparents," a volunteer organization, gives older people a chance to care for small children while their mothers are working. (National Archives)

As director of the OEO for the Johnson administration, Sargent Shriver was given the charge of translating theory into practice. Under Shriver's direction antipoverty programs were created and operated through a policy of "maximum feasible participation." Shriver held the pioneering role as the first director of the OEO from 1964 to 1968. While serving in that capacity he helped create and promote such antipoverty and socially conscious programs as the Volunteers in Service to America (VISTA), Head Start, Community Action Programs (CAP), Foster Grandparents, Job Corps, Legal Services, Indian and Migrant Opportunities, and Neighborhood Health Services. By engaging the poor in creating the solution to their problems, Shriver believed the OEO would offer empowerment. By drawing upon the time-honored American tradition of self-sufficiency, Shriver also believed that the new antipoverty programs would be somewhat insulated from political attacks on the right. Certainly emboldening antipoverty activists, the policy did little to quiet the critics of President Johnson's Great Society, the more general effort to expand the federal government's role in reforming society, creating opportunity, and eradicating poverty. By challenging the existing political and power structure, the policy ensured a confrontation between activists agitating for change and politicians trying to preserve and protect the status quo.

Community Action Programs

The Economic Opportunity Act's Community Action Program (CAP) set out to help all residents of impoverished neighborhoods escape from a culture of poverty by enlisting the poor to participate in solving their community problems. The law described Community Action projects as antipoverty efforts that developed employment opportunities, improved human performance, motivation, and productivity, or bettered the conditions under which people lived, learned, and worked. The act directed communities to award grants to public or private nonprofit agencies. These agencies were then to take this money and use it to run a coherent and effective program that lifted the poor out of poverty and helped them stay out.

It was hard to evaluate the Community Action programs because there were a thousand in operation during the peak of the OEO, with wide variations that defied easy generalizations. The majority worked relatively well with existing institutions and focused on providing educational, legal, and family planning services. In these places Community Action agencies and personnel augmented existing social service agencies and did not make dramatic changes in what had previously been done.

Most of these traditional programs paid lip service to the ideal of "maximum feasible participation." Practically speaking, such participation was hard to achieve given the enormous problems facing the truly poor. Many poor citizens were, in Patrick Moynihan's words, "inarticulate, irresponsible, and relatively unsuccessful."

As a result, it was difficult involving the poorest members of a community in any meaningful way (Patterson, 145).

Even if not immediately successful, though, the presence of a Community Action program built upon the activism of the civil rights movement offered an opportunity for activists and the poor to get politically involved in the fight for social justice and against poverty. This involvement created a conflict between the urban underclass and the power structure of several American cities that erupted into violence and fueled the radicalization of late–1960s revolutionaries.

Citizens Crusade Against Poverty

In the spring of 1964 a new, privately financed organization named the Citizens Crusade Against Poverty (CCAP) dedicated itself to the eradication of poverty and aimed to train community workers to organize the poor and show them how to participate more effectively in local antipoverty programs. The CCAP was a nonpartisan grouping of more than 125 organizations and leaders of religious, civil rights, labor, academic, business, student, and farm groups. Walter P. Reuther, president of the United Automobile Workers (UAW), served as the CCAP's first chairman and announced that his union would commit $1 million to the organization.

The CCAP intended to see that the government's War on Poverty did not falter and that city mayors around the country did not exercise monopoly power over Community Action programs financed by the federal government. The organization proposed to give vitality to a provision in the Economic Opportunity Act that defines community action as one "which is developed, conducted, and administered with the maximum feasible participation of residents of the areas and members of the groups served" (Unger, 170).

The more militant champions of the government's antipoverty campaign believed that community action distinguished the War on Poverty from traditional forms of social work and public assistance. The CCAP contended that making the poor mere recipients of aid would only perpetuate the cycle of poverty. The belief at the heart of this organization was that poverty was more than an absence of money, but actually the presence of hopelessness. To instill hope in the poor, the CCAP created a nationwide information exchange among individuals and groups fighting poverty. It proposed to establish several major centers where local antipoverty leaders could learn organizing and management techniques and where promising young interns from poor neighborhoods and from the Peace Corps and the civil rights movement would be taught how to organize the poor. It would also teach local activists how to attract and manage federal antipoverty grants.

Ultimately this left-of-center organization was taken over by more radical activists such as former OEO advisor and CCAP's executive director Richard Boone, who used the organization to agitate and protest as well as train and educate. For example, CCAP militants disrupted, threatened, and ultimately scared away Shriver at the organization's first national conference in 1966 after he told the audience that he was "not a bit ashamed of what has been done by the War on Poverty" (Unger, 170).

Community Action in Mississippi

OEO operated Community Action programs in all southern states, but it focused its activities most intensely on Mississippi. Nowhere were the lives of the poor more hopeless nor their political poverty greater than in Mississippi where rates of poverty and illiteracy were the highest in the nation, especially among African Americans. Mississippi was also the state most unwilling to let African Americans participate in politics. As late as 1963, Mississippi stood alone among southern states in having no public school desegregation, and its African American voter registration was the lowest in the country.

As federal antipoverty funds became available, the white power structure in Mississippi unsuccessfully sought to control them. OEO bypassed local politicos, siding instead with local African American activists who seized upon the mandate of "maximum feasible participation" to demand that they participate in the Community Action agencies and help decide how to spend the funds. Empowering African Americans meant using federal funds to circumvent local politicians, local educational institutions, and local welfare authorities. Systematic Training and Redevelopment, also called Operation Star, exemplified this circumvention. Initiated by two Catholic priests, Operation Star established an alternative social-welfare system in Mississippi. As one of only two states without a mandatory education law, Mississippi's high illiteracy rates prevented most of the poor from participating in vocational training. Aimed at the hardcore unemployed and functionally illiterate, Operation Star planned to use literacy training followed by vocational training and job referral to make the illiterate employable.

Operation Star received over $5 million from OEO to establish centers throughout the state to train the poor in literacy, arithmetic, and social skills. Operation Star also opened a vocational training center in Greenwood, Mississippi, which offered secretarial training, skilled-trades training in basic wood and metal machines, farm equipment maintenance and repair, and auto engine repair and maintenance. In many communities, Operation Star advisory boards held the state's first racially integrated meetings ever. In order to avoid confrontation with ardent segregationists in the south, OEO appointed mostly moderate African Americans to these advisory boards and Operation Star's board of directors. OEO also feared the disruption African American militants might cause. OEO insisted that Community Action agencies like Operation Star be integrated, distributed resources in a way that undermined the existing political system of patronage, and created new networks that included African Americans.

Community Action in Newark

In a few cities community action went beyond increasing the political participation of the poor to incorporating a more radical vision of social change typified by late–1960s Black Power ideology. One such city was Newark, New Jersey. Here the civil rights movement used the Community Action Program to create an autonomous structure and challenge City Hall.

Newark experienced a rapid influx of African Americans from the south after World War II. By the early 1960s nearly 200,000 African Americans resided there. In response, the white middle class fled to the suburbs. Between 1960 and 1967 Newark lost more than 70,000 white residents; in that period the city moved from 65 percent white to 52 percent African American and 10 percent Puerto Rican and Cuban. In 1962 Hugh Addonizio, a liberal seven-term congressman, forged an African American–Italian coalition to overthrow the Irish who had controlled the city for decades. As mayor, Addonizio proclaimed his door open to African Americans. Despite this promise, the city council and board of education remained dominated by whites and by the mid-1960s the OEO concluded that the city had lost sight of the growing needs of the inner-city poor African American population.

Newark's Community Action program, the United Community Corporation (UCC), was divided into nine area boards, which became pawns in the political struggle between the Democratic Party and the African American community. The area boards were essentially designed to compete with the existing political wards of the city. At the outset of the Community Action program, Addonizio used the UCC to buy off potential opponents. The slightest sign of opposition against his regime resulted in a patronage job that effectively served to quiet potential enemies. Immediately, complaints surfaced that the mayor's handpicked area boards were misusing antipoverty funds. At first, Community Action funds merely filled local patronage coffers while buying off militant activism within the African American community.

The Newark Community Union Project (NCUP), a coalition of three civil rights groups—SDS, CORE, and SNCC—engaged in a political power struggle with City Hall for control of the UCC. Mobilizing quickly, NCUP seized Area Board 2 and Area Board 3, and began competing with the city's central ward for power. Committed to improving the ghetto, NCUP focused on urban renewal as the most important issue to address with OEO funds. The Demonstration Cities and Metropolitan Development Act of 1966, or Model Cities, authorized the federal government to make grants to city agencies to develop programs to improve their physical environments, increase the housing supply to low and moderate-income

African Americans jeer at bayonet-wielding National Guardsmen brought in to quell the riots in Newark on July 14, 1967. (Bettmann/Corbis)

people, and provide educational and social services. In 1967, Newark received Model City funds. The city council voted to use those funds to clear 150 acres of ghetto housing for a medical and dental college.

The Area 2 and 3 boards vehemently denounced the plans for a medical school complex. The plan, they argued, contained no relocation plan for those displaced residents. They also feared that the plan was designed to break up an area that could elect an African American mayor. The controversy came to a head at a tumultuous planning board meeting in June of 1967 when speaker after speaker denounced the city's plan to raze the ghetto. City officials responded that African American nationalists and militants had seized control of the city's antipoverty program. As civil rights activists seized the Community Action program, social policy became a weapon in the battle for racial equality. The numerical dominance of the African American community plus the presence of organized civil rights activists made this possible.

On July 12 cabby John Smith was arrested for driving with a revoked license in a Newark ghetto. Visible to several residents of the Reverend William P. Hayes Housing Project, the police dragged Smith from a police car and into the red-

The Gray Panthers

Although not created until January 1970 and not exclusively focused on economic issues, the Gray Panthers embodied the spirit and political activism of the 1960's anti-poverty movement. Organized by six older professional women and veterans of the civil rights, antiwar, and environmental movements, and spearheaded by Margaret (Maggie) Kuhn, a disciple of the sociologist Charles Elmer Gehlke and a proponent of community action, the Gray Panthers defined its mission as the creation of a better society for all ages. Active in the antiwar movement, Kuhn was a victim of forced retirement from an executive position with the national Presbyterian Church. The other five women were also either recently retired or near retirement: Eleanor French, director of the student division of the YWCA; Helen Smith, an executive with the United Church of Christ; Polly Cuthbertson, director of the American Friends Service Committee College Program; Anne Bennett, religious educator with the Women's Strike for Peace; and Helen Baker, a United Nations reporter.

The Gray Panthers used the tactics of Saul Alinsky's community action to generate cross-generational support for expanded social programs, especially for the elderly. The Gray Panthers organized at a time when the American population was getting older. From 1950 to 1975 the over-65 population expanded from 12 million to 22 million, or from 8.1 percent to 10.5 percent of the total population. Of that elderly population, nearly 25 percent lived below the poverty line, with only 9 percent enrolled in private pension plans. In response to these trends, the Gray Panthers looked to restore the dignity and financial security of the aged. Looking to empower the elderly and preserve their place within the workforce, the Gray Panthers emerged as a loosely organized group of seniors and college-aged youth working to achieve a more equal distribution of power and wealth (Ness, 1230, 1232).

brick building of the Fourth Precinct Police Station. As taxi drivers all over the city began broadcasting reports of his arrest on their radios, a phone call reporting that the police were beating a cab driver interrupted a UCC board meeting. Soon a crowd gathered outside the precinct station. Civil rights leaders tried to keep the growing crowd under control, but when a fire truck arrived on the scene after a young man threw a firebomb, a full-scale riot ensued. The next day anonymous leaflets were distributed in the streets calling for a protest rally at the Fourth Precinct that night. Though the protest began over unfair treatment of African Americans on the police promotion list, it became a riot as a rapidly growing crowd began throwing rocks at the station. The following afternoon the police shot and killed an African American man and as darkness descended on the city, massive looting and vandalism increased. The following day the National Guard moved in with automatic weapons and quelled the riot.

Sensitive to public criticism that the Newark antipoverty programs initiated the riots, OEO recommended that the UCC be abandoned and that an OEO task force be sent to Newark to organize a new Community Action program.

The Newark March for Understanding

In the riot's aftermath, Newark's Democratic mayor, Hugh J. Addonizio, said that the tensions that erupted in racial violence had been "fueled by the rash of wild and extremist statements and behavior of the past 10 or 12 weeks in our city" (*New York Times,* July 19, 1967, p. 1). He directed this statement particularly to those workers in the city's antipoverty agency.

In response to the riot a Committee of Concern comprised of about 60 community leaders, evenly divided between whites and African Americans, organized and immediately called for an independent commission to investigate charges of "violence and terror visited upon the vast majority of the Negro citizens who were in no way involved in the rioting and were shot, beaten and brutalized by military and police forces without regard to wrongdoing." The committee went on to say, "A large segment of the Negro people is convinced that the single continuously lawless element operating in the community is the police force itself in its callous disregard to human rights" (*New York Times,* July 19, 1967, p. 1).

In the wake of the Newark riot, political activists descended upon the city in attempt to gain attention for their cause. The National Conference on Black Power was held in Newark just days after the riot. At this conference Floyd B. McKissick, chairman of the Congress of Racial Equality (CORE), took issue with the concept that African Americans alone were responsible for preventing racial violence. "Bad conditions make for violence. White people control the government, the money and the ghettos. They should be made to answer the question," McKissick said (*New York Times,* July 22, 1967, p. 1).

Asked if he thought rioting would continue in cities across the country, McKissick said he did. "No sane person could say we are not due for more violence," he asserted. "You will have violence as long as you have black people suppressed." Over 900 delegates from mainstream civil rights organizations such as the National Urban League, the Southern Christian Leadership Conference, the National Association for the Advancement of Colored People, CORE, and SNCC attended the conference. In addition, Black Nationalist organizations such as US, from Watts, Harlem's Mau Mau, and the Organization for Afro-American Unity, founded by Malcolm X along with Black Muslims, teachers, laborers, and civil servants from across the country attended the all-African American meeting (*New York Times,* July 22, 1967, p. 1).

Organized by Dr. Nathan Wright Jr., director of urban work for the Episcopal Diocese of Newark, the conference sought ways to give African Americans an effective voice in national, international, and local affairs. On the second day of the conference, July 22, 1967, a dozen young African American activists stormed into a news conference and sent reporters and spectators scurrying for safety. One young African American man involved in the disruption explained, "We had to get the white press out of there. They don't let Negroes cover the John Birch Society or the Ku Klux Klan" (*New York Times,* July 23, 1967, p. 1).

The following spring approximately 25,000 activists returned to Newark amid a far different mood for the "Walk for Understanding." Organized to show the concern and sympathy of the white suburbs for the people of the city's slum, it turned into a massive memorial to the Reverend Martin Luther King Jr., who had been assassinated the week before. Among those in the front line marching were Mayor Hugh J. Addonizio and Nathan Wright; they marched side-by-side holding a banner that proclaimed, "Walk for Understanding . . . People Care." Mr. Wright addressed the cheering crowd at the end of the march by declaring, "The time has come for black and white to get together to bring changes to our society. It has been proven in the past few days that black and white can get together" (*New York Times,* April 8, 1968, p. 1).

Model Cities

In the decade before President Johnson's War on Poverty, urban renewal came to mean forced relocation for mostly poor African American families. For every unit of low-income housing constructed during the 1950s, urban renewal destroyed four units. Urban renewal generally meant the razing of historic structures or bulldozing older sections of cities, followed by the construction of expressways, massive office buildings, or housing projects. By the mid-1960s many city planners believed that urban renewal had done more harm than good.

In 1965 President Johnson created a Task Force on Urban Problems chaired by political scientist Robert Wood of the Massachusetts Institute of Technology. The task force recommended a "demonstration cities" program to address the problems of low- and moderate-cost housing, to link physical construction with social programs, and to cut bureaucratic red tape through more flexible building regulations and trade practices. Although a subsequent task force recommended a limited number of cities be selected as experimental projects, President Johnson decided to propose a bill that would allow virtually all cities and towns to participate in the program. Expanding the application of the program was a political move on the part of the president to secure congressional support, but it diluted the available funds for the various initiatives that would include metropolitan regional planning, a renewed nondiscriminatory housing program, the construction of new communities, rent supplements to provide more low-income housing, and urban mass transportation. The program was to be administered by the new Department of Housing and Urban Development (HUD).

The recommendations of the task force and bill proposed by the president reflected the prevailing view at the time that urban blight and the recent urban riots stemmed from a legacy of economic, political, and racial problems. Instead of a punitive focus of law and order in American cities, these new programs aimed to ameliorate deplorable conditions and enhance opportunity. What later came to be called "Model Cities" tried to not only attack urban blight, but to actually restructure the urban environment. The eventual law that passed in the House and Senate and was signed by the president, the Demonstration Cities and Metropolitan Development Act, put improving the quality of urban life at the top of the government's domestic agenda.

Under the new legislation signed into law on November 3, 1966, cities began planning grants. Once approved, the cities then applied for a range of federal grants and HUD "supplemental grants" to implement their plans. Each "Model City" created a City Demonstration Agency (CDA) whose leadership was appointed by and answerable to the mayor. The act required that neighborhood residents play a significant role in developing and carrying out the program. An elected citizens' board advised the CDA, and successful projects employed local residents. The act required CDAs to employ residents of the community at every stage of the program. Despite this requirement, by 1969 fewer than half of all salaried employees in 77 projects were residents of the targeted neighborhoods.

Model Cities reflected a faith in the social sciences to develop a coordinated vision for urban planning. The magnitude and intransigence of urban decay, the unwillingness of suburbanites to take responsibility for the problem, and the lack of sufficient resources ultimately overwhelmed the policymakers and prevented the complete success of the program. Robert Wood, chairman of the task force that proposed Model Cities, cited four reasons for its failure: presidential and congressional politics and tampering, inadequate resources, complex regulation, and reliance on abstract theory instead of practical realities.

However, despite underfunding, bureaucratic red tape, and uneven levels of citizen participation, some subsequent studies reported that cities receiving grants under the program did concentrate these funds on impoverished neighborhoods for rehabilitation rather than destruction. Among peoples of all races and income levels, Model Cities stimulated greater involvement in local affairs because it mandated community action and gave local governments funds to disburse (Andrew, 131–132).

ANTIPOVERTY MOVEMENT RADICALIZED

From the very beginning, the struggle against poverty in the 1960s reflected politicians' attempts to control the growing social discontent the civil rights movement had unleashed among underrepresented minorities. Politicians spent most of the decade trying to build political coalitions based on both the enthusiastic support for and fear of social change. These efforts typically supported reform in an effort to avoid possible revolution. By the end of the decade, however, the forces of change ushered in an era of radicalism that brought with it an even greater counterforce to maintain the status quo. At each stage of the process stood politicians ready to capitalize on the hopes and fears Americans faced with the very real possibility of political and economic redistribution.

Urban Riots as Class Struggle

By the mid-1960s the urban poor experienced rising expectations amid the bold promises of the Great Society's antipoverty programs. Beginning with the Los Angeles riot of 1965 and continuing with major urban riots in Detroit and Newark in 1967, slum dwellers launched an insurgency against slumlords, tenements, unsanitary conditions, price-gouging storekeepers, and the long hot summer life in the ghetto. Sometimes thought of as "race riots," the violence in these American cities was more akin to the 19th-century uprisings of the white poor.

The Watts (Los Angeles) revolt on August 11, 1965, for example, connected directly to the War on Poverty. The majority of Watts's residents were poor. More than 250,000 people lived in the fifty-square-mile area of Watts—four times as many people per square block as in the rest of Los Angeles. Two-thirds of the residents were on welfare and 34 percent of adult males unemployed. Commentators and residents of the area recognized the connection between poverty and the riot. J. Stanley Sanders, an attorney and Watts native, argued that the main cause of the Watts riot "was the holdup of poverty funds. . . . There was a lot of dissension and ill will on account of that." The Watts riot was a reflection of the growing disenchantment with the city's failure to establish a War on Poverty agency as well as disillusionment with the inclusive possibilities of postwar liberalism (Bauman, 281–282).

Shortly after these riots, money did pour into these cities to maintain the peace and provide jobs, particularly for the unemployed youth. But the more medium-term effects were to escalate white fears of northern urban African American violence and to undermine the success of the civil rights movement. Politicians such as Richard Nixon and Ronald Reagan revived their political careers by capitalizing on these fears by calling for law and order in the streets, self-reliance and accountability among the poor, and the promotion of so-called black capitalism to replace Great Society programs they felt fostered both dependency and the unrealistic expectations that led to violence.

The Detroit Riot of 1967 and the Kerner Report

Like other urban riots in the sixties, the Detroit riot of 1967 began with a police raid that coalesced African American grievances and frustrations. Geographic

*Meeting of the Special Advisory Commission on Civil Disorders (the Kerner
Commission), at the White House on July 29, 1967. From left to right, Roy Wilkins,
Governor Otto Kerner (Chairman), and President Lyndon B. Johnson. (Lyndon
Baines Johnson Museum and Library)*

segregation, lack of recreational facilities, problems with merchants, inadequate
education, poor housing, police behavior, and a lack of jobs topped the list of
African American complaints. Eventually army paratroopers had to be called in
to put down the riot, along with 17,000 troops from the National Guard, the state
police, and the Detroit police department. More than 7,000 persons were arrested,
mostly African American males under age 25 looting downtown stores, and over
600 grocery stores, 500 cleaners, 300 clothing stores, 280 liquor stores and bars,
240 drugstores, and 200 furniture stores were damaged. Convinced that a conspiracy lay at the heart of the Detroit and Newark riots, President Johnson established the Kerner Commission to report on the causes and possible solutions.

Before the Kerner Commission could report its findings, the political mood of
the country had shifted. By the end of the summer of 1967 and after more than
160 riots across the country, President Johnson's approval rating on civil rights
and race had plummeted to 32 percent. Despite the problems of poverty and
race in urban America, Congress now refused to commit any more funds for urban renewal programs, now seemingly more interested in punishing rioters than
in addressing the conditions that spawned riots.

The Kerner Commission report, released in March of 1968, emphasized
both the dangers posed by urban problems and the cost to solve them. The
commission singled out racism as the chief cause of the urban crisis and warned
that the nation increasingly moved toward two societies, one African American

and one white, "separate and unequal." The report recommended a basic principle for change: Government programs designed to solve the problem had to equal the dimensions of the problem, in essence endorsing a broad and costly program of social reform that would dwarf the current Model City program.

President Johnson believed that the Kerner Commission's recommendation would be too costly in the current political climate, especially after the riots and with the rapidly escalating costs of the Vietnam War. The commission argued that economic growth would fund new efforts but failed to consider the state of the economy, the limited funds that such growth would provide, the war's drain on the federal budget, and the conservative political backlash already in full swing. By 1968 public opinion had shifted against the liberal programs of President Johnson's War on Poverty.

Appalachian Volunteers and the Arrest of Joe Mulloy

The sheriff of Pike County, Kentucky, raided the home of social activist Joseph Mulloy on August 11, 1967. A member of the Appalachian Volunteers, an antipoverty organization, Mulloy was a son of working-class parents from Louisville and among an increasingly radical group of activists in Appalachia who believed that to "solve poverty, you [must] change some of the structures that cause that poverty" (Oral History Interview with Mulloy on November 11, 1990). After sheriffs discovered books by V. I. Lenin and Mao Tse-tung, Mulloy and other Appalachian Volunteers were arrested and indicted by a Pike County grand jury for sedition based on Kentucky Revised Statute 432.040 that outlawed the teaching or advocating criminal syndicalism against the state. Although Mulloy and the other volunteers were vindicated three days later when a federal district court declared the law unconstitutional, the incident discredited the Appalachian Volunteers in the eyes of Pike County residents and contributed to the demise of the federal antipoverty programs in eastern Kentucky.

Coal companies dominated the Appalachian economy, monopolized its political resources, and used their abundant resources to effectively mobilize against any threats to their power. For the most part, the oppressed working people of the region resigned themselves to the power of the coal companies. In 1964 President Johnson's War on Poverty moved into this economic and political culture. The Appalachian Volunteers received significant OEO grants and the services of over 100 VISTA workers in 1965. As the War on Poverty, VISTA, and the Appalachian Volunteers received more publicity, they attracted more idealistic young volunteers from all over the nation. In 1966 roughly 150 college students from 30 states descended upon the communities and hamlets of Appalachia to conduct summer-long projects. However, Appalachian Volunteer directors started questioning whether these projects were merely glossing over the symptoms of poverty, but not ending poverty itself. By the end of the summer of 1966 the

Appalachian Volunteers sought a new direction for change that questioned the inclusive, nonconfrontational approach of its umbrella organization, the Council of the Southern Mountains.

Breaking free from the Council of the Southern Mountains, the Appalachian Volunteers adopted a more confrontational approach to ending poverty. The Appalachian Volunteers decided to organize around various issues such as school reform, particularly providing free lunches and qualified teachers, welfare rights, and opposition to strip mining. Through this more confrontational approach, the Appalachian Volunteers hoped to undermine the entrenched political and economic structure of the region. The Appalachian Volunteers declaration that the War on Poverty represented an "extreme hypocrisy" because officials throughout the administration attempted to end human suffering while rendering existing economic and political relationships immune from change exemplified this change in direction.

Acting as the Appalachian Volunteers' new representative in Pike County, Mulloy helped organize a local chapter of the Appalachian Group to Save the Land and People (AGSLP). The purpose of this relatively militant group was to end the destructive practice of strip-mining in the mountains. On June 29, 1967, Jink Ray, a farmer in the Island Creek section of Pike County, blocked a Puritan Coal Company bulldozer from strip-mining on land he had farmed for over 40 years. Mulloy and members of the AGSLP supported Ray at the scene. Despite a court order, the demonstration continued each day until July 18, 1967, when Gov. Edward T. Breathitt suspended the mining permit. Ultimately the permit was permanently revoked due to the land being too steep to mine.

In an effort to reassert their control, local coal operators believed they had to discredit Mulloy and members of the AGSLP by labeling them subversive outsiders. Ten days after Governor Breathitt suspended the permit, Mulloy was arrested. Before his arrest, locals had harassed Mulloy by having his phone disconnected and auto insurance canceled. Many believed that Robert Holcomb, president of both the Pikeville Chamber of Commerce and the powerful National Independent Coal Operators' Association, had engineered Mulloy's arrest.

Legal Aid

While never generously funded, legal services to the poor became an important program in the War on Poverty. Liberals at OEO considered legal services a natural choice for a Community Action program. After all, poor people had greater need for legal advice and lawyers' services than most. They are more often in trouble with the law, victimized by landlords, and in need of help to get their legal due under federal, state, and local welfare and public housing laws. A widely circulated 1964 *Yale Law Journal* article by two young attorneys, Edgar and Jean Camper Cahn, urged the federal government to fund neighborhood legal firms to help the poor. As opposed to the "service oriented" model of privately funded legal aid societies, these federally funded lawyers would serve a "representative function." In effect, the neighborhood lawyers would function as advocates for the poor and as activists for change in the relations of the poor to the larger society. This article represented a new leftist current in the legal profession that saw the law as just another social construct traditionally used by the rich and powerful to protect their wealth and control. These activists believed they should work to change the law to serve the interests of the poor and change the social and economic structure so thoroughly entrenched in the United States.

By July 1966 some $25 million had been committed to OEO Legal Services agencies in 125 communities. The Legal Services program employed 1,800 lawyers in 850 law offices and served almost 500,000 poor people at its peak in 1969. The lawyers worked closely with community spokesmen to challenge discriminatory and stigmatizing aspects of welfare administration. They also made poor people more politically aware and active. As early as 1966, they helped George Wiley form the National Welfare Rights Organization, which aggressively fought the cause of the welfare poor. In addition, the lawyers filed suits to overturn residency requirements and the absent-father rule of Aid for Families with Dependent Children.

Legal Services also exemplified some of the tensions or contradictions inherent in some community action programs. The legal services demanded by the poor conflicted with the larger, rehabilitation-oriented goals of legislators and policymakers. Planners wanted strong families, but the poor wanted legal services to obtain divorces. Planners wanted to end welfare dependency, but the poor wanted legal services to challenge capricious denials of welfare grants. Federally funded lawyers often worked to make the system more permissive, not more oriented toward rehabilitation. In so doing, these lawyers created a conflict between the OEO's goals of reducing dependency on welfare and of instilling in the poor a sense of power.

Legal Services opened access to litigation by poor people for the first time. Lawyers used class-action suits to expand the rights of the poor in several key areas: medical aid, landlord-tenant relations, state housing laws, consumer credit, and welfare administration. But it continually faced opposition from those who did not like its stated goal of legal reform. Even the major professional legal organizations objected to the program's ideology and structure. The Trial Lawyers Association, for example, had no problem with government subsidies for legal services on the Medicare model of paying clients' bills, but it feared a system of full-time, government-employed attorneys that amounted to socializing the bar.

National Welfare Rights Organization

The welfare rights movement began in the mid-1960s as a loosely knit social movement. On August 8, 1966, welfare rights groups around the country formed

Quieting shouts of "sock it to him" from partisans in the audience, Beulah Sanders of the National Welfare Rights Organization waits to tell members of the Democratic Platform Committee that they should back a radical overhaul of the nation's welfare system. Standing beside her are other members of the group, Etta Horn and George Wiley. Chicago, August 22, 1968. (Bettmann/Corbis)

a National Coordinating Committee on Welfare Groups, which began planning tactics for a three-month organizing drive. The organization produced the National Welfare Rights Organization (NWRO). The NWRO embraced many of the tactics used by the civil rights movement: sit-ins, demonstrations, and confrontation with authority. The NWRO demanded increased benefits, jobs, and the removal of rules and regulations that prevented women from receiving benefits. Organizer and welfare activist George Wiley said, "I am not at all convinced that comfortable, affluent, middle-class Americans are going to move over and share their wealth and resources with the people who have none" (Andrew, 85–86). With this in mind, he led the NWRO to exert the political clout of the poor, causing many to fear the onset of class warfare.

While historians have argued that the NWRO and the more general welfare rights movement of the mid- to late 1960s contributed to the increase in the nation's welfare rolls, the rapid rise of recipients began before this movement. Between 1962 and 1967 the number of families receiving Aid for Families with Dependent Children (AFDC) climbed from 3.8 million to 5.3 million. In 1960, 745,000 families received AFDC at an annual cost of less than $1 billion; by 1972, the number of families had become 3 million and the cost $6 billion a year. Conservatives linked this surge with the disintegration of family cohesion during the sixties caused by a more permissive culture. But the causes were more complex. The migration of southern African Americans to northern cities increased the number of poor people dependent on cash incomes and reduced the number of subsistence farmers. Starting in 1961, Congress allowed states to give AFDC to families headed by unemployed male parents. Despite these other causes, though, the welfare rights movement did have an impact.

Richard Cloward and his associate, Frances Piven, fostered the welfare rights movement. Their research showed that twice as many poor families were eligible for relief than were receiving it. They proposed that social workers and other activists should organize a movement with the express purpose of getting more families on the relief rolls. Wiley, a former professor of chemistry at Syracuse University who had quit his job to become associate director of CORE, responded to this call and organized the Poverty Rights Action Center to encourage activists to mobilize an attack on the existing tightfisted welfare structure in order to replace it with a more generous system of welfare for the indigent. This center ultimately evolved into the NWRO.

The NWRO worked at both the local and national levels to challenge strict rules of welfare eligibility and found loopholes that allowed more of the poor to claim public money. They worked to educate the poor about their rights and guided them through the bureaucratic maze of the welfare system. As a result, the proportion of poor families applying for welfare increased dramatically, as did the proportion of applicants accepted for welfare, which skyrocketed from about 33 percent in the early 1960s to 90 percent in 1971 (Katz, 106).

The welfare rights movement successfully recast welfare as an entitlement, reducing its stigma and mobilizing the poor to claim assistance as a right. The federally funded Legal Services Corporation provided poor people with lawyers to act on their behalf. With the example of civil rights victories in the courts, a new generation of poverty lawyers successfully challenged state laws in the Supreme Court. By the early 1970s the number of lawyers focusing on poverty issues had risen by 650 percent, and they appealed 164 cases to the Supreme Court (Andrew, 86).

The welfare rights movement, though, became a victim of its own success. As early as 1967 the American public perceived the nation as trapped in a welfare system marked by fraud, abuse, extravagance, and incentives for the lazy to sponge off the hardworking taxpayers of the nation. In response to these concerns, Congress enacted a Work Incentive Program (WIN) that provided employment, on-the-job training, and work-experience training. Mothers with young children had to participate in job training if daycare was available. During a 1967 Senate hearing held to discuss tighter welfare provisions in the bill, NWRO protesters staged a public and noisy protest that provoked committee chairman Russell Long to tell protesters to get a job rather than sit in the hearing room. House

Democrat Wilbur Mills later remarked, "You would think that the American way of life was built on a dole system to hear some people talk" (Andrew, 109).

WIN did little to stem the rising welfare tide. Most job training for women never got off the ground, and funds for childcare were minimal. By 1970 12.4 million people were on welfare, causing an even greater antiwelfare backlash in states like New York and California.

Cesar Chavez and the United Farm Workers

Born to migrant farm workers, Cesar Chavez dropped out of school in the eighth grade to work full-time as a farm laborer. Following military service in World War II and a decade with the migrant workers' Community Service Organization, Chavez became the first president of the National Farm Workers Association, an organization chartered by the AFL-CIO in 1966 and later renamed the United Farm Workers (UFW).

Chavez led the most visible Chicano struggle for economic justice during the 1960s. Chavez blazed the trail for Chicanismo, a collective identity among Mexican Americans who rejected assimilation. Chicanas and Chicanos formed the La Raza Unida party to advocate for their rights and celebrate their cultural identity in the face of discrimination and exploitation. Mexican Americans involved in this movement reclaimed ancestral lands taken by the federal government or white settlers, staged boycotts, formed the Brown Berets, and organized a student movement. The fight for economic justice waged by Chavez and other migrant workers like Dolores Huerta, represented the most important struggle in this movement's history.

Chavez helped turn the farm workers' plight into a mass movement for social justice. He garnered national prominence when he organized a national boycott of California table grapes in 1968. During the 1968 presidential campaign, Robert Kennedy visited Chavez and the striking farm workers in California and publicly embraced their cause. Kennedy defended the strikers against the charge that they were Communists. Both Chavez and Kennedy shared a belief in nonviolent protest, the struggle for economic justice, and the conviction that Americans must confront economic exploitation. "Today in America," Kennedy wrote, "we are two worlds." The middle class and affluent live in one world, but in the other world "the Negro, the Puerto Rican, and the Mexican American" live in "a dark hopeless place." Chavez believed that Kennedy saw "things through the eyes of the poor. . . . It was like he was ours" (Chafe, 343).

Between 1965 and 1970, Chavez used nonviolent tactics to fight growers who he believed did not provide a livable wage and decent working conditions for the mostly Mexican American farm laborers. Leading Democratic politicians and the United Auto Workers ultimately supported his nationwide boycott of grapes, and later lettuce, which pressured the growers to the bargaining table. In 1970

Chavez and the UFW won their fight with the growers and signed a historic agreement that recognized their union.

Militant Activism for the Poor

The Black Panther Party, founded in Oakland, California, in 1966 as a revolutionary Black Power organization, denounced police brutality, bore arms, and called for the right of armed self-defense and self-determination for African American ghettoes. While best known in the media as a symbol of African American violence, its real political strength came from its efforts to help the poor in urban slum areas. They organized social-welfare programs such as free clinics, free breakfast programs for hungry children, alternative schools, voluntary sanitation projects, and militant protests against slum landlords and local storekeepers. The Black Panthers became a model for other activists among poor minority groups like the Brown Berets (Mexican American activists) and the Young Lords Party (Puerto Rican activists).

The Young Lords Party got its start as a street gang in Chicago in the 1950s, but changed into a militant group working with the Puerto Rican poor through contacts with Black Panther leaders in the mid-1960s. The Young Lords emerged as particularly successful in New York City where they led major protests against police brutality and created voluntary social services for the poor. Less confrontational than the Panthers, the Lords developed relationships with progressive Catholic clergy to help the poor.

In Los Angeles African Americans and Latinos, inspired by the separatist ethos of the Black Power and Chicano movements and encouraged and aided by labor unions, established antipoverty organizations outside the domain of the "official" War on Poverty agency under city and county control. Angered over Mayor Samuel Yorty's refusal to permit significant community participation in the city's official Community Action program, some African Americans in Los Angeles created the Watts Labor Community Action Committee (WLCAC) in 1965 in conjunction with local labor union representatives, particularly from the UAW, to provide services to Watts residents, increase community participation, and build a thriving economic base for the community. Tired of the portrayal of Watts's residents as hopeless and helpless, the WLCAC created a food and clothes bank, childcare and youth centers, health care centers, and a county hospital for the area. Central to the philosophy of the WLCAC and to its connection to the ideas of Black Nationalism were the programs that focused on cultural enrichment and African American pride.

In response to the WLCAC and out of competition with African Americans for War on Poverty funds, Mexican Americans in East Los Angeles created the East Los Angeles Community Union (TELACU), which focused on economic development, and the Chicana Action Service Center, which provided job placement for Mexican American women. TELACU joined the self-determination ethos of the Chicano movement with a community focus and followed a similar community union model as the WLCAC. Organized in 1968, one of TELACU's first efforts at community organization succeeded in the creation of more than 500 new public-housing units. TELACU's first community programs, like the focus of the War on Poverty, were aimed at the youth. They included a summer camp program under the cosponsorship of the WLCAC, Neighborhood Youth Corps programs, and a reading program for young children. In addition, TELACU developed job-training programs for teenagers and young adults in conjunction with the UAW.

ANTIPOVERTY MOVEMENT'S DEMISE

Although the Great Society and community activism were successful in lowering the formal rates of poverty and gave vital aid to African American and other minority middle classes through Affirmation Action-based education and employment programs, the War on Poverty essentially ended with the election of Richard Nixon in 1968. The urban riots, the rise of corrupt Democratic political machines, and growing resentment of moderate- to low-income groups not able to receive social benefits such as Medicaid and Section 8 housing divided the poor and diminished their political effectiveness.

To add to their troubles, Nixon and Spiro T. Agnew exploited white middle-class fears of African American urban violence during the 1968 presidential campaign. They did so by emphasizing three points during the campaign: government should provide adequate welfare for those who cannot work, those who can work should do so, and welfare rolls should not be increased (Burke, 2). The implication was that the current welfare system enabled people not to work, supported irresponsible procreation, and directly contributed to the breakdown of law and order in American cities. The demonstrations at the Democratic Convention in Chicago in August 1968, together with the ensuing massive police repression against the demonstrators, ensured the end of the Great Society and the defeat of Democratic candidate Hubert Humphrey.

The escalation of the Vietnam War, however, was probably the biggest reason for the decline of the antipoverty movement. Despite the enormous victory of liberal Democrats during the 1964 elections, which temporarily broke the veto power that the conservative coalition had enjoyed since World War II, President Johnson found himself negotiating with his political opponents to limit funding for antipoverty programs in order to maintain congressional support for rapidly rising military expenditures. The strongest supporters of the War on Poverty, both in politics and in activist groups and community-based organizations, were also the strongest critics of the Vietnam War. The most ardent enemies of the

antipoverty programs were the most loyal supporters of the Vietnam War and
Cold War politics that demanded increased spending on the military. By 1967
Johnson found himself hated by the very activists whose grassroots support was
necessary to mobilize the poor and educate workers.

Effects of the Vietnam War on the Antipoverty Movement

By the end of the sixties, the Vietnam War affected almost every aspect of politics, public policy, and American life. President Johnson's War on Poverty was
no exception. Some historians divide Johnson's presidency into two categories:
The Great Society and the Vietnam War. But of course a true analysis of this era
cannot divorce the two. These two episodes in American public life dramatically
impacted the social history of the 1960s.

At the most basic level, the Vietnam War siphoned off funds from Johnson's
poverty programs. With the Vietnam War absorbing an ever-increasing share of
the federal budget, the government could ill afford to finance the ambitious
objectives of these programs. Sargent Shriver went so far as to declare, "Vietnam
took it all away, every goddamned dollar; that's what killed the war on poverty."
Between 1965 and 1972 the United States spent more than $128 billion on Viet-
nam compared to only $15 billion on the War on Poverty. For the fiscal year of
1966, the administration submitted to Congress a proposal to cut OEO funding
by nearly 50 percent (Andrew, 81–83).

Not only did the war rob the administration of funds to fight poverty, it also
spent all of President Johnson's political capital. As the war escalated, those in
Congress and the American voters started to lose faith in Johnson's policies and,
maybe more important, his honesty. During the 1964 campaign Johnson promised not to "send American boys nine or ten thousand miles to do what Asian
boys ought to be doing for themselves." Five months later Johnson had launched
a sustained bombing campaign against North Vietnam, quickly followed by the
deployment of the first U.S. soldiers for combat. From that point on he continued to downplay each increment of American commitment and exaggerated the
progress against the enemy. Johnson swept aside concerns of Vietnam through
secrecy, devious rhetoric, and fraudulent budget projections for the conduct of
the war (Unger, 240).

Johnson forestalled a national debate on the war and sustained temporarily
the impression that America could both defeat the Vietcong and simultaneously
end poverty at home. Johnson intentionally misled the American public about
his decisions to dramatically increase U.S. involvement in Vietnam "to avoid un-
due concern and excitement in the Congress and in domestic public opinion."
In retrospect, Johnson knew that he could not continue to fight the war and ad-
equately fund his antipoverty programs. In 1970 he told Doris Kearns:

That I was bound to be crucified either way I moved. If I left the woman I really loved—the Great Society—in order to get involved with the bitch of a war on the other side of the world, then I would lose everything at home. All my programs. All my hopes to feed the hungry and shelter the homeless . . . but if I left the war and let the communists take over South Vietnam, then I would be seen as a coward and my nation would be seen as an appeaser and we would both find it impossible to accomplish anything for anybody anywhere on the entire globe. (Chafe, 292)

Johnson, like liberals before him, believed that true racial and economic equality could be achieved through the economic growth of capitalism without requiring any serious reallocation of resources or power that might pit one group against another. But those within the Johnson administration, especially those working for the OEO, quickly realized that eliminating poverty would be very expensive; far more expensive than anyone imagined in 1964. As long as the War on Poverty rode the crest of economic growth and promised to be relatively cost-free, the American people were supportive. By 1968, this was no longer the case. Johnson's Great Society helped six million Americans out of poverty between 1964 and 1969, but it did so with ever-escalating bureaucratic and financial costs. Forty-five federal social programs spent $9.9 billion in 1961; eight years later 435 programs spent $25.6 billion. Yet the $1.5 billion authorized for antipoverty programs in 1966 represented only 1.5 percent of the total federal budget. Between 1965 and 1968 the federal government spent approximately $50 a year for each American living in poverty. This amount paled in comparison to the costs of the Vietnam War where by 1967 the federal government spent roughly $300,000 for each Vietcong killed (Andrew, 87).

As Johnson continued to spend his political and budgetary capital on the war, congressional Democrats saw little reason to align themselves with the administration. As Republicans turned up the heat on Johnson's Great Society, the Democrats looked to distance themselves from Johnson and therefore proved ineffective and fragmented advocates for the War on Poverty. Frustrated with the toll the war was having on the pursuit for economic justice, longtime ally Martin Luther King Jr., expressed his frustration with Johnson's choices: "35 billion dollars a year to fight an unjust, evil war in Vietnam, and 20 billion dollars to put a man on the moon, it can spend billions of dollars to put God's children on their own two feet right here on earth" (Katz, 54).

Why the 1960s War on Poverty Failed

Ever since the 1960s, social conservatives have held sway on the debate regarding the relative merits of Lyndon Johnson's Great Society generally and the 1960s War on Poverty particularly. The assault on the progressive social programs of the 1960s reached its zenith during Ronald Reagan's tenure as president of the

The Negro Family:
The Case for National Action

Daniel Patrick Moynihan did as much as anyone to define the welfare reform debate from the mid-1960s to the 1990s. When Moynihan was only 10, his father left and the family moved from place to place in an effort to make ends meet. Moynihan ultimately attended City College of New York before entering the navy. After his naval service ended in 1947, Moynihan studied at Tufts University on the GI bill and helped his mother run a saloon in the Hell's Kitchen neighborhood of Manhattan. He began his political career in state government, working for New York's Gov. Averell Harriman in the 1950s before attending graduate school at the London School of Economics on a Fulbright scholarship.

Moynihan's New York political contacts helped him land a job as assistant to the secretary of labor in the Kennedy administration. His position gave him the opportunity to examine the social and economic problems of the day that led to his infamous 1965 report, *The Negro Family: The Case for National Action.* In what has been commonly labeled "The Moynihan Report," he argued that the unstable African American family contributed to "welfare and crime and welfare dependence." He amassed considerable evidence to demonstrate this instability: urban African Americans suffered from high divorce rates, high illegitimate-birth rates, and a high number of families headed by women. He called the instability this data represented the "tangle of pathology" of the urban ghetto. To cure this pathology, Moynihan suggested, the government must develop a program to stabilize the African American family and strengthen the role of African American men. Once this fundamental change in the family structure occurred, the other elements of the civil rights agenda such as legal rights and economic advancement could be achieved. As long as the "Negro family in the urban ghettos is crumbling," Moynihan argued, "the programs that have been enacted in the first phase of the Negro revolution . . . only make opportunities available. They cannot insure the outcome" (Berkowitz, 125).

The report reflected Moynihan's faith in social science as a guide for public policy. Government leaders informed and enlightened by social science could design solutions to the social problems of poverty, ignorance, disease, inequality, teenage delinquency, and racial injustice. Although much later Moynihan developed a powerful critique of its usefulness in informing public policy, while working in the Kennedy, Johnson, and Nixon administrations during the 1960s, he reflected the Age of Liberalism's reliance on social science to solve domestic problems.

The report created a considerable amount of controversy. Some liberal scholars thought that Moynihan failed to appreciate the strength and diversity of the African American family. Others went as far as labeling Moynihan's views as racist. Historians, most notably Herbert Gutman, faulted Moynihan for depending on outdated sources and getting his facts wrong, particularly on the history of the African American family. Moynihan left the Johnson administration distraught and discouraged.

The Negro Family: The Case for National Action, Continued

Nixon called Moynihan back into the political realm by asking him to work in his administration as a domestic advisor. Nixon hoped to demonstrate that conservatives could succeed at fundamental social reform where the liberals had produced only confrontation and resentment. He believed Moynihan could help him in this cause.

Moynihan believed the urban riots of the mid-1960s indicated a breakdown in civility and posed a threat to social order. In response to this challenge to social stability, he helped create Nixon's Family Assistance Plan in 1969 that simply intended to give poor people money instead of more services. Nixon believed that "people should have the responsibility for spending carefully and taking care of themselves. [He] abhorred snoopy, patronizing surveillance by social workers which made children and adults feel stigmatized and separate." As a result, Nixon embraced Moynihan's advocacy for welfare reform that called for an income maintenance plan whereby each family suffering from poverty would receive at least $1,600 per year. Money, not more social workers, offered poor urban African Americans the best chance to achieve economic independence. This was a direct challenge to Johnson's Community Action Program (Berkowitz, 128).

In January 1970 Moynihan sent Nixon a memo that examined the growing alienation between the races and suggested that maybe the issue could benefit from a period of "benign neglect." Leaked to the press, the memo suggested that the Nixon administration was callously indifferent to the plight of African Americans. Moynihan offered his resignation amid the firestorm created by the memo, but Nixon refused to accept it. By the end of the year, however, Moynihan left the administration to return to his faculty position at Harvard.

United States. The social conservative take on the problem is this: the laws passed during the civil rights era of the 1960s brought the playing field of equal opportunity into balance. Social conservatives such as Dinesh D'Souza and Stephen and Abigail Thernstrom argue that minority groups no longer have any excuse for being poor, uninsured, unemployed or underemployed, and uneducated. Poverty is a result of bad personal choices, laziness, and/or bad behavior. They also argue that the poverty programs of the 1960s reinforced this bad behavior by creating perpetual dependency on the public dole.

Critics from the political Left like Michael Brown, *Whitewashing Race: The Myth of a Colorblind Society* (2003), argue that the poverty programs of the 1960s did not go far enough to empower the poor. They argue that the only way to correct the problem of poverty, particularly as it relates to historically discriminated against minority groups, is to have a radical redistribution of resources so as to restore equality of opportunity to all Americans.

There is a third and more balanced view of the struggle against poverty in America. Articulated by the likes of Henry Louis Gates Jr., W.E.B. Du Bois Professor of Humanities at Harvard, this view contends that the problem of poverty, especially as it affects African Americans and other minority groups, is neither wholly behavioral nor wholly structural. Gates challenges Americans to both create opportunities and hold people accountable for their choices, something these critics believe the 1960s' War on Poverty did not do.

The New Federalism

Richard Nixon's victory in the 1968 presidential election reflected, in part, the middle-class disapproval of President Johnson's Great Society policies. Sensing that Johnson's mandate to wage the War on Poverty had expired, Nixon declared that his administration would pursue social justice not by "pouring billions of federal dollars into programs that have failed, but by enlisting the greatest engine of progress ever developed in the history of man—American private enterprise" (Farber and Bailey, 270).

Nixon's New Federalism rejected Johnson's liberal vision that programs like Community Action and Model Cities could produce racial and economic justice. Johnson's Great Society required an interplay between national policy and local initiatives. Communities had the opportunity to fit these federal programs with local needs. In order to receive federal funding, however, local governments had to accept a partial redistribution of political power to the poor. Nixon's plan did not expect any such redistribution of power.

In the wake of the urban riots of 1967, the National Advisory Commission on Civil Disorders (the Kerner Report) reached a conclusion similar to Moynihan's earlier report. This commission concluded that "the condition of Negroes in the central city [was] in a state of crisis because of chronic unemployment among males and because of the concentration of African American males at the lowest end of the occupational scale." Faced with unemployment or underemployment, African American males were "unable or unwilling to remain with their families." The commission asserted that the urban riots of the 1960s were directly related to the instability of the African American family, as "children growing up under such conditions [were likely participants in civil disorder." The commission recommended that the government should work to get African American women off welfare and back in the home by providing income supplements to subsidize those who worked at low-paying jobs and "to provide for mothers who decided to remain with their children" (Farber and Bailey, 270).

With the help of Daniel Patrick Moynihan, Nixon proposed the Family Assistance Plan (FAP) to provide incentives for African American males to become family breadwinners and for African American women to stay at home with their children. In August 1969 Nixon announced his FAP that would guarantee all families with children a minimum of $500 per adult and $300 per child per year, or $1,600 for a two-parent family of four. FAP promised to sustain the incentive to work and supplant welfare dependency. To do this, a poor family could keep the first $60 per month of income without losing any government aid, and half of any income above that, up to specified maximums, at which time benefits would disappear. In practice, the FAP contained an inherent contradiction. It aimed to restore the traditional patriarchal family while encouraging single welfare mothers to work more.

Although the FAP did not become law until 1971, this call for welfare reform, along with other reforms in public assistance like the State and Local Fiscal Assistance Act (1972) and the Housing and Community Development Act (1974) reflected Nixon's New Federalism that awarded public monies in block grants with no target-area requirements or guidelines for spending, thereby returning political authority to local elected officials. Nixon did not decrease federal appropriations to the poor and cities; in fact, federal spending in these areas nearly doubled during his presidency. But Nixon let individuals and local officials decide how to spend the money without any federal guidelines or directives.

When Nixon gave them a choice, municipal governments ignored the social and economic problems of the poor and minorities. Cities used federal block grants for capital improvements and tax reduction and stabilization, and as an alternative to issuing bonds. Expenditures for health and social services averaged only 6 to 7 percent of total Federal Revenue Sharing funds. The poor and minorities, who had not achieved representation in local governments, were hit hard by the loss of federal pressure on local government. For example, childcare planning for welfare mothers was minimal under Nixon's plan. The FAP would create more demand for childcare by pressuring single welfare mothers to work more, but it did nothing to meet this demand. Instead it left the problem of daycare to a market that was not meeting the existing needs. In short, Nixon's New Federalism signaled the end of a national coalition for social change and represented Americans turn away from the problem of poverty and urban destitution.

WELFARE TO WORK

The welfare rights movement continued in earnest until the mid-1970s, but hampered by Nixon's New Federalism and the trend toward welfare-to-work initiatives by Republicans and Democrats alike, it never regained its luster of the mid- to late 1960s. At its height, President Johnson's War on Poverty and the welfare rights movement reflected the spirit of the Age of Liberalism and participatory democracy so prevalent during this decade. But like other experiments in social engineering and grassroots activism of the 1960s, it left a mixed legacy and became a topic that conservatives exploited to their political advantage for the last quarter of the 20th century.

BIOGRAPHIES

Margarita Huantes, 1914–1994

Literacy Advocate

Social worker and adult educator Margarita Huantes founded the San Antonio Literacy Council (SALC) in 1960 and worked tirelessly to end adult illiteracy for three decades. Born in Nueva Rosita, Coahuila, Mexico, Huantes immigrated to San Antonio, Texas, when she was just a baby. She earned an undergraduate degree from the University of Texas in 1939 and a master's in social work degree from Case Western Reserve University in 1948. First a teacher, Huantes later worked in youth programs and community centers in the San Antonio area during the 1950s. While at work in the community centers Huantes recognized the high rate of adult illiteracy, particularly among Mexican Americans, and worked to establish literacy programs. She helped the SALC grow from a single class with a handful of students in one community center to more than 1,500 students in 20 centers. Huantes believed that the inability to read prevented the poor from getting better jobs and ensuring a better quality of life for their children.

Antipoverty advocate and community organizer, Francis Fox Piven. (Courtesy Frances Fox Piven)

Frances Fox Piven, 1932–

Welfare Activist

A provocative commentator of the U.S. social welfare system, Piven was born in Calgary, Alberta, and immigrated to the United States as a baby. She earned her bachelor's, master's, and doctoral degrees from the University of Chicago. She first worked in New York as a city planner and later became a research associate at one of the country's first antipoverty agencies, Mobilization for Youth (a community-based service organization in New York City's Lower East Side). Mobilization for Youth at one point coordinated more than 50 experimental programs designed to reduce poverty and crime. Piven cowrote with Richard Cloward a 1965 article entitled "Mobilizing the Poor: How It Can Be Done," which launched her into the national debate over the welfare state. Their work provided the theoretical base for the National Welfare Rights Organization, the first of many grassroots organizations that Piven founded. She taught in the Columbia University School of Social Work from 1966 to 1972 and in the political science department at Boston University from 1972 to 1982. In 1982 she joined the Graduate Center, City University of New York.

George Wiley, 1931–1973

First NWRO Director

Credited with organizing the poor into a significant political movement during the 1960s, Wiley was educated as a chemist, earning his Ph.D. from Cornell University. In 1960, Wiley became an associate professor of chemistry at Syracuse University and began his work as a social activist, founding a local chapter of the Congress of Racial Equality (CORE) in Syracuse and serving on the National Action Council of CORE. Wiley left Syracuse in 1966 to found the Poverty/Rights Action Center in Washington, D.C., a central communication link for groups of poor people trying to work toward a common goal of ending poverty. Wiley was appointed the first executive director of the National Welfare Rights Organization (NWRO) in 1967. Wiley resigned his position at the NWRO in 1973 to found an organization devoted to tax reform and national health insurance. He died in a boating accident at the age of 42.

Whitney Moore Young Jr., 1921–1971

Civil Rights Leader

A college graduate by the age of 18, Young taught and coached high school, served in the Army during World War II, and studied engineering at the Massachusetts Institute of Technology before earning his master's in social work from the University of Minnesota in 1947. Young then worked with the Urban League in Minnesota before becoming the executive secretary of the Urban League in Omaha, Nebraska, while teaching social work at the University of Nebraska and Creighton University. He later became the dean of the Atlanta University School of Social Work in 1954. In 1961 Young became the executive director of the National Urban League, remaining in that position until his death in 1971. During the 1960s he became a noted civil rights leader committed to eradicating discrimination against African Americans and poor people.

REFERENCES AND FURTHER READINGS

Andrew, John A., III. 1998. *Lyndon Johnson and the Great Society*. Chicago: Ivan R. Dee.

Bauman, Robert. 2007. "The Black Power and Chicano Movements in the Poverty Wars in Los Angeles." *Journal of Urban History* 33: 277–295.

Berkowitz, Edward D. 1991. *America's Welfare State: From Roosevelt to Reagan*. Baltimore: Johns Hopkins University Press.

Brown, Michael K., et al. 2003. *Whitewashing Race: The Myth of a Color-Blind Society*. Berkeley: University of California Press.

Bruns, Roger. 2005. *Cesar Chavez: A Biography*. Westport, CT: Greenwood Press.

Burke, Vincint J., and Vee Burke. 1974. *Nixon's Good Deed: Welfare Reform*. New York: Columbia University Press.

Chafe, William H. 2003. *The Unfinished Journey: America since World War II*. 5th ed. New York: Oxford University Press.

Crook, William H., and Ross Thomas. 1969. *Warriors for the Poor: The Story of VISTA, Volunteers in Service to America*. New York: William Morrow.

D'Souza, Dinesh. 1995. *The End of Racism: Principles for a Multiracial Society*. New York: Free Press.

Farber, David, and Beth Bailey. 2001. *The Columbia Guide to America in the 1960s*. New York: Columbia University Press.

Findlay, James F. 1995. "The Mainline Churches and Head Start in Mississippi: Religious Activism in the Sixties." *Church History* 64: 237–250.

Gates, Henry Louis, Jr. 2004. "Obama Unveils Choices Blacks Make." *San Antonio Express News* (July 20).

Greenberg, Polly. 1969. *The Devil Has Slippery Shoes: A Biased Biography of the Child Development Group of Mississippi*. New York: Macmillan.

Harrington, Michael. 1962. *The Other America; Poverty in the United States*. New York: Macmillan.

Hayden, Tom. 1967. *Rebellion in Newark: Official Violence and Ghetto Response*. New York: Random House.

Hodgson, Godfrey. 2000. *The Gentleman from New York: Daniel Patrick Moynihan, a Biography*. New York: Houghton Mifflin.

Humphrey, Hubert H. 1964. *War on Poverty*. New York: McGraw-Hill.

Jones, Jacqueline. 1992. *The Dispossessed: America's Underclasses from the Civil War to the Present*. New York: Basic Books.

Katz, Michael B. 1989. *The Undeserving Poor: From the War on Poverty to the War on Welfare*. New York: Pantheon Books.

Kiffmeyer, Thomas J. 1998. "From Self-Help to Sedition: The Appalachian Volunteers in Eastern Kentucky, 1964–1970." *Journal of Southern History* 64: 65–94.

Kornbluh, Felicia. 1998. "The Goals of the National Welfare Rights Movement: Why We Need Them Thirty Years Later." *Feminist Studies* 24: 65–78.

Patterson, James T. 2000. *America's Struggle Against Poverty in the Twentieth Century*. Cambridge, MA: Harvard University Press.

Perlstein, Daniel. 1990. "Teaching Freedom: SNCC and the Creation of the Mississippi Freedom Schools." *History of Education Quarterly* 30: 297–324.

Quadango, Jill. 1994. *The Color of Welfare: How Racism Undermined the War on Poverty*. New York: Oxford University Press.

Rothschild, Mary Aickin. 1982. "The Volunteers and the Freedom Schools: Education for Social Change in Mississippi." *History of Education Quarterly* 22: 401–420.

Schlesinger, Arthur Meier. 1965. *A Thousand Days: John F. Kennedy in the White House*. Boston: Houghton Mifflin.

Sundquist, James L. 1968. *Politics and Policy: The Eisenhower, Kennedy, and Johnson Years*. Washington, DC: Brookings Institution Press.

Thernstorm, Stephen, and Abigail Thernstorm. 1997. *America in Black and White: One Nation Indivisible*. New York: Simon and Schuster.

Unger, Irwin. 1996. *The Best of Intentions: The Triumphs and Failures of the Great Society under Kennedy, Johnson, and Nixon*. New York: Doubleday.

United Community Corporation. 1974. *The War on Poverty: One City's Story*. New York: Schneider and Rich.

Zarefsky, David. 1986. *President Johnson's War on Poverty: Rhetoric and History*. Tuscaloosa: University of Alabama Press.

Zigler, Edward, and Susan Muenchow. 1992. *Head Start: The Inside Story of America's Most Successful Educational Experiment*. New York: Basic Books.

The Counterculture Movement

Overview

The term *counterculture* did not appear until rather late in the 1960s. Until then most people used *youth culture* to describe the way adolescents lived. Before the sixties, the principal institutions of this culture were high school and the mass media. But as the sixties progressed, college enrollments exploded to the point where colleges and universities were as influential as high schools in shaping the young. Where once entertainment and amusement defined the youth culture, a new culture began to develop around the recognition that the young could be a distinct force in society with unique values and aspirations. Music became an especially powerful medium for these distinct cultural values. As these new cultural values began to be expressed in new forms of rock-and-roll music, an ideological struggle between the young and old called the "generation gap" emerged. For the first time in American history, social conflict was understood to be a function of age.

The apparent attack on middle-class traditional views and styles broadened so rapidly by the mid-1960s that the term *youth culture* no longer seemed adequate. Though admittedly elastic and vague, *counterculture* seemed to better capture this generational conflict that could be identified by everything from clothing styles to musical taste. Amid the Vietnam War, War on Poverty, urban riots, and New Left politics on university campuses throughout the country, the culture of college-age young people became increasingly oppositional. They felt their parents' generation had clearly lost their way. How else could one explain the growing violence in Southeast Asia and American cities? As a result, everything the counterculture embraced seemed to be aimed at setting itself apart from the values of the previous generation. Instead of bourgeois conformity, the counterculture professed egalitarian individualism. The mantra became, "Do your own thing." Ironically, the counterculture celebrated individualists by embracing many of the same customs, tastes, and styles as a group.

As this chapter indicates, the counterculture of the 1960s was not monolithic. While many hippies of the Haight-Ashbury district in San Francisco espoused an apolitical, nonjudgmental, hedonistic philosophy, others wanted to incorporate the counterculture's music, drug use, and sexual freedoms into a larger political and social agenda. While the counterculture's belief in nonviolence created a natural affinity with the antiwar movement, many hippies were far more interested in the escapism of hallucinogenic drugs, sexual experimentation, and acid rock than political activism. With roots in the beatnik and folk-music revival of the 1950s and early '60s, pioneer musicians like Bob Dylan and Joan Baez gave voice to a new value system of the young that stood in opposition to the postwar conformity of the 1950s. By the time the Beatles arrived in the United States to appear on the *Ed Sullivan Show* in 1964, young Americans were primed to set out on a different course than their mothers and fathers in almost every way imaginable. Movies produced later in the decade like *The Graduate* and *Easy Rider* effectively captured this growing divide between generations and middle-class versus countercultural values.

The counterculture reached its peak from the Summer of Love in 1967 to the Woodstock Rock Festival in August 1969. Tracking the rising death toll of American soldiers in Vietnam and antiwar protests on college campuses, hippies looked for ways to escape the doldrums of a middle-class suburban existence and experiment with alternative ways of living. Drugs, mammoth rock festivals, and communes became manifestations of this experimentation. As the movement grew, the mainstream media increasingly focused on the more outlandish aspects of the counterculture like Abbie Hoffman and Jerry Rubin's Yippies. In the end, the movement died as a result of its own excesses, but for a brief time in American history, a growing youth culture built on the foundation of sex, drugs, and rock-and-roll captured the nation's attention and seemingly threatened the religious, social, economic, and political traditions of American life.

TIMELINE

1960   Timothy Leary experiments with psilocybin in Mexico.

1961   Bob Dylan leaves Minnesota for New York City.
                  Joan Baez releases her first album, *Joan Baez*.

1962	Bob Dylan releases his first album, *Bob Dylan*.
	Leary founds the International Foundation for Freedom.
	Ken Kesey's *One Flew Over the Cuckoo's Nest* is published.
	The Gorda Mountain commune is founded.
	The San Francisco Mime Troupe is organized.
1963	Bob Dylan releases *Freewheelin' Bob Dylan*.
	Leary is fired from Harvard University for drug experimentation with students.
1964	Bob Dylan releases *The Times They Are A-Changin'*.
	The Beatles appear on the *Ed Sullivan Show*.
	The Beatles' first movie, *A Hard Day's Night*, premieres.
	The Beatles release *Meet The Beatles!*
	The Doors begin playing at "Whiskey A Go-Go" on the Sunset Strip.
	Leary's *The Psychedelic Experience* is published.
	The alternative paper, *Los Angeles Free Press*, is first published.
	Ken Kesey begins his "Acid Tests" that become the subject of a Thomas Wolfe book.
1965	Bob Dylan releases *Bringing It All Back Home*.
	The Beatles' second movie, *Help!*, premieres.
	Bob Dylan goes electric at the Newport Folk Festival.
	The Beatles releases two albums, *Rubber Soul* and *Revolver*.
	The commune Drop City is founded.
1966	Bob Dylan releases *Blonde on Blonde*.
	The Jimi Hendrix Experience band is formed.
	Janis Joplin joins Big Brother and the Holding Company.
	The Psychedelic Shop opens in the Haight-Ashbury district.
	The federal government criminalizes LSD.
	The Morning Star Ranch commune is founded.
1967	Bob Dylan releases *John Wesley Harding*.
	The Beatles release *Sergeant Pepper's Lonely Hearts Club Band*.
	The Beatles perform "All You Need is Love" to five continents on the BBC's *Our World*.

Jimi Hendrix releases *Are You Experienced?*

Jimi Hendrix and Janis Joplin appear at the Monterey Pop Festival.

The Doors release *The Doors.*

The movie *The Graduate* premieres.

The Gathering of the Tribes happens in San Francisco's Golden Gate Park.

Abbie Hoffman and Jerry Rubin form the Yippies.

Underground Press Syndicate is organized to support the growing alternative press movement.

The *Rolling Stone Magazine* is first published.

San Francisco is host to the Summer of Love.

Death of Hip ceremony is held in San Francisco at the end of the Summer of Love.

1968   The Beatles release the "White Album."

The White Panther Party is formed.

The Festival of Life is held during Chicago's Democratic National Convention.

Tom Wolfe's book, *The Electric Kool-Aid Test,* is published.

1969   Bob Dylan releases *Nashville Skyline.*

The movie *Easy Rider* premieres.

Over 400,000 attend the Woodstock Rock Festival.

Charles Manson and "the Family" commit infamous murders.

The Rolling Stones host disastrous Altamont Rock Festival.

MUSIC GIVES VOICE TO THE COUNTERCULTURE

Historian Timothy Miller has traced many elements of the counterculture to earlier movements such as the communalism of the 1930s Catholic Worker movement and the literary experimentation and social criticism of the 1950s beatniks. The beatniks in particular bequeathed to the 1960s counterculture an oppositional stance toward mass culture and conventional morality and affinity for slang appropriated from African American jazz musicians and Asian mysticism. From the beats and other avant-garde artists of the 1950s, the hippies inherited a belief that art, particularly music, could serve as a means for uncovering unimaginable possibilities for human relationships.

In many respects, the small number of 1950s bohemians or beatniks who rebelled against 1950s conformity wrote the script for those in the 1960s counterculture who wanted to "drop out." One thing the beats demonstrated was that music influenced young people more than any other popular medium. Mass culture of the 1950s was so bland and predictable that it had little long-lasting or profound effect on young people. Music of the 1960s, on the other hand, captured their imagination and moved them. It started with the folk revival of the late 1950s and transitioned into rock and then acid or psychedelic rock of the mid- and late 1960s.

Large-scale enthusiasm for folk music began in 1958 when the Kingston Trio recorded the song "Tom Dooley," which sold two million records. This paved the way for anticommercial veteran artists like Pete Seeger and newcomers like Joan Baez. Many of these artists sang songs with a politically oppositional message that served to politicize young people. However, even the radical songs of these artists did not offend Middle America because the music was gentle and familiar. This began to change with the emergence of a young artist from Minnesota, Bob Dylan.

Dylan as Bridge between Beatniks and Counterculture

Born on May 24, 1941, in Duluth, Minnesota, into a modest middle-class family, Robert Allen Zimmerman emerged as arguably the most influential musician of the 1960s. Zimmerman changed his name to Bob Dylan while a student at the University of Minnesota where he performed in local coffeehouses. A huge fan of Woody Guthrie, Dylan left Minnesota in January 1961 to visit the legendary folksinger in a New Jersey hospital before moving to Greenwich Village in New York City. Although Guthrie was his principal hero, Dylan was also the heir to the beat tradition of Jack Kerouac, William Burroughs, and Allen Ginsberg, three writers who attended Columbia University after World War II.

Once in New York, Dylan spent a lot of time with folk musicians Pete Seeger and Joan Baez and beat poet Ginsberg. His unique voice and style quickly won him a loyal audience and favorable reviews in the New York press. While his first album, *Bob Dylan,* released in 1962, was a success, his next album, *The Free-wheelin' Bob Dylan,* released in 1963, made him a sensation. With such songs as "Blowin' in the Wind," "A Hard Rain's A-Gonna Fall," and "Oxford Town," Dylan's second album established him as the premier folk-protest songwriter and singer. "Blowin' in the Wind," popularized by the folk-music trio of Peter, Paul, and Mary, became an anthem of the civil rights and antiwar movements. Dylan had written "Talkin' John Birch Society Blues" for the album, but Columbia Records refused to include it out of concern over how the right-wing group might react. When CBS would not permit him to sing the song on the *Ed Sullivan Show,* Dylan canceled his appearance and gained the admiration of the nascent 1960s counterculture.

Bob Dylan plays acoustical guitar in an unidentified studio in 1965. (Library of Congress)

Six of the ten songs on Dylan's third album, *The Times They Are A-Changin',* released in 1964, were songs of protest that earned him recognition as the voice of the student-organized New Left movement. By 1964 Dylan played roughly 200 concerts a year and made regular appearances at important events such as the March on Washington, where he sang "Only a Pawn in Their Game," a ballad inspired by the slaying of African American activist Medgar Evers. Dylan recorded a series of topical songs such as this which paid tribute to the martyrs of the civil rights movement and victims of social injustice.

While recording his 1965 *Bringing It All Back Home* that included the songs "Subterranean Homesick Blues" and "Mr. Tambourine Man," Dylan used a backup band for the first time. At the Newport Folk Festival in July 1965, Dylan shocked and disappointed folk purists when he used an electric guitar. Later that year he released *Highway 61 Revisited,* an album that included the classic, "Like a Rolling Stone." This album proved extremely popular with a mainstream audience. It also confirmed the new direction Dylan was taking his music, with a backup band and rock sound that included the sixties signature combination of electric guitars and organ.

With the release of the mystical double album *Blonde on Blonde* in 1966, Dylan became a counterculture favorite. Just after the release of this seminal album, Dylan suffered a broken neck in a motorcycle accident. While convalescing in Woodstock, New York, he once again experimented with a new sound, recording *John Wesley Harding,* released in 1967, and signaling a return to folk. Two years later he experimented with a country sound in his *Nashville Skyline* album, which reached the top of the rock music charts.

Dylan continued his musical odyssey for the next four decades. Identified by many as the iconic folk musician who brought the civil rights movement to college-aged whites, Dylan refused to be labeled or limited by one theme or genre. Throughout the '60s, and ever since, Dylan has experimented with rock-and-roll, country, and folk music, with varying degrees of commercial success. He has also always embraced social themes and causes in some of his songs. In 1971 he performed at a concert to benefit the new nation of Bangladesh; in 1975 he sang at a concert to publicize the incarceration of ex-boxer Rubin "Hurricane" Carter, who was serving a life sentence for a murder Dylan and others believed the fighter did not commit. In 1985 he participated in the celebrity ensemble recording "We Are the World" to raise money for starving children in Africa. Most perplexing was his late 1970s foray into born-again Christianity. As a testament to his influence on popular American music for over four decades, Dylan won three Grammy Awards for his 1998 *Time Out of Mind,* the American Society of Composers, Authors, and Publishers Founders Award in 1986, and a Rock and Roll Hall of Fame induction in 1988.

Dylan's popularity extends well beyond the borders of the United States; he is possibly even more influential in Europe and Japan. His work has also generated numerous books, articles, college courses, and talks by journalists, critics, and scholars who have analyzed and interpreted his style, lyrics, politics, and cultural significance.

The British Invasion and the American Counterculture

In February 1964, the Beatles, a four-piece British pop band comprised of Paul McCartney, John Lennon, Ringo Starr, and George Harrison, first appeared on the *Ed Sullivan Show* in front of roughly 73 million television viewers. Their first appearance on American television created a sensation. Already widely popular in Great Britain, the Beatles' first single released to an American market, "I Want to Hold Your Hand," skyrocketed to number one on the pop charts. The young American audience, especially women, was taken with the band's mop-top haircuts, elegant "mod"-style clothes, compelling acoustical beat, and lyrics of love. Insipid pop music dominated the airwaves in the early sixties, so the Beatles' appearance on the pop music scene in 1964 signaled a shift in the sensibilities of youth culture. Inspired by African American music, the Beatles revitalized rock music with a British reinterpretation of the genre and a dynamic new group sound.

Beatlemania continued for the next three years with the release of their first movie, *A Hard Day's Night,* in 1964 and second movie, *Help!,* in 1965. Later that year their albums *Rubber Soul* and *Revolver* showed a more introspective side of the group, focusing much more on social issues rather than the more common romantic themes of their earlier work. Always the cultural trendsetters, the Beatles managed to both reflect and shape the cutting edge of youth culture, from the sunny, rebellious antics of *Meet the Beatles* in 1964 to the drug-influenced, mystical, and countercultural *Sergeant Pepper's Lonely Hearts Club Band* in 1967. *Sergeant Pepper* was the ultimate psychedelic pop-culture statement. Recasting themselves as a traditional British concert-hall band, the album took their listeners through a counterculture song cycle featuring acid rivers, Indian sitars, Scottish farm animals, carnival acrobatics, adolescent runaways, leaking roofs, and a British meter maid. At the time of its release it captured the Summer of

English rock 'n roll sensations The Beatles—John Lennon, George Harrison, Paul McCartney, and Ringo Starr (foreground)—wave to several hundred screaming fans before climbing aboard their airplane and leaving Miami, February 21, 1964. (Bettmann/Corbis)

Love ethos like no other rock album. On June 25, 1967, the Beatles performed on the BBC's *Our World* via satellite to five continents the song, "All You Need Is Love," capturing perfectly the counterculture's pacifism, idealism, and faith in the healing power of music.

A year after *Sergeant Pepper,* the group released *The Beatles,* more popularly known as the "White Album," a double-record set containing thirty songs. During the production of this album, the various members started to work separately on some of the songs, and their relationship became more acrimonious. Their next effort, *Get Back,* returned to the band's rock-and-roll roots, but went awry in personal feuds. In January 1969, they appeared together publicly for the last time when they played "Get Back" on their studio rooftop in London. By 1971, when the group had officially announced its dissolution, John Lennon had recorded "Imagine" and, with his wife, Yoko Ono, "Instant Karma." Paul McCartney had released his album, *McCartney,* George Harrison had a top single, "My Sweet Lord," and Ringo Starr had recorded *Sentimental Journey.*

From 1967 to 1969 they led the march into the counterculture. After their breakup, the former members represented both the excesses of the counterculture and its ultimate demise. Lennon went the farthest in his embrace of counterculture values. For example, after he married Ono, the two of them launched a bizarre campaign for world peace and goodness. In doing so, they staged a bed-in for peace and formed a musical group of their own, the Plastic Ono Band, and circulated nude photographs and erotic drawings of themselves. To many, including his former bandmates, this seemed like a peculiar way to end the war in Vietnam.

The Deadheads

The Grateful Dead, more than any other band or artist, symbolized the spirit of the counterculture. The band never sold a large volume of records over its three decades of performance because of the group's anticapitalistic and anti-authoritarian counterculture values. Resisting lucrative recording contracts, the Grateful Dead encouraged their loyal fans, "Deadheads," to bring tape recorders to concerts so they could make their own tapes. When asked what impressed him the most about the 1960s' San Francisco scene, legendary guitarist Eric Clapton said it was the willingness of the Grateful Dead to play for free. "That very much moved me," Clapton said, "I've never heard of anyone doing that before" (Kaiser, 192).

Jerry Garcia formed the band, originally known as the Warlocks, from the group called Mother McCree's Uptown Jug Band. Garcia, who served in the army before being declared unfit for service, grew up on bluegrass, rock-and-roll and the beat poetry of the 1950s. In the late 1950s he played in clubs around the Bay Area with various country and folk groups and quickly earned the reputation as one of San Francisco's best guitar players. By the mid-1960s, Garcia had joined with Bob Weir, Ron McKernan, Phil Lesh, and Bill Kreutzmann Jr. to form the Warlocks. The group changed its name to the Grateful Dead after Garcia saw the phrase in a dictionary while smoking marijuana.

The Grateful Dead became regular entertainers at Ken Kesey's Merry Pranksters' commune in La Honda, California, and regularly participated in Kesey's "Acid Tests," a series of public experimentations with the hallucinogenic drug LSD. These experiments profoundly changed the Dead's music, which infused blues, folk, and rock into a new, improvisational, psychedelic sound. The Dead set out to make their concerts an experience as mind-bending as a trip on the drug of their choice. This is how Garcia earned his nickname, "Captain Trip." Other members of the band also had "far out" nicknames like "Pigpen" (McKernan) and "Reddy Kilowatt" (Lesh).

The group lived together, communal-style, in the Haight-Ashbury district and they became as famous for their hippie lifestyle as their music. In 1970 the band released its best-selling album, *Workingman's Dead,* which reached number 27 in the country and later earned a gold record. Later that year, the band's album, *American Beauty,* reached number 30 on the charts and earned the band another gold record. "Truckin'," the song that became the band's unofficial anthem, was on this record. They did not produce a top 10 hit, however, until the release of their 1987 song, "A Touch of Grey."

Despite the modest success of these albums, the Grateful Dead will always be known for their seemingly interminable concert schedule and cult-like fans who followed them from venue to venue. Into the 1990s, nearly 30 years after the Dead began playing together, their performances still drew thousands of aging hippies and neophytes wanting the social experiential of a live Dead concert. Deadheads typically liked the euphoric experience of hallucinogenic drugs. At a three-day concert in 1991, police in Atlanta, Georgia, arrested fifty-seven people and confiscated 4,856 "tabs" of LSD, 39 bags of "mushrooms," 24 "lids" of marijuana, 1 vial of crack cocaine, and 18 cylinders of nitrous oxide. The death of Jerry Garcia in 1995, the result of lifelong addiction to hard drugs, ended the career of the Dead as one of the most successful touring groups of all time (McWilliams, 110–111).

Jimi Hendrix and the Politics of Race in the Counterculture

Born James Marshall in 1942 in Seattle, Washington, to former vaudeville dancers, Jimi Hendrix had a mixed ethnic background of Cherokee, Irish, and African American. Hendrix dropped out of Garfield High School during his senior year and did some handyman work before enlisting in the Army as a paratrooper in 1959. Two years later he received a medical discharge because of a back injury he sustained during a parachute jump. From 1961 to 1966, using the pseudonym "Jimmy James," Hendrix toured with several rhythm-and-blues acts that included James Brown's Famous Flames and the Isley Brothers. In 1966, he decided to leave the Curtis Knight band and relocate to Greenwich Village, one of the hubs of the emerging counterculture. While there he played in several clubs and became acquainted with other young musicians like Dylan and Bruce Springsteen. During performances in the Village clubs and coffeehouses, the left-handed Hendrix became proficient at playing his Stratocaster guitar while holding it upside down and behind his head, and even playing it with his teeth.

In 1966 he moved to England where he formed the Jimi Hendrix Experience band with bass guitarist Noel Chandler and drummer Mitch Mitchell. The group's "Purple Haze," released in 1967, with its allusions to mind-expanding drugs, became an immediate hit with the counterculture generation. In June 1967, after the release of the group's first album, *Are You Experienced?,* the Jimi Hendrix Experience made its American debut at the Monterey Pop Festival in California. Hendrix's electrifying guitar playing mesmerized the audience and made him an immediate star and icon of the counterculture. Performing to packed houses everywhere he toured, *Billboard* and *Rolling Stone* magazines named Hendrix

1968 "artist of the year." In early 1969 the Experience broke up and Hendrix was arrested in the Toronto airport on charges of heroin possession. Later acquitted of the charges, Hendrix consistently denied he had a drug problem.

In August 1969 Hendrix most memorably closed the Woodstock music festival with an astonishing performance of "The Star-Spangled Banner," one of the most lasting symbols of the 1960s counterculture. When he got to the line "and the rockets' red glare," Hendrix let loose with howling guitar riffs that recreated the sound of bombs bursting in air. As the song drew to a close, Hendrix solemnly plucked a few notes of "Taps" as a memorial to those slain in the Vietnam War. Although the crowd had thinned considerably after the previous night's climactic debauchery, the 30,000 or so remaining were taken by Hendrix's deconstruction of the National Anthem, which simultaneously evoked pride for and rage against the American way of life. Thirteen months later, at the age of 27, Hendrix died in his London apartment from "an inhalation of vomit due to barbiturate intoxication," according to the coroner's report.

Critics and historians have debated the politics of race in the rise of Jimi Hendrix as a hero of the counterculture generation, a largely white middle-class phenomenon. Some critics maintain that Hendrix "sold out" to a white audience with his highly sexual performances and psychedelic music. Hendrix even said that he left Harlem in 1966 for Greenwich Village because "in the Village people were more friendly than in Harlem where it's cold and mean. Your own people hurt you more. Anyway, I always wanted a more open and integrated sound" (Braunstein, 195). Others, such as George Lipstiz, contend that Hendrix's music transcended race. According to this view, Hendrix rose above his personal history to build a new multiracial identity. Yet others claim that this utopian view of Hendrix can reproduce racism in unforeseen ways. For them, race played a factor in every stage of Hendrix's career, and to deny its influence in his music and his music's reception is merely reflecting the white counterculture's naiveté that race can be transcended in America. For these scholars, the view that Hendrix rose above race unconsciously perpetuates racial norms.

Others view Hendrix's meteoric career and music in a less binary way. Critic Paul Gilroy has characterized Hendrix's music as a cultural exchange among Europe, Africa, and North America. Hendrix exchanged and negotiated influences from African American art and the white counterculture while using new technological forms to create a racial hybrid musical style. In experimenting with this new musical and cultural hybrid, Hendrix could intend one thing and mean another. For example, he might have intended his image to, in part, represent sexual and racial freedom, but to some observers it represented racial stereotypes of African American aggressive and supposedly dangerous sexuality. Particularly the often-used image of Hendrix surrounded by naked white women played on the stereotypes and fears of mainstream white America. Some believed Hendrix intentionally exploited this stereotype for commercial gain. Others, like historian Brian Ward, argue that Hendrix played with this white stereotype of African American sexuality for a deeper reason: to gain control over it.

The Doors: Music and Drugs

The Doors, with their fusion of white blues and psychedelic music, embodied the counterculture of the 1960s. Jim Morrison, the band's lead singer and songwriter, was the son of a navy officer. He left Florida State University for Los Angeles in the early sixties where he enrolled at the University of California at Los Angeles (UCLA). Two months after graduating from UCLA, Morrison met keyboardist Ray Manzarek, who recruited two additional members to form The Doors in 1964. The name of the band was an allusion to Aldous Huxley's *The Doors of Perception* (1954), which explored the effects of mind-expanding drugs. Along with Huxley's 1956 book, *Heaven and Hell, The Doors of Perception* was essential reading for the 1960s counterculture movement.

After playing at the Whiskey-a-Go-Go, a notorious psychedelic bar on the Sunset Strip in Los Angeles, the band released their first album, *The Doors,* in 1967, which included such songs as "Break on Through (to the Other Side)" and "Light My Fire," which spent three weeks as the number one song and was *Billboard*'s number two song of 1967. The Doors' music frequently mixed sex with death. As a result, many critics regarded their music as immoral and morbid. In his black-leather jacket and skin-tight vinyl pants, Morrison personified psychedelic rock's sullen, mystical, sexual poet. The Doors' second and third albums, *Strange Days* and *Waiting for the Sun,* more clearly demonstrated Morrison's growing tendency toward self-destruction.

In 1967, Morrison was forcibly removed from a New Haven, Connecticut, stage for allegedly exposing himself. While on tour in May 1968, during a concert in Chicago, Morrison incited a riot and escaped through a backstage door as police tried to stop fans from storming onto the stage and destroying equipment. A similar incident occurred three months later in New York. Morrison was also arrested twice for indecent exposure, most famously after a March 1, 1969, concert in Miami. Morrison supposedly exposed his genitals and simulated masturbation and oral sex while on stage. Six warrants were issued for Morrison's arrest in the concert's aftermath, and he was charged with lewd and lascivious behavior in public, indecent exposure, open profanity, and public drunkenness. After his arrest on these charges, concert promoters shied away from committing the band to future engagements. By this time Morrison could no longer function in the band, dropped out, and moved to Paris. After the Miami concert, which shocked even some of The Doors' most ardent fans, people concerned with the moral effects of Morrison's music, lyrics, and stage antics organized a giant "Rally for Decency" in the Orange Bowl that attracted 30,000.

Morrison died in Paris on July 3, 1971. The official cause of death was listed as a heart attack brought on by respiratory problems. Due to about a four-day delay in the death notice and the fact that few people saw his body, rumors began to circulate that he was still alive. In the Poets' Corner of Pere Lachaise Cemetery in Paris, his gravesite has become a popular tourist attraction and shrine to devoted fans of The Doors and admirers of the counterculture movement.

Janis Joplin and the Challenge to Traditional Standards of Beauty and Musical Genres

After leaving Port Arthur, Texas, at 17 to seek a musical career, Janis Joplin joined the San Francisco music scene of the mid-1960s. In 1966 she joined Big Brother and the Holding Company and sang in clubs in and around the Bay Area. She became famous after the band's performance at the 1967 Monterey International Pop Music Festival, where she made a show-stopping appearance. In February 1968 her East Coast debut in New York City at the Anderson Theater made fans of some of the most cynical music critics. After her performance, critic Robert Shelton wrote in the *New York Times,* "Miss Joplin is as remarkable a new pop music talent that has surfaced in years." After describing her as a "white sister" of Aretha and Erma Franklin, Shelton went on to write, "But comparisons wane, for there are few voices of such power, flexibility and virtuosity in pop music anywhere. Occasionally Miss Joplin appeared to be hitting two harmonizing notes at once. Her voice shouted with ecstasy or anger one minute, trailed off into coquettish curlicues the next. It glided from soprano highs to chesty alto lows" (*New York Times,* February 19, 1968).

Critic Ellen Willis wrote, "Joplin's metamorphosis from the ugly duckling of Port Arthur to the peacock of Haight-Ashbury" meant that "a woman who was not conventionally pretty, who had acne and an intermittent weight problem and hair that stuck out" invented "her own beauty out of sheer energy, soul, sweetness, arrogance, and a sense of humor," and consequently challenged accepted "notions of attractiveness" (Kaiser, 192–193). San Francisco–based freelance writer Michael Lydon described Joplin this way:

> Janis—such a strange, unsettled mix of defiance and hesitancy, vulnerability and strength—doesn't wait; every moment she is what she feels, mean or loving, up or down, stone sober or drunk out of her skull. The intensity makes her always magical, and makes radiant her unpretty face, with its too big nose, too wide mouth, and rough complexion. She consumes vast quantities of energy from some well inside herself that she believes is bottomless, and the heat of it warms everyone who meets her. When she sings all that terrible energy is brutally compressed into the moment. (*New York Times,* February 23, 1969)

A mix of traditional rhythm-and-blues and sixties soul, Joplin had a stage persona that represented both the defiance of the women's liberation movement and the vulnerability that such liberation entailed. She lived life close to the bone and paid a high price for it. Just three weeks after the death of Jimi Hendrix, Joplin succumbed to an accidental heroin overdose in a Hollywood hotel apartment where her guitarist John Cooke found her. She recorded five albums and attracted millions of devoted fans before her death in 1970.

The Ultimate Counterculture Celebration: The Woodstock Music and Art Festival

The counterculture movement came together for three days in August 1969 on Max Yazgur's 600-acre farm in Bethel, New York, at the "Woodstock Music and Art Fair." As *Time* magazine wrote, "the festival turned out to be history's largest happening. As the moment when the special culture of U.S. youth of the '60s openly displayed its strength, appeal and power, it may well rank as one of the significant political and sociological events of the age." No other single event epitomized the spirit and contradictions of the counterculture.

Poster promoting the Woodstock Music and Art Fair in Bethel, New York, on August 15–17, 1969. Over 400,000 people attended Woodstock, making it a popular symbol of the 1960s hippie counterculture. (Library of Congress)

Anticipating 100,000 people, the promoters were overwhelmed when somewhere between 400,000 and 450,000 began arriving on August 14, the day before the festival started. State police had to close the New York State Thruway and arriving hippies had to park their cars and walk for miles to get to the site. Intending to charge $18 for admission, the promoters gave up trying to collect money and allowed everyone in to experience the greatest program of rock talent ever assembled. The music began at 1:00 p.m. on Saturday and continued until Monday morning. Joan Baez, John Sebastian, Arlo Guthrie, and others performed on the first day, designated "folk day." Bands and artists such as Credence Clearwater Revival; Sly and the Family Stone; Canned Heat; the Grateful Dead; Janis Joplin; Santana; Country Joe and the Fish; Blood, Sweat and Tears; Crosby, Stills, Nash, and Young; Joe Cocker; the Moody Blues; and Jimi Hendrix entertained the throngs of dirty, rain-soaked fans. The *New York Times* reported, "most of the hip, swinging youngsters heard the music on stage only as a distant rumble. It was almost impossible for them to tell who was performing and probably only about half the crowd could hear a note" (*New York Times*, August 16, 1969).

The festival's promoters had to deal with several serious problems: insufficient food and sanitation facilities, rain and mud, and excessive drug use that caused hundreds of attendees to suffer bad reactions. Despite these difficulties and the shortage of police security, food, and medical staff, the crowds honored the festival's theme of peace and love and did not riot. Three deaths—two drug related and a third when a tractor accidentally ran over a young man in a sleeping bag—and one birth were reported, but through it the entire crowd formed a sense of community and acted cooperatively and civilly. The police chief in nearby Monticello called the festival crowd "the most courteous, considerate, and well-behaved group of kids that I have ever been in contact with in my twenty-four years of police work" (McWilliams, 75).

Woodstock celebrated the three tenets of the counterculture: sex, drugs, and rock-and-roll. It also represented a transition between eras. For some, its hedonism represented an assertion of the autonomy of the values of youth culture and an open, active rebellion against mainstream values. For those who embraced these mainstream values, Woodstock represented all that was wrong with the excesses of the counterculture movement. Abbie Hoffman mythologized the festival as a gathering of "Woodstock Nation," Joni Mitchell immortalized it with her song, "Woodstock" (performed by Crosby, Stills, Nash, and Young), and Michael Wadleigh celebrated it in his documentary film, *Woodstock*.

The Altamont Rock Festival and the Demise of the Counterculture

If Woodstock represented the apex of the counterculture movement, the Altamont Rock Festival on December 6, 1969, represented its nadir. The Rolling Stones decided to end their whirlwind tour of the United States with a free concert in California. Promoted as a gift to their fans, the Stones actually saw this as a promotional opportunity. Impressed by the moneymaking potential of Woodstock, the Stones decided to stage an all-day rock festival that would be a subject of a documentary film much like Woodstock. They obtained the use of Dick Carter's Altamont Raceway at the last minute. With little time to prepare for the event, the Stones hired a group of Hell's Angels as security guards for $500 worth of beer. The Grateful Dead; Santana; Jefferson Airplane; and Crosby, Stills, Nash, and Young, to name a few, appeared at the festival that attracted roughly 300,000 spectators.

The festival turned tragic when the Hell's Angels, many of them drunk or high on LSD, started to use violence to keep fans away from the stage. Some Hell's Angels even clubbed members of Jefferson Airplane when they approached the stage for their set. When the Rolling Stones finally came on stage, the Hell's Angels surrounded the band with their motorcycles. When tension between the crowd and the Hell's Angels peaked, the Stones inexplicably broke into the song, "Sympathy for the Devil." The crowd surged toward the stage and the Hell's Angels proceeded to stab, beat, and kick to death Meredith Hunter, a young African American man. The concert film, *Gimme Shelter,* captured the horrific event on film. All told, three other people died from various causes.

Initially the incident gained little attention from the mainstream media. *Rolling Stone* magazine, however, published an extensive article that called the event the Altamont Death Festival. The article blamed the tragedy on the Stones and greed. Too cheap to spring for proper security, the Stones even faked the movie-making so as to obscure what really happened at the festival. The *Los Angeles Free Press,* the biggest underground paper, went so far as to run a full-page caricature of Mick Jagger with an Adolf Hitler mustache, arm draped around a Hell's Angel, while long-haired kids gave them the Nazi salute. Ralph Gleason wrote for the *San Francisco Chronicle,* "The name of the game is money, power, and ego, and money is first as it brings power. The Stones didn't do it for free, they did it for money" (O'Neill, 262). Along with the Manson murders, many believed the Altamont tragedy signaled an end to the promise of the counterculture.

DRUGS AND EXPANDED CONSCIOUSNESS

The counterculture's use of drugs most dramatically symbolized the difference between counterculture and establishment values. Those in the counterculture movement used the term "dope" to distinguish between good and bad drugs. Dope was good; drugs were bad. Criticized for indulging in consciousness-altering drugs, the counterculture, as historian David Farber has pointed out, was in fact not alone in their reliance on drugs to change mental process and bodily functions. By the mid-1960s, drug use was endemic in the United States. In 1965, doctors wrote 123 million prescriptions for tranquilizers and 24 million prescriptions for amphetamines. People took "uppers" and "downers" just to cope with the pressures of everyday life. That same year, some 3,000 Americans died from overdoses of legally prescribed drugs. Whether mellowed by Valium, hyped up on speed, drunk, or buzzed on nicotine, Americans had by this time accepted that living life in a quasi-state of altered consciousness was part and parcel of mainstream American culture. But the counterculture's foray into drug use, particularly hallucinogenic drugs like LSD, was distinctive and ultimately alarming to middle-class Americans, local and federal authorities, and the medical profession.

The distinction between dope and drugs, good and bad, was imprecise, but hippies generally believed in the positive qualities of marijuana, hashish, LSD, psilocybin, mescaline, peyote, and morning glory seeds. Psychedelics were good, but uppers and downers were bad. If the substance expanded consciousness, it was good. If the drug dulled your senses and merely helped you get through another day, it was bad. Dope, in theory, altered the consciousness and could provide the foundation for establishing a new culture. But in practical terms, the division between substances was less clear as each individual made his or her own choices on which drugs to take.

Marijuana

Marijuana emerged as the most popular dope for the youth of this era. Gallup polls indicated that from 1967 to 1972 there was a dramatic increase in pot smoking among college students. By the early seventies a reported 60 percent of college students had used marijuana. Lewis Yablonsky conducted a study in 1968 that looked at just the counterculture and found that roughly 90 percent had at least sampled marijuana. The *New York Times* estimated that 99 percent of the crowd at Woodstock smoked marijuana, and a state police officer commented, "As far as I know, the narcotics guys are not arresting anybody for grass. If we did, there wouldn't be enough space in Sullivan County, or the next three counties, to put them in." Even before Woodstock, hippies engaged in "smoke-ins" without fear of arrest. While the psychoactive properties of marijuana had been known since the turn of the 20th century, the 1960s marked the decade when "pot" smoking became a popular activity among a large population of young people (Miller, 27–28).

There were several reasons why marijuana appealed to the counterculture. For one, it was fun. The counterculture was intentionally hedonistic, hence the hippie creed: "If it feels good, then do it so long as it doesn't hurt anyone else." Second, it signaled rebellion. The use of marijuana became a cultural symbol of resisting the social norms of a society the counterculture wanted to reject. Finally, it also offered the hope of healing and insight. Many hippies claimed to have found personal and philosophical insights while under the influence of drugs such as marijuana. Whatever the reason, marijuana and other recreational drugs became a staple in the diet of the counterculture movement by the end of the decade.

LSD as the Consciousness-Raising Drug of Choice

Lysergic acid diethylamide, commonly known as LSD, also became a drug of choice for the 1960s counterculture. Albert Hofmann of Switzerland's Sandoz Pharmaceuticals created LSD in 1943 in hopes of finding a profitable analeptic that might cure migraines. Sandoz discovered LSD did little for headaches, but it did cause hallucinations. Sandoz shipped the drugs to America's burgeoning population of psychiatrists and clinical psychologists in hopes that they might find a use for it. The passage of the Mental Health Act in 1946 signaled the political and military belief that psychiatry and the behavioral sciences should play an important role in national security. Partially due to federal funding, the psychiatric profession exploded after World War II. In 1956 over 15,000 psychiatrists practiced compared to only 3,000 in 1940. These psychiatrists increasingly used medication to try to cure the defective mental processes of unbalanced people. Federally funded psychiatrists experimented with several drugs, including LSD, to see if they could be used to promote a healthier citizenry. Timothy Leary was one of these early federally funded researchers exploring the utility of LSD.

By the early 1960s, mass media celebrated the possibilities of LSD as a cure for psychological problems. Cary Grant reported that LSD administered to him by his psychiatrist had helped him learn to love women more fully. LSD moved from the world of practical medical science to alternative frames of meaning and use in the research of Leary at Harvard between 1960 and 1963 when he started preaching that it could be used to achieve maximum inner exploration. By the mid-1960s, LSD advocates across the country spread the good news of the drug's consciousness-raising effects. Detroit-area rock-and-roll promoter and writer John Sinclair, for example, believed that LSD helped young people move "from alienation to the total embrace of humankind. . . . Acid blasted all the negativism and fear out of our bodies and gave us a vision we needed to go ahead, the rainbow vision which showed us how all people could live together in harmony and peace just as we were beginning to live with each other like that" (Farber, 29). In 1968, Sinclair formed the White Panther Party in hopes that these acid visions would turn the isolation and alienation of their parents' generation into a communal youth consciousness. Allen Cohen, cofounder of the psychedelic newspaper, the *San Francisco Oracle,* believed that acid could point to a lived experience of collective harmony. Extremely naïve in tone, the *Oracle* expressed a Pollyanna faith in the "cosmic consciousness" LSD offered its users and the belief that it offered the hope of turning an entire civilization away from the materialism and competitiveness of industrial capitalism.

Despite its spread throughout the country, LSD became most closely associated with the Haight-Ashbury district of San Francisco. With its bohemian tradition and access to acid due to the work of underground chemist Augustus Owsley Stanley II, this district became the hub of acid-tripping hippies. In January 1966, Ron Thelin, son of the manager of the Haight-Ashbury district's Woolworth's, opened up the Psychedelic Shop at 1535 Haight to make the drug accessible to hundreds of users. After the Swiss pharmaceutical giant Sandoz pulled the plug on the production of LSD in 1965, users became almost completely dependent on these underground chemists and dealers. As a result, "pure"

LSD became unavailable. The reliance on underground LSD also resulted from state and federal governments' decision to make LSD possession and distribution illegal.

By early 1966, the mass media started exploring the counterculture's experimentations with LSD. This coverage gained momentum after the report of LSD-induced psychiatric breakdowns. *Time* magazine, for instance, reported in March of that year that "the disease is striking in beach side beatnik pads and in the dormitories of expensive prep schools; it has grown into an alarming problem at UCLA and on the UC campus at Berkeley." Although the risk of psychotic episodes was overblown, researchers had accumulated enough data to show that LSD usage had its dangers. Ultimately Dr. Stanley Cohen's testimony before a congressional committee paved the way for the 1966 federal criminalization of LSD possession and distribution. In his testimony he said his research into LSD use revealed something alarming: "the loss of cultural values, the loss of feeling of right and wrong, of good and bad. These people lead a valueless life, without motivation, without ambition . . . they are decultured, lost to society, lost to themselves" (Farber, 32).

Criminalization caused users to rely on "street" acid, which was far more dangerous. It also made LSD use an even more powerful symbol of cultural rebellion. Some activists, like Jerry Rubin, claimed that the criminalization of drugs like marijuana and LSD made young people even more disrespectful of the law and the courts. He and Abbie Hoffman formed the Yippies in 1968 in an attempt to bring drug-using hippies into the political arena. These efforts ultimately proved unsuccessful as the experimentation with hallucinogenic drugs and political activism proved to be incompatible endeavors.

The Guru of Psychedelics

Timothy Leary became known as the prophet or guru of the "psychedelic utopians" of the counterculture movement. Due to his bizarre promotion of hallucinogenic drugs, Leary emerged as an icon of the counterculture. Exclusively focused on the transformative power of LSD, Leary intentionally stayed clear of politics and evolved into something of a cross between a pop star and religious cult leader.

Born October 22, 1920, in Springfield, Massachusetts, Leary at age 13 was abandoned by his alcoholic father. A mediocre student through high school, he first attended Holy Cross College in Worcester, Massachusetts. Disenchanted with the strict Jesuit curriculum, Leary dropped out and then attended the U.S. Military Academy at West Point, New York. Not surprisingly, Leary spent much of his 18 months at the Academy in punitive isolation for rules infractions. During this period, Leary began reading Eastern philosophy and developed an interest in Buddhism. After dropping out of West Point in 1941, Leary enrolled at

Timothy Leary was famous for his advice during the psychedelic revolution, "Turn on, tune in, drop out." (Library of Congress)

the University of Alabama where he earned a degree in psychology. After serving at a U.S. Army hospital in Pennsylvania during the last two years of World War II, he earned a master's degree in psychology at Washington State University in Pullman, Washington. He then went on to earn a doctorate in psychology from the University of California at Berkeley in 1950. He served on the faculty at Berkeley for five years and then served as the director of psychological research at the Kaiser Foundation Hospital in Oakland, California, where he developed a personality assessment tool used by both private and public agencies, including the Central Intelligence Agency.

Leary's first of five wives committed suicide in 1958 as a consequence of Leary's perpetual unfaithfulness, leaving him to raise their two children, Susan and Jack. In 1959, Harvard University recruited him to be a lecturer in its psychology program. At Harvard he began researching existential transactional psychology and became critical of the values inherent in bourgeois society. During a trip to Mexico in 1960, Leary first used the psychedelic drug psilocybin, found in what is commonly referred to as "magic mushrooms." Excited by the mind-altering experience, he came back to Harvard to conduct experiments with psilocybin, mescaline, and LSD. Joined by fellow professor Richard Alpert, Leary's research started to include undergraduate students at weekend gatherings. In 1962 he founded the International Foundation for Internal Freedom (IFIF) to train and guide further psychedelic exploration. The IFIF published the *Psychedelic Review;* they advertised with a flyer that began, "Mescaline! Experimental Mysticism! Mushrooms! Ecstasy! LSD-25! Expansion of Consciousness! Phantastica! Transcendence! Hashish! Visionary Botany! Ololiuqui! Physiology of Religion! Internal Freedom! Morning Glory! Politics of the Nervous System!" (O'Neill, 239).

Leary and Alpert, working at the Harvard Psychedelic Research Project, began to publish the results of their experiments. In a 1962 *Bulletin of the Atomic Scientists* they noted that LSD "may produce dramatic changes in personality leading to unprecedented peace, sanity, and happiness." In a 1963 *Harvard Review* article, "The Politics of Consciousness Expansion," Leary and Alpert wrote: "The social situation in respect to consciousness-expanding drugs is very similar to that faced sixty years ago by those crackpot visionaries who were playing around with the horseless carriage. In 1961 the University Health Service at Harvard made Leary promise that he would not use undergraduates in his experiments. In 1963 he was fired for breaking that pledge. That August, he moved into a mansion in Millbrook, New Jersey, that young millionaire and fan William Mellon Hitchcock, heir to the Mellon fortune, allowed him to use gratis. Leary moved into Millbrook with about 60 other adults and children.

Leary believed that LSD enabled people to erase adult middle-class programming. Like other luminaries of the counterculture movement, Leary believed that adults' perception of their environment was shuttered, rigid, and one-dimensional. As a result, their response to stimuli always followed the same pattern, which produced war, injustice, poverty, racism, and sexual repression. Leary represented the hippie belief that being childlike was a sign of mental health. For this reason, hippies had an affinity for acting like children by dressing in costumes, adopting colorful nicknames, and panhandling. Leary and Alpert even took up a brief experiment at Millbrook in collective childrearing. This experiment was based on a scenario taken from Aldous Huxley's book *Island* and aimed to allow adults the opportunity to learn from children and imbibe some of their spontaneity and awe. Not surprisingly, the experiment failed when the work of raising small children became too arduous for those living at the estate more interested in acting like children than grownups. Leary lived at Millbrook for almost five years and published *The Psychedelic Experience* (1964) with Alpert and Ralph Metzner while there. It was also at Millbrook that Leary's two children, who had been passively abused for years, started falling apart.

By 1967 Leary had dropped completely out of society and was living in a tepee with very little income he earned from the occasional lecture. Appearing barefoot, and dressed in white pajama pants in Indian silk shirts with long blond hair, Leary preached of the life-changing potential and mystical experience of LSD usage. With the help of media expert Marshall McLuhan, he coined the famous counterculture slogan, "Turn On, Tune In, Drop Out" to promote the use of LSD. While he meant it as a campaign to promote harmonious living through a detachment with unconscious commitments, the mainstream media quickly took the slogan to mean "get stoned and abandon all constructive activity."

On January 14, 1967, Leary joined other counterculture icons like Allen Ginsberg and Jerry Rubin to hold a "Gathering of the Tribes" in San Francisco's Golden Gate Park. Twenty thousand gathered to hear both antiwar and pro-drug speeches by Ginsburg, Rubin, Leary, and others. Leary was also at the "Human Be-In" to promote the value of LSD. Speaking to an enthusiastic audience, he made his much-quoted proposal: "Turn on to the scene. Tune in to what is happening and drop out—of high school, college and grad school, junior executive, senior executive—and follow me, the hard way" (Kaiser, 204).

In 1969 Leary was arrested on two marijuana possession violations—one in Texas, the other in California. Convicted, he was sentenced to a minimal-security correctional facility near San Luis Obispo, California. He served for six months before escaping with the help of drug dealers and the Weathermen leftist revolutionary group. In October 1970 he turned up in Algiers, where the Algerian government gave him political asylum. When he and his wife, Rosemary, arrived in Algiers, they found themselves wards of the exiled Black Panther leader Eldridge Cleaver. In 1973 he was apprehended in Kabul, Afghanistan, while getting off a plane and extradited to California, and incarcerated until 1976.

In the 1980s, Leary became active on the lecture circuit, including one tour with convicted Watergate conspirator G. Gordon Liddy. In 1990 his daughter, Susan, accused of shooting her boyfriend, committed suicide while in a women's correctional facility. Leary died of prostate cancer in 1996. In July 1999 the FBI confirmed that in 1974 Leary had become an informant on the Weathermen to gain his early release from jail. Despite exemplifying for many all the reasons one would want to stay clear of drugs as he turned from researcher to cult leader and then finally huckster, Leary played a critical role in the unleashing and reconceptualizing of LSD for the counterculture movement.

Ken Kesey and the Merry Pranksters

Ken Kesey, born September 17, 1935, in La Junta, Colorado, moved with his parents to Eugene, Oregon, where they operated the highly successful Eugene Farmers Cooperative. After graduating from the University of Oregon and earning a Woodrow Wilson Fellowship, Kesey enrolled as a graduate student in Stanford University's Creative Writing Program. He married his high school sweetheart and had to take a job as a night attendant in the psychiatric ward of the

Veterans Administration Hospital in Menlo Park to help make ends meet as they prepared for the birth of their first child. At the suggestion of a fellow graduate student, Kesey agreed to take part in an experimental program at the hospital to supplement his income. For $20 a session, Kesey took hallucinogenic drugs, including LSD, psilocybin, mescaline, peyote, Ditran, and morning glory seeds. This experience inspired him to write *One Flew over the Cuckoo's Nest,* which was published in 1962. Set in a mental ward, *Cuckoo's Nest* earned critical acclaim, became the most frequently used contemporary novel in college courses during the 1970s, and became one of the few American works of fiction to be presented as a novel, play, and movie, the last starring Jack Nicholson and winning six Academy Awards in 1975.

Kesey was exposed to various forms of cultural experimentation and radicalism in the late 1950s and early 1960s while living at Perry Lane, a group of cottages near the Stanford campus. As he later recalled, "We pioneered what have since become the hall-marks of hippy culture: LSD and other psychedelics too numerous to mention, body painting, light shows, and mixed media presentations . . . be-ins, exotic costumes, strobe lights, sexual mayhem . . . eastern mysticism, and the rebirth of hair" (McWilliams, 117).

His drug experiences at Menlo Hospital and Perry Lane convinced Kesey that certain substances could heighten consciousness and enhance creativity. In 1964 and 1965, Kesey and his compatriots, the self-styled "Merry Pranksters," began planning public parties called "acid tests," where participants used Day-Glo paint and other visual and audio aids to enhance their hallucinogenic experiences. They went out adventuring, experiencing the world while tripping. The Grateful Dead was the house band for these parties, and Jerry Garcia described the scene as "thousands of people all helplessly stoned, all finding themselves in a roomful of people, none of whom any of them were afraid of. It was magic, far out, beautiful magic" (Farber, 26). In 1964, Kesey bought a 1939 International Harvester school bus, converted it into a camper, painted it with Day-Glo splashes, equipped it with an elaborate sound system, and named it "Furthur." He and the Pranksters used the bus to travel from California to New York for the World's Fair. A sign on the back of the bus read: "Caution: Weird Load." Making stops along their journey, the Pranksters goofed on the crowds and took their acid visions out into the world to create public space where they could play their collective tripping games. The cross-country bus trip and other Prankster adventures became the subject of Tom Wolfe's *The Electric Kool-Aid Test,* published in 1968.

Arrested twice for his drug use, spending five months in jail on one occasion, Kesey moved back to the Eugene area in 1967 where he lost interest in LSD, acid tests, or any other Prankster activities. Later in life he wrote children's stories and several other books including *Sometimes a Great Notion,* which was also adopted into a movie.

The Counterculture Permeates Mass Culture

The term *counterculture* connotes a clear line between mainstream American culture and the increasingly alternative or even oppositional culture of the 1960s' youth movement. This binary view of the 1960s implies a monolithic quality to each category and obscures the fact that both actually shared the same culture. An interesting aspect of the 1960s' counterculture is its rapid cross-fertilization of ideas, sensibilities, and styles with mainstream culture. Mass culture fully displayed this process of exchange and assimilation between the mainstream and oppositional culture of the 1960s.

Journalist and cultural historian Peter Braunstein argues that 1960s popular culture reveals that both the counterculture and mainstream cultures shared a desire for eternal youth through rejuvenation. In short, the music, fashions, movies, and television of the 1960s not only represented youth's opposition to their parents' values and worldview, but also adults' infatuation with the liberating hippie lifestyle. By the 1970s, adults had assimilated the rejuvenation ethos to such an extent that the fascination with youth simply became an accepted part of mainstream culture (Braunstein, 243–273).

Hippies

The definition of a "hippie" is quite vague and imprecise because the hippies themselves lacked a clear sense of purpose. The term *hippie* connoted "junior-grade hipsters," a term supposedly coined by the Beats, hippies' philosophical and cultural forerunners. Perhaps the earliest appearance in the popular press of the word occurred in a late 1964 *New York* magazine article about the "New Bohemia" of Manhattan's Lower East Side. Derived from "hipster," a pre-sixties slang term for an urban male type who often wore his trousers low on his hips, "hippie" referred to someone hip, cool, or "groovy." Norman Mailer, in his essay "The White Negro" (1957), defined a hipster as an existentialist who removed himself from historical consciousness and lived solely in the present.

Often thrown in with other rebellions of that era, hippies, unlike the New Left and other ideological groups of the sixties, had no political aspirations. The major tenet of their faith was that society put too much emphasis on conformity, materialism, and competitiveness. As a result, people became repressed and anxious, unable to enjoy life, live in the moment, and truly love one another. They turned their back on some of the fundamental principles shared by most Americans: Christianity, patriotism, and property ownership. Instead of trying to change a society they saw irreparably damaged, they abandoned it all together.

Due to their pacifism, they sometimes associated with antiwar activists, but generally rejected the strident politics of that movement. To balance the antiwar

Hippies sing and dance at a "love-in" near Los Angeles, California, in March 1967. (Bettmann/Corbis)

activists' seriousness, they often interjected a sense of playfulness to the youth cultural milieu of the sixties.

Like beatniks, hippies chose to drop out of society and exist in the eternal present with the assistance of sex, drugs, communal living, open sexual relationships, and mysticism. Hippies viewed themselves as gentle, peace-loving people. They offered young people the freedom from a rigidly structured work world and a life emphasizing individuality and "doing your own thing."

To a large extent, clothing identified hippies. Women wore flowers in their hair and hand-sewn long and flowing ankle-length skirts. Men wore their hair long, often in ponytails, tie-dyed shirts, and jeans. Both sexes decorated their faces for festive occasions; wore beads and exotic jewelry, ponchos, and serapes; and wore sandals or went barefoot. Even with these distinctive markers, it was not always easy discerning a real hippie from the wannabes who appropriated hippie dress and mannerisms but not the lifestyle. To make matters more confusing, the media and public had a difficult time distinguishing between committed political activists who wanted to influence policy and hippies whose main objective was to seek freedom, fun, and love through sex, drugs, and music.

While hippies' backgrounds varied, many came from families who directly benefited from the postwar economic boom. Raised in ideal nuclear families in suburban developments during the fifties, becoming a hippie was a way to reverse the homogeneous, prevailingly middle-class standards of one's parents. Although true hippies probably never numbered more than 300,000, their

outrageous behavior and unconventional appearance made them media fa-
vorites. The image of the psychedelic dropout became a lightning rod for conservatives who believed deeply in America's middle-class values. In the words
of California governor Ronald Reagan, for example, a hippie was one who
"dresses like Tarzan, has hair like Jane, and smells like Cheetah" (McWilliams, 67).

The Sexual Revolution

During the 1950s two major constraints on sexual freedom were weakened.
Antibiotics made sexually transmitted diseases such as syphilis and gonorrhea
easily and painlessly treatable. Second, improved contraceptives made unwanted
pregnancies less likely. In addition, Alfred Kinsey's studies on human sexuality
broke through the taboo on discussing sex and suggested that more sex, and
more varied sex, occurred than previously believed. In May 1960, the Food and
Drug Administration approved the first contraceptive pill; by 1966, six million
American women took the pill. In *Griswold v. Connecticut* (1964), the Supreme
Court affirmed the right of individuals to have access to contraceptive information (Singleton, 645).

   William H. Masters and Virginia E. Johnson in the mid-1960s went beyond
Kinsey's earlier studies of sexuality by examining the physiology of sexual in-
tercourse. Their 1966 book, *Human Sexual Response,* caused quite a stir by revealing that subjects willingly copulated in the laboratory and by debunking the
Freudian distinction between the "mature" vaginal orgasm and the "immature"
clitoral one. At the same time, there was a general cultural trend toward allowing
printed material to be sold regardless of its sexual content. In 1964, the Supreme
Court pronounced the First Amendment protected Henry Miller's sexually explicit book, *Tropic of Cancer,* and two years later extended the same protection
to William S. Burrough's *Naked Lunch.* This new freedom encouraged publishers to take more chances and sell more sexually explicit and erotic material. The
ruling had a similar effect on plays, movies, and ultimately television.

   As a result of these developments, young people coming of age in the 1960s
experienced a culture not as sexually repressed as earlier generations. Taking
advantage of the progress in contraception and disease control, hippies embraced the philosophies of Herbert Marcuse, which promoted free and open
sexuality as a means to greater freedom and happiness. In the counterculture,
a sexual revolution could be both personally and socially transformative. Some
hippies believed that violence and war were the product of misdirected sexual
energy. To them, the sexual revolution could actually bring peace.

   Critics of the sexual revolution believed it was only a ploy by men to obtain
more sex. As the women's movement grew in the late 1960s, some of its members criticized the revolution because men were pressuring reluctant women into
having sex to prove they were a part of the movement. Other feminists, however,

praised the sexual revolution for making it possible for women to have a more active sex life without suffering social stigmatization.

Counterculture Fashion

The spirit of the counterculture affected the fashion and style of the sixties as young people staged a rebellion against traditional fashion. Fashions started to change radically even before hippies started to appear on America's cultural stage. Not since the 1920s had fashion and style changed so dramatically. And like the twenties, much of the change came from below. Historically fashion has been dictated from above by Parisian couturiers and other authorities, but during the sixties younger people, and relatively unknown designers like Mary Quant and Rudi Gernreich who catered to them, set the pace for changing styles.

Like the emerging counterculture, the new fashions celebrated freedom, sexuality, and choice. Women's clothing flaunted their sexuality like never before. In 1961, some young people started wearing bell-bottom pants and crop tops with a bare midriff (Farber and Bailey, 412). In 1962, the young Quant made Carnaby Street in London the epicenter of the "mod" look with knee-length jumpers, dark eye makeup with heavy eyeliner and white or very pale pink lipstick. In 1964, Gernreich introduced a topless bathing suit for women that had knitted trunks suspended from a cord around the neck. By 1965 miniskirts, go-go boots, and culotte dresses dominated U.S. fashion. Young women wore knee boots with miniskirts and short A-line coats. The boots even made whips a suitable fashion accessory, not so subtly striking a sadomasochism theme. In 1967, women could even buy the very trendy and flammable paper dress.

The unique aspect of sixties fashion, however, was the breakdown of fashion authority and the stylistic anarchy that followed. For example, as skirts got shorter and shorter, an ankle-length "maxiskirt" also became popular. In 1963, Vidal Sassoon introduced geometric, asymmetric, and bob haircuts to accompany the "mod" look, but at the same time young people started growing their hair long. Necklines could go to the throat or the navel. Just about every color, pattern, and design flourished amid this burst of freedom and creativity. Fashion's door swung so wide open that almost anything went. For men, designers like Pierre Cardin started to draw upon this new era of unconventional dress by introducing tight-waisted, long-jacketed suits. The Beatles' 1964 U.S. invasion introduced Prince Valiant hairdos, suits buttoned to the chin, visored caps, and extravagant haberdashery. In 1968, the Nehru coat became popular among the more trendy set.

Even though many of these new fashions predated hippies, they gained their inspiration from the same undercurrent of rebellion that gave rise to the counterculture. In essence, they expressed the same freedom from restraint and embrace of sensuality as the emerging counterculture. As the sixties progressed, some fashion statements were more directly related to counterculture patterns. Iron-ically, socially conscious young people started to wear army and navy jackets, shirts, and bell-bottom pants in the early sixties to symbolize their ostentatious frugality in reaction to consumer culture. Popularized before the rise of the anti-war movement, this fashion statement was not meant to show contempt for the military. Hippies later made handcrafted items popular among young people interested in rejecting materialism. These items implied that the wearer made them, thereby showing his or her independence from the consumer culture while expressing his or her creativity and individuality. Soon, however, the market was so large and the people with skill and patience too limited that handcrafted items were ultimately commercially made and distributed. Bead shops and hip-pie boutiques became commonplace. The "hippie" style became popular not just among counterculture adherents, but young people not particularly interested in making an ideological statement.

Wearing beads, bangles, leather goods, colorful vests and ankle-length hand-crafted dresses reflected the counterculture's affinity with American Indian cul-ture and a back-to-nature ethic. These fashions intentionally signaled peace, love, brotherhood, noble savagery, community, folk artistry, anticapitalism, and even-tually antimilitarism. The hippies' emphasis on costuming in a theatrical sense signaled the counterculture's desire to level the social hierarchy by making every-one look alike. As William O'Neill wrote about the fashion of the counterculture, "In effect, aesthetics were exchanged for ethics. Beauty was no longer related to appearance but to morality" (O'Neill, 249).

Once Middle America made the association between style and political and cultural radicalism, between long hair, beards, beads, and sandals on the one hand and antimilitarism and dope on the other, a war was declared on these physical trappings of the counterculture. School systems across the country started imposing new dress codes and restrictions against long hair in reaction to the new styles. Style became the chief symbol of the generational and cul-tural divide, causing young people, particularly those embracing the counter-culture, to cling even more fanatically to their rebellious fashions.

The Graduate

Directed by Mike Nichols with a soundtrack by Simon and Garfunkel, *The Grad-uate,* released in 1967, became one of the landmark youth culture films of the 1960s. College-age students identified with Benjamin, played by Dustin Hoffman in his first major film role, and his efforts to find himself against the backdrop of his parents' spiritless upper-middle-class existence. The film became 1968's most popular film.

At the beginning of the film, Benjamin's father asks him what he wants to do with his future. Befuddled and unable to articulate what he wants, he merely utters "different." This sets the stage for the movie's plot where the problem of the Generation Gap is memorably dramatized. Similarly, Benjamin is forced to relate to all of his parents' friends in an early party scene. He must answer typical questions from parents of the counterculture generation, with their orientation toward careers and material success. One of his parents' friends tells Ben that the future can be found in one word: "Plastics." Ben asks, "Exactly how do you mean?" He mysteriously replies, "There's a great future in plastics. Think about it." From his reaction, Ben is clearly less interested in his future plans than his parents and parents' friends are.

The tensions between generations and cultures is played out most dramatically in Ben's affair with Mrs. Robinson (Anne Bancroft), the wife of his father's business partner. Like Ben, Mrs. Robinson is looking to rebel against the pointlessness of her suburban upper-middle-class life, but the form of her rebellion, extramarital affairs, is clearly just as pointless and joyless. By reluctantly joining in with Mrs. Robinson's plan to have an affair, Ben is both literally and figuratively screwing the generation that has lost its soul. As Ben tries to lift his relationship with Mrs. Robinson beyond just sex, it becomes clear that she is a victim of her generation's perverted values and expresses nothing but spiritual emptiness. In stark contrast stands Mrs. Robinson's daughter, Elaine (Katharine Ross), who shares Ben's values and authenticity. As a result, Ben falls for Elaine despite Mrs. Robinson's warnings to stay away from her.

As for Elaine, she is engaged to marry Carl (Brian Avery), who reflects the values of her parents' generation. Carl is summed up by his membership with a fraternity that epitomizes the worst of the Greek system, portrayed as sexist and chauvinistic. Leaving Carl at the alter signals Elaine's break with her mother, whose life is empty and unfulfilling in a marriage to a man with similar qualities to Carl's. Her escape with Ben, a sensitive man who also is separating from his parents' generation value system, symbolizes their willingness to live life on their own terms and outside mainstream American culture. The film poignantly makes this point when in response to Mrs. Robinson's warning that it is "too late" for her daughter to change her mind, Elaine simply replies, "Not for me." However, as Ben and Elaine escape from the church on the back of the bus, their jubilant smiles fade to expressions of realization that now they must answer the question they both were trying to avoid: What's next? In that look, the film portrays the inherent challenge to the counterculture's rebellion to their parents' generation: If not their parents' values, culture, and work, whose?

Easy Rider

The movie *Easy Rider* (1969), directed by Dennis Hopper, was a fable aimed at capturing the meaning of the counterculture. Starring Hopper and Peter Fonda, with Jack Nicholson in an important supporting role, and written by Hopper,

Peter Fonda and Dennis Hopper in Easy Rider *(1969). (Bettmann/Corbis)*

Fonda, and novelist Terry Southern, *Easy Rider* portrayed the counterculture in the same manner as Jack Kerouac portrayed the Beat Generation in the book *On the Road*. The film recounts the motorcycle journey across the country by Captain America (Fonda) and his sidekick Billy (Hopper). A portrayal of the counterculture from the inside, it shows its main characters routinely tripping on acid and smoking marijuana. In fact, the money used to fund their cross-country trip to New Orleans came from a drug deal at the beginning of the film.

Early in the journey they arrive at a ranch where they join a rancher and his family for lunch. The rancher provides the outsider's view, wondering how Captain America and Billy can live such unencumbered lives: "It's not every man that can live off the land, you know. Do your own thing on your own time; you should be proud." The film uses the rancher to offer the perspective that the counterculture movement actually expresses American values of individualism, freedom, and self-reliance in an odd, antiwork-ethic sort of way. Along their journey they pick up a hitchhiker who takes them to the quintessential expression of the counterculture, the commune. The hippies who live there are living off the land and indulging in the other aspects of the late-sixties' counterculture communal lifestyle such as smoking dope, casual sex, "guerrilla" theatre (improvisational theatre common among radical political activists of the time), nude swimming, and Tai Chi.

Ultimately, Captain America and Billy wind up in jail in a small, rural town for joining a Fourth of July parade without a permit. It is here that things start going wrong for the three heroes (by this time Captain America and Billy are joined by a third rider, George Hanson, played by Nicholson). The pastoral quality of the opening sequences, with majestic views of the American West, gives way to a more intense melodrama as the protagonists confront the anger and hate of a southern border town. After an unpleasant encounter with some rednecks in a diner, Hanson shakes his head and says, "You know, this used to be a hell of a good country. I can't understand what's going on." In the small town, Hopper depicts a classic culture clash between the wandering hippies and the mainstream culture of a small southern town. "Southern justice" prevails at the end of the movie when Captain America, Billy, and Hanson are shot down by vigilante gunfire not so much for what they have done, but for what they represent. For this small, rural community, the counterculture's embrace of freedom and individualism is not celebrated, but rather envied and feared.

In shooting *Easy Rider,* Hopper attempted to duplicate the experimental drug use of the time and culture. Just as acid rock suggested in music what it was like to trip, *Easy Rider* used wild camera angles and rapid editing to imitate the hallucinatory effects of drugs like LSD. It also marked a fitting end to the decade as it conveyed the self-destructive excesses of the counterculture that ultimately destroyed the antibourgeois utopian movement. After the rednecks shoot Hanson, Captain America engages in a little self-criticism when he tells Billy, "We blew it." Although Billy disagrees, the movie's conclusion seems to reinforce Captain America's point.

An independent production that cost only $365,000, the film grossed $19 million, won a prize at the Cannes Film Festival in Europe, and became a cult classic for its dramatic depiction of the apex of a movement that challenged the values and way of life of mainstream middle-class America.

1960s Situation Comedy and the Counterculture

By the mid-1960s, among the dwindling list of vital television genres, the situation comedy emerged as the lynchpin of network scheduling. More situation comedies finished among Nielsen's Top 25 during the 1960s than all other program types combined. Ironically, television was going through a period of consolidation, contraction, and product rationalization at a time when other expressions of American culture were engaged in experimentation and expansion. Harry Castleman and Walter Podrazik have written about this time that, "the commercial networks seemed to be ignoring a wide range of controversial subjects. . . . Was the toning down deliberate? Were the networks fearful of reprisals by government and industry?" (Castleman and Podrazik, 189). The sitcom was not only the most popular television genre in the mid- to late 1960s, it

Woodstock and the
Co-option of the Counterculture

The documentary film *Woodstock* was an independently produced three-hour documentary about the "peace and music" festival that attracted almost half a million young people to hear the musical icons of the era on a patch of farmland in upstate New York. Producer Bob Maurice and director Michael Wadleigh used state-of-the-art cinematic technology and split-screen effects to portray not only the performers on stage, but also the interesting antics of audience members. Warner Bros., the studio releasing the film, anticipated huge box-office demand and initiated a huge advertising campaign before its 1970 release. The widely circulated *Woodstock* advertisement featured the image of a naked young couple frolicking in a pond, a mildly titillating image that reinforced the earthy sexuality of the counterculture.

Early reviews of the film from the counterculture's underground press were mostly very positive: "You can almost forget that Altamont lay only a few weeks in the future. To watch the film through innocent eyes is to be part of the dream again, to forget the past, and to see a glimpse of the future we will someday build" (*Los Angeles Free Press,* May 8, 1970, p. 20). The film itself, many critics believed, functioned to reassert countercultural youth's visions of a different social order and values. However, the selling of the film ignited a wave of protest from hippies and Yippies: "The brazenness of Warner Bros.' capitalization on the Woodstock phenomenon provided movement writers with a blatant example of cooption for easy deconstruction and attack" (Brodroghkozy, 50). Many adherents of the counterculture's values and lifestyle found it particularly agonizing to have their political stance of opposition so enmeshed in a system they wished to dismantle.

In both Los Angeles and Berkeley, the Yippies organized fairly successful pickets and boycotts of the film. In front of the Los Angeles Warner's Theater on Wilshire Boulevard, protesters chanted, "Woodstock is here on the street, not in the sterile theater on the screen" (*Los Angeles Free Press,* May 22, 1970). In addition to boycotts and picket lines, the movie's premiere experienced a bomb threat. The high cost of tickets, a record high $4 to $5, only exacerbated the hippies' and Yippies' anger. *Variety* wrote, "Hippies, yippies and others think the film makers somehow stole their movement and are keeping [it] captive in a film can." The article went on to describe how the protests were having their desired effect of keeping patrons away from the theater (*Variety,* June 17, 1970).

The underground press felt conflicted over the much-needed revenue from carrying the studio's advertising for the film in their papers and their desire not to support the studio's profit-mongering at the counterculture's expense. Some ran the ads but simultaneously made their outrage over ticket prices known. Others, like the *Kaleidoscope* in Madison, Wisconsin, urged their readers not to go see the film. As Aniko Bodroghkozy has pointed out, "The theaters playing the film frequently served as the tangible evidence of how the process of youth culture exploitation was working" (Bodroghkozy, 54). Many of the targets of campus protests at this time were simply too abstract, like the "military-industrial complex." Local theaters, on the other hand, offered a concrete target of protest.

was also the most thoroughly isolated from current events. The sitcom remained almost completely aloof to the race riots raging in American cities and the war being fought in Vietnam. As David Marc puts it: "The term 'escapism' has long been used by critics to categorize works of popular art. But during the sixties, faced with more cultural ambiguity than the genre dared handle, the sitcom went into what might be called a period of 'deep escapism'" (Marc, 106).

Some of the most popular situation comedies of this era were simply set in the context of fantasy: *Mr. Ed* with a talking horse as the show's main character, *Bewitched* with housewife-witch Samantha Stevens; *The Munsters* and *The Addams Family,* two shows about ghoulish families living their own version of "normal" life in middle-class America; *My Favorite Martian* about a young bachelor taking in a displaced extraterrestrial; and *I Dream of Jeanie* about an astronaut stumbling across a genie in a bottle.

Bewitched, maybe one of the best examples of this era's "magicom," became one of television's all-time hits, finishing among the top 12 prime-time series during its first five seasons. It also offers a good example of how situation comedies softened the hard edges of the real world. With regard to the counterculture, *Bewitched* used Serena, Samantha's cousin, as a stereotypical 1960s hippie. Elizabeth Montgomery played both Samantha, the noble suburban housewife, and Serena, Samantha's free-spirited, miniskirt-wearing alter ego. Serena is typical of the sitcom's treatment of the counterculture. Like the hippies that occasionally showed up in other sitcoms like *The Beverly Hillbillies* or *Gilligan's Island,* Cousin Serena was portrayed as silly, impractical, but ultimately harmless, thus depoliticizing the alternative lifestyle of the counterculture.

It seems as if the producers of these situation comedies effectively tapped into an alternative universe free of the fears that accompanied the nation's confrontations with war, racism, drugs, and poverty. By turning members of the counterculture into caricatures, they downplayed any serious threat that this alternative lifestyle posed to suburban middle-class values and life.

Rolling Stone Magazine

Rolling Stone magazine took some of the sensibility of the underground press and brought it above ground to a mass audience. Jann Wenner, a 21-year-old former Berkeley student who worked on *Ramparts,* the Bay Area Catholic reform magazine turned radical muckraker, started the magazine to celebrate rock 'n roll music. He viewed the new publication as an alternative to both the politics of the mainstream media and the radical underground press. "The bankruptcy of both sides was what I was seeing," Wenner recalled. "There must be a better way out, and rock 'n roll is it."

First published in November 1967, *Rolling Stone* was a for-profit publication that looked cleaner, glossier, and more professional. Wenner kept it out of the

Underground Press Syndicate, opting to publish a magazine with professional standards about primarily rock 'n roll. He had an affinity for the counterculture, but he rejected the most radical forms of the movement. For example, he rejected the antics of the Yippies, believing that Hoffman and Rubin did more harm than good for the cause of a movement searching for an alternative to a morally corrupt political and social system. "A self-appointed coterie of political 'radicals' without a legitimate constituency," Wenner wrote in the May 11, 1968, issue. He declared them "as corrupt as the political machine it hopes to disrupt." "Rock and roll," he continued, "is the *only* way in which the vast but formless power of youth is structured" (Peck, 107).

Like many young people of the time, Wenner believed that the music of that era was powerful enough to change society, and that the politics of either side were corrupt or impossible to implement. "There were three people who were Yippies, except the newspapers were so dumb they were making like this was some big movement," Wenner later said. "Their whole existence depended on the coverage they were getting. The only way they were going to get people to Chicago for the Convention was to claim it was a rock 'n roll event. . . . So we took the lead in calling the bullshit. . . . I thought Abbie and Rubin's activities were extremely destructive, and I was right." For his part, Hoffman called Wenner "The Benedict Arnold of the sixties" (Peck, 107–108).

Drawing up on the New Journalism of the era, publishing work by "gonzo journalists" and critics such as Hunter S. Thompson who were notorious for interjecting themselves into the stories they were covering, *Rolling Stone* started small, selling only 6,000 copies of its first press run of 40,000, but it later became the most successful popular music magazine in the world.

HIP, SEXY, AND DANGEROUS

The counterculture gained thousands of adherents and increased media coverage throughout 1967. This was the year that "hippies" became a part of the nation's consciousness. It all started at the world's first "Human Be-In" at Golden Gate Park in San Francisco on January 14, 1967, a date set by an astrologer as the birthdate of the Age of Aquarius. Roughly 25,000 people responded to the call for "Berkeley activists and the love generation of the Haight-Ashbury" to join with "members of the new nation who will be coming from every state in the nation, every tribe of the young to powwow, celebrate, and prophesy the epoch of liberation, love, peace, compassion, and unity of mankind" (McWilliams, 72). The throng that gathered to celebrate came to do little more than follow Timothy Leary's advice to "tune in, turn on, and drop out." They listened to Allen Ginsberg read poetry and the Jefferson Airplane and Grateful Dead play music while the Diggers, a core group of hippies most committed to creating a counterculture

Allen Ginsberg at the "Human Be-In" in San Francisco, California, in January 1967.
(Karl Sterne)

in Haight-Ashbury, passed out sandwiches and acid. Despite shocking many
with this psychedelic picnic, the hippies not only maintained the peace during
the Be-In, but also cleaned up afterward. Reporters and photojournalists also
congregated at the park to analyze and record these radicals dropping out of
society.

By the end of the decade, the counterculture began to die of its own excesses.
A reaction to the hypocrisies of capitalism, politics, and religion, the counterculture started to disintegrate when it began to mirror the culture it supposedly
rejected. In time, the young proved to be as committed to materialism, power,
and violence as their parents' generation. While they condemned America's militarism and the Vietnam War, the avant-garde increasingly found itself admiring
violent revolutionaries and using hateful and violent rhetoric to promote their
opposition to the mainstream. They decried the immediate gratification of consumerism, yet they embraced the immediate gratification of the sexual revolution.
They mocked the mindless deference to political, corporate, and religious authority, yet thoughtlessly followed their own dubious rock stars and charismatic
leaders. The events of 1969 in particular revealed the extent of the counterculture's hypocrisy, causing a serious backlash among America's "silent majority."

The White Panther Party

The White Panther Party (WPP) of Detroit and Ann Arbor, Michigan, was a radical counterculture group that became a focus of FBI investigations in the late 1960s and early 1970s. Unlike a large segment of the counterculture movement, the WPP was a professedly political organization dedicated to confrontation and a total assault on mainstream American culture. Largely the creation of John Sinclair, the WPP, formed in November 1968, was the political wing of Sinclair's Trans-Love Energies (TLE), an attempted union of counterculture, student, and other alternative groups in Detroit. The selection of the name, White Panther Party, intentionally demonstrated a close identification with the Black Panthers.

The organization's "ten-point program" displayed a mixture of counterculture themes and Yippie-type politics. The platform included such things as full endorsement of the Black Panthers' program; a "total assault on the culture by any means necessary, including rock and roll, dope, and fucking in the streets"; free food, clothes, housing, drugs, music, bodies, and medical care; and freedom from "phony" leaders.

Like the Yippies, the WPP attempted to co-opt the mainstream commercial media. Just as the Yippies Festival of Life in Chicago garnered international press coverage, Sinclair hoped to attract young people to the WPP with both conventional and alternative media coverage. As a result, their press releases were intentionally sensational in hopes of attracting a variety of media outlets. The rock band MC5 served as the more visible promoter of the WPP. In the fall of 1968, Elektra Records signed the band to record a "live" album at the Grande Ballroom in Detroit. Elektra's young publicity director, Danny Fields, recognized the potential commercial value of rebellious youth. MC5's debut album, "Kick Out the Jams," as well as a 45-rpm single were released in early 1969 and immediately entered the Billboard Hot 100. *Rolling Stone* magazine even put the group's lead vocalist, Rob Tyner, on its January 4, 1969, cover.

The formation of the WPP coincided with Richard Nixon's election and an atmosphere of governmental paranoia. As a result, the FBI initiated COINTELPRO (a nationwide secret counterintelligence initiative) designed to disrupt the New Left and counterculture groups. As the WPP presented their predictions of a pending revolution in increasingly militant terms, the organization came under the scrutiny of both state and federal law enforcement agencies. The FBI's interest in the WPP increased after the so-called Ann Arbor riots of June 16–18, 1969, which featured three days of battles between rock-throwing hippies and riot police. FBI Director J. Edgar Hoover had been incensed by the "filthy" and "obscene" lyrics of MC5 (which lost its record deal with Elektra in the spring of 1969 after the group encouraged its fans to kick in the doors of stores that refused to carry its album) and believed the presence of White Panthers at the Ann Arbor riots provided sufficient proof that they had organized the revolt.

On July 28, 1969, Sinclair was sentenced to nine-and-a-half to ten years in prison after his third marijuana offense. Sinclair's incarceration severely impacted the WPP. On October 7, 1969, a federal grand jury in Detroit indicted Sinclair, fellow charismatic leader Pun Plamondon, and Detroit WPP chapter member Jack Forrest on conspiracy charges stemming from the September 29, 1968, CIA office bombing in Ann Arbor. The U.S. Attorney had to wait more than a year to start the trial because Plamondon went underground to elude capture. With Plamondon living underground, the WPP's myth reached its peak. As Plamondon wrote inflammatory articles from the underground, Nixon looked to make examples of as many radical groups as possible. Abandoned by the MC5, who moved away from the WPP to make less revolutionary music, the organization faced a financial crisis. The WPP joined with the Yippies to start a "Free John" movement and convinced noted Chicago conspiracy trial lawyers William Kunstler and Leonard Weinglass to work with the Detroit National Lawyers Guild to defend the White Panthers.

Michigan state police captured Plamondon during the summer of 1970 near Cheboygan, Michigan. Hoover declared the WPP one of the most dangerous militant organizations in America in the wake of Plamondon's arrest. Nixon used the myth of the revolutionary White Panthers leading up to the mid-term 1970 congressional elections in an attempt to overturn Democratic majorities in both Houses. Like the Black Panthers and Charles Manson, the WPP became fodder for conservatives trying to stem the tide of radicalism in America.

The case against the WPP leaders was ultimately dropped in 1972 after the U.S. Supreme Court ruled against Nixon's attorney general, John N. Mitchell, that the president possessed the "inherent constitutional power" to wiretap "domestic radicals" without a court order. Freed from prison, Sinclair and Plamondon returned to Ann Arbor to organize the Rainbow People's Party, a non-militant, grassroots organization that attempted to bring the New Left into mainstream politics (Hale, 125–151).

Haight-Ashbury and the Diggers

Like the East Village in New York, the Haight-Ashbury district in San Francisco became the place to be for new bohemians by the mid-1960s. Lower rents, a less commercialized atmosphere than communities on the beach, and close proximity to Golden Gate Park, made Haight-Ashbury, a former Beat enclave, a place for "serious writers, painters and musicians, civil rights workers, crusaders for all kinds of causes, homosexuals, lesbians, marijuana users . . . and the outer fringe of the outer fringe—the 'hippies'" (*San Francisco Examiner* article quoted in Farber and Bailey, 144). Like the East Village, Haight-Ashbury contained a multiethnic blend of residents, coffeehouses, and boutiques that made it a culturally rich place to hang out. Before long, Haight-Ashbury became the epicenter of the 1960s counterculture. By 1966, the district became known as a psychedelic drug center and the home of hippies dedicated to making their LSD trips an everyday occurrence. "Head" shops, a psychedelic newspaper, *The Oracle,* and the Diggers, a loosely organized group of free-form artists and rebels, contributed to a lively cultural experience.

The Diggers, named for 17th-century utopian English farmers who raised food for the poor, formed a street-theatre group called the Mime Troupe, renounced capitalism, and declared money lust a sickness. They asserted that almost all were exposed to the disease of money in childhood, "but dope and love are curing us." They organized a "Death of Money" parade, burned money, staged free concerts, provided free shelter, and operated a Free Store that gave away clothing. Every day at 4:00 p.m. they distributed free food for those in need. All one needed to do to get the food was pass through a thirteen-foot-square yellow "Free Frame of Reference," a symbolic threshold that separated the way things are from the way things could be (McWilliams, 69–70).

A 1967 *New York Times* article described Haight-Ashbury as the "hippie capital" and the hippies as a group of young people who stand "for nothing." Quite simply, "hippies like LSD, marijuana, nude parties, sex, drawing on the walls and sidewalks, not paying their rent, making noise, and rock 'n roll music." The hardcore hippies, the story went on, even established a "survival school" that taught hippies how to live without money. The story concluded, "While the hippies insist they love just about everyone, nobody here loves the hippies. But they have become a tourist attraction, and traffic jams are not uncommon in Haight-Ashbury as people drive slowly through the area gawking at the hippies, who have, for example, put dimes in the parking meters and lain in the parking space on the street" (*New York Times,* May 5, 1967).

In 1967, Haight-Ashbury attracted as many as 75,000 young people, many lured by media coverage like the *New York Times* story. By 1969, however, most of the original members of this alternative community had left the area, driven out by thousands of runaway teenagers, emotionally disturbed people, and criminals attracted to the district's reputation for promiscuous sex and drug use.

Summer of Love

In June 1967, more than 50,000 came to hear the music of the hippie generation at the Monterey International Pop Festival about 100 miles south of San Francisco. They listened to such artists as Big Brother and the Holding Company, the Grateful Dead, Country Joe and the Fish, the Mamas and the Papas, the Who, the Byrds, Otis Redding, Jimi Hendrix, and Janis Joplin. This kicked off what became known as the "Summer of Love" where thousands of America's youth made a "pilgrimage" to San Francisco upon the invitation of Haight-Ashbury's

Council for a Summer of Love and drawn by the intense media coverage of the district since the "Human Be-In" in January.

Hippies from across the land came for "free love," drugs, and a chance to build a new community of young people. As Joan Didion wrote, "We were seeing the desperate attempt of a handful of pathetically unequipped children to create a community in a social vacuum" (quoted in McWilliams, 70). Unfortunately, many of those arriving were ill-equipped to handle the task at hand. Businesses catering to the hip thrived, but so too did rape, disease, exploitation, violence, and bad drug trips. On October 6, 1967, disillusioned by the rise in crime, drug abuse, and unwanted media attention, the Diggers staged a "Death of Hip" ceremony that included a frolicsome funeral procession through Golden Gate Park. The "corpse" they carried in a gray box labeled "Summer of Love" clutched a zinnia, a symbol of death for the flower children. Yet the numbers of young people calling themselves hippies and seeking a countercultural experience continued to grow.

The Youth International Party: The Yippies

Founded by Abbie Hoffman, Anita Hoffman, Jerry Rubin, Nancy Kurshan, and Paul Krassner in December 1967, the Youth International Party (Yippies) integrated theatre of the absurd, political activism, and the ethos of the counter-culture movement to gain national attention through loosely choreographed events and protests in 1968. The Yippies began publishing in the underground press that "rebels, youth spirits, rock minstrels, truth seekers, peacock freaks, poets, barricade jumpers, dancers, lovers, [and] artisans" should come to participate in their Festival of Life in Chicago during the 1968 Democratic National Convention. For the Yippies, this festival served as an antidote to the Democrats' "Convention of Death" (Farber and Bailey, 258).

Abbie Hoffman and Jerry Rubin were the inspiration and force behind the farcical evolution and demise of the Yippies. A little older and more educated than the average hippie, Hoffman and Rubin used the Yippies to attract the freedom-loving youth of the counterculture movement to the more ideologically based campaign to end the war in Vietnam. Hoffman had earned his master's degree in psychology from the University of California–Berkeley in 1959. He became a political activist in the 1950s at Berkeley and participated in the Student Nonviolent Coordinating Committee's Freedom Summers in Mississippi in 1964 and 1965. In 1967, he became involved in the antiwar movement. By the mid-1960s he had also begun experimenting with drugs and became an enthusiastic member of the counterculture. He earned a reputation for outlandish acts and exploiting mass media to make political points. He helped organize "be-ins" in New York's Central Park, sent 3,000 marijuana cigarettes with instructions on how to smoke them to people he randomly selected from the telephone book, and appeared on the *Merv Griffin Show* wearing an American flag shirt that offended the network censors so much they decided to black out Hoffman's half of the television screen.

Rubin earned his Ph.D. in sociology at Berkeley in 1964. While in school, Rubin was active in the Free Speech Movement and led teach-ins to protest the war in Vietnam. Rubin once appeared before the House Un-American Activities Committee dressed as a soldier from the American Revolution. He also ran for mayor of Berkeley while steadfastly protesting the war. Hoffman and Rubin met in 1967 at a Washington, D.C., antiwar protest where they tried to levitate the Pentagon and exorcise its evil spirits. That December, along with the previously mentioned cofounders, they formed Yippie! The aim of the group was to use street theatre and media manipulation to develop a political consciousness among the growing number of hippies. In short, it sought to blend countercultural freedoms with New Left politics. The "Yippie Manifesto" captured the shock tactics employed by Hoffman and Rubin in their efforts to start a revolution:

Come into the streets on Nov. 5, election day. Vote with your feet. Rise up and abandon the creeping meatball! Demand the bars be open. Make music and dance at every red light. A festival of life in the streets and parks throughout the world. The Amercan election represents death, and we are alive.

Come all you rebels, youth spirits, rock minstrels, bomb throwers, bank robbers, peacock freaks, toe worshippers, poets, street folk, liberated women, professors and body snatchers: it is election day and we are everywhere.

Don't vote in a jackass-elephant-cracker circus. Let's vote for ourselves. Me for President. We are the revolution. We will strike and boycott the election and create our own reality.

Can you dig it: in every metropolis and hamlet of America boycotts, strikes, sit-ins, pickets, lie-ins, pray-ins, feel-ins, piss-ins at the polling places.

Nobody goes to work. Nobody goes to school. Nobody votes. Everyone becomes a life actor of the street doing this thing, making the revolution by freeing himself and fucking up the system . . .

Release a Black Panther in the Justice Department. Hold motorcycle races a hundred yards from the polling places. Fly an American flag out of every house so confused voters can't find the polling places. Wear costumes. Take a burning draft card to Spiro Agnew.

Stall for hours in the polling places trying to decide between Nixon and Humphrey and Wallace. Take your clothes off. Put wall posters up all over the city. Hold black parties. Release hundreds of greased pigs in pig uniforms downtown . . .

Begin now: resist oppression as you feel it. Organize and begin the word of mouth communication that is the basis of all conspiracies . . .

> Every man a revolution! Every small group a revolutionary center! We
> will be together on election day. Yippie!!! (Bloom and Breines, 323–24)

Most famously, Hoffman and Rubin brought the Yippie movement to Chicago
during the Democratic National Convention to stage their "Festival of Life."
Chicago's Mayor Richard J. Daley refused to give the Yippies any permits for
their festival held at Lincoln Park. Young people participating in the festival were
attacked by city police on Mayor Daley's orders. The attack on the Yippies, hippies, and antiwar protesters in Lincoln Park, replete with tear gas, played out
before a national television audience during prime-time coverage of the convention. After Nixon took office in 1969, Hoffman, Rubin, and six other radical
activists were charged with conspiracy to incite a riot for their Chicago protests.
After a lengthy and highly publicized trial and appeal process, the Chicago
Seven (Bobby Seale was tried separately) were acquitted of all major charges
against them.

The Underground Press

The underground press played a major role in the rise of both the antiwar and
counterculture movements. Originating from college campuses embroiled in
social, cultural, and political unrest throughout the country, the underground
press took an antiestablishment view and was consistently critical of the status
quo. In addition to reflecting a view of the world that appealed to young people at the time, the underground press became a popular means of communication among various groups associated with the antiwar and counterculture
movements.

In May 1964, the *Los Angeles Free Press* became the first underground paper
to publish on a sustained basis. By 1968 the *Free Press* had a circulation of
100,000, 150 employees, and a $2 million budget (Ostertag, 120). It and the un-
derground presses that followed offered stories from a dramatically different
perspective than the mainstream press. By 1967, 20 or so black-and-white or
four-color underground papers were being published in the United States via
cheap offset-press technology and a labor pool of mostly current and former
college students. Underground papers, arguably a forerunner to today's Internet
blogs, ran news about protests and demonstrations alongside rock reviews and
The Fabulous Furry Freak Brothers, a comic about three amiable pot-smoking
dudes. The underground papers ran advertisements for rolling paper and LPs
as they criticized the crass materialism of capitalism.

As Abe Peck described them, underground papers used "fledgling, brash underground reporters [who] often lacked skill, and evidence for their conclusions.
Their stories could be self-indulgent, even incomprehensible, and could trample
the tenets of accuracy and fairness. But they knew that some issues do not have
two equally valid sides, and they accepted dissent, experimentation, popular

culture, the breaking of class, race, and national boundaries." By 1969, the apex of the underground press movement, over 500 papers served constituencies worldwide, with 500 to 1,000 more alternative papers in high schools. Besides the *Los Angeles Free Press,* papers like San Francisco's *Oracle* served the Bay region's hippie population while Berkeley's *Barb* angrily communicated to the area's antiwar activists; New York's *Rat* covered and supported the Columbia University student strike of 1968; and the *Seed* reached the growing population of young people experimenting with psychedelic drugs (Peck, xv–xvi).

An extremely loose organization of underground newspapers formed in 1967, called the Underground Press Syndicate, that allowed member papers to reprint each other's material and shared information through a newsletter, the *Free Ranger Intertribal News Service.* Differing agendas created tensions within the organization, and more politically oriented members broke away to form the Liberation News Service (LNS), which itself would break apart within a year. However, in 1969 the LNS served 600 regular subscribers and sent packets of articles to 400 underground, peace, and college newspapers (Ostertag, 120).

San Francisco Mime Troupe and Guerrilla Theatre

Founded by Ronald Guy Davis in 1959, the San Francisco Mime Troupe exemplified a more political strand of the counterculture movement. Davis, a noted figure in the Berkeley Free Speech Movement who was arrested in a San Francisco park in August of 1965 for performing a so-called obscene version of an Italian farce, organized a group of actors who introduced "Guerrilla Theatre" as a tactic against the war in Vietnam. Audiences came to watch the company of actors assuming that they would be watching some variation of the silent white-face routines made famous by Marcel Marceau. The San Francisco Mime Troupe, however, presented an extremely verbal mode of acting that was overtly physical and comic. The Troupe would reconfigure old *commedia dell' arte* plays and stage them as modern farces with running political commentary about racism, capitalism, authoritarianism, and ultimately the Vietnam War.

Davis had long been a part of the San Francisco Bay area progressive scene. But while he embraced many aspects of the burgeoning counterculture movement in the mid-sixties, Davis had become concerned about the apparent contradictions of the hippie life. He felt a tension between the free and easy individualism and egalitarianism of the movement and his pursuit of artistic excellence. His political seriousness, as he later wrote, "made no headway against a tide of long hair, electronic music" and "the democratic notion of amateuristic total participation." He went on to explain,

> The greatest error of the hippie movement is its amateurism, its innocence, and its ignorance. . . . The hippie generation with its acceptance of all with no values, no judgments, is impossible, nay stupid. To attempt to make no

judgments is to deface oneself into a mere potato—just as the style of culture called entertainment does. . . . Where there are no standards or comparisons or judgments, we achieve no style, we receive trash called art, superficiality called inspiration.

Davis contemplated the philosophical question that dogged the counterculture throughout the decade: Where did the unfettered individualism of the hippie movement take you? Davis believed that mainstream American culture lived in a dark haze; those in the counterculture who "dropped out" of society, he feared, were only different in style, not substance. He believed that superior talent and intellect had to engage the world, not drop out. Davis aimed for the San Francisco Mime Troupe to be the best alternative theater company around. Davis wanted the mime troupe "to work at a presentation that talks to a community of people that expresses what you (as a community) all know but what no one is saying: thoughts, images, observations, discoveries that are not printed in newspapers nor made into movies: truth that may be shocking and honesty that is vulgar to the aesthete."

Davis and the San Francisco Mime Troupe took off for a national tour of mostly college campuses during the fall of 1967, after the Summer of Love and amid the rise of the antiwar movement. Davis and his troupe represented the growing tension between the apolitical and political factions of the counterculture (Maraniss, 166–170).

Communes

Communitarian idealism exploded in the mid-1960s. Hundreds of thousands of mostly young people looked to escape from what they perceived to be a decadent and irreparable society in order to rebuild new societies in a wide variety of communes all over the country. The stereotype of the 1960s counterculture hip communes is one of spontaneity, anarchy, rampant drug use, and unconventional sexual relationships. While there were certainly elements of these characteristics at several hip communes, the signature of 1960s collective-living arrangements was its diversity. The thousands of intentional communities that sprung up in the sixties included Asian religious ashrams, group marriage experiments, communal rock bands, "Jesus freak" houses, centers of radical politics, and back-to-the-land experiments in agricultural self-sufficiency. While there is no way to know the number of communes during this era of social and cultural experimentation, they probably ran to tens of thousands.

Sixties-era communes had their roots in the American radical and communal past. In fact, many of the communards of the sixties grew up in families of 1930s and 1940s socialists and communists who already knew the vocabulary and spirit of cooperation and shared ownership. The pages of *The Modern Utopian*, the trade journal of the 1960s communes, regularly ran stories on earlier American communitarianism, and several communards intentionally imitated 19th-century radical social reform communities.

Ken Kesey's Merry Pranksters represented an early outburst of the new communal spirit at the turn of the decade. By 1962, a bohemian encampment called Gorda Mountain began to take shape after Amelia Newell opened her land near Big Sur, California, to anyone who wanted to stay there. This invitation ushered in the new era of the open-land experiment of the communal sixties. A year later, Huw "Piper" Williams established Tolstoy Farm near Davenport, Washington. A Quaker and peace activist, Williams established an intentional community of radical pacifists. Still in existence at the end of the 20th century, Tolstoy Farm could possibly be the oldest surviving sixties commune.

These early experiments in sixties communal living came of age with the founding of Drop City near Trinidad, Colorado, in May 1965. Drop City incorporated most of the themes and characteristics of sixties communal living: anarchy, pacifism, voluntary poverty, sexual freedom, rural isolation, psychedelics, and art. One of the founders, Jo Ann Bernofsky, articulated the boldness of their experiment in this way:

> There was this kind of heady arrogance . . . that we could just do something so outrageous and so far out, that we could pull it off even though none of us had many resources. . . . It was full of vitality, and it was extremely exciting and wonderful. (Miller, 88)

Bernofsky captured the underlying conviction of many communards that modern society had become so materially productive that real scarcity was no more; that you could drop out of society and live off the leftovers of the affluent.

This new wave of communes took another leap in 1966 when several people started moving into Lou Gottlieb's Morning Star Ranch an hour and a half outside San Francisco. Gottlieb, a well-known bassist for the Limeliters, a popular folk-music trio, opened up his 31 acres to all who would come. Convinced that land could not be "owned" by any mortal human but only exist as the common possession of all, Gottlieb deeded the land to God and preached his doctrine of "open land." What ensued was the highly controversial commune that embraced nudity, free love, and psychedelic experimentation. After lengthy court battles, the Sonoma County authorities managed to shut down Morning Star in the early seventies.

From 1967 until the early 1970s, the rise of communal living across the country exploded. The motivations for moving to communes were many: some wanted to escape the city for a more peaceful rural environment, especially with the decline of hip neighborhoods in New York, San Francisco, and other cities after the 1967 Summer of Love; political activists wanted to create a practical base for social causes; religious adherents wanted to pursue the life of the spirit and live with like-minded believers; Woodstock and other rock festivals caused some to believe that those temporary experiences could be made permanent.

Residents share a meal together in a large communal cooking area inside "Drop City," an experimental, countercultural community based around cheaply constructed geodesic dome structures, Trinidad, Colorado, 1967. (Carl Iwasaki/Time & Life Pictures/Getty Images)

Whatever the causes, thousands upon thousands of communes were established between 1967 and 1975.

Rural hip communes certainly got the bulk of media attention during this time. Their colorfulness and counterculture lifestyle centered on sex, drugs, and rock-and-roll certainly made for a far more interesting story than their more spiritual, political, or environmental counterparts. In reality, these hip communes were greatly outnumbered by thousands of religious and spiritual centers and communes for social change. Such communes ran the gamut of social, religious, and political thought. Probably the most numerous of the new Christian communes were those of the Jesus movement, populated by so-called Jesus freaks who took on the appearance and trappings of hippies while espousing a Christian message.

Most of the young people joining communes in the sixties shared the feeling that the United States had lost its way; instead of championing freedom, it had become an oppressor—a belief confirmed by the outrageously immoral behavior exhibited in the execution of the intractable war in Vietnam. Communitarians rejected a system they saw increasingly dominated by the values of greed, materialism, and individualism. They no longer wanted to live in a society obsessed with self-interest; rather, they wanted to live among people committed to the advancement of the common good.

While most communes regarded themselves as tolerant and inclusive, the vast majority was relatively homogeneous. Racially they were overwhelmingly white.

The likely explanation is that sixties communes tended to be populated by people trying to divest themselves of material goods and a bourgeois lifestyle. Disproportionately poor, nonwhites had no interest in the voluntary poverty of the counterculture. Instead, they were searching for greater material wealth. Despite the homogeneity of most communes, their openness attracted several eccentrics and misfits into the fold. Down-and-outers and the mentally ill would find their way to some communes, often driving away some of the more productive and well-balanced members.

For the most part, communes established in the sixties could not be sustained beyond the mid-1970s. By then, the assumption that the age of scarcity was past proved to be wrong. As the war in Vietnam ended, group-centered idealism gave way to the self-interested pursuit of wealth many communitarians had rejected. Over time many communards realized their idealism would not change the world, and that the communes they established ultimately exhibited many of the same ills they observed in the broader society (Miller, 327–349).

Charles Manson and "The Family"

Charles Manson, a sociopath and lifelong criminal, ordered followers he called his "Family" to commit the most infamous murders of the 1960s. One night in August 1969, Manson's "family" sadistically murdered actress Sharon Tate, eight-month-pregnant wife of movie director Roman Polanski, and four of her friends in the secluded Bel Air district of Los Angeles. Other victims included Jay Sebring, a men's hair stylist well known in Hollywood social circles, Voyteck Frykowski, a Polish film director and close friend of Polanski, and Abigail Folger, a member of the Folger coffee family. The victims' mutilated bodies were stabbed 102 times. They left bloody clues like the word "PIG" scrawled in blood on a wall and the word "WAR" carved in one victim's stomach. The following night they slaughtered two members of the wealthy LaBianca family in another expensive Los Angeles suburb, stabbing them fifty-seven times.

Not until December 1, 1969, did police start arresting obscure hippies after one member of Manson's Family, Susan Atkins, started giving several cloudy versions of what happened. Manson was ultimately indicted for murder. Living with about eighteen members of the Family at the Spahn Ranch, a dilapidated riding stable whose Western-style buildings were sometimes used as a movie set, Manson emerged as a strange, hypnotic, and dangerous leader of a cult comprised mostly of teenage girls. A neglected child who became a juvenile delinquent, Manson began compiling a criminal record after a 1960 conviction for forgery. After spending seven years in the penitentiary, he blended into San Francisco's hippie underground during the 1967 Summer of Love and started attracting a harem of young girls. Like other members of the counterculture, he believed in free love, dope, rock music, and mysticism. During this time he unsuccessfully tried to break into the music industry.

Manson thought of himself as a reincarnation of Satan and Christ combined, and he used LSD as a means of mind control over his followers. Although he believed in "free love" in a sexual sense, he preached a doctrine of hatred, claiming that the country was on the verge of a race war between African Americans and whites. Using the code words "helter skelter" from a Beatles' song that he believed contained a hidden message about the upcoming race war, Manson led his followers, aimless drifters who mostly came from middle-class families, to Los Angeles where they set up a commune at the Spahn Ranch and planned the series of infamous murders.

The subsequent trial became a media circus like the so-called Chicago Seven trial after the events of the Democratic National Convention of 1968. The trial lasted for nearly a year, marked by a series of bizarre events, but ultimately Manson received a life sentence for planning and directing the murders even though he actually did not commit any of them. The media coverage of the trial led many Americans to attribute the savage murders to the values and ethics of the counterculture, intensifying middle-class Americans' suspicions and paranoia. Most hippies were not senseless killers, of course, but the establishment saw Manson, a deranged proponent of free love, drugs, and rock-and-roll, and the ritualistic killings as confirmation of their worst fears about the counterculture. The media reinforced this image by referring to Manson as "the hypnotic hippie" and reminding the public of his connection to the antiestablishment culture of Haight-Ashbury. Some radicals, like Students for a Democratic Society activist Bernadine Dohrn, furthered this association by commenting on the murders in dubious terms: "Dig it, first they killed those pigs, then they ate dinner in the same room with them, and they even shoved a fork into the victim's stomach! Wild!" (McWilliams, 37).

Even members of the counterculture questioned what the murders said about the excesses of their movement. The counterculture tended toward extremes, and the Manson Family revealed the dark side of those extremes where victims and victimizers co-existed. Many historians and critics believe that these murders and media attention on the subsequent trial, along with other notorious events like the Altamont Rock Festival, helped bring an end to the counterculture movement of the sixties.

THE COUNTERCULTURE'S UNSUSTAINABILITY

The counterculture was a mass movement comprised mostly of young Americans who began to see the possibilities of new and expanded thinking beyond merely the political and into the realm of how they lived their lives. Though not primarily a political movement, counterculture adherents hoped that a transformation in American life would also change American politics. For the counterculture, rock music served as the anthem for the foray into alternative lifestyles that often included drugs, sex, communal living, egalitarianism, and individualism. In the words of John Sinclair, manager of the Detroit political rockers MC5, rock 'n roll became "a weapon of cultural revolution." For Sinclair and others, music and drugs offered a way for people to break free from the "monstrous funeral parlor of western civilization" and live life free from the shackles of money and ego (Bloom and Breines, 243–244).

The counterculture essentially subscribed to the principles of hedonism. Sex, drugs, and rock-and-roll offered a way for young people to experience their lives through their senses and feel good. Hence the counterculture's slogan: "If it feels good, do it." They believed that capitalism had brainwashed people into unthinkingly accepting the tenets of greed, competition, militarism, and social conformity. Reflecting the anxiety and frustration of the Vietnam War era, the counterculture expressed a desire to start over on principles antithetical to a Protestant work ethic and market-driven society.

Linked to other more explicitly political elements of sixties life such as the antiwar movement, the counterculture proved to be naïve, radical, and utopian. As a result, it could not be sustained. However, its concerns over the environment, discovering personal fulfillment in a materially based culture, and America's role in the world as an economic and military superpower have remained deeply rooted concerns about American life ever since. In the end, youthful self-indulgence trumped revolutionary zeal and caused the counterculture to be a subject of derision and ridicule by politicians and the media. But beneath some of the silliness of the movement rested a deeply philosophical question about how Americans should live their lives.

BIOGRAPHIES

Joan Baez, 1941–

Folk Singer

Born in New York, Joan Baez moved with her parents to Palo Alto, California, in the early 1950s. Sensitized to racism as a result of the taunts she received because of the dark skin she inherited from her Mexican father, Baez participated in the civil rights movement at an early age. Her pacifism also came from her father, a Quaker whose belief in nonviolence motivated him to quit a lucrative job in the defense industry. After Joan graduated from high school in 1958, the family moved back East where Joan's father, a physicist, taught at Harvard and the Massachusetts Institute of Technology. Baez dropped out of Boston Univer-

Bob Dylan and Joan Baez sing at the 1963 March on Washington. The pair were again featured in D. A. Pennebaker's 1967 documentary, Don't Look Back. *(National Archives)*

sity's School of Fine and Applied Arts and began singing in coffeehouses in nearby Cambridge. By 1959 she had obtained a national following, bolstered by an appearance in front of 13,000 people at the Newport Folk Festival in Rhode Island. In 1961 she signed a record contract and released her first album, *Joan Baez.* She then toured the country with fellow folk artist Bob Dylan, performing for crowds up to 20,000 people.

Baez entered the consciousness of mainstream America in November 1962 when she became the subject of a *Time* magazine cover story as a representative of the country's folk-music revival. Baez often led civil rights and later antiwar protesters in singing motivational songs at public demonstrations. Baez refused to sing on ABC's new show *Hootenanny* in 1963 when the network refused to allow her hero and activist Pete Seeger to appear. Later that year she stirred 200,000 people when she led them in "We Shall Overcome" at the March on Washington on August 28, 1963.

To protest the Vietnam War, she informed the Internal Revenue Service (IRS) she would withhold 60 percent of the federal income taxes she owed. As a result, the IRS filed a $50,182 lien against her in 1964. In 1966, Baez and 55 other people filed a suit against the IRS for refunds of those portions of their 1965 and

1966 income taxes that were used for military purposes. Baez personally asked for a refund of $36,528.37 from her 1965 taxes.

Baez opened a school to teach techniques of nonviolence, including sit-ins and picket lines, in Carmel, California. She also performed at the Students for a Democratic Society's March on Washington to End the War in Vietnam on April 17, 1965, to a surprisingly large crowd of 25,000 people. In October and December 1967, she was arrested and jailed for participating in a sit-in outside the draft induction center in Oakland. While demonstrating against the draft, she helped finance the Resistance, an organization founded by David Harris, whom she married in 1968 and divorced three years later. To encourage males to resist the draft, some pacifists used a poster featuring Baez that read, "Girls say yes to guys who say no." As an act of protest against the war, she later recorded an album in Hanoi in 1972 while American planes bombed the city.

Although she remained active in antiwar activities and a prominent spokesperson for the cause, by 1968 she had fallen out of vogue with the younger counterculture movement. While her political activism remained relevant to a college-aged audience, her style of music did not. By the end of the 1960s, Janis Joplin, the hard-drinking, tough-talking dynamic singer with roots in the blues tradition, eclipsed Baez as the iconic female performer of the counterculture.

Herbert Marcuse's critique of capitalism became popular among university students in the United States and abroad during the 1960s. During that decade, Marcuse became known as the "father of the New Left." (Courtesy Marcuse family)

Herbert Marcuse, 1898–1979

Social Theorist

A philosopher, social theorist, and political activist, Herbert Marcuse was the son of upper-class German Jews Carl Marcuse and Gertrud Kreslawsky. Marcuse fought in the German army during World War I. After his service in the military, he went to Freiburg to pursue his studies. Marcuse earned his Ph.D. in literature in 1922 and went back to school in 1928 to study with the philosopher Martin Heidegger. Marcuse became an American citizen in 1940 and worked for the State Department during World War II. In 1955 he published *Eros and Civilization,* which attempted to synthesize Marx and Freud in an effort to outline the vision of a nonrepressive society. Marcuse's idea of a nonrepressive civilization involved libidinal and nonalienated labor, play, free and open sexuality, and production of a society and culture that would further freedom and happiness. His vision of liberation anticipated and influenced many of the values of the 1960s' counterculture, making him a major intellectual force during the decade.

Joe McDonald, 1942–

Antiwar Rocker

Born in 1942 in Washington, D.C., McDonald grew up in El Monte, California, just outside Los Angeles. McDonald's parents fled the nation's capital after World War II because of their leftist politics during the postwar Red Scare. In the early 1960s, McDonald moved to Berkeley, California, to attend school, but instead ended up playing in a number of musical groups around town. Exposed to all forms of music growing up, McDonald joined forces with Barry Melton in 1965 during the Berkeley Free Speech Movement to form the rock bank Country Joe and the Fish. The band played regularly at Berkeley's Jabberwock coffeehouse and at the Avalon and Fillmore Auditorium in San Francisco. In the summer of 1966 they released a three-song extended-play album that got a lot of airplay on Bay Area progressive radio stations and caught the attention of East Coast listeners. As a result, the band signed a contract with Vanguard Records in December 1966. The band's first two albums, *Electric Music* and *I Feel Like I'm Fixin' to Die* were moderately successful as the group toured the college and ballroom circuit around America. They played at the Monterey Pop Festival and introduced a light show to their concerts that offered their audiences a "psychedelic" experience. In 1968 and 1969 Country Joe and the Fish released their third and fourth albums, *Together* and *Here We Are Again.* Although the other members came and went, McDonald and Melton remained fixtures of the band. The band's appearance and performance of "I Feel Like I'm Fixin' to Die Rag" at the Woodstock Festival in upstate New York brought them great notoriety and forever linked the group to the counterculture and antiwar movements.

Carolee Schneeman, 1939–

Performance Artist

Schneeman graduated with a B.A. from Bard College and an M.F.A. from the University of Illinois. She then became a famous performance artist known best for her discourses on the body, sexuality, and gender. A member of the avant-garde of the 1960s, she burst onto the scene in the mid-1960s and became representative of the sexual and gender revolutions. Her most famous works include *Eye Body: 36 Transformative Actions* (1963), *Meat Joy* (1964), and *Interior Scroll* (1975). In 1964 she produced a film, *Fuses,* that incorporated a mixture of collage and painting featuring Schneeman and her boyfriend having sex. Considered pornography by some, *Fuses* is viewed as a "proto-feminist" film that visually challenges tradition and taboos while empowering women to celebrate their sexuality.

John Alexander Sinclair, 1941–

Activist

Born in Flint, Michigan, John Sinclair enjoyed a middle-class childhood in Davison, Michigan, a small town a few miles from Flint. His father worked all of his life for the local Buick plant, starting on the assembly line in 1928 and working his way up to midlevel management positions. Sinclair attended Albion College where he became acquainted with the beatnik culture, becoming a devoted listener to avant-garde jazz and Beat poetry. He also started smoking marijuana, something that had been a part of the urban jazz scene since the 1920s. Like others in the counterculture, Sinclair believed that marijuana heightened his awareness of the world around him, promoted togetherness, and expanded his creativity. He dropped out of Albion after two years and moved back to Flint, where he continued his exploration of African American culture and jazz, frequenting clubs in the town's North Side ghetto. After completing a bachelor's degree at the Flint branch of the University of Michigan in 1964, Sinclair moved to Detroit and enrolled in the graduate school at Wayne State University. Hanging out in beatnik clubs such as the Red Door Gallery, Sinclair came into contact with jazz musicians, poets, and other hipsters. He also met his future wife, Madalene "Leni" Arndt, a photographer from East Germany who had immigrated to Detroit in 1959 and also attended Wayne State. Sinclair, Leni, and their friends began discussing the formation of a new organization for area poets, musicians, and other artists. Soon afterward, the Artists' Workshop was established on the ground floor of a two-story house in Detroit. Every Sunday members would gather for poetry readings, jazz performances, exhibitions of photographs and original art, and screenings of avant-garde films. Sinclair performed in an experimental jazz group known as the DC-4 and Leni began experimenting with photography and filmmaking. The Artists' Workshop flourished and regularly interacted with bohemian communities on the two coasts. After his incarceration for marijuana possession in 1966, Sinclair created the Trans-Love Energies in 1967, an attempted union of counterculture, student, and other alternative groups in Detroit. The Trans-Love Energies' most significant modes of cultural expression became the underground press and the rock band MC5. After the Detroit riots of 1967 and subsequent police reaction, the Trans-Love Energies relocated to Ann Arbor in May 1968 and formed a commune of 28 people, including three children and the members of MC5. Sinclair helped create the White Panther Party as the political wing of the Trans-Love Energies in November 1968.

REFERENCES AND FURTHER READINGS

Bailey, Beth. 2002. "Sex as a Weapon: Underground Comix and the Paradox of Liberation." In *Imagine Nation: The American Counterculture of the 1960s and '70s*. New York: Routledge.

Barsness, John A. 1969. "Ken Kesey: The Hero in Modern Dress." *The Bulletin of the Rocky Mountain Modern Language Association* 23, no. 1: 27–33.

Bloom, Alexander, and Wini Breines. 1995. *Takin' it to the Streets: A Sixties Reader*. New York: Oxford University Press.

Bodroghkozy, Aniko. 2002. "Reel Revolutionaries: An Examination of Hollywood's Cycle of 1960s Youth Rebellion Films." *Cinema Journal* 41: 38–58.

Braunstein, Peter. 2002. "Forever Young: Insurgent Youth and the Sixties Culture of Rejuvenation." In *Imagine Nation: The American Counterculture of the 1960s and '70s*. New York: Routledge.

Brevard, Lisa Pertillar. 2002. *Womansaints: The Saintly Portrayal of Select African-American and Latina Cultural Heroines*. New Orleans: University Press of the South.

Castleman, Harry, and Walter J. Podrazik. 1992. *Watching TV: Four Decades of American Television*. NY: McGraw-Hill.

Chafe, William H. 2003. *The Unfinished Journey: America since World War II*. 5th ed. New York: Oxford University Press.

Chalmers, David. 1996. *And the Crooked Places Made Straight: The Struggle for Social Change in the 1960s*. 2nd ed. Baltimore: Johns Hopkins University Press.

Chenoweth, Lawrence. 1971. "The Rhetoric of Hope and Despair: A Study of the Jimi Hendrix Experience and the Jefferson Airplane." *American Quarterly* 23: 25–45.

Cohen, Allen, ed. 1991. *The San Francisco Oracle: The Psychedelic Newspaper of the Haight-Ashbury, 1966–1968*. Facsimile edition. Berkeley, CA: Regent.

Dickstein, Morris. 1989. *Gates of Eden: American Culture in the Sixties*. New York: Penguin Books.

Digger Archives. http://www.diggers.org.

Doyle, Michael William. 2002. "Staging the Revolution: Guerrilla Theater as a Countercultural Practice, 1965–68." In *Imagine Nation: The American Counterculture of the 1960s and '70s*. New York: Routledge.

Farber, David. 2002. "The Intoxicated State/Illegal Nation: Drugs in the Sixties Counterculture." In *Imagine Nation: The American Counterculture of the 1960s and '70s*. New York: Routledge.

Farber, David, and Beth Bailey. 2001. *The Columbia Guide to America in the 1960s*. New York: Columbia University Press.

Filene, Benjamin. 2000. *Romancing the Folk: Public Memory and American Roots Music*. Chapel Hill: University of North Carolina Press.

Garman, Bryan K. 2000. *A Race of Singers: Whitman's Working-Class Hero from Guthrie to Springsteen*. Chapel Hill: University of North Carolina Press.

Greenfield, Robert. 2006. *Timothy Leary: A Biography*. New York: A James H. Silberman Book/Harcourt.

Hale, Jeff A. 2002. "The White Panthers' 'Total Assault on the Culture.'" In *Imagine Nation: The American Counterculture of the 1960s and '70s*. New York: Routledge.

James, David E. 2002. "The Movies Are a Revolution: Film and the Counterculture." In *Imagine Nation: The American Counterculture of the 1960s and '70s*. New York: Routledge.

Kaiser, Charles. 1988. *1968 in America: Music, Politics, Chaos, Counterculture, and the Shaping of a Generation*. New York: Grove Press.

Laffan, Barry. 1997. *Communal Organization and Social Transition: A Case Study from the Counterculture of the Sixties and Seventies*. New York: P. Lang.

Lee, Martin A., and Bruce Shlain. 1985. *Acid Dreams: The CIA, LSD, and the Sixties Rebellion*. New York: Grove Press.

Loss, Archie K. 1999. *Pop Dreams: Music, Movies, and the Media in the 1960s*. Fort Worth: Harcourt Brace.

Maraniss, David. 2003. *They Marched Into Sunlight: War and Peace, Vietnam and America, October 1967*. New York: Simon and Schuster.

Marc, David. 1989. *Comic Visions: Television Comedy and American Culture*. Malden, MA: Blackwell.

McWilliams, John C. 2000. *The 1960s Cultural Revolution*. Westport, CT: Greenwood.

Michals, Debra. 2002. "From 'Consciousness Expansion' to 'Consciousness Raising': Feminism and the Countercultural Politics of the Self." In *Imagine Nation: The American Counterculture of the 1960s and '70s*. New York: Routledge.

Miller, Timothy. 1991. *The Hippies and American Values*. Knoxville: University of Tennessee Press.

O'Neill, William L. 2005. *Coming Apart: An Informal History of America in the 1960s*. Chicago: Ivan R. Dee.

Onkey, Lauren. 2002. "Voodoo Child: Jimi Hendrix and the Politics of Race in the Sixties." In *Imagine Nation: The American Counterculture of the 1960s and '70s*. New York: Routledge.

Ostertag, Bob. 2006. *People's Movements, People's Press: The Journalism of Social Justice Movements*. Boston: Beacon Press.

Peck, Abe. 1985. *Uncovering the Sixties: The Life and Times of the Underground Press*. New York: Pantheon Books.

Perry, Charles. 1985. *The Haight-Ashbury: A History*. New York: Vintage.

Singleton, Carl, ed. 1999. *The Sixties in America*. Pasadena, CA: Salem Press.

Veysey, Laurence. 1973. *The Communal Experience: Anarchist and Mystical Counter-Culture in America*. New York: Harper and Row.

Young, Marilyn B. Foreword. 2002. In *Imagine Nation: The American Counter-culture of the 1960s and '70s*. New York: Routledge.

Politics of Gender and Sexuality

Overview

President John F. Kennedy's establishment of the President's Commission on the Status of Women signaled the federal government's assumption of a new responsibility with regard to equal treatment for women in the labor force. The establishment of this commission, the enactment of equal pay legislation, and the prohibition of discrimination against women in the federal civil service all occurred, much to President Kennedy's credit, before the start of a widespread feminist movement. President Kennedy's support for these initiatives is all the more remarkable given the fact that attention to equal pay legislation and the Equal Rights Amendment (ERA) actually declined during the previous decade.

Yet some important demographic changes in the workforce during the 1950s set the stage for President Kennedy's action and a subsequent vigorous wave of feminism in the mid- to late 1960s. According to Census reports, the proportion of women who worked for wages rose from 31.4 percent in 1950 to 34.8 percent in 1960. The proportion of married women who were employed outside the home increased from 23.8 percent in 1950 to 30.5 percent in 1960. In 1950, 52.1 percent of women in the labor force were married, but by 1960 the percentage had increased to 59.9. Most significantly, women who had children under the age of six increased their participation in the workforce by 50 percent (Harrison, 631).

The Equal Pay Act, civil service reform, and the establishment of the commission during the Kennedy administration constituted minor successes that helped lead to more meaningful change. The creation of the commission particularly added legitimacy to the fight against discrimination based on sex and initiated a national discussion that continued for the next two decades. As Betty Friedan wrote in *The Feminine Mystique,* "the very existence of the President's Commission on the Status of Women, under Eleanor Roosevelt's leadership, creates a climate where it is possible to recognize and do something about discrimination against women, in terms not only of pay but of the subtle barriers to opportunity" (Friedan, 361).

In the wake of the commission's work, every state instituted similar commissions that spawned the creation of the Interdepartmental Committee on the Status of Women and the Citizens' Advisory Council on the Status of Women, which hosted annual conventions and offered networking opportunities for their women members. The desire to be free from federal and state control led to the organization of the Third National Conference of Commissions on the Status of Women in 1966, which provided the impetus for the formation of the National Organization for Women (NOW), the organizational base for the feminist movement for the remainder of the 20th century. The founders of NOW established the organization to start "a civil rights movement for women" that would fight law and custom to earn women the "right to be fully free and equal human beings" (National Organization for Women, "A Statement of Purpose" [1966] in Kraditor, 363–369).

NOW focused on the public life of women, but by the end of the decade a radical branch of the women's movement began placing the private lives of women at its core. Inspired by the Black Power movement of the late sixties, these women started what became known as the women's liberation movement. They furiously attacked the cultural definitions of women as secondary, inferior sexual objects. As a result, they mounted a sweeping and aggressive challenge to cultural definitions of womanhood and femininity. The Jeanette Rankin Brigade, a planned demonstration against the Vietnam War in January 1968, offered a chance for these "radical" feminists to express their objection to maternal feminism as a condition for political activism. At a planning meeting for the Brigade held in Chicago, members of the newly formed West Side Group expressed their disagreement with any claim that women's authority derived from their roles as mothers and wives.

Women from the West Side Group and the New York Radical Women showed up at the Jeanette Rankin Brigade to declare their opposition to any representation of women as dependent on their relationship to men. Some of the New York women showed up with props like a coffin and banners that announced the "burial of traditional womanhood." This event marked the beginning of radical feminism and signaled the beginning of the fight over the woman's movement's relationship with other leftist groups.

Regardless of these women's feelings about their relationship to the "male-dominated left," the rise of radical feminism in 1968 signaled a clear separation of the women's liberation movement from all other movements, including the anti-war movement. This understanding that the women's liberation movement was revolutionary and distinctive emerged from the rise of "consciousness-raising" small-group discussions where women started sharing their stories of discrimination and oppression with each other, creating an opportunity to redefine the world using their own lives as a template. One radical feminist group, the Redstockings, put it this way in their manifesto:

> We regard our personal experience, and our feelings abut that experience, as the basis of an analysis of our common situation. We cannot rely on existing ideologies, as they are all products of male supremacist culture. We question every generalization and accept none that are not confirmed by our experience.
>
> Our chief task at present is to develop female class-consciousness through sharing experience and publicly exposing the sexist foundation of all our institutions. (Evans, 27–30)

Throughout 1968 and 1969 the women's liberation movement grew at a rapid rate, fueled by the belief among its founders that they were starting a revolution. Grappling with many issues with regard to how the movement should proceed and what should be the ultimate aim of the cause, participants of this revolution engaged in passionate debates and expressed their ideas through a proliferation of articles, manifestos, newsletters, and new journals. Riding the wave of revolutionary zeal so much a part of the late-sixties' leftist political culture, these radical feminists carried the banner of the women's liberation movement into the seventies until it collided with a cultural backlash.

The gay rights movement of the 1960s followed a similar trajectory. At the beginning of the decade, ONE, Inc., the Mattachine Society, and the Daughters of Bilitis were the gay rights movement's standard bearers. Though all three disagreed about particulars, they all agreed that education was their most important and immediate goal. ONE published a magazine directed to a gay audience that deliberately sought to provoke its readers and unapologetically put itself at odds with the culturally dominant view about gay men and women. A forerunner to gay pride, ONE, in defiance of the dominant culture, preached a positive self-image for homosexuals. Mattachine and the Daughters of Bilitis, on the other hand, took a more moderate position by arguing that homosexuals had to accommodate themselves to a society that excoriated homosexual behavior.

Activists working within these organizations found the goal of gaining large numbers of new members to the cause slow going until the Stonewall riot of 1969. This singular event, occurring in the context of the rise of the radical movement that captured the passions of so many American young people at the end of the 1960s, galvanized the movement behind the call for gay pride and gay liberation. The concept of gay liberation is best captured in the words of Carl Wittman's *Refugees from Amerika: A Gay Manifesto:* "Liberation for gay people is to define ourselves how and with whom we live, instead of measuring our relationships by straight values. . . . To be a free territory, we must govern ourselves, set up our own institutions, defend ourselves, and use our own energies to improve our lives." Gone were expressions of accommodation, replaced by the rhetoric of self-determination and pride in the tradition of Black Power. Mattachine and the Daughters of Bilitis could not match the energy or enthusiasm of new radical organizations like the Gay Liberation Front. By 1973, over 800 gay rights organizations existed as the gay liberation movement achieved what the leaders of Mattachine and the Daughters of Bilitis could not: a large-scale grassroots movement for gay rights.

TIMELINE

1960   Federal government approves the use of the birth control pill.

1961   Illinois becomes the first state to repeal sodomy laws.

Women Strike for Peace conducts national strike on November 1 to protest the nuclear arms race.

John F. Kennedy establishes the President's Commission on the Status of Women.

1962   The Equal Pay Act is passed.

The House Committee on Un-American Activities (HUAC) holds hearing to question Women Strike for Peace activists.

The American Law Institute issues model penal code that decriminalizes homosexual behavior.

1963   Betty Friedan's *The Feminine Mystique* is published.

Howard Becker's *Outsiders* is published.

Erving Goffman's *Stigma* is published.

1964   President Johnson signs the Civil Rights Act of 1964, which includes Title VII's prohibition against sex discrimination.

The Council on Religions and the Homosexual forms in San Francisco.

The Society for Individual Rights is created in San Francisco.

1965   Casey Hayden and Mary King write "Sex and Caste: A Kind of Memo."

Edwin Schur's *Crimes without Victims* is published.

1966   National Organization of Women organizes.

1968   The Jeanette Rankin Brigade protest against the Vietnam War is held on January 15 in Washington, D.C.

The Miss America Pageant in Atlantic City, New Jersey, is disrupted by a feminist protest on September 7.

Women's International Conspiracy from Hell (WITCH) is organized.

Martin Hoffman's *The Gay World* is published.

1969   The Redstockings are organized.

The Redstockings interrupts a New York state legislature committee hearing on abortion law reform in February.

WITCH and other women's liberation groups stage protests against the institution of marriage on February 15.

The Stonewall riot breaks out in June.

Texas attorney Sarah Weddington begins legal research on abortion which will culminate in *Roe v. Wade* (1973).

Gay Liberation Front is organized.

National Abortion Rights Action League is organized.

Lesbians walk out of the Congress to Unite Women in November.

SETTING THE STAGE FOR A WOMEN'S LIBERATION MOVEMENT, 1960–1964

The women's liberation movement did not gain public notoriety until the late 1960s, yet the stage was set early in the decade by a growing awareness of women's marginalized status in American society. Since women obtained the right to vote with the ratification of the Nineteenth Amendment in 1920, the issue of women's rights had taken a back seat to other pressing issues such as the Great Depression, World War II, the Cold War, and the civil rights movement. Although by the early sixties more women attended college than had in 1920, they actually made up a smaller percentage of the undergraduate population. The proportion of women earning graduate degrees in the early 1960s was smaller than it was in 1930. While more women worked, they did so at declining rates of pay as compared to their male counterparts. Inspired by the civil rights movement and benefiting from the work of the president's commission in 1961 and the publication of *The Feminine Mystique* in 1963, the foundation for a new wave of feminist activism was laid.

The Changing Lives of Women in the Sixties

By the early 1960s the lives of women had changed greatly. Better contraception, more educational and economic opportunity, and the liberalization of attitudes toward divorce were altering the American social milieu. Women were marrying later, having fewer children than the previous generation, and seeking divorces more often. As a result, an increasing number of women could expect to spend some part of their lives supporting their families or themselves.

As of March 1963, 41.5 percent of mothers with children between the ages of six and seventeen worked for wages, compared with 30.3 percent in 1950. Mothers with children under the age of six raised their labor force participation from 14 percent in 1951 to 22.5 percent in 1963. By 1961, approximately 24 million women were working, 34 percent of all workers. At the time, the Department of Labor predicted that this number would swell to 30 million by the end of the decade. One Labor Department economist in 1963 stated that the growing incidence of married women workers represented "the most significant employment trend in the country" (Harrison 1988, 90).

Although the employment of married women created more egalitarian marriages and greater political participation on the part of women, it did not increase women's employment choices or their wages. Women were still relegated to work as clerks, service workers, factory operatives, domestic workers, teachers, and nurses. In 1960, the wages of full-time year-round women workers averaged only 60.6 percent of their male counterparts, actually down from 63.6 percent in 1957. African American women fared much worse by earning only 42 percent of men's earnings (Harrison 1988, 90–91).

Women Strike for Peace

On November 1, 1961, an estimated 50,000 women in over sixty cities across the United States walked out of their homes and off their jobs to participate in a one-day women's strike for peace. From coast to coast these women marched, took ads out in local papers, and visited government officials demanding they take immediate steps to "End the Arms Race—Not the Human Race" (the central slogan of the strike taken from a promotional flyer, "Help Wanted," October 25, 1961). The organization of this strike seemed to come from nowhere. Most involved did not belong to a unifying organization, and its organizers were not recognized public figures. The women strikers actually responded to a call from a small group of Washington, D.C., women who had become concerned by the acceleration of the nuclear arms race between the United States and the Soviet Union. Disenchanted by the inaction of the traditional peace groups, they sent a call to women friends and contacts across the country urging them to abandon their regular routine of home, family, and work and join the one-day strike to end the arms race.

Word of the planned strike spread quickly through typical female networks: word of mouth, chain letters, personal telephone calls, and Christmas card lists. Organizations such as the Parent Teacher Associations, the League of Women Voters, church and temple groups, and more established peace groups such as the Women's International League for Peace and Freedom (WILPF) and the Committee for a Sane Nuclear Policy (SANE), also helped to spread the word.

Within one year of this strike for peace, its primary organizers and participants transformed the one-day event into a national women's movement with local groups in 60 communities and offices in 10 cities. With no paid staff or designated leader, thousands of women from all over the country managed to establish a loosely structured communications network that could quickly mobilize the forces to participate in protests. From its inception, the Women Strike for Peace (WSP) was a nonhierarchical participatory network of activists opposed both to rigid ideologies and formal organizational structure. WSP used the not-so-artful phrase, "our un-organization," to describe the structure. The lack of structure served multiple purposes: First of all, coming at the end of the McCarthy era, the absence of a membership list avoided at least one aspect of political intimidation by the House Un-American Activities Committee (HUAC) or some other government agency. Second of all, it avoided the hierarchical and bureaucratic structure of the other peace groups like WILPF and SANE that required all action proposals to be cleared by state and national offices. This demand often served as a roadblock to spontaneous and direct responses to an international crisis. Finally, the WSP never had to accurately assess the numerical strength of the organization, thereby allowing the legend of the group to grow.

By using the tactics of lobbying and petitioning alongside demonstrative action and civil disobedience, the WSP successfully put women's political demands on the front pages of newspapers, from which they had largely disappeared since the suffrage campaign of the early 20th century. President Kennedy even gave public recognition to the WSP after its first antinuclear march at the White House, on January 15, 1962:

> I saw the ladies myself. I recognized why they were here. There were a great number of them; it was in the rain. I understand what they were attempting to say; therefore, I consider their message was received. (*New York Times,* January 16, 1962)

They were even given credit for pushing President Kennedy toward signing the limited Test Ban Treaty of 1963.

Women Strike for Peace v. HUAC

At the end of 1962 the WSP planned to escalate their commitment and protests, but HUAC built a roadblock to these efforts when it issued subpoenas to 13 women peace activists. Even though by 1962 the Cold War hysteria had abated, the HUAC investigation into WSP still possessed enough clout to command headlines, cast suspicions by labeling individuals as subversives, and to destroy careers, reputations, and organizations. Well before the subpoenas, the WSP had decided to reject political screening of its members, deeming such a process a relic of Cold War thinking. With this principle firmly established at the organization's founding, the WSP had no problem with the decision to support and embrace every woman summoned before HUAC, regardless of past affiliations. This decision was in sharp contrast to other peace organizations such as SANE that had gone through similar congressional scrutiny. The decision of WSP to allow each member to act according to the dictates of her conscience was bold and based on a sense of sisterhood.

WSP prepared for the HUAC hearings by going on the attack and basing their campaign against nuclear armament on the most sincere form of patriotism. Americanism, they proclaimed, should be measured by one's dedication to saving America's children from nuclear extinction. With regard to the charges of Communist infiltration into their group, they declared, "Differences of politics, economics or social belief disappear when we recognize man's common peril . . . we do not ask an oath of loyalty to any set of beliefs. Instead we ask loyalty to the race of man. The time is long past when a small group of censors can silence the voice of peace" (WSP public statement quoted in Swerdlow, 500).

The HUAC hearing occurred only three weeks after the arrival of the first subpoenas. In that time, the WSP developed a legal defense, a national support system for those testifying, and a broad national public protest campaign against HUAC. The hearings opened on December 11, 1962, with each woman testifying in such a way as to capture the sympathy and support of large sections of the national media. They courageously articulated the danger of nuclear holocaust to the committee and explained women's rights and responsibility to work for peace. As Amy Swerdlow has

Over 800 members of the Women Strike for Peace group gather in front of the United Nations building in New York City to protest the Cuban Missile Crisis in 1962. (Library of Congress)

written, "For the first time, HUAC was belittled with humor and treated to a dose of its own moral superiority" (Swerdlow, 504). They garnered this support, in part, by embracing a traditional "feminine" persona that emphasized their roles as mothers. These hearings represented how the WSP, a movement of middle-class, middle-aged, white women mobilized to counter the red-baiting of HUAC in a bold, grassroots, pragmatic, moralistic, and maternal way. The University of Wisconsin–Madison's student paper, the *Daily Cardinal,* described them as "the bourgeois mother's underground" (December 14, 1962).

Elise Boulding, a sociologist who edited the *Women's Peace Movement Bulletin,* an information exchange for WSP groups, composed a questionnaire that was sent to every eighth name on the mailing lists of 45 local groups to determine the make-up of this loosely structured women's movement. Just before the HUAC hearings, 279 questionnaires had been returned to Boulding that revealed that the overwhelming majority of the WSP women were well-educated mothers, and that 61 percent were not employed outside the home. She concluded that the women who went out on strike back on November 1, 1961, were more complicated and complex than the image of the "buggy-pushing housewife" that the movement conveyed. Most of the women strikers had been liberals, radicals, or pacifists in the 1940s. They believed in social transformation through the direct political action of ordinary people. By the early 1960s, many of these women had school-aged children who no longer required full-time care, freeing them up to get involved in the PTAs, League of Women Voters, Democratic Party politics, churches, and ultimately the WSP. Propelled into the political sphere, these women found their moral outrage over the threat to their children's future by the nuclear arms race. These women saw motherhood not only as a private function, but also as a contribution to society in general and to the future (Boulding).

In the repressive climate of the early 1960s, the WSP relied on traditional gender roles to legitimize its opposition to Cold War politics. But by their protest they also implied that men could no longer be trusted with their traditional gender role of protector. The performance of the WSP witnesses at the HUAC hearings also raised women's sense of political power and self-esteem. However, their heavy reliance on the politics of motherhood alienated an emerging generation of women who saw its acquiescence to traditional gender roles as regressive. Yet the WSP helped start the transformation of women's role in American politics and society (Swerdlow, 493–520).

President's Commission on the Status of Women

When John F. Kennedy took office as president, he appointed Esther Peterson director of the Women's Bureau and relied on her as his advisor for women's affairs. Peterson and Secretary of Labor Arthur Goldberg persuaded Kennedy

Eleanor Roosevelt (left), the head of the President's Commission on the Status of Women, poses in 1962 with Esther Peterson (right), the commission's vice president. (Franklin D. Roosevelt Library)

to form by executive order a President's Commission on the Status of Women (PCSW). Established on December 14, 1961, the president's executive order, written by the Women's Bureau, contended that "prejudices and outmoded customs" prevented the "full realization of women's basic rights" and hindered their ability to make their fullest contribution to the national welfare. The creation of the commission, the order stated, recognized that women had the right to "develop their capabilities and fulfill their aspirations on a continuing basis irrespective of national exigencies." The 26-member commission would review the progress and make recommendations on six issues: employment policies and practices in the federal government; employment policies and practices of federal contractors; social insurance and tax laws; labor legislation; political, civil, and property rights; and new and expanded services necessary for women as wives, mothers, and workers. In a politically savvy move, President Kennedy named former first lady Eleanor Roosevelt as the commission's chair (Harrison, 109–115).

The PCSW served the purpose of reaching out to an important constituency while avoiding the far more contentious alternative: supporting the Equal Rights

Amendment (ERA). After the suffrage amendment was ratified in 1920, Alice Paul, the leader of the National Woman's Party (NWP), submitted the ERA to Congress in 1923. The NWP sought formal equality with men and believed that in order to achieve this, a constitutional amendment was necessary. The amendment, which simply said, "Equality of rights under the law shall not be denied or abridged by the United States or by any State on account of sex," had remained a contentious issue ever since. Women activists remained deeply divided over the issue of its ratification. For women like Peterson who came out of a labor union tradition, the ERA posed a threat to protective legislation for working women. Protective legislation regulated the hours and conditions of women workers, and Peterson and other labor and leftist activists believed those laws prevented female laborers from extreme exploitation. So Peterson and other women in the Democratic Party pushed President Kennedy to establish the commission rather than support the ERA. For Kennedy this suggestion was a blessing because labor constituted an important part of his political base.

Peterson, though personally opposed to the ERA, knew that if the commission opposed the amendment at the outset, the pro-ERA groups would refuse to cooperate and make consensus on an effective plan impossible to achieve. Peterson wanted to keep the conflict over the ERA from destroying the effort of the commission to address the many conflicts, burdens, and obstacles confronting American women. As a result, she insisted that the president's order not overtly declare opposition to the ERA. Instead, Peterson promised that the commission would objectively examine the merits of the amendment.

In October 1963, the commission presented its report, *American Women*, which offered evidence to show that women faced discrimination in every facet of American life. Most notably, the report showed that women earned up to 40 percent less than men on the same job. Although the PCSW report did not support or reject the ERA, the commission took the position that equality of rights under the law for all persons must be in the Constitution. However, in the view of the commission, equality under the law was already embodied in the "equal protection" clause of the Fourteenth Amendment, and it expressed the belief that legal challenges would soon lead the Supreme Court to affirm this interpretation.

Although the report came out after President Kennedy signed the Equal Pay Act, which mandated equal pay for equal work in the private sector and ordered federal agencies to hire and manage their employees on a gender-blind basis, the examination of this issue by the PCSW created the political climate for the law. However, perhaps the most important legacy of the PCSW was not in the area of legislation at all, but in the mandate to convene commissions on the status of women at the state level. In the report's aftermath, every state in the union created such a commission. Most of the state commissions on the status of women were created at the urging of women already active in politics and therefore became a simple way for political leaders of both parties to pay back those women who had worked so hard on their campaigns.

The Feminine Mystique

In 1963, Betty Friedan, housewife and former labor union journalist, published the results of interviews she had conducted with women who had graduated from Smith College. Friedan graduated from Smith in 1942, joined the intellectual world of leftist politics, worked as a journalist for the *UE News,* the newsletter of the United Electrical, Radio and Machine Workers of America, married Carl Friedan in 1947 and settled into a suburban life in which she experienced firsthand domestic isolation. In her interviews with other Smith graduates, she discovered that she was not alone in her feelings of isolation. Blessed with successful husbands, nice homes, and healthy children, these women often blamed themselves for their unhappiness and resisted sharing the depths of their despair. To quell this internal struggle, some of the interviewees took tranquilizers, cooked gourmet meals, smothered their children, sought out sexual affairs, or volunteered their time to churches, schools, and charitable organizations.

Friedan concluded that these educated women had nurtured dreams and talents that were never realized due to the postwar conviction that women should limit their lives to home and hearth, thereby closing opportunities and crushing their spirits. Her analysis of the existence of American middle-class women's existence actually derived from Simone de Beauvoir's 1949 *The Second Sex.* More academic in nature and therefore never finding a wider audience, *The Second Sex* found in Friedan a "translator" who could boil down its ideas, and its theory, into a less radical, more readable text, so that its message could be communicated to the masses.

Historian Gerda Lerner and others have criticized Friedan for exclusively focusing on the plight of white suburban housewives. As a result, she ignored the obstacles faced by working-class and minority women. Others have also taken her to task for not fully examining the systemic obstacles facing women who sought well-paid, meaningful work in a sex-segregated workforce or challenging the basic presumption that women bore the primary responsibility for all domestic work. Friedan, a longtime activist for the working class, ironically consciously chose to focus on the middle class so as to avoid being discredited by holdovers from the red-baiting McCarthy era. She chose this politically safer focus so as to get her message of female self-realization out to as many readers as possible. The tactic worked. While Friedan's analysis incited widespread hostility, several American magazines and journals also positively reviewed the book. Excerpted in several women's magazines, read by three million people, and publicly debated, the book reached a huge population of American women and men and fostered an empathetic reaction by thousands of women who wrote Friedan desperate letters of their own isolated existence.

In fact, the postwar retreat of women into the domestic sphere was not as universal as Friedan portrayed by her focus on Smith graduates. Although the 1950s saw the revitalization of family life, it also witnessed a doubling of women's employment outside the home. In spite of the media's focus on the "housewife-mother" distinction, many women rejected this role in daily life. Or, at the very least, they were confronted more with the conflict of trying to fulfill dual roles. Nevertheless, Friedan's book successfully broke the silence of women's struggles in American life caused by idealized notions of women's roles as wives and mothers.

Charged with gathering data on the roles and resources of women and with documenting areas of discrimination in the laws and practices of state government, these state commissions offered an opportunity for their members to share common concerns. The data they gathered often opened their eyes to the impact of discrimination on women. State commissions started sharing their findings in hearings, news releases, reports, and media interviews. The state commissions could more effectively disperse data gathered through the Federal Interdepartmental Committee and Citizens' Advisory Council, which became clearinghouses for information.

Empowered to think about and recommend policy changes, the women serving on these commissions enjoyed a period of community building and political consciousness-raising. President Kennedy never intended to start a movement with the formation of the PCSW, but the subsequent establishment of state commissions created a network of politically active women who now had a mechanism to create a sense of community and political awareness about the plight of women.

National Woman's Party and Title VII of the 1964 Civil Rights Act

The National Woman's Party (NWP) had fought for the ERA since the early 1920s because its members believed that it would eliminate all legally based barriers to women's advancement. The debate over the ERA had class and ideological overtones that pitted affluent, business-oriented, and politically conservative women against poor, union-oriented, and politically liberal women. The former supported the amendment, while the latter opposed it out of fear that it would do great harm by eliminating laws that favored women, such as those that set minimum wages and maximum hours, which they believed aided working-class women. The PCSW's opposition to the ERA angered the NWP because the most prestigious national panel ever to report on the status of women had rejected their primary objective of the last 40 years. As a result, the NWP looked for alternative means to achieve its objective. Alice Paul, the key figure of the NWP since the 1920s, had the idea to include a sex amendment to the 1964 Civil Rights Act.

The NWP's struggle to include women in the law aimed to protect against discrimination because of race, color, religion, or national origins represents the historic ambiguity of the women's movement. In this advancement of women's rights, the civil rights movement opened the door, but it was ultimately the opponents, not the supporters, of federally mandated civil rights for African Americans who championed the inclusion of gender in this landmark legislation. At times, the NWP members employed implicitly racist, anti-Semitic, and xenophobic tactics to achieve their objectives. On December 16, 1963, the NWP

President Lyndon B. Johnson signs the Civil Rights Act of 1964, legislation intended to eliminate racial discrimination in places of public accommodation and in employment. (Lyndon Baines Johnson Museum and Library)

unanimously adopted a resolution calling for inclusion of sex in the civil rights bill: "the Civil Rights Bill would not even give protection against discrimination because of 'race, color, religion, or national origins,' to a *White Woman,* a *Woman of the Christian Religion,* or a *Woman of United States Origin,* according to the construction that appears to have been placed on the words . . . in Orders and Statements by Government officials." Privately, some NWP members went further in appealing to the fears of many white Americans by emphasizing the perceived threats to white, native-born Christian women in the civil rights bill. NWP member Nina Horton Avery wrote to a Virginia congressman that the inclusion of women in the civil rights bill was "merely a tool of strategy to take the pressure off the passage of any Civil Rights Bill" that she believed would be unconstitutional and unacceptable to the American public. She wrote, "Thank God for the Members of Congress who are from the South . . . who will use their brains and energies to prevent a mongrel race in the United States and who will fight for the rights of white citizens" (Brauer, 43).

Eventually the NWP was successful in attaching the sex amendment to the bill, and President Johnson signed the Civil Rights Act of 1964 in July. Afterward Alice Paul wrote a fellow NWP activist that the NWP "bore the entire burden of this battle and with absolutely no help of any kind from other women's organizations" (Brauer, 55). The prohibition of sexual discrimination in employment represented a convergence of conflicting and ambiguous aims. Unimaginable without the rise of the civil rights movement that forced presidents Kennedy and Johnson to seek legislation banning racially discriminatory practices, the addition of the ban on sex discrimination cleared Congress because of the support it received from southern opponents of the legislation as a whole. The motives of these lawmakers are difficult to determine, but it appears as if it involved a combination of a desire to thwart the civil rights legislation and to protect the honor of white women. Thus, the new ban on sex discrimination resulted from both NWP's political will and, ironically, congressional sexism.

In the first year of the Equal Employment Opportunity Commission (EEOC), the governmental authority charged with enforcing the Civil Rights Act of 1964, this agency received nearly 2,500 complaints (27 percent of the total) from women charging sexual discrimination in the workplace.

THE WOMEN'S MOVEMENT GOES PUBLIC

Emboldened by the awareness of their shared experience as a repressed if not oppressed class of American citizens, women in the mid-1960s began using their experiences with the civil rights and New Left movements to build an organizational base by which to advocate demands for equality. Still willing to work for reform within the existing social, cultural, and economic system, they started a movement that sought to challenge assumptions but not alienate potential political allies. However, from 1965 to 1968 these founding mothers of the new wave of feminism confronted internal challenges around race, class, and sexual orientation that threatened to destroy the new women's movement before it started. The debates around some of these issues set the stage for a more radical brand of feminism at the end of the decade and into the 1970s.

Women in the Civil Rights Movement

The *New Left* is a term used to describe a variety of groups and organizations of the 1960s comprised mostly of college-aged men and women interested in challenging traditional American values and institutions. Among their targets were universities, the military, racism, materialism, capitalism, modern politics, and economic imperialism. Sexism, however, was missing from the agenda of most New Left organizations. Unlike the Old Left of the 1930s, the New Left of the 1960s never embraced an ideological commitment to equality for women.

Before the escalation of the Vietnam War, several of these groups found their inspiration in the civil rights movement of the 1950s and 1960s. Moved by African Americans' willingness to fight and sacrifice everything to change society, young white people started joining organizations such as SNCC, SCLC, and later SDS.

The introduction of young white women into the civil rights movement caused a certain amount of racial tension. African American women who were leaders in organizing their communities often found themselves confronted with the aggressively sexist style of the young African American men who for the first time found themselves in positions of power. Both African American and white women found a common cause in confronting the sexism of the movement, but it also drove a wedge between them. White women could walk away from the struggle easier than African American women who were accused of abandoning the greater cause of civil rights. Those white women who remained more readily tolerated the sexist behavior of the movement's leading men, leaving African American women resentful and scorned. To make matters worse, African American men often accepted white standards of beauty that only further demeaned the status of African American women within the movement.

Yet African American and white women alike created a social space within which women could develop a new sense of their own potential. As historian Sara Evans has written, "a critical vanguard of young women accumulated the tools for movement building: a language to describe oppression and justify revolt, experience in the strategy and tactics of organizing, and a beginning sense of themselves collectively as objects of discrimination" (Evans, 10). Many of the white women who joined the civil rights movement came from the South. Their very willingness to join such an embattled movement signaled their declaration of war on a culture that celebrated the ideal of the "Southern Lady." It also evoked talents, energies, and a sense of independence that many of these women did not think they possessed.

Despite the divisiveness of sexual politics within these organizations, white women drew inspiration from the African American women in the movement. With the help of African American women, white women developed a sense of how their own sex was used as a basis for discrimination by men both outside and inside the movement. Women of both races, but particularly African American women, were upset during the Freedom Summer Project of 1964 by the frequency of interracial sexual relationships and the general sexist attitudes among men in the movement. In the fall of 1964 a number of SNCC women prepared a paper on the sexist attitude of the men within the organization. Written primarily by Casey Hayden and Mary King, the paper charged that the women in SNCC experienced the same sort of discrimination as African Americans in American society. The "assumption of male superiority," they wrote, is "as widespread and deep-rooted and as crippling to the woman as the assumptions of white supremacy are to the Negro" (quoted in Chafe, 323). Despite the importance of women in organizing and running the movement's day-to-day operations, the paper had little effect.

The following year Hayden and King made one last effort at creating a gender-based solidarity with African American women by writing "Sex and Caste: A Kind of Memo." They argued that women had learned from the movement a new sense of personal worth and dignity. They once again drew parallels between the racism African Americans experienced in society and the sexism women experienced in the movement. They wrote that women "in the movement seem to be caught up in a common-law caste system that operates, sometimes subtly, forcing them to work around or outside hierarchical structures of power which may exclude them. . . . It is a caste system which, at its worst, uses and exploits women" (Chafe, 323). Although they never realized the sort of "community of support" they advocated for within the civil rights movement, their analysis of sexism within SNCC presented the first public manifesto of women's liberation that ultimately generated a response from women having similar experiences in other New Left organizations.

Ella Baker was a founder of the Student Nonviolent Coordinating Committee during the civil rights movement of the 1960s. (Library of Congress)

The incipient civil rights movement also contributed to the rise of feminism in the sixties by producing many experienced female activists who grew into leaders. Fannie Lou Hamer and Ella Baker, for example, became two of the great orators and organizers of the civil rights movement and inspired a generation of young civil rights activists to feel proud of powerful female leadership. Dorothy Height, president of the National Council of Negro Women, lawyer Pauli Murray, and union leaders Aileen Hernandez and Addie Wyatt all played decisive roles in explaining the double jeopardy that African American women faced in American society as women and as minorities.

Women in the New Left

Assumptions of male superiority dominated SDS and the fledgling antiwar movement. As with the civil rights movement, women within SDS and other antiwar organizations similarly bore the primary responsibility for community organization. Yet the intellectual and political style of these organizations militated against women's equality being recognized. Symptomatic of this attitude was the popular antiwar slogan, "Girls say yes to guys who say no." Women were

Women's Liberation and the Problem of Race

Aware of their "double jeopardy" in gender and racial/ethnic terms, African American women and Chicanas wondered if feminism could offer them liberation. As Flora Davis has pointed out in *Moving the Mountain,* African American women supported feminist goals earlier and in greater numbers than white women, but did not become active in the women's movement because they did not trust white women. To them, the women's movement of the 1960s used the white, middle-class, heterosexual woman as the female norm. This new wave of feminism seemed like a movement focused on the problem of bored, white, middle-class housewives. This problem paled in comparison to the problems caused by racism and poverty. By the mid-1960s, certain African American periodicals had cautioned that the women's liberation movement could usurp African American women's support for the fight against racism.

With the rise of the Black Power movement in the late sixties, African American women activists continued to express disdain for what they perceived as a predominantly white women's liberation movement. Fearing cooptation, the subordination of the goals of African American liberation, and a division between women and men in the African American movement, African American women questioned the motives behind the women's liberation movement. One militant black woman of the 1960's put it this way: "I don't think any of them are real people involved in anything real. . . . God only knows what their goals are. To me, maybe a lot of publicity for white women to say aren't we great" (Evans, 33). As historian Alice Echols has pointed out, the rise of Black Power ironically played an important role in fostering feminist consciousness among white women, but it caused some African American women to be generally unsympathetic to women's liberation because they thought racism was by far the more pressing issue.

Over time, African American women and Chicanas involved in racial and ethnic struggles started to push back against the male privilege inherent in their movements. Black Power, for example, laid claim to masculine privileges denied them by white supremacist society. Within the African American liberation movement, African American women were expected to play a domestic, submissive role so African American men could express their male prerogatives. Within the Chicano movement, those women involved in the women's liberation movement were characterized as "man-haters, frustrated women, and 'aggringadas,' Anglo-cized" (Evans, 33). As a result, African American women and Chicanas became increasingly uncomfortable with their submissive roles within their respective movements. Within the Chicano movement, women began to hold workshops in 1969. Angela Davis, one of the best-known female activists in the Black Power movement, contended that she was attacked as "domineering" by African American men who feared that she was out to "rob them of their manhood." Frances Beale of SNCC pointed out that while the African American militant male was quick to renounce many white cultural values, "when it comes to women he seems to take his guidelines from the pages of *Ladies Home Journal*" (Echols, 106–107). For their part, Shirley Chisholm, the first African American woman elected to Congress, and Fannie Lou Hamer claimed they experienced more discrimination as a result of being women than as being African American (Chalmers, 162).

expected to cook, clean, do clerical work, and willingly have sex with male activists.

By the end of the decade and at the height of the antiwar movement, women within organizations like SDS suffered a series of humiliations that served to raise their political consciousness and become more active in fighting for gender equality. At the Chicago Democratic Convention in 1968, the Yippies suggested that "their" women pose as prostitutes and spike the delegates' drinks with LSD. In January 1969, the National Mobilization Committee sponsored a "counter-inauguration" in Washington, D.C., one day before Richard Nixon's inauguration. Meant primarily to serve as a rally against the Vietnam War, the male organizers chose speakers from various groups, including SDS veteran Marilyn Salzman Webb. Webb began by declaring, "We as women are oppressed. We, as women [who] are supposedly the most privileged in this society, are mutilated as human beings so that we will learn to function within the capitalist system" (quoted in Rosen, 134). Even though pandemonium broke out below the stage, Webb continued to describe how women were treated as objects and property. She then watched in horror as men in the crowd started yelling, "Fuck her! Take her off the stage! Rape her in a back alley!" The experience traumatized her and other women within the movement. For a core group of women active in New Left groups, this public humiliation caused them to realize that they had to break free from organizations like SDS and create an autonomous movement.

Experiencing sexism while fighting for egalitarian values within the civil rights and New Left movements inspired women and offered them an alternative vision of society. Women working within these movements acquired the experience and skills that enabled them to feel strong enough to move out on their own and fight for their own distinct cause of gender equity.

The National Organization for Women (NOW)

On October 29, 1966, the National Organization for Women (NOW) convened its first meeting by a group of 28 women who had attended a conference in Washington, D.C., on the status of women. They selected Betty Friedan as its first president and former EEOC commissioners Aileen Hernandez and Richard Graham as its vice presidents. Determined to avoid the separatism of the fledgling Black Power movement, the group adopted a "Statement of Purpose" that began, "We men and women," and called for a "fully equal partnership of the sexes." Modeled on civil rights organizations, NOW stated its objective as "to bring women into full participation in the mainstream of American society now, assuming all the privileges and responsibilities thereof in truly equal partnership with men."

The founders envisioned NOW as a pragmatic organization that would perform traditional lobbying functions to gain the enforcement of legislation against

National Organization for Women president Betty Friedan and feminists march in New York City on August 26, 1970, on the 50th anniversary of the passing of the Nineteenth Amendment which granted American women full suffrage. The National Organization for Women (NOW) called upon women nationwide to strike for equality on that day. (JP Laffont/Sygma/Corbis)

sex discrimination and passage of the federal Equal Rights Amendment (ERA). Despite the inclusion of Title VII in the Civil Rights Act of 1964, the economic status of women continued to decline. By 1966, the wages of full-time year-round women workers averaged only 60 percent of those of men, a drop of 3.6 percent in a decade. African American women, hit with the double discrimination of sex and race, earned even less. Although nearly 50 percent of American adult women worked, roughly 75 percent still labored in traditional clerical or sales jobs or as household workers, cleaning women, and hospital attendants. Women constituted 53 percent of the population, but represented only 1 percent of federal judges, less than 4 percent of attorneys, and about 7 percent of doctors. To make matters worse, since World War II, men had been replacing women in the professional fields of elementary and secondary school administration, librarians, and social workers (Rosen, 78–79).

NOW's Statement of Purpose criticized the United States for falling behind other industrialized countries in offering social services such as health care, childcare, and pregnancy leave that supported women's domestic and work needs. It questioned the "assumption that these problems are the unique responsibility of each individual woman, rather than a basic social dilemma which society must solve." To challenge this assumption, the statement called for a national network of childcare centers and government programs for retraining mothers who had been outside the workforce due to childrearing responsibilities. The statement also challenged the acceptance of traditional gender roles within a marriage, suggesting instead that a "true partnership between the sexes demands a different concept of marriage, an equitable sharing of the responsibilities of home and children and of the economic burden of their support."

The adoption of NOW's Statement of Purpose and Bill of Rights caused a schism within the fledgling modern women's liberation movement. On the left, feminists such as Rita Mae Brown left the organization because of NOW's failure to explicitly support lesbianism as a feminist issue. Many UAW members left the organization because of NOW's support for the ERA, which the union saw as undercutting legislation protecting women workers. Some more conservative members ultimately left NOW because of its support for reproductive freedom that they saw as too radical an issue for the American public to accept. The latter group of feminists formed the Women's Equity Action League (WEAL) with the goal of achieving equality through the conventional means of lobbying and lawsuits. In time, the UAW backed the ERA, WEAL supported a woman's right to choose, and NOW endorsed lesbian rights.

NOW's first cause was supporting the sex discrimination lawsuit brought by flight attendants (then called "stewardesses") that challenged the airlines' policy of forcing them to retire upon marriage or at age 30 or 35. It also supported the claim that sex-segregated employment advertising in newspapers did not constitute discrimination. Although the EEOC resisted hearing these claims, NOW's media-savvy public demonstrations ultimately pressured the federal regulatory committee to hold hearings on both issues. After the EEOC ruled in favor of NOW's position on both cases, President Lyndon Johnson issued an executive order barring discrimination by all federal contractors.

NOW quickly became an effective organization for women's rights, but throughout the sixties its leaders continued to confront the most basic and persistent challenges of the women's liberation movement, which were defining the movement's ultimate goals. Would NOW fight to improve women's opportunity within the existing social and economic structure or would it champion a broader and more controversial goal of confronting and eliminating sexism throughout society? (Ferree, Marx, and Hess, 65–66).

1968 Miss America Pageant Protest

A protest outside the Atlantic City convention hall at the Miss America Pageant on September 7, 1968, became the first nationally visible protest of the modern women's liberation movement. Primarily organized by Robin Morgan, a former child star best known for her role as Dagmar in CBS's series *I Remember Mama,* the protest signaled a growing disgust with the degradation implicit in beauty contests. The protesters, mostly from New York but also from places like Washington D.C., New Jersey, Detroit, Florida, and Iowa, believed the pageant represented women in a doll-like ideal of what men wanted them to be: inoffensive, bland, mindless, wholesome, and apolitical. Morgan had become active in the New Left as a college student but became enraged over how women were treated by male leaders of the SDS. As a result, she became active in the fledgling women's liberation movement.

More than 200 women responded to the flyer "No More Miss America" and attended the protest that began the afternoon of the pageant. Television cameras caught them marching down the boardwalk, singing and shouting slogans like "Atlantic City is a town with class; they raise your morals and they judge your ass!" Some held placards that read "No More Beauty Standards—Everyone is Beautiful," "Welcome to the Miss America Cattle Auction," "I Am a Woman—Not a Toy, a Pet or a Mascot," and "Liberation now!" The protesters marched their way to a receptacle marked "Freedom Trash Can" that contained a fire so that symbols of their oppression could be tossed and burned: Dishcloths, girdles, false eyelashes, copies of *Playboy, Vogue, Cosmopolitan, Ladies Home Journal,* high-heeled shoes, laundry detergent, girdles, and bras. On the other side of police barricades stood antiprotestors who jeered at the women with chants of "Lesbians!" and "Screwy, frustrated women!" One even suggested that the protesters throw themselves into the Freedom Trash Can. Some observers objected to the more vulgar placards like "Miss America Sells It!" and "Up Against the Wall, Miss America!"

The protesters then auctioned off an eight-foot-high wooden Miss America puppet. They introduced the puppet as "the best scapegoat yet invented for man." The puppet had chains hanging from her red, white, and blue bathing suit. The women said she represented "the chains that tie us to these beauty standards against our will." They then trotted out a live sheep with a big bow strapped to its tail, draped it with a banner, and crowned it Miss America.

After an hour or so, some counterpickets arrived among the spectators. The leader was Terry Meewsen, a runner-up in the 1967 Miss America contest and a former Miss Green Bay from Wisconsin. She wore a hand-painted sign that read: "There's Only One Thing Wrong with Miss America: She's Beautiful." The placard was pinned to her dress with a Nixon-for-President button.

By 8:30, as the pageant began, a few of the protesters made their way into the convention hall, watched closely by a contingent of policewomen, troopers, and plainclothesmen. Two hours into the pageant, a putrid smell wafted through the hall as police pounced on a protestor spraying butyric acid from a hair-spray bottle. At midnight, as 18-year-old Judith Ann Ford, Miss Illinois, was being crowned the new Miss America, shouts burst out in the hall: "Down with Miss America!" and "Freedom!" About that time, a great, white bed sheet floated slowly down from the balcony that boldly proclaimed: women's liberation. That night millions of American viewers learned about the women's liberation movement for the first time.

Several blocks from the convention hall where the all-white Miss America pageant was being held, the country's first Miss Black America Pageant was held at the Ritz-Carlton Hotel. The organizers called it "a positive protest" against the Miss America Pageant's bias toward white beauty standards. "There's a need for the beauty of the black woman to be paraded and applauded as a symbol of universal pride," said organizer J. Morris Anderson. Unlike the white Miss America pageant, the eight Miss Black America finalists left the Ritz-Carlton to ride in open convertibles around the business district and into the African American community. They waved their white-gloved hands, smiled perfect smiles, and showed off their elegant evening gowns in the afternoon sun. They were cheered everywhere they went, but they were most enthusiastically greeted by the African American community (*New York Times,* September 8, 1968, and Cohen, 149–153).

THE RISE OF RADICAL FEMINISM

The emergence of radical feminism at the end of the decade represented a rejection of liberal feminism's pursuit of gaining equality for women in America's existing social and economic structure. Radical feminism was a political movement dedicated to restructuring society. To them, male dominance was the original and most basic form of domination from which all other acts of oppression flowed. Unlike liberal feminists who organized around the principle of female difference and aimed to mount a movement that reversed the cultural valuation of the male and the cultural devaluation of the female, radical feminism aimed to completely change the sex-class system by promoting the similarity of men and women. Liberal feminism sought to include women in the mainstream; radical feminism rejected the mainstream.

Between 1967 and 1969, the women's liberation movement experienced a schism between what Alice Echols calls the "feminists" and the "politicos." The politicos wanted to remain connected to the Left while the feminists had grown tired of what they perceived to be the subordination of women's liberation to the Left. Echols points out that this divide became known at the Jeannette Rankin Brigade (named for the first woman elected to Congress who voted against U.S. involvement in both world wars). The older, liberal women who had closer ties to the civil rights movement wanted to ensure that their demonstrations remained peaceful, whereas younger women believed nonviolent protests had outlived their usefulness. Members of the newly formed New York Radical Women, such as Shulamith Firestone, criticized the Brigade for reinforcing the cultural assumptions about women's passivity and called for a forceful show of political power. Five thousand women showed up in Washington, D.C., on January 15, 1968, to protest the war on the first day of Congress. Unfortunately, the protest was as feeble as the young radicals had predicted. The Brigade was prevented from petitioning Congress when Vice President Hubert Humphrey invoked precedent to bar Congress from conducting any business until the president delivered the State of the Union address. The protesters were reduced to standing outside in the snow while singing, "We Shall Overcome." In the aftermath of the Jeannette Rankin Brigade debacle, radical feminists started developing a body of literature that more clearly articulated their differences with liberal feminism.

Consciousness-Raising

In 1968, Carol Hanisch, a civil rights worker in Mississippi and member of the Gainesville Women's Liberation and later the New York Radical Women, coined the slogan, "The personal is political." By this she intended to convey that one's private life had political dimensions, that power relations shaped life in marriage, in the kitchen, the bedroom, and at work. Kathy Sarachild, a Harvard peace activist, civil rights worker in Mississippi, and member of the New York Radical Women and later the Redstockings coined the term *consciousness-raising*. The term described the process by which women in small groups explored the political aspects of their personal lives. Derivative of SNCC's tradition of "speaking truth to power," Sarachild believed that women could only see the reality of their existence when they understood that their problems were not theirs alone. Consciousness-raising meant not only looking at your life through your own eyes by reflecting on the choices you had made, but also recognizing who had encouraged and discouraged your decisions, and identifying the obstacles and constraints put in your way that had little or nothing to do with individual temperament or talent.

Women would gather in each other's homes to share their stories and realize that their problems were a result of deep cultural, social, and economic forces and assumptions. Consciousness-raising also took place in novels, essays, and new forms of artistic expression. Not surprisingly, consciousness-raising ended up fueling a lot of repressed anger. In many cases, small group meetings turned individual depression into collective anger. As women experienced epiphanies about their own struggles, they also experienced an unexpected sense of exhilaration and empowerment that gave them a stronger sense of community and political purpose. Consciousness-raising was a critical part of the women's liberation movement in the late 1960s and early 1970s.

The Redstockings

Founded in New York by Ellen Willis and Shulamith Firestone in 1969, the Redstockings represented the rise of a more militant and radical version of feminism at the end of the decade. Although the Redstockings rejected the Marxist view that gender inequality would disappear with the eradication of capitalism, in every other way they subscribed to Marxist ideology by developing a "female class consciousness through sharing experience and publicly exposing the sexist foundation of all our institutions" (Redstockings Manifesto). They argued that all women should renounce their privileges and unite to defeat the dual forces of capitalism and patriarchy.

In February 1969, the Redstockings interrupted a New York State legislative committee meeting on abortion law reform and offered to give firsthand testimony about their experiences with illegal abortions. The committee, composed of 14 men and a nun, refused the offer and moved their meeting to another room where they could continue their work behind closed doors. One month later, the Redstockings held a "speak-out" organized by Kathie Sarachild at which twelve women spoke publicly about their backstreet abortions before an audience of roughly 300 people. Gloria Steinem, a journalist at the time, was assigned to cover this event that ultimately transformed her life. While listening to these women share their stories, Steinem felt as though a "great blinding light bulb" had just been turned on. At that moment, "all the humiliation of being a woman from political assignments lost to less-experienced male writers to a lifetime of journalists' jokes about frigid wives, dumb blonds and farmers' daughters" suddenly made sense to Steinem (Rosen, 209).

Abortion Rights and the Politics of the Body

The movement for abortion reform began long before the 1960s women's liberation movement. Abortion had been illegal for nearly a century when in 1959 the American Law Institute recommended that abortion should be available when the mother or child might suffer if the pregnancy continued. Throughout the sixties, a variety of activists joined the reform movement. However, abortion reform made little headway until the women's movement joined the cause. When the women's liberation movement joined the abortion rights campaign in the late 1960s, feminists rejected the more moderate call for the "reform" of abortion laws and instead insisted upon the "repeal" of all laws that limited a woman's right to an abortion. For example, feminists testifying before the New York legislature passed out a copy of their proposed abortion law: a blank sheet of paper (Rosen, 158).

Advocates for abortion rights estimated that close to one million women had illegal abortions each year until the procedure became legal in 1973. Often desperate to end a pregnancy that would dramatically change their lives or end the pursuit of their dreams, women would try an astonishing array of abortifacients. Hospitals would admit thousands of women whose wombs were forever scarred by self-induced abortions. They would pump air into the uterus, ingest turpentine, force soap or detergent up the cervix, push potassium permanganate tablets up their vagina to stimulate bleeding, among other things, just to end an unwanted pregnancy. The names of "abortionists" spread by word of mouth, but women could not be sure of their reliability or reliance on sterile instruments.

As the women's movement joined the cause, an underground network of ministers, women activists, and doctors formed to direct pregnant women to competent physicians willing to illegally perform abortions. The Society for Humane Abortion, founded by longtime abortion rights advocate Patricia Mc-Ginnis, reportedly helped roughly 12,000 women go to Mexico for abortions by the end of the decade (Rosen, 55). In Chicago, members of the Chicago Women's

Abortion rights advocate Patricia Maginnis and supporters in 1970. (Bettmann/ Corbis)

Liberation Union in 1969 started offering doctor referrals for women seeking illegal abortions. Calling themselves "Jane," they helped thousands of women gain access to competent doctors to perform safe abortions. By late 1970, they began to shift from just making referrals to performing the abortions themselves. By the time they disbanded in 1973, members of Jane estimate that they performed over 11,000 illegal abortions with a safety record that matched doctor-performed abortions (Evans, 47).

Non-Catholic clergy also played an important role in the development of these underground networks. The Clergy Consultation Service on Abortion (CCSA), for example, represented close to 1,000 ministers willing to risk arrest in order to help women gain access to safe abortions. About the same time "Jane" formed, a consciousness-raising group of Austin, Texas, women formed an alliance with the CCSA to help raise money for the cause. In September 1969, Sarah Weddington, a recent law school graduate and member of the group, decided to begin legal research on the legalization of abortion. Thus began the process that resulted in the landmark Supreme Court case, *Roe v. Wade* (1973), in which Weddington argued her first case at the age of 25.

The National Abortion Rights Action League (NARAL) formed in 1969, originally named the National Association for the Repeal of Abortion Laws. It changed its mission from the repeal of such laws to keeping "abortion safe, legal, and accessible for all women" after the *Roe v. Wade* decision. The fight for abortion rights by women's liberation groups grew out of a broader effort to increase women's sexual autonomy. In 1960, the federal government approved the use of the birth-control pill, shifting the incipient sexual revolution into high gear. A growing number of women began to claim their right to enjoy sex for pleasure rather than merely for procreation. By the late sixties, consciousness-raising groups across the country began openly discussing female sexuality. Enlightened by such books as *Our Bodies, Ourselves,* women started to stress the need for sexual self-determination. No longer taboo within the safety of these groups, issues such as orgasms and masturbation became regular items for discussion at consciousness-raising sessions. Like admitting to abortions, women would confess to faking orgasms with their husbands and partners. The faked orgasm became a symbol of female repression. Susan Lydon, a Berkeley feminist, wrote an article, "The Politics of Orgasm," that summed up the sexual predicament of many women: "With their men, they often fake orgasm to appear 'good in bed' and thus place an intolerable physical burden on themselves and a psychological burden on the men unlucky enough to see through the ruse."

Demanding sexual openness and pleasure became yet another important way for women to achieve equality.

Lesbianism within the Women's Movement

Lesbian feminists played an important role promoting the idea that women should have the right to control their own body. Historian Liz Craven traces the history of lesbian organizing, beginning in 1955 with the formation of the secret organization, the Daughters of Bilitis (DOB). The DOB published a newsletter, *The Ladder,* which shared research and personal stories dealing with the assimilation of lesbians into society. At a time when homosexuality was still a felony, DOB attempted to rid lesbians of a deviant status within American society. In the early 1960s, the DOB allied themselves with gay men; however, the male organizations at that time, ONE, Inc., and Mattachine, wanted them to remain an auxiliary organization. Craven describes how the publication of *The Feminine Mystique* in 1963 made lesbians more aware that gender definitions and gender roles are built into the social structure. If gender behavior is a social construct, as Friedan suggested, lesbianism is not necessarily the result of a psychological flaw.

In the late 1960s, lesbians had to choose to be a part of the gay movement or the women's liberation movement. They faced chauvinism within the gay movement and silence within the women's liberation movement. Lesbians who joined NOW felt outraged by Betty Friedan's characterization of them as a "lavender menace" that would provide the enemies of the women's liberation movement ammunition to dismiss all feminists as man-haters. The NOW leader-ship simply did not want to deal with the issue of lesbianism. NOW's omission of DOB as an institutional sponsor of the November 1969 Congress to Unite Women represented its homophobia. Shortly thereafter, Rita Mae Brown, the leading activist trying to raise the issue of lesbianism within NOW, was inex-plicably relieved of her duties as editor of the New York NOW's newsletter. Brown angrily resigned from NOW along with two other lesbians and issued a statement concerning the homophobia within the organization:

> The leadership consciously oppresses other women on the question of sex-ual preference—or in plain words, enormous prejudice is directed against the lesbian. Lesbian is the one word that can cause the Executive Com-mittee a collective heart attack. (Quoted in Marotta, 235)

In late 1969, Brown set about organizing a lesbian-feminist movement. Brown initially joined the Redstockings' consciousness-raising group, but soon quit after she discovered they too did not want to deal with the issue of lesbianism. She moved on to the Gay Liberation Front where she persuaded women to form consciousness-raising groups and to make common cause with lesbians from women's liberation.

In 1969, Martha Shelley began to articulate the political importance of lesbian feminism in an essay titled, "Notes of a Radical Lesbian." She wrote,

> Lesbianism is one road to freedom—freedom from oppression by men. . . . The woman who is totally independent of men—who obtains love, sex, and self-esteem from other women—is a terrible threat to male supremacy. She doesn't need them, and they have less power over her. (Quoted in Rosen, 167)

Lesbian feminism advanced the notion that to value both the female body and oneself as a woman is related to the ability to love oneself and to love other women, either platonically or sexually.

Yet even radical feminism at the end of the sixties felt conflicted about the issue of lesbianism being connected to the cause of women's liberation. Most early radical feminists believed the sexual revolution of the 1960s was in many ways more exploitive than liberating. Most commonly dismissed lesbianism as a sexual movement and not a political movement. One radical feminist declared that the task of feminism was to get women out of bed rather than change the gender of their partners (Echols, 211).

Women's International Conspiracy from Hell

A faction of the New York Radical Women broke off to form the Women's Inter-national Conspiracy from Hell (WITCH) in the fall of 1968, a move inspired by

Abbie Hoffman and Jerry Rubin's Youth International Party's use of guerrilla-theatre tactics designed to gain media attention for their cause. Their outlandish protest at the 1968 Democratic Convention inspired women to organize WITCH around the plan to stage outrageous acts to draw media attention to the women's liberation movement. To other feminists the Yippie approach to political activism seemed elitist and frivolous. Women who came out of the civil rights movement had a far more generous view of ordinary people and continued to put their faith in consciousness-raising rather than the shock and offend tactics of WITCH.

WITCH did such things as a public hexing of Wall Street that symbolized their objection to the inherent patriarchal nature of American capitalism. The stock market inexplicably declined. They also spearheaded a national protest against the institution of marriage that specifically targeted bridal fairs. On February 15, 1969, women's liberation groups disrupted large bridal fairs on both coasts. In New York, members of WITCH plastered the city with 10,000 stickers urging other women to join them in a protest against a bridal fair held at Madison Square Garden. At the fair they chanted, "Confront the Whoremakers," cast a "hex" on the "manipulator-exhibitors," sang "Here Comes the Slave, Off to Her Grave," and distributed free "shop-lifting bags" which several prospective brides eagerly took. They held signs that read, "Always a Bride, Never a Person" and "Ask Not for Whom the Wedding Bell Tolls." The Women's Liberation Front and the San Diego State Guerrilla Theater conducted similar protests at a bridal fair in San Diego on the same day.

The antics of WITCH, while derided by some within the movement, inspired other feminists to take a more radical approach to their cause. By 1969, for example, women at the University of California—Berkeley, the hub of university feminist activism, began to protest the "patriarchal" nature of their educations and started demanding the inclusion of women's history and literature into their curriculum. Undergraduate women held a rally where they distributed leaflets that declared, "We've been burned. We thought we were free human beings." Like SDS and the student movement before them, these young feminists started to view themselves as brainwashed victims, "trapped in an educational institution that refused to allow them to challenge the basis of knowledge." At this rally they demanded that the ROTC building be converted into a space for women's studies and that the university provide childcare, and that funds for "war-related research" be converted into financial support for women's education (Rosen, 204–205).

SEXUAL POLITICS IN THE ERA OF CIVIL RIGHTS

Until the 1960s, gay men and women could not effectively mobilize a political constituency large enough to alter conditions of gay life. The prevailing view was that homosexuals and lesbians were psychologically flawed and individually responsible for their predicament. This view made it difficult for gay men and women to develop a group consciousness. In addition, it justified the criminal penalties attached to homosexual behavior. Without a mass movement, the hopes of improvement in the status of gay men and women seemed unlikely. At the same time, without a significant change in attitude, it appeared unlikely that a mass movement could develop. During the 1960s, however, a noticeable shift occurred in both the amount of discourse about homosexuality and the social and psychological interpretation of the condition. A significant amount of the discourse and analysis of this era started to view lesbians and homosexuals, not as aberrant individuals, but as members of a group. This minority view started to lay the foundation for the formation of a group consciousness and mass movement.

In the 1960s, everything from pornography to mass media started publishing images and descriptions of the lifestyle and sexuality of gay men and women. Even though some was derogatory and exploitive, the sheer quantity of the material that portrayed, examined, and debated about the gay experience in American life began to expose the experiences of this minority group to the mainstream. The emergence of gay life in the public view brought opportunities to redefine homosexuality. Inherent in the ideology that made homosexuality a sin, sickness, and crime was the assumption that gay men and women possessed maladjusted pathological personalities and therefore lived in relative isolation from the rest of society. However, as these more public portrayals started to reveal, gay subcultures actually existed and even thrived in the urban environments of American cities, thereby making it possible to conceptualize homosexuality from the vantage point of social science.

Howard Becker's *Outsiders*

Sociologists in the 1960s started to mount the most pointed attack on the traditional view of homosexuality as socially pathological. After World War II, social scientists adopted a relativist approach that viewed deviance not as evidence of social disorganization but rather as a sign of alternative norms of behavior. Howard Becker's 1963 book, *Outsiders,* became the standard text on this relativistic view of so-called deviant behavior. Becker asserted that social groups "create deviance by making the rules whose infraction constitutes deviance. . . . Deviance is not a quality of the act the person commits, but rather a consequence of the application by others of rules and sanctions to an 'offender.'" Becker warned sociologists who study deviant populations, such as homosexuals, to resist adopting the majority viewpoint that established and enforced the rules. Instead, they should "see it simply as a kind of behavior some disapprove of and others value" (Becker, 8–9, 176).

Social scientists started to examine homosexuality from Becker's minority view. Erving Goffman's *Stigma* (1963) and Edwin Schur's *Crimes Without Victims* (1965) are two examples of how the majority viewpoint had stigmatized certain segments of the population by penalizing their behavior even if there were no victims. Martin Hoffman in *The Gay World* (1968) offered the first book-length portrayal of an urban homosexual community. Based on three years of observing gay male life in San Francisco, Hoffman described the network of institutions that bound the community together and the impact of legal penalties on gay men's lives.

The Decriminalization of Sodomy

The works of Becker, Hoffman, and others began the public debate over the criminalization of homosexual acts. During the 1960s the legal profession considered these dissenting opinions about criminalization in a growing debate about the role of the state in regulating morality, the right to privacy, violations of due process, and arbitrary, capricious law enforcement. Jurists and attorneys began joining the cause to decriminalize private, consensual, adult homosexual relations. The American Law Institute (ALI) completed work in 1962 on a model penal code that eliminated the sodomy statutes. Two years later, the International Congress on Penal Law endorsed the position of the ALI. The reasoning of the ALI was based on the assumption that state criminal laws were meant to protect the person and property of citizens; sexual conduct in private endangered neither. Another rationale for the change was that the laws were impossible to enforce. Some legal experts also based their objections to these laws on the inherently changing nature of sexual morality. What is condemned today might be accepted tomorrow.

Despite this growing chorus of objection to sodomy laws, little change occurred during the 1960s. However, Illinois in 1961 and Connecticut in 1969 adopted the model penal code of the ALI and repealed their sodomy laws. But the changes in these laws revealed that sodomy laws had little effect on the lives of gay men. Homosexuals rarely got arrested for private sexual acts; instead, they were more often arrested for vagrancy, disorderly conduct, public lewdness, and solicitation. Still, the change in the ALI model penal code and its adoption by Illinois and Connecticut signaled a break from centuries of tradition and custom that considered homosexuality deviant and punishable.

Mattachine Society

Because of the dominant culture's view of homosexuality as a sin, sickness, or crime, gay men and women traditionally viewed their situation as a personal problem and not a cause for political action. Social pressure caused most homosexuals to "pass," the choice to keep one's sexual identity a secret. The anti-homosexual impulse of the 1950s' McCarthy era created a particularly inhospitable political climate to transformative social movements. Yet the founding of the Mattachine Society in Los Angeles in 1951 marked the beginning of what would grow into the gay rights movement of the second half of the 20th century. The society derived its name from the court jesters of the Middle Ages who were permitted to utter frank social commentary from behind masks.

The society's leadership came from gay men who were either communists or traveled in left-wing circles. Accustomed to their role of social and political outsiders, they broke away from the accepted notions of homoerotic behavior and began thinking of homosexuals as an oppressed minority. The Mattachine Society worked to develop a group consciousness free of the guilt and negative attitudes most gay men and women had internalized. Instead, members tried to instill a sense of pride in belonging to a minority group that had made significant contributions to society. The Mattachine Society created a secret society that protected its members from public exposure and allowed them to organize and create a group consciousness in relative safety.

During the 1950s the Mattachine Society made only minimal progress in establishing chapters throughout the country. Mattachine established communities in San Francisco, Los Angeles, New York, Boston, Denver, and Philadelphia, and for a time in Detroit, Chicago, and Washington, D.C. By 1960 membership stood at only 230 (quoted in D'Emilio, 115). Almost a decade after its founding, gay activists still had few political achievements to encourage them. By the beginning of the 1960s, the gay rights movement remained at best marginal to the lives of homosexuals. In fact, the nascent movement and Mattachine Society had factionalized over disagreements about structure and objectives. Living in a society where their proclivities were labeled perverted and sinful, many homosexuals at the turn of the decade lacked the assuredness to step out and participate in an unapologetic movement for gay rights. As the 1950s wore on, Mettachine became increasingly conservative, primarily interested in gaining acceptance on the mainstream's terms.

The relatively passive and inconspicuous gay rights movement of the 1950s became more aggressive when radicals like Franklin Kameny became involved with the Mattachine Society. A Harvard educated astronomer, Kameny lost his job with the U.S. Army Map Service in 1957 after investigators discovered a 1956 arrest on charges of lewd conduct. After failing to regain his job through the internal appeals process and the courts, Kameny formed a Mattachine chapter in Washington, D.C., in 1961 and started to push the organization toward a more aggressive and resistant approach to gaining equality and acceptance for homosexuals. He declared in a 1964 speech to the New York Mattachine Society, "It is absolutely necessary to be prepared to take definite, unequivocal positions upon supposedly controversial matters. We should have a clear, explicit, consistent viewpoint and we should not be timid in presenting it. . . . This is a movement, in many respects, of down-to-earth, grass-roots, sometimes tooth-and-nail politics" (quoted in D'Emilio, 152).

Due to Kameny's forceful leadership, the Washington, D.C., Mattachine chapter took a much more aggressive approach to initiating change. Starting in 1962, the Washington Mattachine relentlessly pursued federal officials in order to obtain meetings to discuss issues such as the federal government's employment policies that discriminated against homosexuals. The Washington Mattachine also started to effectively challenge the police harassment of gay men. When Kameny heard of a case of police harassment, he would interview the victims and lodge complaints with the police department and the D.C. board of commissioners. The American Civil Liberties Union would also file complaints and provide attorneys for arrested and harassed men.

In the same way and at about the same time, Randy Wicker radicalized the New York Mattachine. A former student at the University of Texas in Austin, Wicker made his first contact with the movement when he found a copy of Mattachine's magazine, *One*. After watching several of his friends and roommate get expelled from the University of Texas for being homosexuals, Wicker was convinced that homosexuals needed a militant movement. Already very active in the southern civil rights movement, Wicker moved to New York City in 1961 and became involved in Mattachine. Wicker effectively used the media in New York to make the lives of gay men and women more visible. Wicker started writing a column called "The Wicker Basket" for the organization's newsletter that expressed his militant approach to obtaining gay rights. His call for a more radical approach started to catch on with the rank-and-file of the still fledgling gay rights movement in New York.

Daughters of Bilitis

The Daughters of Bilitis (DOB) came into existence in 1955. Named for Pierre Louys's poems on lesbian themes, the DOB was founded by four couples in San Francisco and was the first postwar lesbian organization. Led by its president, Del Martin, and editor of the *Ladder* (started in 1956), Phyllis Lyon, DOB stated its objectives as:

- "Education of the variant"
- Development of a library on sexual deviance
- Coordinating public discussion on sexual deviance by leading members of the legal, psychiatric, religious, and other professions
- Advocating a mode of behavior and dress for lesbians acceptable to society
- Participation in research projects and the investigation of the penal code as it pertains to homosexuals

1963 *New York Times* Article on "Overt Homosexuality"

A December 17, 1963, lengthy *New York Times* article by Robert C. Doty with the headline "Growth of Overt Homosexuality in City Provokes Wide Concern" examined the "increasing openness" of New York's homosexual population. The article described the presence of "what is probably the greatest homosexual population in the world" as the city's "most sensitive open secret." It went on to state that until recently, the "problem" of homosexuality had "grown in the shadows, protected by taboos on open discussion that have only recently begun to be breached." The article declared, "The overt homosexual . . . has become such an obtrusive part of the New York scene that the phenomenon needs public discussion."

Some experts at the time believed the number of homosexuals in the city to be growing, while others merely claimed that as public attitudes became more tolerant, homosexuals became less concerned with concealing their deviant lifestyles. Although the article gave both sides to the homosexual debate, the thrust of the piece gave more weight to the dominant psychoanalytic view of the time that homosexuality was a pathological disorder. The homophile position that "homosexuality is an incurable, congenital" condition that should be "treated by an increasingly tolerant society" was dismissed as flying in the face of "the bulk of scientific evidence." The article gave more credence to the view of 1960s' analytical psychiatrists who believed the "overwhelming evidence that homosexuals are created—generally by ill-adjusted parents—not born." Dr. Charles W. Socarides, a New York psychoanalyst, articulated this position: "The homosexual is ill, and anything that tends to hide that fact reduces his chances of seeking and obtaining treatment." Despite the slant toward the traditional, negative view of homosexuality, the *Times* article served as a marker in ending the public silence over the issue (Doty, 1).

- The promotion of changes of the penal code through the due process of law in the state legislatures (Adam, 64)

At the height of the McCarthy era, DOB believed accommodation the only realistic approach. Homophiles believed that they had to placate their oppressors by being law-abiding, deferential, and inconspicuous.

Around the same time Kameny and others started influencing Mattachine to be more oppositional in its approach, members of DOB started to argue for a more activist stance. Barbara Gittings, the founder of the New York DOB in 1958, in particular led this charge when she became editor of the *Ladder* in 1962 and moved the journal toward an "antisick," mass-movement position. As other gay rights organizations embraced a more militant approach, the DOB leadership withdrew from the conference of East Coast Homophile Organizations (ECHO) and removed Gittings from the *Ladder* in 1965. The militants within the organization responded by expelling the conservative leadership of DOB in favor of its first African American president, Ernestine Eckstein. However, the old leadership regained control in 1966, causing the more radical members to leave the organization for Mattachine (Adam, 71–72).

Throughout the rest of the decade, DOB continued to work behind the scenes to change the law as it related to so-called sexual deviance. A November 17, 1969, *New York Times* article reported that the DOB held meetings in "unprepossessing quarters on an unprepossessing street in midtown Manhattan" (Nemy, *New York Times,* November 17, 1969) and that the national membership was only 500, according to its president, Rita Laporte. Laporte said that many more women came to their meetings but were afraid to be on DOB's mailing list. DOB meetings offered a safe space for lesbians to socialize without fear of social or legal retribution.

Council on Religion and the Homosexual

In the early 1960s the Reverend A. Cecil Williams, pastor of San Francisco's Glide Memorial Methodist Church and veteran of the long struggle for racial justice and civil rights, operated a Young Adult project to serve the needs of a growing population of teenaged runaways living on the streets of San Francisco's Tenderloin district. In 1962 Reverend Williams hired Ted McIlvenna, a young minister and social worker from Kansas City to lead the project. McIlvenna's work quickly caused him to deal directly with the issue of homosexuality. Uneducated on issues related to sexual identity, McIlvenna turned to the Mattachine Society for guidance and discovered that the organization, fearful of charges of corrupting youth, did not allow any members under the age of 21. McIlvenna learned through his contact with Mattachine and other gay rights organizations that homosexuals had real grievances against the church.

Under McIlvenna's leadership, a group of ministers in the San Francisco area began to work for social justice for homosexuals. The ministers promised to initiate a discussion in their denominations on the church's stand on homosexuality. After a series of meetings between the ministers and homophile leaders of San Francisco, they formed the Council on Religion and the Homosexual (CRH) in December 1964. To raise funds for the organization, the leaders planned a New Year's Eve dance for San Francisco's gay community. Several police arrived with paddywagons at California Hall, the site of the dance, to harass the well-intentioned liberal ministers. As the police sought entrance into the hall, CRH lawyers stood at the door and demanded a search warrant. Three lawyers and a ticket-taker were then arrested on charges of obstructing an officer.

Although gays and lesbians had grown accustomed to this sort of harassment, the ministers had not. As a result, on January 2 the ministers held a press conference at Williams's church and accused the police of harassment, intimidation, and bad faith. The American Civil Liberties Union saw this as an example of police harassing attorneys who represented unpopular groups and quickly volunteered to represent the defendants. At the trial in February, the gay community felt vindicated for the first time in the eyes of the law when the judge directed the jury to return a not-guilty verdict due to a lack of evidence. Gay activists believed that the New Year's Eve dance signaled a turning point in the movement in San Francisco:

> This is the type of police activity that homosexuals know well, but heretofore the police had never played their hand before Mr. Average Citizen. It was always the testimony of the police versus the homosexual, and the homosexual, fearing publicity and knowing the odds were against him, succumbed. But in this instance the police overplayed their part. (Quoted in D'Emilio, 195)

Society for Individual Rights

Organized in San Francisco in September 1964, the Society for Individual Rights (SIR) aimed to create a homosexual community that resisted the centralized decisionmaking of Mattachine and other gay organizations in favor of a more democratic process that would promote the "worth of the homosexual . . . and [his] right to his own sexual orientation." The SIR organizers believed that for the gay rights movement to grow, it had to embrace the impulses that brought homosexuals together in gay bars. As William Beardemphl, SIR's first president, asserted, "Our work is to create a community feeling that will bring a 'Homophile Movement' into being" (quoted in D'Emilio, 190).

In contrast to Mattachine, SIR encouraged public and social activities such as dances, parties, brunches, drag entertainment, bridge clubs, bowling leagues, meditation groups, and art classes. In April 1966 SIR opened a gay community center in San Francisco, the first of its kind in the country. SIR's willingness to engage in activities that encouraged the fellowship of gay men caused membership to rapidly grow to roughly 1,000 by the end of 1967. As membership grew, the gay community could claim a more powerful political constituency that could start making demands on public officials.

The North American Conference of Homophile Organizations

In the mid-1960s, gay and lesbian groups recognized the need for building broad national coalitions, first through an affiliation of East Coast groups and then through the National American Conference of Homophile Organizations

January 21, 1966, *Time*
Essay on Homosexuality

Time magazine ran an unsigned two-page essay entitled, "The Homosexual in America," in its January 21, 1966, issue. The essay offered a contemptuous view of the homosexual's place in American life and a negative psychological analysis of homosexuality's cause. The essay claimed, "The once widespread view that homosexuality is caused by heredity, or some derangement of hormones, has been generally discarded. The consensus is that it is caused psychically, through a disabling fear of the opposite sex." The essay presented the classic Freudian dominant mother/subservient father explanation for homosexuality. It asserted that both gay men and lesbians are examples of "arrested development, a failure of learning, a refusal to accept the full responsibilities of life. This is no more apparent than in the pathetic pseudomarriages in which many homosexuals act out conventional roles—wearing rings, calling themselves 'he' and 'she.'" The essayist then concluded with a vicious attack, writing that homosexuality "is a pathetic little second-rate substitute for reality, a pitiable flight from life. As such, it deserves fairness, compassion, understanding and when possible, treatment. But it deserves no encouragement, no glamorization, no rationalization, no fake status as minority martyrdom, no sophistry about simple differences in taste—and above all, no pretense that it is anything but a pernicious sickness."

Despite this extremely negative portrayal of homosexuality, the publicity in *Time* represented improvement over the recent past when nothing—good or bad—about gay people appeared in print. The essay mentioned several homosexual organizations, such as the Mattachine Society, thereby inadvertently providing free publicity for these underfunded groups. It also showed that the organized demonstrations of the early homophile movement, though small, were beginning to bring the issue of homosexuality from out of the closet. These demonstrations, modeled after the civil rights movement's demonstrations, started in 1964 when 10 women and men picketed the U.S. Army induction center on Whitehall Street in New York City. The demonstrators demanded that homosexuals be allowed to serve in the military and protested the dishonorable discharges issued to gay men and lesbians who had served in the military.

The Mattachine Society of Washington organized a demonstration that included nine men and three women on May 29, 1965. The protestors picketed the White House to protest government discrimination against homosexuals. Mattachine pronounced at the demonstration that it was acting on behalf of "the nation's second largest minority"—15 million homosexuals. The pickets said the protest concerned the treatment of homosexuals in the military, particularly that they were given less than honorable discharges, the refusal of government officials to hire homosexuals, and the rejection of government officials to discuss these issues with Mattachine leaders.

(NACHO). At a 1968 NACHO conference in Chicago, delegates from 26 different gay and lesbian organizations adopted the slogan, "Gay is Good," representing the adoption of gay pride as a galvanizing concept. Delegates at this conference also adopted a five-point Homosexual Bill of Rights that presented the immediate goals of the still nascent gay rights movement:

- Private consensual acts between persons over the age of consent shall not be an offense.

- Solicitation for any sexual act shall not be an offense except upon the filing of a complaint by the aggrieved party, not a police officer or agent.

- A person's sexual orientation or practice shall not be a factor in the granting or receiving of federal security clearances, visas, and the granting of citizenship.

- Service in and discharge from the armed forces and eligibility for veteran's benefits shall be without reference to homosexuality.

- A person's sexual orientation or practice shall not affect his eligibility for employment with federal, state, or local governments, or private employers. (Quoted in Marcus, 75–76)

SEXUAL POLITICS IN THE ERA OF RADICALISM

The homophile movement, like most other social movements of this era, was affected by the radical politics of the late 1960s. By 1967 one could see evidence of a new approach to gay rights that went beyond the civil rights integrationist orientation and into the more militant stance that employed more confrontational or oppositional demonstrations against social and legal discrimination. Like the Black Power and antiwar movements, the energy for this stage of the movement emerged on radicalized university campuses. Premised on the special needs of a distinctive gay community, young activists within the movement were ready to take their cause to the streets. Dick Michaels and Bill Rand started publishing the *Advocate* in 1968 to serve as a hard-hitting newspaper for the gay community that expressed an aggressive pride in being gay. This publication served as the oracle of a movement no longer willing to remain in the shadows of American public life.

Quickening Pace of Law Reform

Although only Connecticut had followed the lead of Illinois in repealing its sodomy statute, by the end of the decade a growing chorus of legal experts advocated for decriminalization. Despite the Supreme Court's 1967 decision to sustain the constitutionality of an immigration law that denied citizenship to aliens on the grounds of homosexuality, homophile activists won an increasing number of appellate court decisions, particularly in the realm of employment discrimination. More significantly, the number of gay-related cases making it to the federal courts grew from 12 in the first half of the decade to 30 between 1965 and 1969. This increase offered hope that legal appeals might bring victory for gay rights advocates.

The legal status of gay bars offered a clear sign of progress. By the end of the decade, courts in New York, New Jersey, and Pennsylvania had followed California's lead in establishing the constitutional right of lesbians and gay men to assemble and be served in places selling alcohol. The movement received a boost when the ACLU took on the cause of gay rights earlier in the decade. By the late 1960s the ACLU was leading the fight in the courts against employment discrimination, violations of due process, and unequal enforcement of law (D'Emilio, 211–213).

Stonewall Riot

On Friday, June 27, 1969, the police of Manhattan's Sixth Precinct initiated a raid on Stonewall Inn, a gay bar on Christopher Street in the heart of Greenwich Village, during a New York City mayoral campaign. Incumbent John Lindsay had recently lost his party's primary and considered this a good time to boost his popularity by cracking down on homosexuals. Police harassment and repression of homosexuals increased in the city, particularly Greenwich Village, as gay life became more visible and gay men, women, and organizations became more assertive. Police would conduct the raids of gay bars based on a New York State Liquor authority ruling that a bar could allow no more than three homosexual patrons at any given time. The Stonewall Inn presented an inviting target for a police raid. It operated without a liquor license, allegedly had ties to organized crime, and offered scantily clad go-go boys as entertainment. On this particular night, however, the police were met with unexpected resistance.

As the police released the patrons one by one from inside the bar, a crowd began to grow outside on the street. Onlookers began to jeer the police as they led the bartender, bouncer, and three drag queens into a paddywagon. The last customer removed from the bar, a lesbian, put up a struggle, causing the crowd to react with even more hostility. Beer cans, bottles, and coins rained down onto police. All of a sudden, an uprooted parking meter was used as a battering ram on the Stonewall door as some of the resisters set the bar on fire. The police estimated that 200 mostly young men had been removed from the bar, but the crowd quickly grew to roughly 400 during the melee, which initially lasted approximately 45 minutes. This did not end the protesting as rioting continued well into the night as gay men and transvestites led charges against rows of police before regrouping in Greenwich Village alleys and side streets. The rioting and protests lasted throughout Friday and Saturday night as homosexuals vented years of frustration over bar raids, entrapment, and other forms of police harassment.

The Stonewall riot became the nation's first large-scale gay media event. Because it took place in New York City, the country's communication capital, news of the riot was broadcast throughout the country. Although much of the coverage about the Stonewall riot was negative, the word that gay people had fought back inspired the formation of several new, more radical, gay rights organizations throughout the nation. By the end of the weekend, gay liberation, a new form of collective action, had begun in earnest. The Mattachine Action Committee responded to the riot by issuing a call for organized resistance, and within a few days students at the Alternative University were providing space for Gay Liberation Front meetings. By 1973 an estimated 800 openly gay organizations existed in the United States. The anniversary of Stonewall is still recognized by the gay community in celebrations of Gay Pride from coast to coast.

Gay Liberation Front

The most noteworthy organization to form in the wake of Stonewall was the Gay Liberation Front (GLF). Founded in July 1969, the GLF fashioned itself in

Gay Liberation Front member holds poster under a banner, about 1970. (Evening Standard/Getty Images)

the mold of the New Left radicals. In order to get the word out about the new gay liberation movement, the GLF took advantage of the various political events young radicals staged across the country. New York's GLF, for example, sent a contingent of activists to a large antiwar demonstration held in the city on October 15, 1969. The GLF sent an even larger number of representatives to the November moratorium weekend in Washington, D.C., where almost half a million activists rallied against the United States involvement in Vietnam. GLF radicals also showed up on university campuses across the country during the fall of 1969. Gay radicals at the University of California–Berkeley performed guerrilla theatre on the campus during orientation and carried banners in a San Francisco antiwar march that November. The GLF also organized workshops at the 1969 annual convention of the National Student Association.

Gay liberationists working within the GLF attracted many young radicals not only because of a shared sexual identity, but also because of a shared political philosophy. As John D'Emilio has written, "Gay liberationists spoke in the hyperbolic phrases of the New Left. They talked of liberation from oppression, resisting genocide, and making a revolution against 'imperialist Amerika'" (D'Emilio, 234).

WOMEN'S AND GAY RIGHTS: ONLY THE BEGINNING

The feminist and homosexual struggles of the 1960s had their origins in the activism of the civil rights and New Left movements. These movements created a climate where injustice could be challenged. But as the decade evolved and entered an era of radicalism in reaction to the expanding conflict in Vietnam and the civil unrest of inner cities, a new wave of feminists began to separate themselves ideologically and culturally from their predecessors. To these radicals, equality in a fundamentally unequal society was no victory. Liberation, not equality, became their goal.

Radical feminists and gay liberationists, like radicals within the antiwar movement and Black Power movement, began to question liberalism's assumption that the system could be repaired. They also feared liberalism's apparent ability to co-opt and contain dissent. In this way, radical feminists of the late sixties shared new leftists' and African American separatists' hostility toward liberalism. Feminists of NOW sought women's inclusion in the public sphere, whereas radical feminists focused on the sexual politics of personal life. The women's liberation movement at the end of the decade got caught up in the countercultural milieu of utopian community building where they would build an alternative society free of hierarchy and centralized decisionmaking. Radical feminism remained the dominant ideology of the women's liberation movement into the early 1970s, when the movement became the victim of a cultural backlash in the mid-1970s.

In the same way, the gay liberation movement that formed after the Stonewall riots of 1969 rejected the more gradualist, integrationist approach of the Mattachine Society of the 1950s and early 1960s and began unapologetically demanding their rights to live and associate in a manner they, and not the dominant society, chose. Like adherents to the Black Power movement, homosexuals started calling for "Gay Power." Instead of begging for a place on the margins of society, gay radicals took to the streets as a part of the broader radical movements that had so inflamed much of American youth during the 1960s. Gay liberation boldly moved the homophile movement from the private into the public sphere. Infused with a sense of purpose and righteous indignation, the post-Stonewall gay liberation movement poured gasoline onto the homophile rights cause. Representative of this invigoration was the 5,000 to 10,000 men and women who showed up in June 1970 to commemorate the first anniversary of the Stonewall riot with a march from Greenwich Village to Central Park. The 50 homophile organizations that existed in the United States in 1969 exploded to more than 800 just four years later. In a relatively short amount of time, the gay liberation movement achieved what the more modest homophile movement could not: the active involvement of large numbers of homosexuals and lesbians in the gay rights movement.

BIOGRAPHIES

Heather Booth, 1945–

Abortion Activist

In 1963 Heather Booth went to the University of Chicago and became very involved in the civil rights movement. Her efforts to help coordinate the South Side Freedom Schools to campaign for integrated schools caused her to become active in Chicago's Coordinating Council of Community Organization. She then decided to set up a campus chapter of the Student Nonviolent Coordinating Committee. As a result of her extensive involvement in Chicago's civil rights movement, she was recruited to go to Mississippi during the summer of 1964 to work on the Freedom Summer Project. In 1965, during her sophomore year at the University of Chicago, Booth's ex-boyfriend told her that his sister was pregnant and needed an abortion. She called the civil rights' physician support team, Medical Committee for Human Rights, to find a doctor willing to do the abortion. After that experience, Booth started getting calls from other pregnant women needing help. She began telling people that callers should ask for Jane. Recognizing the need to support women during a crisis pregnancy, Booth formed JANE, one of the country's first abortion-counseling services. Very involved in

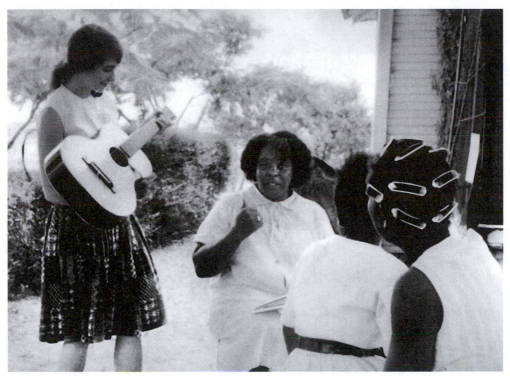

Heather Booth playing the guitar for Fannie Lou Hamer by her home in Ruleville, Mississippi, during the Mississippi Freedom Summer Project of 1964. (Wally Roberts)

the early women's movement of the mid-1960s, Booth has devoted her entire life to activism and community organizing. In addition to abortion rights, she has fought for affordable childcare and healthcare for working women.

Shulamith Firestone, 1945–

Radical Feminist

Born in Ottawa, Canada, Shulamith Firestone became a key figure in the early radical feminist movement. She attended Yavney of Telshe Yeshiva, Washington University, and the Art Institute of Chicago, where she earned a BFA in painting. While in Chicago, Firestone worked with Jo Freeman to organize the Westside Group, later called the Chicago Women's Liberation Union. In 1967 she moved to New York City and helped start the New York Radical Women. After a political split in the organization in 1969, Firestone led a group of more radical feminists in the founding of the Redstockings. It did not take long for Firestone to abandon Redstockings to form the New York Radical Feminists in late 1969. As with her previous associations, however, Firestone broke from this group over disagreements about its direction. She published *The Dialectic of Sex: A*

Case for Feminist Revolution in 1970 and then slid into obscurity while suffering from various forms of mental illness.

Franklin Kameny, 1925–

Gay Activist

Born in New York City, Franklin Kameny served in World War II and later became an astronomer in the Army Map Service in Washington, D.C. Dr. Kameny lost his job with the Map Service in 1957 for being a homosexual. In 1961, he and Jack Nichols cofounded the Mattachine Society in Washington, D.C., an organization that fought for gay rights, particularly in the area of equal employment rights within the federal government. Dr. Kameny and Nichols organized the first public protests by gays and lesbians at the White House on April 17, 1965. With the support of other gay and lesbian rights' organizations, the protest expanded to the Pentagon, the U.S. Civil Service Commission, and Philadelphia's Independence Hall. To mark this date in history, gay activists participate in protests, marches, and celebrations each year. In 1963, Dr. Kameny helped start a campaign to overturn sodomy laws and remove homosexuality as a mental disorder from the American Psychiatric Association's manual of mental disorders. In the 1970s, Dr. Kameny became the first openly gay man to run for U.S. Congress and created the Gay and Lesbian Alliance of Washington, D.C., a group that lobbies government for gay and lesbian rights.

Gerda Lerner, 1920–

Historian

Born in Vienna, Austria, to an affluent Jewish couple, Robert and Ilona Kronstein, she joined the anti-Nazi resistance in the 1930s, spending six weeks in jail for the cause. Lerner and her family escaped Nazi persecution by immigrating to the United States in 1939. After divorcing her first husband, Lerner married Carl Lerner, a theatre director who was a member of the Communist Party. The couple moved to Los Angeles where Carl became a successful filmmaker. Lerner joined the Community Party in 1946 and remained active in the party during the 1950s' McCarthy era. A latecomer to academia, Lerner went back to school at the age of 38. She earned her bachelor's degree from the New School for Social Research in 1963 and an M.A. (1965) and Ph.D. (1966) in history from Columbia University. Lerner developed one of the first women's history courses in the nation in 1963 as an undergraduate. She was a founding member of the National Organization for Women and later became president of the Organization of American Historians. She developed women's history curricula and programs at Long Island University (1965–1967), Sarah Lawrence College (1968–1979), Columbia University (1979–1980), and the University of Wisconsin–Madison where she is a professor emerita of history. She developed and directed the first graduate program in women's history at Sarah Lawrence College. In 1979, she developed the Summer Institute in Women's History for Leaders of Women's Organizations that ultimately gained presidential approval for a nationally recognized "Women's History Week." In 1987 it was expanded into Women's History Month.

Esther Peterson, 1906–1997

Labor Activist

Born to Danish immigrants, Peterson (maiden name Eggertson) grew up in a conservative Mormon family in Provo, Utah. She later graduated from Brigham Young University and moved to New York City where she married Oliver Peterson. The couple moved to Boston in 1932 where she taught at a prep school. While volunteering at the local Young Women's Christian Association, Peterson became aware of the problem of unequal pay for women. She eventually became involved with the International Ladies Garment Workers Union (ILGWL) and spent summers working at the Summer School for Women Workers in Industry. The school's mission was to bring young workingwomen from around the world to classes in everything from economics to poetry. In 1938, Peterson became a paid organizer for the American Federation of Teachers. That year she also had the first of four children. Because she continued to work after she became a mother, she became even more sensitive to the demands placed on underpaid workingwomen. In 1939, she joined the Amalgamated Clothing Workers Union and became its first lobbyist in Washington, D.C., in 1944. Assigned to work with a young U.S. representative from Boston, John F. Kennedy, Peterson fought for raising the minimum wage and the inclusion of more industries covered by the Fair Labor Standards Act, the law that established minimum wages and work hours. In 1948 she followed her husband to Sweden after his appointment as a diplomat for the State Department. For 10 years she lived in Europe and became active in the Swedish Confederation of Trade Unions and the International Confederation of Free Trade Unions. After she returned to the United States in 1957, Peterson became a lobbyist for the Industrial Union Department of the AFL-CIO. After Kennedy decided to run for president, Peterson left the AFL-CIO to work for his campaign in Utah. After Kennedy became president, he appointed Peterson to lead the Women's Bureau in the Department of Labor. While in that role she established the President's Commission on the Status of Women to study the status of women and develop recommendations to promote gender equality. The commission's final report addressed the lack of daycare for working mothers, equal pay for equal work, and the concentration of women working in low-wage jobs. The commission also helped prepare the way for the National Women's Committee on Civil Rights to provide a voice for African American women in the struggle for civil rights. Peterson was instrumental in the passage of the Equal Pay Act of 1963. In 1963, she was named assistant secretary for labor standards, making her the highest-ranking woman in the Kennedy administration. In 1981, Peterson received a Presidential Medal of Freedom, the nation's highest civilian award.

Randolfe "Randy" Wicker, 1938–

Gay Activist

Born Charles Hayden Jr. in 1938, he became active in the Mattachine Society in New York in 1958. He unsuccessfully tried to push the Mattachine Society to use more aggressive tactics in its fight for gay civil rights. He changed his name to "Randy Wicker" at the request of his father. After his failed efforts to radicalize the Mattachine Society, Wicker took off on his own in an effort to use the media to get the word out about discrimination against homosexuals. In 1962, he successfully hosted the first radio talk show in New York City that focused on homosexual-related issues. In 1964, he organized a picket at the New York Army induction center. Starting in the 1960s, Wicker began contributing numerous articles to gay periodicals in New York City and Washington, D.C. In 1971, Wicker cofounded the GAA-NY Video Committee in an effort to document gay celebrations and protests. These videos became the basis for a New York cable access television series devoted to gay issues.

REFERENCES AND FURTHER READINGS

Adam, Barry. 1987. *The Rise of a Gay and Lesbian Movement*. Boston: Twayne.

Boulding, E. 1962. *Who Are These Women?* Ann Arbor, MI: Institute for Conflict Resolution.

Brauer, Carl M. 1983. "Women Activists, Southern Conservatives, and the Prohibition of Sex Discrimination in Title VII of the 1964 Civil Rights Act." *Journal of Southern History* 49, no. 1: 37–56.

Chafe, William H. 2003. *The Unfinished Journey: America since World War II*. 5th ed. New York: Oxford University Press.

Chalmers, David. 1996. *And the Crooked Places Made Straight: The Struggle for Social Change in the 1960s*. 2nd ed. Baltimore: Johns Hopkins University Press.

Chauncey, George. 2004. *Why Marriage? The History Shaping Today's Debate Over Gay Equality*. New York: Basic Books.

Cohen, Marcia. 1988. *The Sisterhood: The True Story of the Women Who Changed the World*. New York: Simon and Schuster.

D'Emilio, John. 1983. *Sexual Politics, Sexual Communities: The Making of a Homosexual Minority in the United States, 1940–1970*. Chicago: University of Chicago Press.

Dijkstra, Sandra. 1980. "Simone de Beauvoir and Betty Friedan: The Politics of Omission." *Feminist Studies* 6, no. 2: 290–303.

Doty, Robert C. 1963. "Growth of Overt Homosexuality in City Provokes Wide Concern." *New York Times* (December 17).

Duberman, Martin. 1993. *Stonewall*. New York: Plume.

Echols, Alice. 1989. *Daring to Be Bad: Radical Feminism in America, 1967–1975*. Minneapolis: University of Minnesota Press.

Evans, Sara M. 2003. *Tidal Wave: How Women Changed America at Century's End*. New York: Free Press.

Farber, David, and Beth Bailey. 2001. *The Columbia Guide to America in the 1960s*. New York: Columbia University Press.

Ferree, Myra Marx, and Beth B. Hess. 1995. *Controversy and Coalition: The New Feminist Movement Across Three Decades of Change*. 3rd ed. New York: Routledge.

Friedan, Betty. 1963. *The Feminine Mystique*. New York: Norton.

Harrison, Cynthia. 1988. *On Account of Sex: The Politics of Women's Issues, 1945–1968*. Berkeley: University of California Press.

Harrison, Cynthia E. 1980. "A 'New Frontier' for Women: The Public Policy of the Kennedy Administration." *Journal of American History* 67, no. 3: 630–646.

Kisseloff, Jeff. 2007. *Generation on Fire: Voices of Protest from the 1960s*. Lexington: University Press of Kentucky.

Kraditor, Aileen, ed. 1968. *Up From the Pedestal: Selected Writings in the History of American Feminism*. Chicago: Quadrangle Books.

Marcus, Eric. 2002. *Making Gay History: The Half-Century Fight for Lesbian and Gay Equal Rights*. New York: Perennial.

Marotta, Toby. 1981. *The Politics of Homosexuality*. Boston: Houghton-Mifflin.

Murdoch, Joyce, and Deb Price. 2001. *Courting Justice: Gay Men and Lesbians v. The Supreme Court*. New York: Basic Books.

Rosen, Ruth. 2000. *The World Split Open: How the Modern Women's Movement Changed America*. New York: Viking.

Ryan, Barbara. 1992. *Feminism and the Women's Movement: Dynamics of Change in Social Movement, Ideology, and Activism*. New York: Routledge.

Swerdlow, Amy. 1982. "Ladies' Day at the Capitol: Women Strike for Peace versus HUAC." *Feminist Studies* 8, no. 3: 493–520.

Timmons, Stuart. 1990. *The Trouble with Harry Hay: Founder of the Modern Gay Movement*. Boston: Alyson Publishers.

Identity Politics

As the civil rights movement hit its crescendo in the 1960s, other ethnic minority groups beside African Americans began to reassess their own place in the political, economic, and cultural landscape of the United States. Mexican Americans, American Indians, and Asian Americans were three such minorities who began to organize and express their resistance to racial and ethnic discrimination. The trajectory of the politics of ethnic identity by these and other groups during the 1960s mirrored the civil rights movement's transformation from a call for integration to a call for independence and self-determination. This chapter will explore the rise and radicalization of ethnic identity politics during the decade.

The increasingly xenophobic political environment of the 1950s caused the largest segment of the Latino population, Mexican Americans, to organize a unified ethnic class movement. Mexicans were excluded from the restrictive immigration legislation of the 1920s because Americans believed that they would be transitory migrants and would return to Mexico, and therefore the United States could benefit from their labor while avoiding the problems of having to absorb them into society. But with a 2,000-mile border it proved impossible to control the flow of migrant workers with the spiraling demand for cheap labor, especially during World War II. A constant flow of Mexicans into the United States expanded a minority group whose cultural values and language were constantly reinforced by new waves of immigrants. For this reason, Mexicans proved culturally resistant to assimilation.

Inclusive organizations in the 1950s such as the Community Service Organization and Asociacin Nacional Mexico-Americana tried to bring Mexican Americans together on the grounds of ethnicity and class regardless of their status as U.S. citizens. These groups began working on the housing, educational, and economic needs of Mexican Americans, particularly in the Southwest. While celebrating Mexican American culture, they also identified police brutality as a major problem for all people of color. By combining the campaign for Mexican American civil rights with the rights of Mexican alien workers, the work of these organizations signaled a crucial ideological change for Mexican American political and labor groups that set the stage for the rise of ethnic politics in the 1960s.

The growing sense of awareness of cultural identity and a feeling of exploitation and discrimination could no longer be contained by the mid-1960s when the Chicano movement emerged among Mexican American students on California university campuses. As an outgrowth of a more general student revolt of this decade, the Chicano movement was in part a generational phenomenon. The Chicano movement represented the most radical group within the larger American population of Mexican origin. Some Mexican Americans completely identified with the United States while others more closely identified with their Spanish heritage. Chicanos, influenced by the Black Power movement and a general heightened awareness of a Latin American revival ignited by the Cuban Revolution, asserted their Mexican and Hispanic origins and traditions in opposition to the American white bourgeois culture. The Chicano movement was a part of a wider revolt against the values of the establishment also expressed by African Americans and Indians. In fact, unlike older generations of Mexican Americans, Chicanos also embraced their Indian origins and believed their "brownness" was an important part of their culture.

Along with the Chicanos, American Indians best represent the new ethnic politics of the 1960s that was a part of this wider revolt against the establishment. After World War II, federal policy toward Indians changed. Thousands of Indians served in the military during the war only to return to the reservation with limited economic opportunity. In 1953 the U.S. Congress issued a joint resolution to end federal supervision and control of Indians and adopt a policy of assimilation. The so-called policy of emancipation and assimilation quickly became one of termination as the federal government began to disband several Indian communities and distribute their assets to individual tribal members while discontinuing federal services like health care and education. Indians fell deeper into poverty and lost thousands of acres as a result of this federal policy until in the 1960s it was declared a failure.

Operating concurrently with the policy of termination was the policy of relocation that aimed to move Indians from the reservation to urban areas in search of better educational and economic opportunities. Recognizing the oppressive poverty of the reservation, the Bureau of Indian Affairs believed that relocation offered a better chance of social betterment and integration. By the end of the

1960s almost half of the Indian population lived outside of reservations, but their economic condition did not improve. The policy of termination and relocation, however, did serve to politicize Indians now living in cities by exposing them to other groups struggling for social change and reinforcing a group consciousness in opposition to the dominant culture.

Indians began their protest in the early to mid-1960s by targeting whites' use of their land and what they viewed as other violations of century-old treaties between Indian tribes and the U.S. government. By the end of the decade, politically active Indians had followed the path of other social movements to assert a more radical agenda. "As the policymakers of the Kennedy and Johnson administrations sought to include them in their programs, Indians themselves were becoming increasingly self-reliant in articulating their agenda" (Sayer, 27). With the establishment of the American Indian movement in 1968, Indians sought to reclaim their identity by aggressively asserting their traditions, spiritual beliefs, treaty rights, land reform, and a call for Indian nation sovereignty.

With the rise of the Chicano movement and the American Indian movement, Mexican Americans and American Indians exemplified the rise of ethnic politics that emerged out of a 1960s' culture of revolt against economic, political, and cultural discrimination. Following the example of the African American civil rights movement, Chicanos and Indians asserted their rights and paved the way for other ethnic groups such as Asian Americans.

TIMELINE

1958   Tuscarora Indians protest against the New York Power Authority.

1959   Mexican American Political Association (MAPA) is organized.

1961   The American Indian Chicago Conference is held.
National Indian Youth Council is organized.

1963   Alianza Federal de Pueblos Libres is organized.
The first southern California Chicano youth conferences are held.

1964   The National Indian Youth Council begins a series of "fish-ins" in the Pacific Northwest.
Indians seize Alcatraz.
Indians take over Fort Lawton in Seattle.

1965   President Johnson signs the Immigration Act.

The Agricultural Workers Organizing Committee (AWOC) initiates a strike by Filipino migrant workers.

Caesar Chavez and the National Farm Workers join the AWOC strike.

1966   Fifty Mexican Americans walk out of a meeting with the Johnson administration's Equal Employment Opportunities Commission (EEOC), called the "Guarache Out."

Mexican American Ad Hoc Committee is created within the EEOC.

Vicente Ximenes is appointed to the EEOC. Ximenes later appointed head of the newly created Interagency Committee on Mexican-American Affairs.

Chavez is named president of the newly formed United Farm Workers (UFW).

Alianza Federal de Pueblos Libres 62-mile protest march from Albuquerque to Santa Fe.

UFW organizes a boycott against grape growers.

1967   La Raza Unida is organized.

The Brown Berets are organized.

Reies Lopez Tijerina and Alianza Federal de Pueblos Libres Tierra Amarilla courthouse seizure.

Mexican American Youth Organization (MAYO) is organized.

1968   The Mexican American Legal Defense and Education Fund (MALDEF) is created.

Crusade for Justice protests are held in Denver.

Students participate in "Blowout" at Los Angeles area high schools.

Chicana Welfare Rights is organized.

The Indian Civil Rights Act signed by President Johnson.

American Indian Movement (AIM) is organized in Minneapolis, Minnesota.

1969   Students participate in West Side High walkout.

El Plan Espiritual de Aztlan is adopted at the Chicano Youth Conference.

Students participate in Crystal City High School Boycott.

MAYO organizes the Winter Garden Project (Texas).

MAYO organizes Del Rio, Texas, demonstrations.

The Hijas de Cauhuhtemoc group and the Chicana Symposium are organized.

"Indians of All Tribes" seize Alcatraz.

Custer Died for Your Sins is published.

1970   American Indian Tribal Court Judges Association is organized.

MEXICAN AMERICANS STRUGGLE FOR ASSIMILATION

During the 1960s Mexican Americans represented the nation's largest and fastest-growing minority group. Concentrated mainly in the Southwest and Midwest, they totaled approximately 5.6 million by the end of the decade. California had the largest concentrations of Mexican Americans of any state in the nation, and Los Angeles of any city. Even though Census statistics typically undercounted the number of Americans of Mexican descent, it reported that the Mexican American population in California had tripled in size since 1940. The Los Angeles area showed even greater increases; the "Spanish surname" population in the county jumped from 576,000 (9.54 percent of the total) in 1960 to 1,289,000 (17.24 percent of the total) in 1970 and in the city from 260,000 (10.5 percent) in 1960 to 545,000 (19.4 percent) in 1970 (Grebler, Moore, and Guzman, 106).

Mexican Americans suffered from racial discrimination well before these demographic changes of the sixties. Although the Mexican-American War of 1848 caused many Mexicans to live within the U.S. borders, the barrios that exist in cities throughout the Southwest and Midwest emerged when 1.5 million Mexicans immigrated to the United States between 1900 and 1930. Upon their arrival these immigrants discovered that they would be restricted to the lowest-paying, most menial jobs, segregated in underfunded schools, and provided inadequate housing and inferior public accommodations. In response to these conditions, these immigrants formed political organizations such as the League of United Latin American Citizens (LULAC) to fight for equality and civil rights.

During the Great Depression, Mexican American workers became scapegoats for massive unemployment. By World War II, employment opportunities for Mexican Americans expanded, but discrimination and racial stereotypes, especially those that regarded Mexicans as inherently criminal and lazy, persisted. During wartime hysteria a fictional wave of Mexican American juvenile delinquency led to the Zoot Suit riots of 1943 and institutionalized a fervent hostility between police and the Mexican American community.

By the 1960s Mexican Americans could relate to the plight of African Americans as they suffered lower levels of educational attainment and experienced rigid occupational stratification and inferior housing. Mexican Americans had even less political representation than African Americans. Organizations such as LULAC, the G.I. Forum, and the Mexican American Political Association (MAPA) served as Mexican Americans' best hope to respond to these conditions. While these were not monolithic groups, they fought against discrimination in three distinct ways: by engaging liberal politics in order to end the most offensive forms of discrimination; by claiming Mexican Americans were a part of the white race; and by adopting a pluralistic vision of American society in which they could be integrated into the mainstream of American life while holding on to aspects of Mexican culture. Because they considered themselves white, they essentially rejected any classification system that equated them with African Americans. As a result, by the mid-sixties the leading Mexican American political organizations had defined themselves out of the civil rights agenda (Escobar, 1483–1490).

The Mexican American Political Association

In April 1959 150 delegates gathered in Fresno, California, to organize the Mexican American Political Association (MAPA). Identifying the need for a Mexican electoral organization, these delegates established MAPA to emphasize ethnic identity, direct electoral politics, electoral independence, and the concerns of the Mexican community. Its slogan was "Opportunity for All through MAPA." The founders organized MAPA partially due to the Democratic Party's disregard for the Mexican community and the defeats of Mexican American office-seekers. MAPA's major figure was Ed Roybal, who represented a significant constituency in urban Southern California.

MAPA existed throughout the 1980s, but reached its peak between 1960 and 1965. According to historian Juan Gomez-Quinones, MAPA contributed partially to the election of two assemblymen, one congressman, and six judges in California during the 1960 election. However, the organization could not capitalize on this early success and quickly faded into political irrelevance. In fact, between 1960 and 1966 the total number of Mexican American voters in California declined. It suffered from a loose organizational structure, a split between moderate and progressive factions, and power struggles between competing leaders. Often accused of lacking sharply informed and well-reasoned positions, reacting too late and too ineffectively to critically important issues affecting the Mexican community, and subverting the populist concerns of the membership to the careerist interests of its leaders, MAPA suffered most acutely from a lack of resources and effective outreach.

Although somewhat effective in influencing local cases of police brutality and discrimination, MAPA could never mount a large-scale voter registration drive. Its biggest defeat came in 1960 when it was unable to prevent the gerrymandering of the Democratic-controlled legislature that diluted the influence of the Mexican American vote throughout California.

The Immigration Act of 1965

Immigration laws passed in the 1920s created quotas based on "national origins" that favored immigrants from northern and western Europe. Subsequent legislation somewhat altered the immigration profile, but the Immigration Act of 1965 represented the first major departure from the restrictionist intent of earlier immigration policy. The act replaced national origins with hemispheric "ceilings," established a preference for professionals and skilled technical workers, and emphasized family reunification. In effect, the Immigration Act of 1965 dramatically altered the demographics of the American population by encouraging immigration from Asia and the Americas.

From 1930 to 1960 about 80 percent of the immigrants to the United States came from Europe or Canada. By the late 1970s, only 16 percent of the immigrants came from Europe or Canada while 40 percent came from Asia and Latin America. The authors of the Immigration Act of 1965 expected the continued

President Lyndon B. Johnson signs the Immigration Act of 1965 on Liberty Island, New York. (Lyndon Baines Johnson Museum and Library/Yoichi R. Okamoto)

The "Guarache Out"

Due to complaints that the Equal Employment Opportunities Commission (EEOC) paid little attention to the employment problems of Mexican Americans, the Johnson administration directed the EEOC to call a meeting with Mexican Americans in March 1966 in Albuquerque, New Mexico. Although the commission, headed by Franklin Roosevelt Jr. promised to focus attention to the employment problems of Mexican Americans, no action was taken. Tired of being ignored, approximately 50 Mexican Americans walked out of the meeting because, although the commission advocated equal employment, it did not propose any action or include a single Mexican American on its staff. In fact, Roosevelt and all but one of the commissioners did not even attend the meeting. This act of protest was later called the "guarache out."

When asked why no Mexican Americans were on his staff, EEOC Executive Director Herman Edelman blamed the disorganization of Mexican Americans, pointing out that only 12 of the 300 complaints filed with the EEOC since 1965 had come from Mexican Americans. In response to the walkout and the claims of disorganization, Mexican Americans formed the Mexican-American Ad Hoc Committee in Equal Employment Opportunity. President Johnson later agreed to meet with selected Mexican American leaders at the White House on May 26, 1966, where he charmed these leaders and in 1967 appointed Vicente Ximenes to the EEOC. Shortly thereafter Ximenes was named head of the newly created Interagency Committee on Mexican-American Affairs.

The meeting and these appointments mollified middle-class Mexican American activists, but it did little to appease the growing chorus of young Mexican Americans who saw little accomplished by these hollow gestures. President Johnson held a Cabinet committee hearing in El Paso, Texas, in October 1967 but, fearing another walkout, refused to invite the more oppositional Chicano leaders of that time like Cesar Chavez and Rodolfo Gonzales. Instead, activists representing those Mexican Americans ignored by the American mainstream and caught in the underclass picketed the Cabinet hearing, calling themselves La Raza Unida.

flow of Europeans, but improved economic conditions in these countries made immigration to the United States less attractive. It was evident by the late 1960s that Mexican immigration was increasing, mostly to rural areas and the barrios of cities in the Southwest. This increased flow of Mexican immigration increased the political clout of Mexican Americans living in the Southwest.

The United Farm Workers

Cesar Chavez was the first president of the AFL-CIO–chartered National Farm Workers Association, later renamed the United Farm Workers (UFW), in 1965. As the leader of the UFW, Chavez led the most visible Chicano struggle for economic justice of the decade. Chavez brought national attention to the struggle of migrant farm workers when he organized a strike and national boycott of California grapes. Leading up to the California primary for the 1968 presidential election, Robert Kennedy, favored Democratic presidential candidate, visited Chavez and the striking workers to publicly support their cause.

The grape pickers of California were among the most exploited workers in the country. They had no job security, fringe benefits, or retirement program. Due to the powerful state and federal farm lobby, growers did not have to bargain collectively with them. The strike actually began in September 1965 with Filipino workers organized by the Agricultural Workers Organizing Committee (AWOC) of the AFL-CIO. Eight days later Chavez' National Farm Workers joined them.

Chavez had previously worked with Saul Alinsky's Community Services Organization for 10 years, learning Alin-

Cesar Chavez organized the first effective migrant worker union in the United States. His political skill and his unswerving dedication to one of society's most unprotected sectors made him a popular hero. (Library of Congress)

sky's technique of building local organizations from the inside out. Chavez worked in the fields around the Delano, California, area for three years before the strike began. In that time he was able to organize 300 of the approximately 5,000 vineyard workers in the area (AWOC represented about 200 workers). The strike quickly became an impetus for a broader civil rights movement for Mexican Americans. Six months into the strike approximately 10,000 people marched to the steps of the state capitol in Sacramento to support what had now become something more than a strike; it had become a cause, "La Causa."

In December 1965 the AFL-CIO recognized Chavez' organization and changed the name to the United Farm Workers (UFW). The union began contributing $10,000 a month to the strike while local churches and charitable organizations also threw their support behind the cause. In 1966 the UFW organized a boycott against the principal wine grape growers, most notably the Schenley and DiGiogio corporations. Several major wine-grape growers reluctantly agreed to negotiate a contract with the workers instead of continuing to watch their businesses and reputations suffer. The table-grape growers proved more obstinate. Even though these growers only spent roughly 2 to 5 percent of total production costs on labor, they insisted that they needed the cheap labor some 350,000 Mexican nationals with California work permits provided. Chavez responded by asking that all Mexicans with green cards be sent home and that immigration laws be strictly enforced. He said, "The growers are using the poorest of the poor of another country to defeat the poorest of the poor in this country."

As the struggle with growers continued, militants from the Brown Power movement became involved in the cause. Concerned about the prospects of violence by the intrusion of these radicals, Chavez reinforced his commitment to non-violence by going on a 25-day fast that permanently injured his health but served the purpose of bringing national attention to the fight. Robert Kennedy joined Chavez when he ended the fast at an ecumenical mass and declared Chavez "one of the heroic figures of our time." The national attention on Chavez' fast and the grape workers strike helped launch the national boycott against the table-grape industry. Many food store chains stopped carrying grapes, but the growers continued to claim profits (the Pentagon helped the growers by placing large orders). By the middle of 1969, however, 10 growers producing about 10 percent of the California grape crop negotiated a contract with the UFW. This proved a major victory for Chavez, the UFW, and the Mexican American cause. Chavez' leadership of the grape strike made him an icon for the emerging Chicano movement (O'Neill, 393–395).

Mexican American Legal Defense and Education Fund (MALDEF)

The Ford Foundation helped establish the Mexican American Legal Defense and Education Fund (MALDEF) in 1968 to help address the needs of the Mexican American community, particularly in the Southwest. Modeled after the NAACP Legal Defense Fund, the Ford Foundation committed $2.2 million over eight years to hire lawyers able to fight discrimination against Mexican Americans. The Ford Foundation had concluded that Mexican Americans were the most disorganized and fragmented minority in the United States, and they needed a national organization of lawyers to serve their social, economic, and political needs. McGeorge Bundy, president of the Ford Foundation, in announcing the grant, underscored the Mexican American community's needs:

> In terms of legal enforcement of their civil rights, American citizens of Mexican descent are now where the Negro community was a quarter-century ago. There are not nearly enough Mexican-American lawyers, and most of them have neither the income nor experience to do civil rights works.

He went on to explain why the Mexican American community had not sought recourse in the courts: "Because the law has often been used against Mexican-Americans, as well as other minority groups, they are suspicious of legal processes" (*New York Times,* May 2, 1968, p. 38).

The Ford Foundation felt compelled to respond to a request for assistance by a group of Mexican American lawyers after examining studies that showed Mexican Americans living in the Southwest were recruited for lower-paying jobs, were discriminated against in employment in government and private industry, and were often denied equal pay. One-third of all Mexican American families lived below the poverty line and were the most poorly educated demographic in the Southwest, with a dropout rate of approximately 50 percent. In addition, they suffered from school segregation and the indignity of being classified "retarded" because of language and cultural differences that caused them to do poorly on aptitude tests that did not take these differences into account.

Young law school graduates came to work for MALDEF and began seeking to use the courts to advance the social and political welfare of the Mexican American community. MALDEF attorneys launched scores of lawsuits to challenge vestiges of segregation and discrimination in the Southwest. Perhaps the most important case was *Cisneros v. Corpus Christi Independent School District* (1970), which decided that Mexican Americans constituted an identifiable ethnic group for desegregation purposes.

THE RISE OF THE CHICANO MOVEMENT

The origins of new political activity among Mexicans living in the United States can be traced to the political climate, material conditions, and cultural milieu of the early 1960s. The Mexican population increased more dramatically at this time due to both birthrate and immigration. Because of this increased presence, particularly in the Southwest, Mexicans living in the United States gained more scholarly, media, and political attention. At the time, Mexicans were recognized as the second-largest minority group and typically worked the least desirable jobs and lagged behind the income and schooling levels of both whites and African Americans. As a result, amid the rise of New Left politics, the social and economic conditions of Mexican Americans increasingly attracted the attention of political activists.

In 1960 Mexican Americans on average made it only through the eighth grade as compared with the tenth grade for other nonwhites and twelfth grade for white Americans. Their per capita yearly income remained extremely low at $968, compared with $1,044 for other nonwhite minorities, such as African Americans and American Indians, and $2,047 for white Americans. These statistics were even worse for areas of chronic poverty like rural New Mexico and southern

Texas. The social and economic conditions of Mexican Americans at the beginning of the decade suggest that these statistics were a portent for future civil disturbances.

As President Lyndon Johnson's Great Society programs were established, Mexican Americans contact with government services increased both in relation to services received as well as services demanded. As governmental contact increased, Mexican Americans experienced the hostility of agencies more interested in regulating their behavior than providing services. As service became slightly more accessible amid the wave of Great Society programs, hostile government attitudes and practices continued to be the norm and therefore became the focus of Mexican American political protest and mobilization.

The civil rights movement of the 1960s also contributed to the beginning of this new political activism. While primarily focused on the plight of African Americans living in the South, it brought awareness to other minorities problems. Both the Kennedy and Johnson administrations seemed willing to consider the increased demands by Mexican Americans for equal citizenship rights. In addition, the Cuban Revolution, and later the African and Vietnamese liberation wars, brought awareness about the conditions of third world peoples living within the United States. Within this social, political, and ideological context rose what became identified as the "Chicano movement."

Chicanismo

In the early 1960s, a strand of radical political and ethnic populism rose to challenge accepted assumptions, politics, and principles of the establishment both inside and outside the Mexican community. As liberal and reformist movements dominated the political landscape of the early 1960s, most closely identified with the civil rights movement, early strands of radicalism appeared in the separatist and anticorporation tendencies of young "Chicanos," a word used to identify Mexicans as a group with an overt identity. "Chicano" or "Chicana" denoted the person and group, while "Chicanismo" referred to a set of beliefs and political practice. The word "Chicano" dates back to the early 16th century when Spaniards invaded Mexico and conquered the Aztecs. The uneducated rural Mexicans who lived in the mountain villages, isolated from urban areas, referred to themselves as "Meh-shee-kah-nos." When many living in these isolated rural villages later migrated to urban areas and the United States, they dropped the "Me" and shortened the word to "Shicano," which later became "Chicano" (Castro, 131–132).

"The emphasis of 'Chicanismo' upon dignity, self-worth, pride, uniqueness, and a feeling of cultural rebirth made it attractive to many Mexicans in a way that cut across class, regional, and generational lines" (Gomez-Quinones, 104). Having experienced social and economic discrimination for some time, Chicanismo especially appealed to young Mexicans looking for a sense of pride and empowerment by emphasizing Mexican cultural consciousness, heritage, and language. The political right and middle class rejected the term as pejorative while the laboring class preferred "Mexicano," but to the young, "Chicano" became the rallying cry for a new, more oppositional political activism. This newfound ethnic consciousness accompanied a more confrontational politics that included demonstrations, boycotts, strikes, sit-ins, and street fighting. The point of this activism was to promote the conceptualization of a national identity, advocate for full political rights, and achieve increased economic and social participation.

The Brown Berets

Several young Mexican Americans in the 1960s rejected assimilation in the dominant culture of the United States and instead celebrated their Mexican heritage. Referred to as "Brown Power," derived from Stokely Carmichael's militant call for "Black Power," the Brown Berets best exemplified this radical movement. Brown Power advocates urged Mexican Americans to embrace their Spanish and Indian traditions while calling for state and federal support for equal employment opportunities and bilingual and bicultural education. The Brown Berets, founded in East Los Angeles by David Sanchez, acted as the vanguard of this movement. The organization rallied militant youth from 1967 through 1972 in nearly 30 chapters across mainly the Southwest, especially in Texas and California. They published a newspaper, *La Causa,* to promote their political, social, and cultural agenda. In principle nonviolent, like the Black Panthers they emphasized the right to self-defense in the face of aggression.

Carlos Montes, cofounder of the Brown Berets, speaks during a rally of the Poor Peoples' March to Washington, in Kansas City, May 20, 1968. (AP Photo/William Straeter)

The Brown Berets in particular protested police brutality and discrimination against Chicanos while also questioning the disproportionate number of Chicanos serving in Vietnam. Allied with the Black Panthers and the Students for a Democratic Society on many issues in the late 1960s, they emphasized self-determination, adequate housing, justice, and equal employment and education opportunities for Mexican Americans.

Crusade for Justice

Founded in the mid-1960s by Rodolfo "Corky" Gonzales, a former boxer and liberal Democrat who worked for the John F. Kennedy campaign in 1960, the Crusade for Justice offered direction for the confrontational politics of the Chicano movement. Based out of Denver, the Crusade for Justice found its focus and energy through a protest against discrimination by the administration for the city of Denver in April 1966. Growing up in a migrant farm-worker family and becoming a Golden Gloves boxing champion gave Gonzales credibility among the barrio youth, college students, and the ex-inmate population.

The Crusade for Justice organized protests that would often attract thousands of protesters. The demonstrations concentrated on civil rights, discrimination in schools, police brutality, and cultural programs. The Crusade promoted cultural consciousness among Mexican Americans and the creation of a society based on humanism, "La Familia," and self-determination rather than competition. Instead of working within the existing social and political structure, the Crusade for Justice developed alternative institutions such as its school, Tlatelolco, social center, bookstore, and newspaper, *El Gallo*.

The Crusade for Justice provided national leadership for the Chicano movement and remained highly active from 1968 until 1978. On June 29, 1968, the Crusade for Justice headed a march on Denver's police headquarters to protest the police shooting and killing of 15-year-old Joseph Archuleta. In 1969 when students walked out of West Side High School, the Crusade for Justice organized a march in support of the students and their parents. Gonzales and several others were arrested following an altercation with police during the walkout. At the trial, films showed that the altercation was best characterized as a "police riot" and all defendants were acquitted.

El Plan Espiritual de Aztlan

The Crusade for Justice strengthened its impact by organizing the Chicano Youth conferences of 1969 and 1970. At the 1969 youth conference the term "Chicano" was adopted as a symbol of cultural resistance. The roughly 2,000 participants at the 1969 conference adopted "El Plan Espiritual de Aztlan," a revolutionary plan in the tradition of Mexican history. The 1969 conference and plan it produced signaled a clear break at a national level from the assimilationist "Mexican American" consciousness and politics of earlier decades.

El Plan Espiritual de Aztlan was a national plan for liberation that articulated nationalism as its method and self-determination as its goal. The preamble of the plan called for liberation through solidarity based on culture and nationality. Although ideologically vague, the plan's call for a "Bronze Nation of Aztlan" created a foundation for much of the subsequent ideological and political developments of cultural nationalism among young Mexican Americans. The very term

The Crystal City High School Boycott

Approximately 1,600 Mexican American students in Crystal City, Texas, put the principle of self-determination into action by boycotting school to protest discriminatory practices by the "gringo"-dominated school board. Mexican Americans comprised 80 percent of the population of Crystal City, a town located forty miles from the Mexican border and 100 miles southwest of San Antonio. Over 2,500 of Crystal City High School's 2,900 students were Mexican American.

The student unrest began in the spring of 1969 when a committee of the faculty, which had 97 white teachers compared to only 30 Mexican American teachers, began selecting cheerleaders, class representatives, and other class honors. The faculty committee, for example, picked three white students and only one Mexican American student for the cheerleading squad. Two students presented a petition to the high school principal that demanded equal representation on the squad. Rejected by the principal, the school superintendent agreed that two additional Mexican American cheerleaders should be added. Buoyed by the success of the petition, another student wrote a pamphlet decrying the method used to pick the homecoming queen. School rules required that the queen be a daughter of a graduate from Crystal City High, essentially eliminating most Mexican Americans from contention. In support of the pamphlet, thousands of students took to the streets in a planned demonstration. Incited by some racist comments from local business owners and school officials, the 1,600 students decided in December 1969 to begin a boycott of classes.

In late December, investigators for the Department of Health, Education, and Welfare and the U.S. Civil Rights Commission came to Crystal City amid reports that the schools could lose more than $300,000 in federal funding and even more in state monies due to the decline in average daily attendance at the school. The boycotts ended in early January 1970 when school officials ratified an agreement to abolish many of the "ethnic inequalities" of the school system. More important, in the wake of this student protest, a newly formed citizens' organization decided they would work to take over the school board in the spring elections of 1970. In April 1970, Mexican Americans won four out of seven seats on the Crystal City Board of Education, and all of the Mexican American city council candidates were elected.

Aztlan referred back to the ancient Aztec myth of a homeland somewhere to the north of present-day Mexico City. For the Chicano students, Aztlan meant that Chicanos and Mexicans shared a common historical origin and identity. The plan referred to all people living in the United States with a Mexican heritage as La Raza Bronze, or the Bronze People, a Mestizo people proud of their Indian roots. In a call for unity among all with Mexican origins, the plan poetically declared: "With our heart in our hands and our hands in the soil, we declare the independence of our mestizo nation. We are a bronze people with a bronze culture. Before all of North America, before all our brothers in the bronze continent, we are a nation, we are a union of free pueblos, we are Aztlan. *Por La Raz todo. Fuera de la Raza nada*" (Del Castillo and Leon, 131).

In an effort to carry out El Espiritual Plan de Aztlan, college and university students organized another conference at the University of California at Santa Barbara in 1969. They tried to bring all Chicano student organizations under one umbrella called MEChA that would pressure universities to recruit more Chicano students and faculty, establish Chicano studies programs, and serve the general interests and needs of the Chicano community.

Bilingual Education

In an article published in 1969 in the *National Education Association Journal,* Joe Bernal made the case for bilingual education in response to the growing problem of diminishing educational opportunities for Mexican Americans. In the 1960s, the average Mexican American dropped out of school by the seventh grade. In Texas, almost 80 percent of students with Spanish surnames dropped out before finishing high school. In California, 73.5 percent of the state's Mexican American students did not complete high school. Bernal argued that school failure for Mexican American students could be traced to how white educators put the Spanish speaking and listening skills of these students in direct conflict with English proficiency.

Bernal explained that unlike other immigrant groups, Mexican Americans had clung to their mother tongue, Spanish, for three, four, and five generations. The close proximity of the Mexican border and therefore the availability of Spanish language television, newspapers, radio, and movies in part explained the continued reliance on Spanish by Mexican Americans living in the Southwest. Accustomed to communicating in Spanish with friends and family in the barrios, Mexican American students were then punished for speaking Spanish in the schools. Bernal and those involved in the bilingual movement argued that the use of Spanish in the educational process could help in overcoming this language conflict for Mexican American students. "In some cases," he wrote, "Spanish can be used as the teaching language. For instance, bilinguists can be taught mathematics in Spanish. Admittedly, this will not improve their abilities in English, but at least their mathematical learning will not be held back because of their deficiency in English."

Activists within the Chicano movement who advocated for bilingual education believed the emphasis on English proficiency in so-called intelligence tests caused teachers and counselors to inadvertently classify bright bilingual children as slow learners. The push for bilingual education became a part of the larger Chicano movement that resented being a minority on land that belonged to their ancestors and forced them to live in a society dominated by Anglo governmental, educational, and economic institutions. Chicanos expressed this resentment by withdrawing from the dominant culture and clinging to their Mexican American traditions, including their language. Bernal and others emphasized that in light of this larger cultural context, it was important for educators to show respect for the language their Mexican American students cherished. He expanded his case for bilingual education to include Mexican American heritage into the curriculum of Mexican American–dominated school systems: "They should study histories of Latin America. United States history ought to emphasize Mexican contributions. School libraries should make available biographies of Spanish-speaking leaders. Students need to have the opportunity to learn about contemporary Mexican-Americans who are contributing to the American scene" (Bernal).

Alianza Federal de Pueblos Libres

Reies Lopez Tijerina organized the Alianza Federal de Pueblos Libres in New Mexico in 1963 in order to reclaim lost lands and the creation of a Confederation of Free City-States that would exist in the socioeconomic context of rural utopian simplicity. The Alianza became a part of Mexican American efforts to reclaim or retain land and water rights. These efforts became increasingly difficult after a 1960 court ruling stated that Congress and not the courts had ultimate authority in determining issues raised with regard to land rights based on the Treaty of Guadalupe Hidalgo. After the Mexican-American War of 1848 the Treaty of Guadalupe Hidalgo gave Mexicans in the Southwest citizenship, land rights, and cultural autonomy. Over time, governmental agencies, wealthy white individuals, or corporations took the land grants. By emphasizing their right to land, language, and culture, Alianza did much to shape the character of the Chicano movement's cultural nationalism.

Within three years of its founding, the Alianza claimed 20,000 members, with the bulk of its support coming from New Mexico's northwestern Rio Arriba region. Its rapid growth owed much to the charisma and rhetorical skills of Tijerina, who laid claim to millions of acres of land originally owned by Mexicans and threatened to make this claim the basis for a secessionist movement. In 1966, to dramatize Tijerina and Alianza's goal of repossessing land and creating a stronger group identity among Mexican Americans, he organized a 62-mile march from Albuquerque to the state capitol at Santa Fe over the July 4 weekend. Upon arrival at the state capitol, the marchers presented Gov. Jack Campbell with a petition asking support for a bill to investigate the land-claims issue. Producing no results, aliancistas planned an act of civil disobedience that would bring more attention to their cause. In October they attempted to take over part of the Kit Carson National Forest, which they claimed as their own. Forest Service

Reies Lopez Tijerina gestures during a speech in Albuquerque, New Mexico, in 1972.
Tijerina and the Alianza Federal de Pueblos Libres, the organization he founded in
1963, demanded that the U.S. government recognize the provisions of the 1848 Treaty
of Guadalupe Hidalgo. (Bettmann/Corbis)

rangers ignored their declaration of the Republic of San Joaquin del Rio de Chama
and attempted to remove the aliancistas. In the process, Alianza members seized
the rangers, setting off a series of events that led to the arrest of Tijerina and
four others.

On June 5, 1967, Tijerina and other Alianza members stormed the courthouse
in the little northwestern New Mexico town of Tierra Amarilla. They went there
to look for District Attorney Alfonso Sanchez and sought the release of fellow
aliancistas who earlier had been arrested. During the raid, Tijerina's supporters
opened fire on police, wounded two deputies, released eleven aliancistas from
jail, and fled town with two hostages. State and federal officials commenced a
massive manhunt that included helicopters, tanks, 200 state troopers, and about
400 members of the National Guard. Eventually they captured Tijerina and other
Alianza members who were charged with assault with intent to commit murder,
kidnapping, and other crimes. Tijerina stood trial for the Tierra Amarilla courthouse raid, defended himself, and was acquitted of the charges of kidnapping
and assault to commit murder.

While awaiting trial on indictments stemming from the courthouse raid, Tijerina and four other members of the Alianza were tried on earlier charges of as-

saulting forest rangers. Tijerina was found guilty in that trial and sentenced to two years in prison. He remained free on bail while he appealed the conviction. The time he was out on bail signaled a period of violence that culminated in the murder of the chief prosecution witness against Tijerina. Tijerina went to jail between June 1969 and July 1971, effectively debilitating the Alianza by removing its inspirational leader. As Juan Gomez-Quinones writes, during Tijerina's imprisonment the Alianza "failed to expand its membership in New Mexico or to other states, or to develop ideas beyond those it had begun with, and had never mustered the minimum of organizational discipline, structure, or resources apart from money collected at rallies" (Gomez-Quinones, 117).

Blowouts

The Los Angeles Human Relations Commission, staffed by Richard Villabos, Mike Duran, and others, helped ignite the Chicano youth movement in southern California by sponsoring annual Chicano student conferences in 1963. By 1964 these conferences were held at Camp Hess Kramer and pushed identity politics among young Mexican Americans by conducting seminars, inviting speakers, and identifying potential student leaders from barrio junior and senior high schools. At these sessions, students discussed and compared grievances with their schools. The students were most alarmed by the 50 percent dropout rate for Chicanos at Los Angeles area high schools.

These conferences developed into a significant part of the nascent Chicano movement when student activists effectively focused community attention on the abysmal conditions within the city's public school system in the spring of 1968. After several months of organizing, thousands of Mexican American students staged a walkout with a list of demands directed at the Board of Education. This list became the group's points of negotiation. The so-called blowouts, as the demonstrations were called, involved mainly five area high schools in the East Los Angeles area. Their impact, however, reverberated throughout the Southwest. With the support of older Chicano activists and one of their teachers, Sal Castro, the students drew attention to the racist attitudes held by many white teachers and to the inferior educational conditions that plagued their schools.

The blowouts caused a wave of community outcry and a series of confrontations between the local Mexican American community and the Los Angeles Board of Education and the police. Students and the community demanded quality education that included bilingual and bicultural school programs. In response, Mexican Americans participating in the demonstrations were subjected to police harassment and a grand jury indictment for actions supposedly protected by the First Amendment of the U.S. Constitution. In the end, the blowouts brought increased attention to the inequality of the public education system in inner cities and helped give voice to a marginalized minority.

Mexican American Youth Organization

Five Chicano youths organized the Mexican American Youth Organization (MAYO) in 1967 while students at St. Mary's University in San Antonio. José Angel Gutiérrez, Mario Compean, Willie Velasquez, Juan Patlan, and Ignacio Perez chose the name MAYO partly because the word means "May" in Spanish, and several successful Mexican revolutions culminated in that month. Followers of the tough, middle-aged Bexar County commissioner Albert Pena Jr., the five founders of MAYO, who were in their early to mid-twenties, set out to end wage, job, and educational discrimination, obtain better welfare and housing programs, and energize the Mexican American electorate to vote for politicians supportive of their causes.

Under the leadership of Gutiérrez, MAYO recruited the young and preached confrontational politics: "It is the gringo who we need to fight. He is the real enemy and cause of our miserable plight. We have to be revolutionary in our demands and make every sacrifice necessary, even if it means death, to achieve our goals" (Castro, 154). MAYO gained some political clout by indirectly receiving a $10,000 grant from the Ford Foundation. With the help of this money, MAYO initiated the Winter Garden Project, whose purpose was to redirect political, social, and economic resources in a 10-county South Texas area to benefit residents and maximize Mexican American political representation. They focused on barrios of South Texas because it represented one of the poorest Mexican areas in the United States, a place where ethnic and class identities were still clearly drawn. Through the Winter Garden Project, MAYO effectively mobilized several student protests in 1969 and almost got enough support that same year for their San Antonio mayoral candidate, Mario Compean, to get into a run-off election with the city's eighty-year-old mayor, W. W. McAllister.

On March 30, 1969, MAYO organized a demonstration by thousands of Mexican Americans in the border town of Del Rio, Texas. The demonstrators marched through the streets yelling, "Ya basta," which means "enough already." They primarily went to Del Rio to protest police brutality and job, education, and housing discrimination. After adopting a manifesto that demanded "self-determination" for the 5.6 million Mexican Americans living north of the border, the demonstrators paraded through the streets of the town, population 26,000, and pasted the manifesto on the door of the Val Verde County Courthouse.

Due to the hyperbolic rhetoric of its leader, Gutiérrez, who once declared at a press conference, "We have got to eliminate the gringo, and what I mean by that is if the worst comes to the worst, we have got to kill him," the Ford Foundation received a lot of heat for its support of MAYO (Castro, 149). Even the liberal Mexican American Democratic U.S. Representative Henry B. Gonzalez criticized MAYO and the Ford Foundation for what he described as the organization's "racial hatred." The conflict between MAYO and Gonzalez was significant because it marked the first major confrontation between the established old-style "liberal" Gonzalez and the new style "militant" Gutiérrez, in determining the direction of Mexican American politics.

By mid-1969, the Ford Foundation pulled back its funding, but MAYO continued to extend its reach. By doing so, they continued to threaten the long-standing civil rights organizations and leaders of that region. These groups and leaders, such as Gonzalez, believed MAYO threatened not only their standing, but also the gains they had made over the years with the entrenched Texas Democratic Party. In January 1970, members of MAYO filed for party status on behalf of "El Partido de la Raza Unida" in three South Texas counties in order to gain representation on school boards and city councils.

Chicanas in the Movement

Chicanas, women involved in the Chicano movement, played mostly a hidden role in the movement during the sixties. The movement was almost completely male-dominated and did not give prominence to female activists. During the early years of the movement, Chicanas felt excluded from decisionmaking power due to the traditional outlook of most of the Chicano leadership. These attitudes subordinated women to roles as wives and mothers. Even in the 1960s, Mexican and Chicana women were expected to be submissive and not seek roles outside of family life. Rural Mexican culture and the Catholic Church reinforced these attitudes.

As the feminist movement gained momentum in the late sixties, Chicanas became more visibly active in the movement. The late sixties witnessed an increasing emphasis on full participation in all aspects of Mexican American life and especially on issues that directly related to women. New women's groups included the Chicana Welfare Rights organization of 1968, the Hijas de Cauhuhtemoc group and the Chicana Symposium of 1969, and the Houston Conference Las Mujeres Por La Raza of 1971.

INDIAN CIVIL RIGHTS

Despite the passage of the 1946 Indian Claims Commission Act, which was meant to compensate Indians for unjust expropriation of their lands, only a small fraction of the claims were ever recognized. Indians gained a mere 5 percent of the total amount of land they requested. During the 1950s, Indians felt the pressure of the postwar conformist mood that translated into federal policy that encouraged assimilation. By 1953, the government had terminated all federal benefits for Indians as a distinct group and had abolished the tribes' legal standing under federal law. Not long thereafter, the federal government started encouraging the relocation of Indians from reservations into cities. The Bureau of Indian Affairs

(BIA) described this relocation policy as a "New Deal" for Indians that would serve to improve their educational and economic status. In practice the relocation into cities did just the opposite while causing Indians to experience traumatic cultural shock. Urban life stood at odds with Indian culture, causing them to struggle with such things as stoplights, clocks, elevators, telephones, clothing styles, and English language skills. As a result, Indians who moved to the city often became highly disoriented and isolated. Relocation officers had to be hired to help them with the transition and teach them basic life skills. Forced to take low-paying jobs that demanded monotonous work and lacked the promise of advancement, Indians became discouraged and often quit, causing employers to become more skeptical about hiring them.

Racism, homesickness, poverty, and substandard housing caused many Indians to leave the city and go back to the reservation. Despite the challenges, however, approximately 12,600 Indians relocated to cities by mid-1956, which prompted Congress to appropriate almost $3.5 million in 1957 to continue these relocation efforts. Although many Indians remained on the reservations in an effort to maintain their cultures, languages, and right to economic and political self-determination, the experience of relocation by thousands of Indians made them aware of their marginalized status in American society. In 1960, Indians annual family income was roughly $1,000 less than that of African Americans. Indians' unemployment rate was 10 times higher and life expectancy 20 years less than the average American. The suicide rate among Indians was 10 times higher than that of white Americans, and they suffered from the poorest housing and lowest educational achievement of any group in American society.

This growing awareness of their plight awakened a political consciousness among Indians that grew into a mass protest movement by the end of the 1960s. American Indians participated in more than 20 major demonstrations or acts of protest during the 1950s. By the 1960s these events became commonplace. The 1961 American Indian Chicago Conference kicked it off, followed shortly by the founding of the National Indian Youth Council (NIYC), the first of the major militant Indian rights activist organizations. By 1963, urban Indians took to the streets against BIA policies, initiating a wave of protest that lasted over a decade (Chafe, 169–170).

The New York Power Authority v. Tuscarora Indians

In 1946 Congress created the Indian Claims Commission to adjudicate cases in which Indian land had been taken in violation of treaty agreements. Touted as a good deal for Indians, the commission was used as a means of terminating Indian title to land by paying cash to puppet tribal councils in lieu of returning the land to Indians. Throughout the 1950s the commission brokered deals between state power projects and tribal councils to acquire even more Indian lands. Ultimately the federal government adopted a "termination" program that offered tribal councils the chance to accept payoffs by the government for the title of Indian land holdings, thereby ending tribal sovereignty. By 1958 several tribal councils had accepted cash payments under the termination program. Over 40,000 Indians had been affected by the termination program by the end of the decade, leading Montana congressman Lee Metcalf to declare, "The Bureau of Indian Affairs has used duress, blackmail, and pressure" on tribal councils to gain acceptance of termination (Weyler, 38).

Mad Bear, a Haudenosaunee Indian from the Tuscarora reservation that straddled the New York–Canadian border, in 1958 emerged as a leader of resistance to this process of termination. The New York Power Authority had sent a team of engineers to the home of Tuscarora Chief Clinton Rickard to gain permission to take soil samples. The power company planned to expropriate 1,383 acres of Tuscarora land for flooding, but Chief Rickard refused the tests. The resistance quickly spread throughout the Haudeno-

As part of a protest against government plans to build a reservoir on their reservation, members of the Tuscarora Nation—including Wallace Mad Bear Anderson on the lower right—warn the New York Power Authority to stay off their land. In Federal Power Commission v. Tuscarora Indian Nation, *however, the Supreme Court ruled that Tuscarora land could be taken by the government with just compensation. (Buffalo and Erie County Historical Society)*

saunee reservations in New York where Indians set up camps on disputed land, challenging state officials to remove them. On April 16, 1958, 100 armed state troopers and police invaded the Tuscarora lands in an effort to gain access for the engineers of the New York Power Authority. Mad Bear led a nonviolent protest of 150 men, women, and children who laid down or stood in front of government trucks. Police ultimately arrested Mad Bear and two other protesters, but the media captured the images of armed police fighting Indian women on their own land. This exposure caused the power company to back down as the Tuscarora Indians refused a $3-million offer by the Claims Commission for the land.

Indians in America and Canada took notice of this victory and realized that visibility would be important in their fight against the erosion of Indian lands. Mad Bear came away from this encounter as a leading activist in the emerging Indian rights movement and traveled the country helping to organize similar standoffs with the federal government. With the help of Mad Bear, Indians throughout North America now had a model of resistance (Weyler, 38–40).

Action Anthropology and the American Indian Chicago Conference

In the summer of 1960, those interested in the "Indian Problem" expressed optimism by the prospect of a change in the national administration. The two presidential candidates, Richard Nixon and John F. Kennedy, had committed to the current federal policy on Indian relations and both parties expressed the need for special attention to Indian affairs. To some, this seemed like an opportune time to influence a potentially sympathetic administration to adopt sound new policies acceptable to Indians.

Among those concerned with the future of American Indians was Sol Tax, a University of Chicago anthropologist who had for years been working with his students on techniques for effective community development. Tax had developed a concept of community action emphasizing self-determination that he had termed "Action Anthropology." Action anthropologists would work with the Indians to determine what they could do on their own behalf. Tax envisioned a representative group of Indians working with anthropologists and other experts to develop an acceptable and workable program. If a workable program were to be developed, somehow all Indians would have to be involved so that ideas could be exchanged, points of agreement discovered, and satisfactory recommendations produced. Tax and his colleagues gradually formed the concept of an all-Indian conference based on prior exchanges of ideas. Assisted by a grant from the Emil Schwarzhaupt Foundation that supported the study of problems of education and citizenship, Tax set out on the difficult work of organizing the American Indian Chicago Conference (AICC).

The AICC provided a forum to discuss the aggravated state of Indian discontent, the increasing concern and development of new skills on the part of scholars and scientists in resolving social problems, and the favorable political climate to initiate positive change. Held at the University of Chicago during the week of June 13–20, 1961, the AICC boasted a final registration of 467 Indians from 90 bands and tribes. Many Chicago Indians who did not all register but visited the conference with friends who had come to town grew the number of Indians on campus during the week to 800 (Lurie, 489–490).

The AICC produced a "Declaration of Indian Purpose" they hoped the new Kennedy administration would adopt. The document in its final form showed the Indians' overwhelming inclination to seek solutions to their problems within the existing political and administrative framework, leaving radical alterations to the federal bureaucratic structure to the more distant future. The Indians at the AICC believed that the Indian Bureau did not necessarily need overhauling.

Rather, they believed it was the attitude of government personnel that needed changing. They also recognized the need to bring their case before the American people in the hope that an informed citizenry would understand and support their contentions.

The Declaration expressed the principle that Indians have a right to retain their spiritual and cultural values. The one constant theme of all conference discussions and the Declaration was the insistence on Indian participation in planning their own programs and carrying them out. The Declaration also emphasized the "good citizenship" of the Indian people and asked for a new federal policy that would fulfill longstanding federal commitments to Indians. Although considered rather daring and innovative for the time, some questioned if the Declaration could really express the sentiments of the some 600,000 Indians in the United States that comprised about 200 separate tribes and bands. Many young Indians who participated in the AICC believed that while good publicity, the Declaration did not give voice to the real concerns of most Indians living on the reservation. The disparity between what most Indians felt and what the Chicago conference allowed the delegates to express prompted several young Indians in attendance to organize into the National Indian Youth Council and push for a "Greater Indian America."

How Do Ethnic Identities Form and Persist?

The rise of ethnic identity political movements in the 1960s caused historians and sociologists to examine the reasons for such a strong and persistent ethnic consciousness amid a diverse and complex racial and ethnic population. Prior to the 1960s, many historians bought into the all-encompassing myth of the "melting pot" that completely eradicated ethnic identity. The rise of ethnic political movements in the sixties caused many scholars to step back and re-examine the straight-line assimilationist theorists.

In studying the Chicano student movement of the 1960s and 1970s, historian Carlos Munoz Jr. views the rise of ethnic political movements of this era as a conscious rejection of Americanization. Opposing American cultural imperialism and the values of capitalism, Munoz argues, young Mexican Americans in the 1960s returned to the humanistic cultural values of the Mexican working class that led to a nationalist ideology. Other historians, such as Gilbert Gonzalez, reject that the rise of ethnic politics in the 1960s emerged from an anti-American impulse. To Gonzalez and other historians, ethnic politics is American politics. To these historians, the cultural nationalism of the Chicano movement did not signal a rejection of assimilation, rather it evidenced the assimilation of Chicanos into the political culture of the United States. Whereas Munoz views a Chicano identity as the antithesis to Americanization, Gonzalez views it as a demand for greater cultural and social integration as evidenced by Chicanos' demand for entrance into the social, cultural, and intellectual life of public universities.

Sociologist Joane Nagel emphasizes the social construction of ethnic consciousness in her examination of the formation of an ethnic identity among American Indians during the 1960s. She points to the Red Power movement and its reaction to federal programs and policies amid the increase in the Indian population during the 20th century as major factors causing American Indians to realize an ethnic identity. As a result, American Indians joined other ethnic groups in claiming a collective identity that for the first time transcended separate and diverse tribal identities. Scholars like Nagel, Michael Omi, Howard Winant, Frederick Barth, and Yasuko Takezawa have contributed to more recent sociological treatments that challenge an objective and clearly defined concept of race, ethnicity, assimilation, and acculturation. Their studies of racial formation and ethnic groups envision a more dynamic and flexible understanding of group identity that can vary depending on the social and historical contexts.

Takezawa, for example, in examining the formation of a Japanese American identity, argues that while there is a primordial attachment to a group identity resulting from ascribed statuses like kinship, language, and religion, ethnic identities really persist because they function and have meaning within a social and historical context. In short, ethnic identity is formed as a group reconstructs and reinterprets the past to find relevant meanings in the present. In other words, the exposure to discrimination by American Indians, Mexican Americans, and Japanese Americans led to a stronger ethnic identity that caused each group to critique the Americanization process. In the case of Japanese Americans, their experiences in internment camps during World War II caused a somewhat assimilated group to step back and reclaim their ethnicity despite earlier generations' efforts to blend into mainstream America.

National Indian Youth Council

In the early 1950s students at the University of New Mexico in Albuquerque founded an Indian club they named "The Kiva Club." Initially a social organization intended to bring together Indian students who, for the most part, had come to college directly from the reservation, a group of these students and others gathered in Santa Fe in 1954 to discuss Indian education and Indian affairs with older tribal leaders. The gathering led to similar clubs at other schools, scattered regional youth councils, and eventually a series of youth conferences that addressed a variety of Indian issues. The largest, in 1960, drew 350 Indians from fifty-seven tribes.

After the National Congress of American Indians at the University of Chicago, many young Indians identified a disparity between what the delegates expressed and what most Indians felt. As a result, a few months after the Chicago conference, they decided to organize themselves and push for a "Greater Indian America." With the help of this loose federation of student clubs, regional youth councils, and youth conferences, college-aged Indians decided to organize the National Indian Youth Council (NIYC), with an aim to resurrect a sense of national pride among Indians. Although the NIYC began slowly, its message and objective were clear: Indians would no longer defer to the Bureau of Indian Affairs or other institutions of white society. The NIYC started the more radical phase of the Indian rights movement that called upon Indians to look back at their own great traditions and make decisions based on their values as opposed to the values of white America. In essence, they called for self-government.

The NIYC's later call for "Red Power" paralleled the Black Power movement. The impact of the NIYC far exceeded the actual number of its participants. Once the ideology of traditionalism and Red Power was embraced by Indian youth, it slowly spread across the age spectrum of Indian society, creating a more aggressive tone to Indians' relationships with non-Indians. As a result, by the mid- to late 1960s Indian activists of all ages began seeking political and cultural sovereignty and social and economic equality. The term "Red Power" expressed pan-Indian unity exemplified by the NIYC and later the American Indian Movement.

Indians and the War on Poverty

President Lyndon Johnson announced on January 20, 1964, that Indian welfare would be placed in the forefront of his war on poverty. Speaking in the East Room of the White House to tribal representatives in Washington, D.C., for a meeting of the National Congress of American Indians, President Johnson said that Indians suffered more from poverty than any other group in the country. Walter Wetzel of Montana, president of the congress, offered President Johnson a plan to combat poverty, unemployment, and educational problems among the Indians. The plan included a request for special consideration to Indians in the allocation of jobs under public works and other federal programs. Speaking to about 100 members of the congress, President Johnson noted that the per capita income of Indians was less than one-third that of the rest of the country and their unemployment rate averaged more than 50 percent. He also pointed out that the average age of death among Indians was 42 years of age and the average educational attainment for adult Indians was the eighth grade with about a 60 percent dropout rate. He then called for Secretary of the Interior Stewart L. Udall to make specific recommendations to him about how the War on Poverty could attack this problem.

President Johnson ultimately declared Indian tribes eligible as local sponsoring agencies for the multitude of social welfare programs authorized by Congress as a part of the Great Society. The War on Poverty required that the poor be organized into Community Action Programs (CAPs). Once organized into a CAP, tribes could access federal money for educational services, economic development, and public housing. Vine Deloria Jr. of the Standing Rock Sioux and two other tribal representatives told a Senate subcommittee in April 1967 that the federal antipoverty program had "brought a sense of dignity, responsibility, enthusiasm and desire to people who were almost completely without hope in the depths of poverty." Deloria explained how when Indian tribes became sponsoring agencies for the Office of Economic Opportunity, other agencies such as the Bureau of Indian Affairs suddenly felt in competition with the Indian Community Action Program. "No longer would an Indian be required to wait, hat in hand, outside an office of the Bureau of Indian Affairs or Public Health Service waiting for a few crumbs to fall his way. Instead he could form his own programs and get funding through the OEO and begin to make real plans for progress for his people" (*New York Times,* April 25, 1967, p. 31).

The first taste of self-determination gave tribes enough confidence in their own talents in management and political organization that by the early 1970s they began to pressure the federal government to give them more flexibility in controlling the activities on their reservations. The 1972 Indian Education Act and the Indian Self-determination and Education Act of 1975 were legislative expressions of the Indian desire for more freedom in the activities of government.

RED POWER

A more radical stage of the American Indian movement began after the National Indian Youth Council's call for "Red Power." Indians, particularly young Indians, joined the more general wave of radicalism sweeping the African American civil rights, women's liberation, and gay rights movements from the mid- to late 1960s. Tired of living as colonial people, they began calling for self-determination and political independence. Tribes started filing lawsuits about ownership of land granted long ago by U.S.-Indian treaties. Red Power gained public attention through a series of "fish-ins" in 1964 organized by NIYC activists in the Northwest that dramatized the Indians' struggle to reclaim their land. In 1965 Cherokees in Oklahoma organized to defy state restrictions on Indian hunting land. Over the next few years, Indians from Maine to California organized to protest white use of their land, the education of their children, and what they viewed as other violations of century-old treaties.

During the rest of the 1960s, Indians protested Thanksgiving and Columbus Day holidays and the theft and display of ancestral bones and sacred artifacts, called for Indian studies programs at universities, and communicated their agenda in such books as Vine Deloria's *Custer Died for Your Sins* and activist newspapers like *Akwesasne Notes.* By the end of the decade the civil rights, Black Power, and student movements had either slowed or splintered into ineffective factions, but the "Red Power" Indian movement was just gaining momentum.

After the Kennedy and Johnson administrations included them into their policies and programs, Indians had become increasingly self-reliant in setting their own agenda, which for some meant treaty rights as distinct from civil rights.

Fish-Ins

Beginning in 1964 with a series of "fish-ins" on rivers in the state of Washington, the NIYC adopted more militant or aggressive tactics to protest those institutions and individuals who had traditionally dominated Indian Affairs for over 100 years. These fish-ins in the Pacific Northwest offered a way for Indians to assert their treaty rights by fishing in traditional sites in defiance of state regulations.

At times these fish-ins turned violent as several Indians were arrested for their involvement. For example, in the fall of 1965, state fish and game enforcement officers in the state of Washington arrested 23 Indians in a three-month span in

Movie star Marlon Brando joins an American Indian "fish-in" demonstration at the Nisqually and Puyallup rivers in Washington State on March 2, 1964. The protest supports American Indian fishing rights. (Seattle Post-Intelligencer Collection; Museum of History and Industry/Corbis)

an effort to enforce court orders banning off-reservation net-fishing on the choice Salmon and Steelhead streams. State agents also confiscated about 50 nets, seven boats, and other fishing equipment. Some of the staged fish-ins attracted famous civil rights activists such as the African American comedian Dick Gregory. On February 15, 1966, Gregory was arrested and put in jail in Olympia, Washington, on two counts of illegal net fishing. Gregory had been fishing with Nisqually Indians to help focus attention on the Pacific Northwest fishing-rights controversy and decided to go to jail instead of posting a $2,000 bond. The Nisqually Indians contended that a 110-year-old treaty gave them the right to fish the same streams and rivers as their ancestors. Expressing the growing alliance between minority groups, James Farmer, the national director of the Congress of Racial Equality, said, "The arrest of Dick Gregory and his wife, Lillian, in the state of Washington once again exposes the unjust treatment of America's longest oppressed minority, the American Indian" (*New York Times,* October 16, 1966, p. L46). These fish-ins in the Pacific Northwest from 1964 to 1966 set off a wave of similar protests throughout the country by the emerging and expanding American Indian movement.

1964 Takeover of Alcatraz Island

As Indians migrated to urban areas, tribal identities and histories somewhat artificially merged. For example, the 1868 Sioux treaty with the U.S. government became the common property of all Indians. Claims based on this treaty often relied on memory and the oral tradition of the Sioux. That tradition asserted that the U.S. government, after its cavalry troops had been defeated several times by Red Cloud's freedom fighters, begged the Lakota for a peace treaty in 1868. As Sioux tradition tells it, the U.S. Senate ratified a treaty that gave the Sioux the right to claim any federal facility or real estate for which the government had ended appropriations. No article existed in the 1868 treaty that gave the Sioux, or any other tribe for that matter, rights to federal surplus property. However, traditional elders believed their right to abandoned government property existed because Red Cloud had burned abandoned federal forts along the Bozeman Trail, instilling the belief that Red Cloud had negotiated a treaty promising the transfer of federal surplus property to the Sioux.

In the early 1960s the federal government closed the prison on Alcatraz Island and ended its appropriations. Before the island could be turned into a national park, however, in 1964 a group of Indian college students of varying tribal backgrounds invaded Alcatraz Island in San Francisco Bay and later Fort Lawton near Seattle, Washington. The occupation force first gathered at the Indian Center near Sixteenth and Mission in San Francisco before making its way to Fisherman's Wharf where they had chartered a boat. Accompanied by lawyers, the Indians held a press conference before embarking for the island where Chalk

Group of Sioux Indians protest at Alcatraz in an attempt to claim the land under the allowances provided in an 1868 treaty with the U.S. government, March 8, 1964. (Bettmann/Corbis)

Cottier, an American Indian from Pine Ridge, South Dakota, who moved to the Bay Area in 1952, and the lawyers explained the legal basis for their claim to Alcatraz. Once on Alcatraz they put up a tipi and began a celebration of singing and dancing. A young Russell Means remembered accompanying his father on this mission and "getting into the spirit of things" by running around "laying claim to various parts of the island, just as the many whites who had come to our land had claimed our rivers, forests, hills, and meadows. For a few exhilarating hours, I felt a freedom that I had never experienced, as though Alcatraz were mine" (Means, 106).

The U.S. marshals soon arrived, forced the press to leave, and ultimately convinced the Indians' lawyers to persuade the protesters to leave and take up their claims in the courts. They gathered back at the Indian Center to wait for early editions of the next day's papers to read the front-page article: "Wacky Sioux

Indian Civil Rights Act of 1968

Attached as an amendment to the Fair Housing Act of 1968, the Indian Civil Rights Act radically changed the nature of tribal courts and life on the reservation. This act turned the tribal court into a formal institution that resembled the federal judiciary. It incorporated the First Amendment and Fourth through Eighth Amendments into a package of enumerated rights tribal governments could not violate. In practice, though, the Indian Civil Rights Act greatly complicated Indians' lives and raised many questions about tribal sovereignty.

The Indian Civil Rights Act's premise was the belief that with the inclusion of certain protections derived from the Bill of Rights, the tribal courts would have the same relationship to both tribal citizens and the tribal government as did the federal courts to American citizens and the federal government. In practice, however, the act destroyed the informality of Indian life that had been the repository of cultural traditions and customs. In the place of this informality now existed a rigid and formalized process that required individuals to identify those instances in which the tribal government impinged upon the rights of tribal members. The Indian Civil Rights Act distorted reservation life because it imposed certain rules and procedures with respect to tribal courts that did not exist in any other part of reservation life or reservation institutions.

Traditional Indian society functioned on the basis of responsibilities and duties, but the Indian Civil Rights Act subverted this tradition by transposing this belief in responsibilities and duties into a society based on rights against government. The act made these responsibilities impossible to perform because it inserted the tribal court as an institution between the people and their responsibilities. In short, tribal courts became a competitor with more traditional ways of resolving disputes between Indians. Symbolizing the institutionalization of dispute resolution on the reservation, the American Indian Tribal Court Judges Association was founded in 1970 to assist tribal courts in meeting the new procedural requirements that many people believed the act instituted.

Raid Alcatraz." Although frustrated by the racist coverage that characterized the protesters as "wacky," the young Indians were also emboldened by the amount of print and television coverage the protest received. They had hit upon a tactic that could bring attention to their agenda of self-determination and political independence.

American Indian Movement

Clyde Bellecourt, a member of the Ojibwa tribe, was released from the Minnesota Stillwater State Prison in 1964 after three jail terms for burglary and armed rob-

*Dennis Banks (left) and preacher Carl McEntire during the 1972 "Trail of Broken
Treaties" occupation of the Bureau of Indian Affairs' headquarters in Washington,
D.C. (Bettmann/Corbis)*

bery. While in prison he helped organize 46 Indian prisoners to study Indian
traditions and heritage. Bellecourt said of the group, "I guess we had the first
real Indian Studies Program in the country." Upon his release from jail, Bellecourt tried to replicate what he achieved in prison by attempting to organize
the large "red ghetto" population of Minneapolis. In the tradition of the other
political and social movements of the sixties, Bellecourt envisioned a civil rights
movement that would work to increase the opportunities for each urban Indian
to "enjoy his full rights as a citizen of these United States." Later he recognized
that Indians' citizenship meant nothing and that the pursuit of civil rights was
the wrong approach. Civil rights meant working within the system and Bellecourt and other Indians transplanted from the reservation to the cities had little
interest in that. They instead desired complete independence and the right to
self-determination. In July 1968, Bellecourt, Eddie Benton Banai, an Ojibwa Bellecourt had met in prison, Mary Jane Wilson, George Mitchell, and another
ex-convict, Dennis Banks founded "Concerned Indian Americans" but quickly
changed the name to the "American Indian Movement" (AIM) because of the
preferable acronym (Matthiessen, 34).

Custer Died for Your Sins

Vine Deloria Jr., former executive director of the National Congress of American Indians, published his book, *Custer Died for Your Sins,* in 1969. Extremely popular, the book played an important part in introducing the American people to an alternative view of the past that reminded its readers that Columbus did not discover America. The simple fact that Indians had lived on the continent for over 20,000 years before European settlers arrived had somehow eluded most Americans and the narrative of American history taught in schools. Deloria explained that this fact had been ignored because the English settlers of this continent did not regard the Indians as people or human beings but simply as a part of the wildlife.

Intending to fill in the many little gaps in school textbooks on American history, Deloria accused the U.S. government of ignoring or violating some 400 treaties made with Indian tribes. In recounting the long history of Indian grievances against the U.S., Deloria carefully made connections to the questionable justifications for the war in Vietnam: "History may well record that while the United States was squandering some one hundred billion dollars in Vietnam while justifying this bloody orgy as commitment keeping, it was also busy breaking the oldest Indian treaty, that between the United States and the Seneca tribe of the Iroquois Nation" (Deloria, 29). Specifically he referred to the Pickering Treaty of 1794, signed by President George Washington but broken in the early 1960s by the construction of the Kinzua Dam on the Allegheny River, which flooded the Senecas out of their ancestral homeland.

Deloria not only recounted the history of Indian-U.S. relations, he wrote about more contemporary afflictions suffered by Indians at the hands of white Americans such as misguided anthropologists, well-meaning missionaries, and ignorant bureaucrats of the Bureau of Indian Affairs and other government agencies—not to mention the wrong-headed policies of "termination," by which the government attempted to eliminate medical and educational services, and "relocation," where surplus reservation Indians were transplanted to big-city slums and left to fend for themselves.

Despite the grim past injustices Deloria recounted, his book was mostly void of the deep bitterness most would expect, helping to expand the book's readership. In fact, reviewer Edward Abbey noted Deloria's hopefulness and good humor in the face of such a long history of what some Indians described as a policy of genocide against their people (*New York Times,* November 9, 1969, pg. BR 46).

Although inspired by the fish-ins of the Northwest and the land protests of Ontario and New York and other "Red Power" activity around the country, particularly on the West Coast, AIM came into existence as a result of the termination and relocation programs of the 1950s that forced thousands of disoriented Indians into the cities. Even those who received job training often found themselves facing racism and discrimination that caused them to take the least desirable jobs in the workforce—work that paid the lowest wages and that forced them to live in the worst conditions of urban blight. In its first year, AIM's main concerns were jobs, housing, and education. Bellecourt also set up a street patrol to protect Indians from police abuse and violence, filming arrests and advising those taken into custody of their rights against self-incrimination, to counsel, and a jury trial. The patrol quickly reduced the number of Indians arrested, but as a result Bellecourt suffered at least 30 beatings by outraged police officers.

AIM spread throughout the nation in 1969 and 1970, helping to organize the second occupation of Alcatraz Island in San Francisco Bay in 1969, a July 4, 1971, countercelebration atop Mount Rushmore, a Thanksgiving Day takeover of the Mayflower replica, and the 1972 "Trail of Broken Treaties" in which hundreds of Indians marched to Washington, D.C., to air their grievances against the federal government. In 1973, AIM protesters barricaded themselves inside a trading post at Wounded Knee (site of the 1890 massacre of over 150 Sioux by the United States Army). Federal agents responded with overwhelming force leaving two Indians killed and one U.S. marshall paralyzed in sporadic fighting during a three-month standoff.

Seizure of Alcatraz Island, Part 2 (1969–1971)

"Indians of All Tribes," a loosely affiliated group promoting Red Power, decided to revisit the 1964 takeover of Alcatraz Island by planning a second seizure of the island based on Indians' claim to surplus land taken by the U.S. government for military purposes. Indians believed the land must revert to its previous owner once abandoned by the military. Indian activists believed the takeover of Alcatraz appropriately symbolized their cause to reclaim land that had been taken from Indians from the East Coast to the West Coast. The idea of retaking the country from west to east, like the "wagon train in reverse," developed into AIM's "Trail of Broken Treaties" in 1972 (Weyler, 42).

The second seizure of Alcatraz Island began on November 4, 1969, with 14 Indians occupying the site. Two weeks later, 79 Indians occupied the island, claiming it as free Indian land. In press releases the occupiers offered to pay the U.S. government $24 for the island, mocking the 1626 purchase of Manhattan Island by Dutch settlers. They also offered to establish a Bureau of Caucasian Affairs to manage any problems that whites might have with the Indian takeover of the island. They also issued a proclamation: "To the Great White Father and All His People":

> We, the native Americans, reclaim the land known as Alcatraz Island in the name of all American Indians by right of discovery. . . . We feel that this so-called Alcatraz Island is more than suitable for an Indian Reservation, as

determined by the white man's own standard. By this we mean that this place resembles most Indian reservations that:

1. It is isolated from modern facilities, and without adequate means of transportation.
2. It has no fresh running water.
3. It has inadequate sanitation facilities.
4. There are no oil or mineral rights.
5. There is no industry, and so unemployment is very great.
6. There are no health care facilities.
7. The soil is rocky and unproductive, and the land does not support game.
8. There are no educational facilities.
9. The population has always exceeded the land base.
10. The population has always been held as prisoners and kept dependent upon others.

Further, it would be fitting and symbolic that ships from all over the world, entering the Golden Gate, would first see Indian land, and thus be reminded of the true history of this nation. This tiny island would be a symbol of the great lands once ruled by free and noble Indians. (Quoted in Matthiessen, 37–38)

During the occupation the number of occupiers rose to about 400 as President Richard Nixon maintained a "hands-off" policy but did not accede to any of the Indians' demands, which included:

1. A center for Native American Studies aimed at imparting skills and knowledge to improve the lives and spirits of all Indians.
2. A spiritual center where Indians could practice ancient tribal religious and healing ceremonies.
3. A center of ecology to train young people to restore lands and waters to their natural state.
4. A museum that would depict Indian food and cultural contributions and show the "noble and tragic events of Indian history, including the broken treaties, the documentary of the trail of tears, the massacre of Wounded Knee, as well as the victory over yellow hair Custer and his army." (*New York Times,* April 8, p. 38)

At the one-year anniversary of the takeover, the Indians held a news conference that described plans for a $6-million Indian center and the establishment of Thunderbird University. At the news conference they announced their intention to make Alcatraz an "international outlet" for Indian art (*New York Times,* November 22, 1970, p. 38).

Yellow Power

In 1969 Amy Uyematsu wrote "The Emergence of Yellow Power" as a call for Asian Americans to join other minority groups in "their own cause to fight, since they are also victims—with less visible scars—of the white institutionalized racism." She asserted that the new "Yellow Power" movement "is relevant to the black power movement in that both are part of the Third World struggle to liberate all colored people." She identified Asian Americans' ability to achieve middle-class status as obscuring their subordinate status in American society. While maybe not a movement in the same sense as the Chicano and American Indian movements, both of which had programmatic agendas, Yellow Power in 1969 is what Uyematsu called "an articulated mood" that had as its immediate goal the creation of a "yellow consciousness" that called for an end to "the process of Americanization" Asians had undergone since arriving in the United States. Instead of trying to act and look white, she called for Asian Americans "to be proud of their physical and cultural heritage. Yellow power advocates self-acceptance as the first step toward strengthening personalities of Asian Americans" (Bloom and Breines, 145–147).

Uyematsu's call for a yellow power movement was a strike against the stereotype of Asian Americans as being passive, silent, and accommodating. She feared that Asians had allowed white America to use the "silent Oriental" stereotype as ammunition against other minority groups, particularly African Americans. "Fearful whites tell militant African Americans that the acceptable criterion for behavior is exemplified in the quiet, passive Asian American." She envisioned a new role for Asian Americans in the fight for the rights of all people of color in her manifesto: "It is a rejection of the passive Oriental stereotype and symbolizes the birth of a new Asian—one who will recognize and deal with injustices. The shout of Yellow Power, symbolic of our new direction, is reverberating in the quiet corridors of the Asian community." (Excerpt of "The Emergence of Yellow Power," from Bloom and Breines, 145–147.)

The standoff with the federal government ended on June 11, 1971, when U.S. federal marshals stormed the island and removed the remaining 15 activists still on the island. This highly publicized 19-month occupation of Alcatraz Island sparked a series of occupations of government facilities by other Indian activists throughout the country.

CONCLUSION: GROUP IDENTITY AND SOCIAL ACTIVISM

The 1960s witnessed an emphasis on group identity as the fulcrum for social activism for various ethnic communities, particularly Mexican Americans and

American Indians. The activism of the 1960s emphasized a pride in the distinctive traditions and identities of various ethnic minority groups. Mexican Americans represented the oldest and greatest number of Spanish-speaking Americans. The 1960s witnessed the emerging spirit of Chicanismo, a populist pride in Mexican heritage, among young Mexican Americans, one of the most economically deprived groups in American society. Similarly, Indians relocated into urban areas built their political activism on their belief and pride in cultural and spiritual traditions. Yet they differed from their African American and Mexican American counterparts in that they based their claim for self-determination and independence on a series of treaties between the U.S. government and Indian tribes. Both cases, however, represent the end of the myths of the melting pot and political consensus that had been promulgated in American schools for most of the 20th century.

BIOGRAPHIES

Dennis Banks, 1930–

Indian Activist

An Anishinaabe from the Leech Lake Indian Reservation in Minnesota, Banks, with George Mitchell and Mary Jane Wilson, founded the American Indian Movement (AIM), an intertribal organization initially aimed at protecting Indians transplanted to cities from police harassment. Involved with several of AIM's protests in the late 1960s, Banks most famously was involved in the 1973 Wounded Knee standoff with federal agents in which he was a defendant in a closely watched and sensational trial.

Vine Deloria Jr., 1933–2005

Indian Activist

The author of two very influential books, *Custer Died for Your Sins* (1969), and *God Is Red* (1973), which presented Indian history and metaphysical concepts to the American public, Vine Deloria also served as the executive director of the National Congress of American Indians from 1964 to 1967 and worked with several Indian rights organizations. Deloria argued in his books and with his activism that Indians should resist assimilation but instead study their tribal traditions and religious practices and pursue self-determination.

Henry B. Gonzalez, 1925–

U.S. Representative

In 1956 Henry Gonzalez was the first Mexican American elected to the Texas state Senate. In 1961, at the age of 35, he became the first Mexican American ever elected to the U.S. Congress from Texas. In the late 1950s and early 1960s, Gonzalez built a reputation as a radical within the state's conservative-dominated political circles. Gonzalez's election to the House of Representatives was a major achievement by a Mexican American at that time, but he never assumed the role of spokesman for the millions of Mexican Americans in the Southwest. Instead, Gonzalez saw himself as a representative of all his constituents. In this vein, his most famous confrontation was with the MAYO organization at the end of the sixties. In denouncing the oppositional politics of this young Chicano organization, he declared, "I cannot stand silently by if an organization like the Mexican-American Youth Organization . . . publishes hate sheets containing statements like: 'the gringo took your grandfather's land. He took your father's job, and now he's sucking out your soul.' . . . MAYO styles itself as the embodiment of good and the Anglo-American as the incarnation of evil. That is not merely ridiculous; it is drawing fire from the deepest wellsprings of hate" (Castro, 152). In this confrontation, Gonzalez represented the old guard liberals against the rising tide of the more militant Chicano movement at the end of the decade.

Rodolfo "Corky" Gonzales 1928–2005

Poet

From his roots in a migrant worker family, Corky Gonzales developed into a Golden Gloves boxing champion, fought as a professional fighter from 1947 to 1955 as a featherweight, and became active in Democratic Party politics by working for the John F. Kennedy presidential campaign of 1960. In 1966 he founded the Crusade for Justice in Denver, Colorado, to promote Mexican American pride and an end to discrimination against Chicanos. Also a poet, he wrote "Yo Soy Joaquin" (1969), which inspired Chicano pride and activism. Known for rallying young people, college students, and ex-inmates to the Chicano movement, Gonzales inspired thousands of young people to become politically active at his Chicano youth conferences in Denver in 1969 and 1970.

José Angel Gutiérrez, 1944–

Founder of La Raza Unida

The son of a doctor who had fought with Francisco "Pancho" Villa in support of Carranza's insurrection against the government of Gen. Victoriano Huerta,

Gutiérrez was only 12 when his father died. The family had little money because the doctor had treated many of his Mexican American patients in Crystal City, Texas, for free. As a result, Gutiérrez's mother went to work in the fields alongside other Mexican Americans. In high school, Gutiérrez became interested in politics because he had a keen awareness of the discrimination and racism suffered by Mexican Americans at the hands of white Americans. He gained his political education by volunteering to assist the Political Association of Spanish-Speaking Organizations (PASSO) in 1963 to get five Mexican Americans elected to the Crystal City Council. While working on this campaign, Gutiérrez suffered a beating by the Texas Rangers who had been called into the area to monitor the election. This experience shaped Gutiérrez's radical politics. He received national attention for his organization and leadership of the Mexican American Youth Organization (MAYO) in 1969. It was at this time that he returned to Crystal City to plan the Winter Garden Project and help mobilize about 700 high school students to walk out of school in protest of the discrimination Mexican Americans suffered in the public school system. In 1970, Gutiérrez organized a new political party in South Texas: La Raza Unida. In 1970, La Raza Unida won control of the school boards in Crystal City, Carizzo Springs, and Cotulla, the town where Lyndon Johnson had first taught in a small Mexican American school. By 1974, Gutiérrez had become the school board president in Crystal City and had filled 23 of the 24 administrative positions with Mexican Americans, changed the composition of the faculty to 70 percent Mexican American, and increased the school district's annual budget from $1 million to $3 million.

Dolores Huerta, vice president of United Farm Workers, during a grape pickers' strike in 1968. (Time & Life Pictures/Getty Images)

Dolores Huerta, 1930–

UFW Activist

Huerta helped found and served as the executive vice president of the United Farm Workers, tirelessly lobbying for the union and negotiating contracts with employers. Her father's experiences as a migrant laborer and coal miner inspired her union activities. She traveled constantly to give speeches and secure support for the workers' boycott activities. Cesar Chavez depended on her as both a key negotiator and political strategist during the 1960s grape strike and lettuce boycott.

Elizabeth "Betita" Martinez 1925–

Chicana Activist

After graduating from Swarthmore College, Martinez worked as a researcher for the United Nations on colonialism in the late 1950s. In the sixties she participated in the Student Nonviolent Coordinating Committee (SNCC) in Mississippi and as coordinator of SNCC's New York office. Later in the decade she worked with the Black Panthers before moving to New Mexico in 1968 to publish *El Grito Del Norte* for five years and work on various barrio projects. Martinez represented a growing number of Chicanas who became active in the Chicano movement at the end of the decade. Her experiences at the United Nations helped define the oppression suffered by African Americans and Mexican Americans in the context of colonialism and the multinational struggle of the day. She later wrote six books, including her best-known work, *500 Years of Chicana History in Pictures,* a bilingual history that became the basis for a video she directed.

Russell Means, 1939–

Indian Activist

An early leader of the American Indian Movement (AIM) in the late 1960s, Means played an important role in both the 1972 "Trail of Broken Treaties" and the takeover of the Bureau of Indian Affairs (BIA) building in Washington, D.C. He helped organize AIM's standoff with federal marshals and agents at Wounded Knee, South Dakota, in 1973, that ended in a highly publicized trial.

Reies Lopez Tijerina, 1926–

Mexican American Activist

Tijerina grew up in the poverty of migrant farmworkers and sharecroppers in the Southwest. Although he only received six months of formal education,

Russell Means, American Indian Movement (AIM) leader, speaks to a crowd of followers in South Dakota in 1974. (Bettmann/Corbis)

he possessed natural rhetorical skills. In his mid-teens he received a New Testament from a Baptist minister, felt called into the ministry, and attended an Assembly of God college in Ysleta, Texas. After three years of study, he began preaching in Victoria, Texas. Due to disagreements with church officials, Tijerina lost his Assembly of God credentials in 1950. Throughout the fifties he traveled the southwest, south, and California as a fundamentalist tent evangelist. Tijerina moved to New Mexico in the late 1950s and discovered audiences of Christians apparently more concerned with reclaiming their land than saving their souls. Tijerina began leading Mexican Americans living in New Mexico on their quest to reclaim land lost after the Mexican-American War. He eventually rejoined the Catholic Church of his youth to better identify with his followers. After an earlier marriage had failed, he married a 15-year-old land claimant, believing it showed his followers his profound interest in land issues. In his effort to reclaim lost land, Tijerina relied on the 1848 Treaty of Guadalupe Hidalgo that promised protection for the civil rights and land grants of former Mexican citizens in the United States. During the early 1960s he traveled throughout New Mexico organizing a land-grant association called La Alianza Federal de Mercedes Libres (the Federal Alliance of Free Land Grants). The Alianza became the catalyst for many militant actions, such as the occupation of Kit Carson National Forest and the proclamation of the Republic of San Joaquin de Chama in 1966, a courthouse raid and shootout at Tierra Amarilla and a massive military manhunt for Tijerina and his followers in 1967, and lengthy legal battles that ended with the federal courts sentencing him to prison in 1970.

REFERENCES AND FURTHER READINGS

Acuña, Rodolfo. 2000. *Occupied America: A History of Chicanos.* 4th ed. New York: Longman.

Bernal, Joe. 1969. "I Am Mexican-American." *National Education Association Journal* (May).

Bloom, Alexander, and Wini Breines. 2003. *"Takin' It to the Streets": A Sixties Reader.* New York: Oxford University Press.

Castro, Tony. 1974. *Chicano Power: The Emergence of Mexican America.* New York: Saturday Review Press.

Chafe, William H. 2003. *The Unfinished Journey: America since World War II.* 5th ed. New York: Oxford University Press.

Cornell, Stephen. 1988. *The Return of the Native: American Indian Political Resurgence.* New York: Oxford University Press.

Del Castillo, Richard Griswold, and Arnoldo de León. 1996. *North to Aztlán: A History of Mexican Americans in the United States.* New York: Twayne Publishers.

Deloria, Vine, Jr., and Clifford M. Lytle. 1984. *The Nations Within: The Past and Future of American Indian Sovereignty*. New York: Pantheon Books.

Escobar, Edward J. 1993. "The Dialectics of Repression: The Los Angeles Police Department and the Chicano Movement, 1968–1971." *Journal of American History* 79, no. 4: 1483–1514.

Farber, David, and Beth Bailey. 2001. *The Columbia Guide to America in the 1960s*. New York: Columbia University Press.

Gómez-Quiñones, Juan. 1990. *Chicano Politics: Reality and Promise, 1940–1990*. Albuquerque: University of New Mexico Press.

Griswold del Castillo, Richard and Arnoldo de Leon. 1996. *North to Aztlan: A History of Mexican Americans in the United States*. New York: Twayne Publishers.

Hammerback, John C., Richard J. Jensen, and José Angel Gutiérrez. 1985. *A War of Words: Chicano Protest in the 1960s and 1970s*. Westport, CT: Greenwood Press.

Hennessy, Alistair. 1984. "The Rise of the Hispanics I: Chicanos." *Journal of Latin American Studies* 16, no. 1: 171–194.

Hood, Susan. 1972. "Termination of the Klamath Indian Tribe of Oregon." *Ethnohistory* 19, no. 4: 379–392.

Lurie, Nancy Oestreich. 1961. "The Voice of the American Indian: Report on the American Indian Chicago Conference." *Current Anthropology* 2, no. 5: 478–500.

Machado, Manuel A., Jr. 1978. *Listen Chicano! An Informal History of the Mexican-American*. Chicago: Nelson Hall.

Matthiessen, Peter. 1991. *In the Spirit of Crazy Horse*. New York: Penguin Books.

Means, Russell, and Marvin J. Wolf. 1995. *Where White Men Fear to Tread: The Autobiography of Russell Means*. New York: St. Martin's Press.

Meier, Matt S., and Feliciano Rivera. 1972. *The Chicanos: A History of Mexican Americans*. New York: Hill and Wang.

Mirandé, Alfredo, and Evangelina Enriquez. 1979. *La Chicana: The Mexican-American Woman*. Chicago: University of Chicago Press.

Moquin, Wayne, and Charles van Doren, eds. 1971. *A Documentary History of the Mexican Americans*. New York: Praeger.

Munoz, Carlos, Jr. 1989. *Youth, Identity, Power: The Chicano Movement*. London: Verso.

Nagel, Joane. 1996. *American Indian Ethnic Renewal: Red Power and the Resurgence of Identity and Culture*. New York: Oxford University Press.

O'Neill, William L. 1971. *Coming Apart: An Informal History of America in the 1960s*. New York: Quadrangle.

Sayer, John William. 1997. *Ghost Dancing the Law: The Wounded Knee Trials*. Cambridge: Harvard University Press.

Takezawa, Yasuko I. 1995. *Breaking the Silence: Redress and Japanese American Ethnicity*. Ithaca, NY: Cornell University Press.

Uyematsu, Amy. 1995. "The Emergence of Yellow Power," in Alexander Bloom and Wini Breines, eds., *"Takin' It to the Streets": A Sixties Reader*. New York: Oxford University Press.

Weed, Perry L. 1973. *The White Ethnic Movement and Ethnic Politics*. New York: Praeger.

Weyler, Rex. 1982. *Blood of the Land: The Government and Corporate War Against the American Indian Movement*. New York: Vintage Books.

The Environmental Movement

OVERVIEW

After World War II, the American conservation movement focused on the efficient use of natural resources in the context of an industrial age. By the 1960s, the focus on the conservation of natural resources like water, trees, and soil shifted to a new emphasis on environmentalism that incorporated concerns about air and water pollution, overpopulation, and nuclear energy. Building on an era of grassroots movements, environmental advocates redirected the nation's attention to the dangers of rapid population and technological growth.

As the decade progressed, an increasing number of Americans became convinced of the imminent threats of massive chemical pollution and nuclear apocalypse. By the dawn of the 1970s, concerns about ecological degradation, wilderness preservation, consumer protection, and resistance to the dominance of big business had cohered around the banner of environmentalism. Wilderness-preservation organizations such as the Sierra Club, established in 1892 by California poet, naturalist, and back-to-the-land advocate John Muir, attracted a large number of new members and adopted a much more aggressive campaign for wilderness preservation. David Brower, the Sierra Club's director during the 1960s, used the group's publishing arm and lobbying efforts to promote environmental preservation and move the club's focus away from the more conservative post–World War II goal of conservation.

Sierra Club coffeetable books and calendars that contained the sublime photographs of Ansel Adams aroused concern about threatened rivers and forests and made the wilderness relevant to the baby-boom generation largely raised in the American suburbs. Brower, the Sierra Club, and these picture books and calendars presented wilderness as a desperately needed place for spiritual seclusion and meditative reflection in a world dominated by technology, business interests, and competition.

Rachel Carson's *Silent Spring,* first appearing as a series of articles in the *New Yorker* in 1962 and then a best-selling book, explained in an accessible and evocative way how the postwar chemical industry and the harmful and indiscriminate use of inorganic chemical pesticides like DDT could destroy the earth's ecological processes and therefore the interrelated human and environmental worlds. Carson's description of chemically tainted foods encouraged grassroots consumer activism and revealed the permeable boundaries between humans and nature. It also pierced the façade of suburban tranquility by revealing ecological dangers lurking in the local grocery store and on the front lawn.

This new concern for the environment not only strengthened existing groups like the Sierra Club, but also spawned new organizations like the Chesapeake Bay Foundation (1966), the Population Crisis Committee (1965), and the Environmental Defense Fund (1967). These new groups and their lobbyists found a receptive climate during the early years of the Johnson administration. The environment played an important part of President Johnson's vision for a "Great Society" as evidenced by his signing of the Wilderness Act in 1964 that aimed to protect natural and scenic places. President Johnson would also later support legislation to limit air, water, and solid-waste pollution. In 1966 he created the Council on Recreation and Natural Beauty that ultimately recommended increased government intervention in the preservation and management of nature. Prior to the 1968 Presidential election, President Johnson and Congress passed a number of preservation-related legislation such as the National Wildlife Refuge System (1966), the National Wild and Scenic Rivers Act (1968), and the National Trails Act (1968).

Ironically, it was technology that helped Americans become aware of the environmental degradation caused by industry, chemicals, and the lifestyle of millions of people living in a technologically developed country. Visions of the effects of Dow Chemical Corporation–produced incendiaries like napalm and defoliants like Agent Orange broadcast on television sets across the country helped convince an increasing number of people of the fears expressed by environmental activists. Likewise, the ubiquitous photograph of planet Earth floating alone in the darkness of space made possible by President Kennedy's Apollo space program evoked feelings of ecological vulnerability. Viewing this tranquil image in the context of a series of hideous environmental disasters at the end of the decade, including massive oil spills in the English Channel and Pacific Ocean and a fire *on* the severely polluted Cuyahoga River in Ohio, rallied support for even more environmental protections. In the last months of 1968 and the first half of 1969, more than 130 environment-related bills were introduced before Congress.

Rachel Carson was a noted biologist whose books played a major role in launching the modern environmental movement. Carson's book Silent Spring, *published in 1962, became a best seller and touched off a controversy that led to a fundamental shift in the public's attitudes toward the use of pesticides. (Library of Congress)*

Other social and cultural movements of the decade contributed to the explosion of a nascent modern environmental movement. Those in the counterculture at the end of the 1960s, for example, turned to nature as an escape from the ills of American society. Hippies often idealized nature and looked to the wilderness as a way to have transformative experiences that would help elevate their consciousness above the experiences of a repressive bourgeois American culture. Inspired by Eastern religion and the works of Gary Snyder and others, many young people set out to change themselves and saw the wilderness as a place where they could locate a natural self. Charles A. Reich in a best-selling 1970 book described this process of personal liberation through nature as "the greening of America." The "green" politics of the counterculture embraced an antimodern, utopian, and escapist strand of the environmental movement that shared a great deal with the antiprogressive and romantic origins of groups like the Sierra Club. Like John Muir, many of the late-sixties hippies looked to "drop out" of the urban and suburban rat race for a rural communal existence in idyllic locations. As historian Rusty L. Monhollon perceptively points out, the communards "choice to search for authentic alternatives within a more natural setting had similarities to 'white flight' from urban America" as young people raised in the suburbs now looked for "the next ideal place" and relief from the complexities and anxieties of modern life (Farber and Bailey, 279).

By the 1970s, environmentalism had entered the American mainstream as television shows, magazine articles, and popular books focused on the problem of the earth's resources. Population control, pollution, and endangered species became the concern of middle-class Americans as exemplified by Wisconsin senator Gaylord Nelson's proposal for a massive Earth Day. On April 22, 1970, the nation celebrated its first Earth Day with massive demonstrations taking place in several major cities across the country. As much as any one event, Earth Day convinced politicians like President Richard Nixon of the political value of the environmental movement.

TIMELINE

1960   The Multiple Use-Sustained Yield Act broadening the defined purpose of the national forests to include nonmaterial benefits.

1961   U.S. chapter of World Wildlife Fund is established.

1962   Rachel Carson publishes *Silent Spring*.

President John F. Kennedy and Secretary of the Interior Stewart Udall host a White House Conference on Conservation.

1963   The Bureau of Outdoor Recreation is established with the Department of the Interior.

The Clean Air Act is passed.

President Kennedy takes Conservation Tour.

The Nuclear Test-Ban Treaty is passed.

1964   The Wilderness Act passed and establishes the National Wilderness Preservation System.

Canyonlands National Park is established in Utah.

1965   The Land and Water Conservation Fund Act makes money available for local, state, and federal acquisition and development of park land and open space.

President Lyndon B. Johnson hosts White House Conference on Natural Beauty.

Environmental Pollution Panel is convened.

1966   The National Historic Preservation Act is passed.

The Endangered Species Act initiates federal involvement in habitat protection and rare species identification.

President's Committee on Recreation and Natural Beauty is formed.

Barry Commoner's Center for the Biology of Natural Systems is established.

1967   The Environmental Defense Fund is established.

The Air Quality Act is passed.

1968   Paul Ehrlich publishes *The Population Bomb*.

National Wild and Scenic Rivers Act and national Trails System Act are passed.

Proposal for Grand Canyon dams is defeated.

The first manned flight to circle the moon produces photographs of Earth that become a symbol for the environmental movement.

Redwoods National Park is established.

1969   An oil spill in Santa Barbara, California, dramatizes the problem of pollution.

David R. Brower establishes Friends of the Earth after his ouster from the Sierra Club.

Greenpeace is organized.

Oily wastes and debris on the Cuyahoga River catch fire.

Gary Snyder's "Four Changes" essay argues for a more environmentally responsible civilization.

Paul Ehrlich and others found Zero Population Growth.

BIRTH OF THE MODERN ENVIRONMENTAL MOVEMENT

Prior to the 1960s, activists and policymakers expressed their concerns about the environment with a utilitarian or resource-oriented conservation. After 1960 Americans began to expand their understanding of nature to include not only its scenic and recreational qualities, but the health of the habitat as well. As an indication of this change, activists began calling themselves environmentalists as opposed to conservationists. After the publication of Rachel Carson's *Silent Spring* in 1962, Americans began understanding the world in ecological terms. By the end of the decade, many activists subscribed to what could be called a "gospel of ecology." Although many Americans could not give an accurate definition of ecology as the study of interrelationships between organisms and their environment, they began to understand that human health and welfare were directly linked to the protection of the earth.

As environmental historian Roderick Frazier Nash has written, "fear catalyzed modern environmentalism" (Nash 1990, 188). Unlike earlier fears centering on the exhaustion of useful natural resources that inspired the utilitarian conservationists of the early 20th century, or fears that focused on the aesthetic qualities of nature that played a major role in calls for preservation as early as the 19th century, this fear developed from an understanding of ecology; that the careless use of technology and chemicals could catastrophically impact the health of the entire ecosystem. Although still anthropocentric, the new environmentalism of the 1960s recognized that immediate self-interest had to take a back seat to concerns about the long-term health of the planet. Pollution, no matter how useful for a productive industrial economy, had to be abated.

The World Wildlife Fund

Founded in 1961, the U.S. chapter of the World Wildlife Fund for Nature reflected this new trend in conservation with a mission "to preserve the diversity and abundance of life on Earth and the health of ecological systems" (Bosso, 38). The organization would raise money for the International Union for Conservation of Nature and Natural Resources (now called the World Conservation Union), formed in 1957 by European scientists, naturalists, and business and political leaders, to foster conservation around the world. The World Wildlife Fund raised money through national appeals and provided technical support to appropriate national and local organizations, particularly those focused on preserving endangered species and habitats in less developed nations. The recently retired Dwight D. Eisenhower was the U.S. chapter's first honorary president.

Like the Nature Conservancy (founded in 1951 to purchase sensitive ecosystems) and Defenders of Wildlife (founded in 1947 to protect endangered species), the World Wildlife Fund focused on supporting research, raising the public's awareness, and purchasing land to keep it from degradation and development.

Rachel Carson's *Silent Spring*

The publication of Rachel Carson's *Silent Spring* in 1962 helped launch the modern environmental movement. About half of the book was first published as a series in the *New Yorker,* creating a lot of prerelease interest and controversy. Carson was a marine biologist who had published two bestsellers in the 1950s, *The Sea Around Us* and *The Edge of the Sea*. Her concern in *Silent Spring* was the indiscriminate and profligate use of chemical pesticides, particularly the insecticide DDT, and their devastating effects on wildlife and public health. The book created a sensation and became a bestseller in the United States and Great Britain and was ultimately translated into 30 languages.

Carson's *Silent Spring* made the problem of pesticides relatable to the ordinary person by demonstrating DDT's and other pesticides' potential effects on human health. As important, she cast her argument in scientific language, developing a technical case for her assertion that DDT was responsible for some natural disasters, which she chronicled in some detail. At the same time, she offered an alternative to chemical pesticides, biological methods of insect control that could just as effectively sustain modern agriculture. In offering this alternative, she presented an ecological basis for environmentalism that would shape the movement's future. This view challenged the prevailing assumptions about the relationship between humans and nature that put humans firmly in control of nature. The ecological view instead presented a complex and integrated system of relationships between living things that had to be protected and maintained. Chemicals such as DDT threatened to destroy the ecological system, thereby threatening the very basis of human existence. By the end of the decade, the environmental movement had adopted Carson's ecological perspective.

The book directly stimulated legislation that regulated the use of pesticides and virtually eliminated the widespread use of DDT; it also provided political support for the protection of federal wilderness areas in the Wilderness Act of 1964. The agricultural chemical industry waged an aggressive campaign to challenge her science and assumptions, stating that Carson presented a one-sided case and chose to ignore the benefits in increased food production and decreased incidence of disease that had accrued from the development and use of modern pesticides. P. Rothberg, president of the Montrose Chemical Corporation, for instance, said that Carson wrote not "as a scientist but rather as a fanatic defender of the cult of the balance of nature" (*New York Times*, July 22, 1962, p. 87).

Why Environmentalism Emerged in the 1960s

Historians and sociologists have debated why the modern environmental movement emerged as a force at the end of the 1960s. Sociologist Robert Gottlieb, for example, contends that environmentalism was a cluster of social movements that converged in response to the urban and industrial forces of the previous hundred years. Diminishing the role of the ecological movement represented by *Silent Spring,* Gottlieb argues that the beginning of the modern environmental movement went back into the 19th century with such things as the public response to urban blight during the industrial revolution and the rise of the public health professions.

Victor Scheffer, on the other hand, argues that the environmental movement is rooted in both conservation and ecology. To Scheffer, the rise of the environmental movement is a single, coherent narrative that connects Gifford Pinchot's 19th-century commodity-approach conservation ideals with Rachel Carson's ecology. He contends that the environmental movement grew out of a united front that "swept across boundaries of age, sex, intellect, and class" (Scheffer, 6). Taking a rather simplistic view of the past, Scheffer portrays the rise of the environmental movement as a "good guy versus bad guy" story and ignores the complex, multifaceted aspects of the movement. But unlike Gottlieb, Scheffer does see Carson's ecological justification for environmentalism as an important part of the movement's evolution.

Historians John McCormick and Samuel P. Hays offer a multipart explanation for the powerful emergence of the environmental movement in the 1960s. They believe fear for survival in a polluted world and changing social and economic priorities after World War II served to ignite the movement. But while they, particularly McCormick, suggest that advances in scientific thinking played a major role in this growing anxiety about the environment's future, they minimize the significance of the rise of the ecological perspective.

The environmental historian Roderick Frazier Nash suggests that the environmental ethics of "deep ecology" gave the environmental movement its moral perspective and served to link it to the other social movements of this era. If viewed in this way, it was logical for environmentalists to see the connection between the rights of blacks and women and the rights of natures. To Nash, ethics and morals, not fear for survival, inspired the philosophers and environmentalists of this era.

The National Audubon Society

Like other longstanding environmental groups, the National Audubon Society reflected the shift from a conservationist to ecological focus. Founded at the turn of the 20th century to protect birds from slaughter at the hands of plume hunters, the National Audubon Society in the 1960s adopted an agenda much more expansive than bird protection. In fact, the organization played an important role in introducing the ecological perspective to the environmental movement. Richard Pough, a respected ornithologist, wrote the *Audubon Bird Guide* and sounded the alarm as early as 1945 regarding government experiments with DDT and its early effects on birds. By 1960, two years before the publication of *Silent Spring,* the National Audubon Society began documenting the decline of bird species, including the bald eagle, and attributing it to the use of DDT.

Like other conservation groups going through this transition to a more expansive, ecological, and preservationist agenda, the National Audubon Society experienced exponential growth in the 1960s. With roughly 32,000 members in

Table 7.1. Membership Trends of Selected Environmental Organizations, 1950–1971

Organization	1950–1951	1960–1961	1965–1966	1970–1971
Sierra Club	7,000	16,500	31,000	124,000
National Audubon Society	17,000	32,000	40,500	115,000
National Parks Conservation Association	5,400	15,000	31,000	49,000
The Wilderness Society	5,000	10,000	28,000	62,000
National Wildlife Federation	—	—	256,000	540,000

Source: Christopher J. Bosso, *Environment, Inc.: From Grassroots to Beltway* (Lawrence: University Press of Kansas, 2005).

1960, the organization could boast a membership of 232,000 by the early 1970s (see Table 7.1). During that time the National Audubon Society played an active role in almost every public and political fight to preserve more wilderness, including the successful campaign in support of the 1964 Wilderness Preservation Act. In 1969 the organization opened its public policy office in Washington, D.C., and effectively lobbied Congress for a series of important laws aimed at protecting the environment such as the National Environmental Policy Act of 1969.

The Sierra Club

In 1892 the Scottish immigrant, amateur botanist, and naturalist John Muir founded the Sierra Club to support efforts to protect the forests of the Sierra Nevada and Yosemite Valley from development. For more than a half century, the organization remained small and regional. Each new member had to be sponsored by two current members and approved by a membership committee. Militantly preservationist, the Sierra Club fought to preserve wild areas in the Sierra Nevada, most famously losing their fight to keep the Hetch Hetchy Valley from being flooded to serve as a reservoir for the San Francisco area.

Immediately following World War II the Sierra Club focused its attention on the conservation of natural resources, but during the 1950s the Sierra Club went through a period of change as its leaders began to take on new threats to America's wilderness. It became national in scope, opening an Atlantic chapter in 1951, and joined the Wilderness Society in trying to stop the construction of the proposed Echo Park Dam that would threaten the Dinosaur National Monument in Utah and Colorado. The Sierra Club really started to change, though, after it hired David Brower as its first executive director in 1952. Brower convinced the board that he could effectively sell preservation and raise money for the club. As the Sierra Club's first full-time professional-level employee, Brower aggressively pursued a campaign in defense of wild areas, most notably one to save the Grand Canyon from being flooded by proposed downstream dams. These

American environmental activist David Brower (1912–2000) (center, foreground),
executive director of the Sierra Club, leads a protest against the proposed construction
of dams on the Colorado River in Grand Canyon National Park, Arizona, 1966.
(Arthur Schatz/Time & Life Pictures/Getty Images)

campaigns brought greater awareness to public land-use issues and united conservationists behind preservationist goals. In 1966 the Sierra Club moved beyond concerns of preservation to include population and "urban amenities" to
its action agenda (Mitchell, 87).

Brower's more expansive and aggressive approach brought greater attention,
more membership, and increased funds to the Sierra Club. From 1960 to 1969,
conservation and preservation groups in general experienced a sevenfold increase in membership, from 124,000 to 819,000, as they became more aggressive
and outspoken about threats to scenic national treasures and wildlife. Abolish-
ing its restrictive membership practices helped the Sierra Club go from 16,500
members in 1960 to 124,000 members in 1970. Similarly, the National Audubon
Society grew from 32,000 members in 1960 to 115,000 members in 1970, and
the Wilderness Society grew from 10,000 members in 1960 to 62,000 members in
1970 (see Table 7.1).

As the Sierra Club celebrated its seventy-fifth anniversary in 1967, it pledged
to expand its activities even further in a worldwide education enterprise. Dr.
Edgar Wayburn, serving as its president, likened the Sierra Club to "a small
school of conservation which now is ready to become a university, possibly a
multiversity" in dealing with planetary environment. As for the ambitious Brower,

he wanted "to see it become an action arm for the International Union for the Conservation of Nature. I don't want to see us back away from our responsibilities anywhere in the world. There is very little left on this planet that man hasn't done something to." At the club's diamond jubilee, leaders proved to be prescient as they predicted that membership could exceed 200,000 within five years. In fact, in 1972 the Sierra Club would boast 232,000 members (*New York Times,* December 9, 1967).

The Sierra Club in 1960 inaugurated a series of beautifully printed books of photographs related to the theme of preservation to increase awareness of the nation's natural resources and beauty and to the continuing threat to their existence. Ansel Adam's "This Is the American Earth" published in 1960 and Eliot Porter's "In Wildness is the Preservation of the World" published in 1961 proved to be huge successes and served as a foundation to the club's expanded publishing efforts.

In 1969, Brower resigned as executive director of the Sierra Club to form a new national organization to lobby for preservation causes at the legislative level. As the embodiment of the Sierra Club's growth and more aggressive stand on preservation, Brower's departure signaled a clear divide in the seventy-seven-year-old organization. Brower's departure followed the decisive defeat of a Brower-led slate of candidates for vacancies on the club's board of directors. Although wildly successful, Brower had angered a board majority and many of the rank-and-file membership by his aggressive, freehanded leadership of an organization he helped to transform from a parochial hiking group into a large-scale advocate for global preservation.

The Wilderness Society

David Brower had pushed the Sierra Club into the wilderness movement, but the cause of wilderness preservation had originated with a small group of easterners of considerable means two and a half decades earlier. The group's leader, Robert Marshall, had organized the Wilderness Society in 1937. The group led the fight for the preservation of wilderness areas that culminated in the Wilderness Act of 1964 (see below). At first this small group of wilderness advocates identified only a few large areas in the West as worthy of federal protection.

Like the Sierra Club and other environmental groups, the Wilderness Society experienced exponential growth during the 1960s. As Table 7.1 indicates, it went from a modest-sized organization of 10,000 members in 1960 to 62,000 members in 1970. Almost immediately after successfully fighting for the Wilderness Act of 1964, members began demanding an expansion of federal wilderness designations. While the old guard within the Wilderness Society maintained that many of the newly proposed areas were not of sufficient wilderness quality, new members effectively argued for expansion. In some cases special-interest factions within the Wilderness Society created new organizations such as the Oregon Natural Resources Council that effectively made the case for the inclusion of the Cascades, the Oregon Coast Range, and large forested areas in eastern Oregon into the National Wilderness System.

EARLY POLITICAL RESPONSES TO THE GROWING ENVIRONMENTAL MOVEMENT

As a result of the growing concern over lost wilderness and the possibility of irreparable damage to the earth's ecosystem, the 1960s marked the beginning of legislative initiatives that would be fine-tuned over the remainder of the 20th century, partially in response to the tremendous growth of the environmental movement and organizations. Politicians responded to the growing fear among the American people over the health and sustainability of the environment. The proliferation of legislation regulating human behavior's effects on the environment reflected this fear and the growing impact and effectiveness of organizations like the World Wildlife Fund for Nature, the National Audubon Society, the Sierra Club, and the Wilderness Society.

As a carryover from the postwar period, parks and wilderness remained high on the public and legislative agenda. For example, by 1960 the number of National Park visitors had grown to 70 million, and Congress responded by creating the Land and Water Conservation Fund, which added new wilderness areas and national parks.

For his part, President Johnson called his environmental policy "the new conservation." This policy included support for more urban parks and a highway beautification program spearheaded by his wife, Lady Bird Johnson. Although several environmental laws were passed during the 1940s and 1950s, many of the hallmark pieces of antipollution and wilderness legislation were enacted during the 1960s in response to the growing momentum of the environmental movement (Switzer, 17–20).

The Wilderness Act of 1964

The conservation lobby began pressing Congress for a wilderness protection bill as early as 1957. In 1959, David Brower made the case for a Wilderness Preservation System that represented the views of groups like the Wilderness Society, the Sierra Club, and the Audubon Society:

> The most important source of the vital organic forms constituting the chain of life is the gene bank that exists in wilderness, where the life force has gone on since the beginning uninterrupted by man and his technology.

For this reason alone, it is important that the remnants of wilderness that we still have on our public lands be preserved by the best methods our form of government can find. . . . A growing economy will have availed us nothing if it extinguishes our all-important wilderness. A gross misunderstanding of wilderness, in which it is evaluated according to the number of hikers who get into it, has been fostered for the past several years, to the great detriment of all the future. There must be no more needless losses. There is no substitute for wilderness. What we now have is all that we shall ever have. (Brower, 271–272)

After a series of compromises, Congress passed the Wilderness Act in 1964. The major challenge to the legislation came from the mining, lumber, and grazing industries. In response to industry's call for access, Carl W. Buchheister, president of the Audubon Society, said no methods of mining or exploration should be permitted "that would ruin the wilderness character of the area. We preserve furniture, coats of armor and paintings jealously, and at great expense, but have so far neglected the most important museum of them all, the wilderness" (*New York Times,* April 30, 1964, p. 21). Opponents of the bill held that the economic growth of large regions, mostly in the West, rested on the mineral, fuel, and grazing potentials of the area.

The compromise program put 9.1 million acres of government land into a wilderness conservation system. The program initially involved 54 areas in 12 states—areas where, the bill stated, "the earth and its community of life are untrammeled by man, where man himself is a visitor who does not remain. . . . An area of undeveloped Federal land retaining its primeval character and influence, without permanent improvements or human habitation, which is protected and managed so as to preserve its natural conditions" (*New York Times,* April 30, 1964, p. 21).

This removed the power to designate wilderness area from the Forest Service. The congressional designation deprived the Forest Service of the right to reallocate such lands for other uses and imposed a set of stringent standards, such as the prohibition of structures and use of motorized vehicles that determined the management of wilderness. The Wilderness Act represented a shift away from the old era of administrative discretion and expertise to an era of legislative skepticism toward federal land-management policies and bureaucracies. This removal of power from the Forest Service was ironic given that innovative and extraordinary Forest Service employees Aldo Leopold and Robert Marshall initially championed the idea of wilderness designation. But due to a series of questionable decisions to reallocate wilderness areas for other uses, conservationists and preservationists alike supported diminishing agency discretion and setting out explicit legislative standards to guide and control administrative action. With the passage of the Wilderness Act, an agency that hardly ever had to defend its decisions in court would now become a familiar defendant in lawsuits aimed at getting more land designated as wilderness under this new congressional mandate.

Clean Air

The Clean Air Act of 1955 signaled the federal government's tentative first steps toward a nationwide promotion of clean air by funding state and local air-pollution prevention and control programs. Until this time, responsibility for clean air in the United States rested solely with the states and local communities. In the 1960s both the House of Representatives and the Senate responded to the growing attention to environmental issues by considering bills that would establish federal air quality criteria to serve as guidelines for states and localities in planning and instituting their own air-pollution control programs. Prodded along by President Kennedy, the freshman senator from Maine, Edmund S. Muskie, chaired a Subcommittee on Air and Water Pollution and held hearings in September 1963 to consider a new federal air-pollution control bill. As a result of these hearings, the subcommittee determined that air pollution was a national, worsening problem that demanded federal intervention. In December 1963, after Kennedy's assassination, President Johnson rammed the 1963 Clean Air Act through Congress as a memorial to the slain president.

The Clean Air Act of 1963 expanded the research-oriented program that allowed the federal government to help with funding but still gave it no enforcement power. After its passage, Muskie's subcommittee held field hearings in various cities to determine how well this law served the needs of different localities. They heard testimony from conservationists that pointed to a need for auto exhaust controls and regional air-pollution control agencies. These hearings pitted the environmental concerns of environmentalists against industry, in this case the auto industry. They also revealed the inherent conflict between Americans' love affair with the automobile and their desire for clean air and a safe environment. By the 1960s, vehicular emissions accounted for up to half the nation's total air pollution. With 85 million cars on the roads, conservationists and lawmakers looked not to Americans, but to the auto industry to change its behavior. In January 1965, Muskie introduced a bill to strengthen the Clean Air Act of 1963 by calling for the establishment of federal vehicular emissions standards similar to those California had already adopted.

Despite having already produced 1966 model cars that met California's emissions standards, the auto industry balked at this bill and claimed there was insufficient evidence to prove the problem of auto exhaust was serious enough to warrant nationwide controls. Deflecting attention away from auto pollution, they asserted that taxpayers' dollars would be better spent on expanding controls on pollution from industrial plants and homes. Despite this opposition, the auto manufacturers recognized the inevitability of vehicular exhaust controls and promised they could meet these standards by the 1968 model year.

A dense layer of smog sits among the skyscrapers of Los Angeles, California, and the surrounding urban sprawl. Air pollution from auto emissions became a major concern in California during the 1960s, leading to air quality legislation. (Getty Images/PhotoDisc)

California, however, recognized that these new national standards established in Muskie's proposed Air Quality Act (which became law in 1967), while modeled after their existing standards, would not be restrictive enough to meet its worsening air-pollution problem. Although the auto industry had earlier supported multiple standards, it now resisted California's demand that states be allowed to impose stricter standards than the federal minimum. Muskie, although generally in favor of a uniform standard, supported the bill the Senate ultimately passed that gave only California the right to require stricter controls. This made California the locus for the growing fight between the environmental movement and the auto industry.

Conservationists and legislators started to push the auto industry even further by wondering whether more progress could be gained against air pollution through different approaches to the problem. For instance, as a part of the developing, more ambitious vision of environmentalists, some argued that the solution to auto emissions lay not in trying to clean up the inherently polluting internal-combustion engine but in replacing it altogether. There were numerous alternatives drawing attention in both California and Washington, D.C., during the mid- to late 1960s, such as the gas turbine engines, modern steam engines, and fuel cells; vehicles designed to run on compressed natural gas, propane, or

The President's Committee on Recreation and Natural Beauty

In response to growing concerns about the environment, the threat to the nation's natural beauty and wilderness areas, and population growth, President Lyndon B. Johnson in May 1966 established the Committee on Recreation and Natural Beauty, composed of six Cabinet members, other government officials, and a twelve-member Citizens Advisory Committee. In announcing the committee, President Johnson said, the United States had "just begun to scratch the surface of ugliness, neglect and decay" in city and countryside (*New York Times,* May 5, 1966, p. 18).

President Johnson named Laurance S. Rockefeller to head the citizens' committee and said the committee's job would be to chart a course for the nation in helping to provide recreation areas nearby to bring relief from the noise and congestion of cities. The new committee was an outgrowth of recommendations from a White House Conference on Natural Beauty held in 1965. The committee reported on subjects ranging from highway billboards and automobile junkyards to the underground installation of utilities.

Both the 1965 conference and 1966 creation of the committee demonstrated that the power and prestige of the executive office was now engaged in some of the most pressing environmental issues. Lady Bird Johnson, the first lady, was a prominent figure at the conference as well as in the national beautification movement. In a special message on natural beauty sent to Congress on February 8, 1965, President Johnson wrote:

> A growing population is swallowing up areas of natural beauty with its demands for living space. . . . The increasing tempo of urbanization and growth is already depriving many Americans of the right to live in decent surroundings. . . . The modern technology, which has added much to our lives can also have a darker side. Its uncontrolled waste products are menacing the world we live in, our enjoyment and our health. The air we breathe, our water, our soil, and wildlife, are being blighted by the poisons and chemicals which are the by-products of technology and industry. . . . To deal with these new problems will require a new conservation. . . . In this conservation the protection and enhancement of man's opportunity to be in contact with beauty must play a major role. (Nash, *American Environmentalism,* 181–186)

even hydrogen; battery-powered electric and hybrid vehicles (cars that could operate on electricity in the city but could switch to traditional gasoline in rural areas). However, while many of these technologies promised lower emissions than the traditional combustion engine, they were not at a stage of development to compete in terms of range, reliability, cost, convenience, or power.

The Environmental Pollution Panel

Rachel Carson's *Silent Spring* brought public attention to the pesticide menace contaminating the environment, but this only dealt with one portion of the problems Americans started referring to as "pollution." Evidence of this growing national concern was the appointment of an Environmental Pollution Panel by the President's Science Advisory Committee. In 1965 the panel produced a report that chronicled the concerns that dominated environmental policy and legislation for the remainder of the 20th century.

The report started with a simple declarative statement: "The production of pollutants and an increasing need for pollution management are an inevitable concomitant of a technological society with a high standard of living. Pollution problems will increase in importance as our technology and standard of living continue to grow" (Nash, *American Environmentalism,* 195). The panel explained that air, water, and land pollution threatens the "health, longevity, livelihood, recreation, cleanliness and happiness of citizens" who cannot escape their influence. Because of the pervasive nature of pollution and its disregard of political boundaries, the panel argued that it was "mandatory that the Federal Government assume leadership and exert its influence in pollution abatement on a national scale" (Nash, *American Environmentalism,* 196).

Consistent with Carson's explanation of the dangers of DDT, the panel made an ecological argument for the necessity of federal environmental management. "Because living things are interdependent and interacting," the report explained, "they form a complex, dynamic system" and tampering with that system can produce "unexpected results, or side effects" that pose a serious threat to the earth's habitability. "Pollutants tend to reduce the numbers of species and to make the relationships of those that remain less stable" (Nash, *American Environmentalism,* 197).

After explaining the nature of the problem, the panel argued that the lack of federal authority to act reveals a lack of "ecological foresight." The panel made an important and compelling case for minimum environmental quality standards industry must adhere to with federal governmental oversight. The report concluded by giving the government the responsibility to guarantee a "clean, healthy, and happy environment" (quoted in Nash 1990, 195–201).

CAUSES FOR ALARM

At the end of the decade, a series of hideous environmental disasters horrified a broader spectrum of American society. Oil spills in the English Channel and Pacific Ocean, the severely polluted Cuyahoga River in Ohio catching fire, and the declaration by biologist Barry Commoner that Lake Erie had "died" as a result of chemical and sewage pollution offered a compelling case for dramatic action. In addition, images of the Vietnam War broadcast on the evening news in households across the nation brought not only terrifying images of war, but also of environmental degradation through the use of incendiaries like napalm and defoliants like Agent Orange. For many Americans, witnessing the destruction of a third world's landscape and people by a technologically advanced, industrial war machine confirmed the case for linking environmental concerns with social and political critiques.

The Fight to Preserve the Grand Canyon

In 1964 a federal plan to build two dams that would flood part of the Colorado River in the Grand Canyon sparked an intense debate. The government asserted the construction of the dams was imperative to meet the arid Southwest's growing need for water for a burgeoning population, agriculture, and industry, and as a source of hydroelectric power.

Officially known as the Pacific Southwest Water Plan, the government proposal included constructing the Marble Canyon dam roughly 12 miles above the upstream boundary of the Grand Canyon National Park and the Bridge Canyon dam a little over two miles upstream from Lake Mead. The first 53 miles of the reservoir would be in the Lake Mead National Recreation Area. The water would then back up through the Grand Canyon National Monument for 40 miles. The upper 13 miles of the reservoir would have flooded an inner gorge between the Grand Canyon Park and Monument.

The debate over the plan pitted Stewart L. Udall, secretary of the Interior and self-proclaimed conservationist, against David Brower, charismatic executive director of the Sierra Club and ardent preservationist. These two figures represented a growing split in the environmental movement. Secretary Udall favored what he called "conservation for use" while Brower represented a group some referred to as ultraconservationists, purists, or preservationists. This latter group held inviolate certain parts of the national landscape as sanctuaries of the human spirit. In recommending the plan, Udall recognized the problem and expressed regret that there was no other way to meet the water crises of the Southwest: "If there were other dam sites on the Colorado," he wrote in a letter to President Johnson, "the problem could be readily resolved, but regrettably such is not the case. The urgency of the water crisis in the Pacific Southwest has caused me to favor the plan submitted herewith, when weighed against the peripheral impairment of scenic values." Brower countered that together the two dams would drown nearly half of all the flowing river of the canyon beneath deep, still lakes, silencing what he called the "pulsing heart of the place" (Quoted in the *New York Times,* December 12, 1965, pp. SM 56 and 122).

The debate intensified and became personal when the Internal Revenue Service (IRS) began examining the tax-exempt status of the Sierra Club. Brower believed the IRS bowed to political pressure in agreeing to investigate while so little evidence of a violation existed. He then accused Udall of "assisting the demise of the great park system he was pledged to protect" (*New York Times,* July 13, 1966, p. 35). While denying Brower's charges, Udall and the federal government eventually shelved the plan to construct the dams, giving Brower, the Sierra Club, and a growing number of preservationists a significant victory.

Ralph Nader's Study Group on Air Pollution

The young consumer advocate Ralph Nader organized a study on the problem of air pollution that ultimately criticized the federal government's passive response to what he considered an inevitable global crisis. Nader's harsh criticism of the federal government revealed a growing public agitation over dirty air at the end of the decade. Hailed as progressive and responsive to the concerns of environmentalists at the time of its passage, Senator Muskie's Air Quality Act of 1967 quickly came under heavy criticism for its moderation, gradualism, and reliance on state and local initiatives. Nader's study blamed Muskie, once championed as "Mr. Clean," for introducing an excessively moderate bill. The group's report went as far as implying that Muskie was a corporate sellout and criticized him for being a conciliator, not a fighter. It also blasted Muskie's vision of "creative federalism" in air-pollution control, given the states' demonstrated reluctance to act.

"Nader's Raiders" condemned the Air Quality Act as a perpetuation of the old system of delays before the federal government would intervene: "Do we have twenty, thirty, or forty years before major areas will be literally uninhabitable? Can we wait for the mechanisms of the Air Quality Act to be implemented? If we can wait, will the Act work when it is implemented?" (quoted in Dewey, 242). The criticism reflected the overall radicalization of public environmental attitudes by 1969 and stung a politician with presidential ambitions who had to a large extent built his political career on the issue of pollution control.

The Environmental Defense Fund and the National Resources Defense Council

Dennis Puleston became an active environmentalist in the 1960s when he noticed that ospreys were disappearing from Long Island, New York, where he lived. He remembered that when he first visited Gardiner's Island in 1948 there were more than 300 active osprey nests, producing an average of more than two fledglings per nest. During the 1950s he noticed the number of nests dropping steadily until by the early sixties the drop had reached collapse proportion. Puleston saw this drop as a sort of a "canary in the coal mine," a warning about the health and welfare of people living in the area. After reading Rachel Carson's *Silent Spring*, Puleston gathered several unhatched eggs, which tested positive for the presence of high concentrations of DDT. This discovery caused scientists to focus more attention on the almost total disappearance of the blueclaw crab from the island's bay, and the diminished populations of reptiles, amphibians, and species of birds, butterflies, and honeybees.

It did not take long to identify the cause of these increased levels of DDT on Long Island. For twenty years, the Suffolk County Mosquito Control Commission had sprayed DDT in a largely unsuccessful effort to reduce the mosquito populations. The commission ignored requests from concerned citizens to stop the spraying, so they hired a local lawyer, Victor Yannecone, to file a class-action lawsuit claiming the citizenry had a right to the cleanest possible environment consistent with the general welfare. Yannecone filed the suit in 1966 against the Suffolk County Mosquito Control Commission and did so mostly without outside funding. Athough he received volunteer scientific assistance from several concerned biologists in the area, Yannecone had no official relationship with any organization. With the help of the scientists, Yannecone demonstrated that the use of DDT polluted and disturbed the environment. At the same time, the commission failed to show that there was an economic necessity to use DDT, causing the court to issue a temporary ban on DDT use for about a year, at which time the judge ruled that a permanent ban must come from the state legislature. Despite the judge's order of a temporary ban, the county administration stepped in and made the ban permanent.

Emboldened by this victory, Yannecone, a group of concerned scientists, and conservationists like Puleston decided to follow their courtroom tactics on a broader scale. In 1967, Yannecone and the group of scientists formalized their association by founding the Environmental Defense Fund, the first environmental law group. Despite Yannecone's talents as a litigator, he was unpredictable and difficult to work with, which led to his departure from the association by 1969. The scientists then approached the Ford Foundation for funding to hire a legal staff so they could pursue litigation on environmental hazards all over the country. Although interested in funding social reform projects and protecting the environment, the Ford Foundation was not yet convinced that the nascent Environmental Defense Fund was a viable organization. Instead, Ford Foundation officials informally brokered a merger between several prominent New York attorneys and seven Yale law school students to create a new organization, the National Resources Defense Council. Ford then gave the new National Resources Defense Council a $100,000 initial grant in 1970, followed by a series of grants totaling $2.6 million by 1977. The success of the National Resources Defense Council grant prompted the Ford Foundation to start making similar grants to the Environmental Defense Fund.

Throughout the 1970s the Environmental Defense Fund tended to focus on issues related to toxic chemicals, wetlands, water quality, and power generation.

For their part, the National Resources Defense Council concentrated on air pollution, nuclear power, and solid waste. At its conception the Environmental Defense Fund was a membership group dominated by scientists but used litigation to achieve its ends. The National Resources Defense Council, on the other hand, was originally a law firm run by lawyers and not a membership organization. However, within a few years the two organizations became more similar as the National Resources Defense Council developed a membership and hired some scientists while lawyers took on a larger role within the Environmental Defense Fund.

Oil Spills

The environmental movement gained support after two highly publicized oil spills: one off of Britain's southwest coast and the Scilly Isles in March 1966 and the other off the coast of Southern California in February 1969. Environmental groups effectively used these human-made disasters as evidence that short-term corporate interests were threatening the long-term health of the earth's delicate ecological systems.

Tons of crude oil poured into the Atlantic from an American-owned tanker, the *Torrey Canyon,* after it went aground on the Seven Stones reef at the western entrance to the English Channel in the spring of 1966. The tanker, owned by the Union Oil Company of California and on charter to the British Petroleum Company, hit the reef despite receiving warnings by the nearby Seven Stones lightship. At least half of the 118,000 tons of oil on board spilled into the sea through holes torn in the hull by the rocks. The tanker ultimately broke in two approximately a week and a half after it had struck the reef, causing even more of the oil to spill into the ocean and causing the massive pollution of Britain's coasts.

Less than three years later a huge oil slick oozed from an offshore well in the Pacific Ocean about five miles from Santa Barbara, California. The well, also owned by the Union Oil Company of California, developed a leak in late January 1969, causing a thin film of oil to reach land along a 16-mile stretch of scenic shoreline south of Santa Barbara. The media covered the story with images of birds—mostly gulls and grebes—covered with oil, raising the ire of local residents and conservation groups. The massive spill rekindled an intense debate from the previous year when the Department of the Interior auctioned oil-drilling rights on nearly 1,000 square miles of ocean floor off Santa Barbara to a dozen of the country's major oil companies for $603 million. Local residents and conservationists complained that exploitation of the Continental shelf would besmirch the renowned beauty of the affluent beach community. One angry conservationist asked, "how far do we go in sacrificing the pleasantness of everyone's surroundings for short-term economic gains for a relatively few?" (*New York Times,* February 2, 1969, p. 1). At the time of the debate, environmentalists

The oil tanker Torrey Canyon *breaks apart after running aground on a reef off Land's End, England, in March 1967. The tanker spilled about 31 million gallons of crude oil into the sea, contaminating vast areas of coastline between England and France. (AFP/Getty Images)*

warned that the deal paved the way for a Southern California equivalent of the *Torrey Canyon* disaster. The fears expressed in 1968 proved correct as the nation faced the fact that one cannot measure in dollars the damage resulting from the mass slaughter of birds, fish, whales, and seals, not to mention the value of sparkling beaches.

Secretary of the Interior Walter J. Hickel found himself in the middle of this controversy only two weeks after assuming the position. He responded by first requesting a voluntary cessation of drilling in the area by all oil companies. The next day he ordered the resumption of drilling only to be followed the next day by another order to stop all offshore drilling in the polluted Santa Barbara Channel. His ultimate order to stop the drilling came after a considerable protest from anxious officials, environmentalists, and residents of the Santa Barbara area. As the order was issued, some 200,000 gallons of crude oil continued to spread over the ocean off Santa Barbara, soiling nearly 30 miles of beaches. Experts estimated that approximately 20,000 additional gallons of oil had spurted up from the ocean floor each day.

Fire on the Cuyahoga

On June 22, 1969, the Cuyahoga River located in northeastern Ohio caught fire, dramatizing the extent of the river's pollution and the ineffectiveness of Cleveland's pollution-abatement program. Witnesses reported that the fire reached as high as five stories and lasted about 20 minutes before being brought under control. The fire was allegedly caused by an accumulation of oily wastes and debris on the river directly under two wooden trestles at the foot of Campbell Road hill in southeast Cleveland. A subsequent investigation by Cleveland's Bureau of Industrial Wastes determined that the fire erupted due to a discharge of highly volatile petroleum derivatives with a sufficiently low flash point.

The fire prompted *Time* magazine to describe the Cuyahoga as the river that "oozes and flows," which added to Cleveland's reputation as a negligent pollutant of Lake Erie just a year after biologist Barry Commoner had declared the lake dead (Lake Erie flows into the Cuyahoga). The publicity surrounding this fire helped gain public support for a series of pollution-control legislative measures, like the Clean Water Act and the Great Lakes Water Quality Agreement, as well as the creation of the Environmental Protection Agency (EPA). Although due to this attention the river's water quality has improved dramatically over the last three decades of the 20th century, the fire on the Cuyahoga remains a symbol of environmental degradation caused by industrial waste. Randy Newman's song "Burn On" in 1972 and R.E.M.'s "Cuyahoga" in 1986 are but two examples of the fire's enduring symbolic significance to the environmental movement.

The *Torrey Canyon* spill, followed by the Santa Barbara leak, helped garner more political support for the wave of environmental protection laws Congress passed in the early 1970s.

Zero Population Growth

Founded in 1968, the organization Zero Population Growth worked to raise awareness of the relationship between environmental degradation and uncontrolled population growth. A small group of environmentalists energized by the publication of Dr. Paul R. Ehrlich's *The Population Bomb* (1968) founded the group and started using such slogans as "The pill in time saves nine" and "This line is too long. Join ZPG" to make its point and attract new members. By 1972, Zero Population Growth claimed 35,000 members in local chapters across the country.

Ehrlich's *The Population Bomb* served as the inspiration and justification for this movement. The controversial and polemical writings of Ehrlich, a Stanford

Graduate student using arguments from Paul Ehrlich's The Population Bomb *to debate attorney Stephen Foley, who opposes abortion reform, at Rutgers University. (Art Rickerby/ Time Life Pictures/Getty Images)*

University biology professor, argued for unilateral action by the United States in densely populated nations like India in order to enforce a low birth rate. He wrote, for example, that the United States should have seized on a proposal in India for compulsory sterilization and offered logistical support in the form of helicopters, vehicles, surgical instruments, and platoons of doctors and paramedical personnel to implement the plan. Ehrlich believed that the ends justified such drastic means. He wrote that the United States had to shift its efforts away from treating the symptoms to curing the cause of the planet's environmental degradation. He went on to argue that a real solution to the population problem would require apparently heartless and brutal decisions such as not intervening to prevent famines in nations whose population explosions had become unmanageable and enforcing migration control at the borders to ensure that the starving millions did not swarm into the United States.

Critics of the Zero Population Growth movement challenged both Ehrlich's analysis of the problem and his method for a solution. While the American mainstream and even President Richard Nixon acknowledged that more had to be done to control population growth, few believed that the situation was as dire as Ehrlich claimed. For his part, President Nixon in 1969 emphasized the absolute right of couples to make their own decisions about the size of their families, promising that the government would never "infringe on the religious convictions, personal wishes and freedom of any individual" (*New York Times,* July 19, 1970, p. 174).

Others worried about the moral overtones of the Zero Population Growth message. To them, it sounded like a prosperous nation like the United States, which had only 5 percent of the population but consumed nearly half of the world's natural resources, could continue to serve its own gluttony by telling poor nations like India, Indonesia, and China to stop procreating. Although acknowledging that the greatest challenge to population growth existed where the population was densest and poorest, realists countered that the chances of actual control over the population in such places was remote. In such societies traditional values such as measuring a man's wealth by the number of sons he has would not give way easily.

THE MATURATION OF THE ENVIRONMENTAL MOVEMENT

The emphasis on ecology by public scientists like Rachel Carson and Barry Commoner and the political activism of pioneers like David Brower set the stage for the expansive, politically powerful environmental movement of the late 20th and early 21st centuries. The explosion of new advocacy organizations aided by a change in the political structure of the late 1960s that lowered the barriers of access to the federal judiciary, combined with the new legal concept of "class action," gave attorneys representing the public's interest unprecedented opportunities to use lawsuits as advocacy tactics. In addition, new and old environmental advocacy groups alike learned new tactics to strengthen their memberships, raise money, and advocate for environmental protection legislation. The environmental movement also benefited from an era of grassroots movements and alternative cultures that challenged the values, assumptions, and effects of industrial capitalism. As a result of these developments, concern for the environment had gone mainstream by the turn of the decade.

The Counterculture and the Environment

As traditional environmental activists, government bureaucrats, and environmental lawyers toiled to create legislation to protect the environment, a growing counterculture in the late 1960s began to incorporate nature and wilderness into their alternative lifestyle. Not so concerned with practical politics, the counterculture viewed nature as an escape from the ills of modern American society. As historian Jeff Sanders has written, "idealized nature and antimodernism had been strong features of environmentalism since the Progressive era, and it is not surprising that some members of the counterculture would look to nature in their attempts to create a more authentic and transformed consciousness" (Sanders in Farber and Bailey, 278).

The counterculture blended this idealized view of nature with Eastern religious principles as an avenue to change themselves and possibly the culture of mainstream America. Nature became a place to locate one's true self. As described by Charles A. Reich in his 1970 bestselling book, *The Greening of America,* personal liberation and being green became synonymous for counterculturalists. The green worldview of the counterculture could be antimodern, utopian, and escapist. Reminiscent of the Sierra Club's founder, John Muir, the counterculture's love of nature stemmed from an antiprogressive, romantic impulse. Like Muir, many hippies wanted to drop out of the rat race inherent in American cities by escaping to the bucolic and serene lifestyle experienced through communal living arrangements in idyllic settings.

The writings and poetry of Pulitzer Prize–winning author Gary Snyder possibly best illustrate the counterculture's romantic view of nature. After studying anthropology and living as a bohemian in San Francisco, Snyder took an extended trip to Japan where he steeped himself in non-Western ways of thinking about humans' relationship to nature. In 1969, he wrote the essay "Four Changes" as an argument for radical alterations in American thought, government, and culture with the intent of making our civilization more environmentally responsible. He envisioned a world where humans viewed other creatures as equal partners. He also believed that the interests of nonhuman life forms should be represented in human systems of government.

Friends of the Earth

After transforming the Sierra Club into a national political force, David Brower formed a new advocacy organization, named Friends of the Earth after a John Muir quotation. While at the helm of the Sierra Club, Brower had provoked a schism over his leadership style and inability to run the organization within a budget. After years of increasingly acrimonious conflict, the election of a new board backed by Brower's critics led to his resignation. Brower took several senior Sierra Club staffers with him to run Friends of the Earth.

Brower conceived Friends of the Earth as a broad-spectrum national environmental organization that would combine scientific research, major publication campaigns to raise public awareness, and direct lobbying. Brower wanted to take his concerns for the environment and support for increased wilderness to a global level. Almost immediately after the main group formed, affiliates were established in Canada and Great Britain. Burdened over the Sierra Club's tax-exempt status while serving as its executive director, Brower generated revenues for Friends of the Earth from a direct-mail mass membership drive and foundation grants to its tax-exempt John Muir Institute in addition to publication revenues. (The Sierra Club similarly established a separate foundation to help with its fundraising efforts after the organization lost its tax-exempt status.)

In 1970, leaders of the Friends of Earth created the League of Conservation Voters as a nontax-exempt political action committee. As such, the League of Conservation could pursue overtly partisan activities, including making campaign contributions to candidates.

National Environmental Policy Act

Responding to growing public pressure for action to solve the nation's growing environmental problems, Congress in 1968 and 1969 held joint and separate

House and Senate committee hearings to consider how to legislate a national policy for the environment. These hearings demonstrated recognition that the government's actions made large and sometimes indelible footprints on the environment. They also showed that Congress now realized environmental concerns should be treated equally and contemporaneously with economic and technical considerations.

As a result of these hearings, the House drafted a bill to establish a Council on Environmental Quality within the Executive Office of the President, similar to the Council of Economic Advisors, with the responsibility to prepare an annual report on the state of the nation's environment. A Senate bill contained a strong declarative statement of national environmental policy as well as a provision to compel federal agencies to document their efforts to comply with the policy set forth in the law. A conference committee later combined the House and Senate provisions into what became the National Environment Policy Act (NEPA), signed into law by President Nixon on January 1, 1970. Sometimes referred to as the nation's environmental Magna Carta, the NEPA articulated a concern for environmental quality rooted in the philosophies of early conservationists, but also tempered by more recent utilitarian and scientific perspectives.

The NEPA established the framework for environmental impact assessment. The NEPA declared that:

> it is the continuing responsibility of the Federal Government to use all practicable means, consistent with other essential considerations of national policy, to improve and coordinate Federal plans, functions, programs, and resources to the end that the Nation may . . . fulfill the responsibilities of each generation as trustee of the environment for succeeding generations; assure for all Americans safe, healthful, productive, and esthetically and culturally pleasing surroundings; attain the widest range of beneficial uses of the environment without degradation, risk to health or safety, or other undesirable and unintended consequences; . . . maintain, wherever possible, an environment which supports diversity and variety of individual choice; achieve a balance between population and resource use . . . ; and enhance the quality of renewable resources and approach the maximum attainable recycling of depletable resources. (National Environmental Policy Act, 1969)

The NEPA essentially directed all federal agencies to consider the environmental impact of proposed government action. The NEPA also provided the public an opportunity to influence the shape and breadth of a proposal for action. Federal agencies must include an environmental impact statement that discusses any adverse environmental effects of the proposed action, of alternatives to the proposed action, of the relationship between local short-term uses of the environment and long-term productivity, and of any irreversible and irretrievable commitments of resources that the project would involve.

The NEPA set the stage for much of the environmental legislation of the 1970s. By requiring all federal agencies to monitor, evaluate, and control their activities to protect and enhance the quality of the environment, the NEPA has had an impact on economic and technological development in the United States broader than any other environmental legislation. In the wake of signing the NEPA into law, President Nixon made environmental issues a major focus of his first State of the Union address on January 22, 1970:

> The great question of the seventies is, shall we surrender to our surroundings, or shall we make our peace with nature and begin to make reparations for the damage we have done to our air, to our land, and to our water?
>
> Restoring nature to its natural state is a cause beyond party and beyond factions. It has become a common cause of all the people of this country. It is a cause of particular concern to young Americans, because they more than we will reap the grim consequences of our failure to act on programs which are needed now if we are to prevent disaster later.
>
> Clean air, clean water, open spaces—these should once again be the birthright of every American. If we act now, they can be.

Earth Day

Although the first Earth Day celebration occurred on April 22, 1970, it represented the culmination of the 1960s environmental movement. The event marked a high point in popular concern about environmental issues and the beginning of a populist push for government regulation on activities and products that had a negative impact on the environment, and it served as a catalyst for a decade of environmental action on the local, national, and international levels.

The brainchild of Sen. Gaylord Nelson of Wisconsin, conservationists in Congress, Environmental Action, Inc., an organization made up of a small cadre of young people based in Washington, and thousands of volunteers in schools, colleges, and communities across the country helped organize and promote Earth Day. The purpose of the event was to increase public awareness of pollution and other ecological problems that threatened the earth's habitability. The Earth Day manifesto declared:

> Earth Day is a commitment to make life better, not just bigger and faster, to provide real rather than rhetorical solutions. . . . It is a day to re-examine the ethic of individual progress at mankind's expense—a day to challenge the corporate and governmental leaders who promise change, but who shortchange the necessary programs. . . . April 22 seeks a future worth living. (Quoted in the *New York Times,* April 21, 1970, p. 36)

Senator Nelson came up with the idea shortly after a series of November 1969 national demonstrations protesting the Vietnam War. He believed that if public sentiment could be galvanized on a negative theme, it could be mobilized even more forcefully toward the positive goal of an improved environment.

The principal organizers later claimed that Earth Day was "the largest organized demonstration in human history—with as many as fifteen hundred colleges, ten thousand schools, and an estimated twenty million people around the nation participating in various activities, marches, and demonstrations, including the closing of New York City's Fifth Avenue to automobile traffic so that a hundred thousand people could hear speeches on environmental topics" (Dewey, 250). Congress adjourned for the day and a 12-hour demonstration at the Washington Monument attracted as many as 100,000 people.

A group of participants celebrate the first Earth Day on April 22, 1970. An estimated 20 million people participated in rallies, concerts, and workshops across the nation in an effort to raise awareness about the environment. Earth Day has been celebrated annually ever since. (Hulton Archive/Getty Images)

Conclusion: Environmental Legislation at the Turn of the Decade

The success of the 1960s' environmental movement is reflected in the rash of environmental legislation approved by Congress from the late 1960s to the early 1970s. These laws included the Land and Water Conservation Fund Act (1965), the first Endangered Species Act (1966), the Wild and Scenic Rivers Act (1968) that aimed to protect the natural characteristics of streams that had outstanding scenic, recreational, historic, scientific, or cultural values, and the National Trails Act (1968). In addition to this more traditional preservation-related legislation, Congress, with increasing public pressure and awareness of environmental problems, also passed the Water Quality Act (1965), the Solid Waste Disposal Act (1965), and the Clean Air Act (1965). In 1968 the Sierra Club also won its decade-long battle with the Bureau of Reclamation to defeat the Grand Canyon dams bill with the support of a Congress and administration sensitized to wilderness preservation and environmental concerns. However, by the end of Johnson's term, his activist stance on environmental issues dissipated as the Vietnam War took his focus away from his domestic agenda.

The immediate legacy of the 1960s' environmental movement can be seen in the increased amount of attention the environment received from policymakers, legislators, and the Executive Branch in the early 1970s. Because the movement successfully raised public awareness about the immediate threat to the nation's natural resources and beauty, politicians had little choice but to respond. Even President Nixon, who had shown little interest in the environment during the 1968 campaign, recognized that the environment had become an immensely popular issue Republicans could not afford to abandon to the Democrats. The following are some examples of politicians' responses in the early 1970s to the environmental movement's demand for increased federal regulation:

- Senator Muskie's Clean Air Act Amendments of 1970, which finally gave federal officials ultimate authority, responsibility, and direct enforcement power for air-pollution problems throughout the nation and provided for the setting of federal emissions and air-quality standards that the states would have to meet.

- The creation of the Environmental Protection Agency (EPA) in 1970, which brought together most federal programs related to pollution and many of those related to other environmental issues that had previously been divided among various federal departments and agencies. This created a larger, more powerful federal umbrella agency covering most environmental matters.

- The Clean Water Act of 1972, amending the Federal Water Pollution Control Act of 1948, strengthened earlier legislation aimed at preventing or reducing water pollution and laid the foundation for future efforts to preserve the nation's wetlands.

- The second Endangered Species Act of 1973 committed the federal government "to conserve to the extent practicable the various species of fish or wildlife and plants facing extinction." The debate and enforcement of this act has often pitted the rights of property owners and other financially interested parties against environmentalists fighting for the preservation of endangered species. The fight to protect the endangered snail darter (a rare species of perch) on the Little Tennessee River and the spotted owl in the forests of the Northwest to the detriment of local industry are but two examples used by opponents to exemplify the absurdity of the act's enforcement. However, the act also has a history of success as ospreys, brown pelicans, bald eagles, and peregrine falcons have all moved from the brink of extinction as a result of the act's enforcement.

- DDT was outlawed in 1972 after the public accepted the growing scientific case against its use.

Between 1950 and 1970, the U.S. population grew by 37 percent, to 200 million people, and the gross domestic product rose by more than 50 percent in real, inflation-adjusted dollars. A doubling of gross energy consumption and the generation of massive amounts of air and water pollutants and other toxic chemicals accompanied these gains with adverse effects on human health and the environment. With the publication of Rachel Carson's *Silent Spring* in 1962, the American public started to pay attention to these adverse effects. The 10 years that followed the book's publication witnessed the burgeoning environmental movement and aforementioned increased federal oversight of the nation's natural resources, wilderness, and wildlife. Concerns over how human behavior and industry's economic interests have negatively affected the environment persist as the debate over such issues as global warming reflects ongoing worries about the future of the earth's habitability. Several of the environmental organizations and groups that found a voice in the 1960s remain at the center of this critically important fight for a healthy and sustainable environment.

BIOGRAPHIES

David Brower, 1912–2000

Environmental Activist

During Brower's tenure as the first executive director of the Sierra Club (1952–1969), the Sierra Club's membership rose from 2,000 to 84,000. He resigned from his position in 1969 after members complained about his management style. In 1969 he founded Friends of the Earth along with the League of Conservation Voters and initiated the founding of independent Friends of the Earth, which operated in 63 countries at the time of his death in 2000. Through the years, Brower helped to create national parks and seashores in Kings Canyon, the North Cascades, the Redwoods, Great Basin, Alaska, Cape Cod, Fire Island, and Point Reyes. He also played a major role in keeping dams out of Dinosaur National Monument, the Yukon, and the Grand Canyon, and in establishing the National Wilderness Preservation

David Brower was founder of the Earth Island Institute, Friends of the Earth, and a leading member of the Sierra Club. (Tom Turner)

System. In 1982, Brower founded the Earth Island Institute, an organization that worked to bring peace, environmental, and social justice together. He was nominated for the Nobel Peace Prize three times. Frustrated with the Sierra Club's passivity in fighting threats to the environment, he resigned from its board in 2000 just before he died.

Rachel Louise Carson, 1907–1964

Writer

A marine biologist who had earned her master's degree in zoology from Johns Hopkins University in 1932, Rachel Carson was also an established author who wrote radio scripts and publications for the U.S. Fish and Wildlife Service and popular books and articles on marine biology, earning her a National Book Award in 1952. Carson helped launch the modern environmental movement with the publication of her book, *Silent Spring,* in 1962. The book drew attention to the effects of chemical pesticides and focused on the ecological impacts of human action. After she helped shape the pesticide report issued by the Kennedy administration's Science Advisory Committee in 1963, Carson died of cancer in 1964.

Barry Commoner, 1917–

Eco-socialist

Born in Brooklyn, Commoner received his bachelor's degree from Columbia University (1937) and his master's and doctoral degrees from Harvard University (1938, 1941). After serving as a lieutenant in the U.S. Navy during World War II, Commoner became a professor of plant physiology at Washington University in St. Louis, where he taught for 34 years. He became a renowned cellular biologist and helped initiate the modern environmental movement. During the 1950s he became concerned over the environmental effects of radioactive fallout from nuclear weapons testing in the Nevada desert. While trying to research the possible health risks from such testing, he discovered that much of the data were classified and unavailable for analysis. As a result, he formed the St. Louis Committee for Nuclear Information, which gathered its own data for research. The Committee for Nuclear Information did an analysis of children's baby teeth that demonstrated that nuclear testing did in fact cause radioactive buildup in humans. This research contributed to the implementation of the 1963 nuclear test-ban treaty that phased out atmospheric nuclear testing. During the 1960s Commoner broadened his study to pollution and ozone-layer depletion. Among other things, he was one of the first who advocated the use of solar and other types of renewable energy. In 1966 he established the Washington University Center for the Biology of Natural Systems to study humans' relationship with the environment. He garnered a lot of attention when in 1968 he declared Lake Erie had "died" as a result of contamination from chemical and industrial waste. In a 1970 cover story, *Time* magazine called him the "Paul Revere of Ecology." In 1971 he published *The Closing Circle,* which examined the high environmental cost to American technological development. In that book he recounted his four laws of ecology: 1) Everything is connected to everything else; 2) Everything must go somewhere; 3) Nature knows best; 4) There is no such thing as a free lunch. In 1980 he unsuccessfully ran for president under the banner of the Citizen's Party.

Paul Ehrlich, 1932–

Professor of Population Studies

After earning his Ph.D. in 1957, Ehrlich joined the Biology Department at Stanford in 1959, earning the rank of full professor in 1966. Although the author of numerous books and articles on ecology, entomology, and other subjects, he is best known for his book, *The Population Bomb* (1968), written at the suggestion of David Brower after Ehrlich had written an article about overpopulation in the *New Scientist* magazine where he predicted the world would suffer from a series of catastrophic famines between 1970 and 1985 due to population growth and the exhaustion of natural resources. He predicted that hundreds of millions of people would starve to death as a result of these famines. After a chorus of criticisms from the scientific community, some of his dire predictions were removed in the 1971 edition of the book. Ehrlich founded the Zero Population Growth organization in 1968, along with Richard Bowers and Charles Remington. Many credit *The Population Bomb* and the Zero Population Growth movement with raising awareness about the problems associated with overpopulation and the need for making controls on reproduction more easily available. Critics point to his dubious predictions of uncontrollable famines, declining life expectancies, and increasing food prices to discredit him and other environmental theorists as alarmists who base their conclusions on pseudo-science. Ehrlich's predicted famines never materialized.

Edmund Muskie, 1914–1996

Senator

A graduate from Bates College (1936) and Cornell University Law School (1939), Muskie became governor of Maine in 1954 after serving as a lieutenant in the Navy during World War II and serving in the Maine House of Representatives for four years. Largely responsible for revitalizing the Democratic Party in Republican-dominated Maine, Muskie defeated incumbent Republican senator

Senator Edmund Muskie of Maine, circa 1966, was one of the first politicians to actively support legislation aimed at protecting the environment. (Library of Congress)

Frederick Payne in 1958 for a seat in the U.S. Senate. He was reelected in 1964, 1970, and 1976. During the 1960s he became the first active environmentalist in Congress, earning the nickname "Mr. Clean." He became the leading author and advocate for new and stronger measures to curb pollution and provide a cleaner environment. He ran for vice president in 1968. Perceived as the leading contender for the 1972 Democratic Presidential nomination, his campaign faltered after an emotional defense of his wife in response to the *Manchester Union-Leader* attacking her character. He later served as secretary of state in 1980 as a part of Jimmy Carter's administration.

Ralph Nader, 1934–

Political Activist

After graduating from Princeton University (1955) and Harvard Law School (1958), Ralph Nader served in the U.S. Army for six months in 1959 and then practiced law in Hartford, Connecticut. He taught history and government at the University of Hartford from 1961 to 1963. In 1964, Nader moved to Washington, D.C., where he got a job working for Assistant Secretary of Labor Daniel Patrick Moynihan. In the 1960s he developed his reputation as a consumer-protection activist after he published *Unsafe at Any Speed* (1965), an exposé of the American automobile industry. Hundreds of young activists, inspired by Nader's work, came to Washington, D.C., to help him investigate other projects; they became known as "Nader's Raiders." Led by Nader, they investigated governmental and corporate corruption and published dozens of reports. Several of these reports focused on the environment: *Vanishing Air* (air pollution), *The Water Lords* (water pollution), *Destroy the Forest* (destruction of global ecosystem). His consumer protection and environmental advocacy played a significant role in the establishment of several governmental agencies charged with the oversight of corporate practices that threaten the environment and consumers' health. Nader unsuccessfully ran for president in 1992, 1996, 2000, 2004, and 2008. He ran on the Green Party ticket in 1996 and 2000.

Gaylord Nelson, 1916–2005

Environmentalist

With a bachelor's degree from San Jose State College (1939) and law degree from the University of Wisconsin (1942), Nelson served as a first lieutenant in the Army during World War II and fought in the Battle of Okinawa. After serving in the Wisconsin state Senate for 10 years, he was elected governor of Wisconsin in 1958. In 1962, he won a seat in the U.S. Senate, where he served from 1963 until 1981. Throughout the 1960s he searched for ways to focus public attention on the environment. In 1963, he convinced President John Kennedy to take a nationwide conservation tour where he talked about the need to conserve natural resources. The tour through Pennsylvania, Michigan, Minnesota, Wisconsin, Wyoming, Utah, Washington, and California, however, did not receive a lot of media coverage. Searching for another way to promote environmental concerns, Nelson gained inspiration from antiwar protests, particularly the teach-ins, to come up with the idea of Earth Day. Nelson raised funds and wrote letters to all 50 governors and the mayors of major cities asking them to issue Earth Day Proclamations. He also promoted the event through college newspapers and *Scholastic Magazine,* a publication sent to most high schools and grade schools throughout the country. The first Earth Day, held on April 22, 1970, was a major success with an estimated 20 million people around the world participating in educational activities and community events concerning environmental protection. In addition to founding Earth Day, Nelson produced a legislative record that demonstrated his commitment to the environment. As Wisconsin's governor he created the Outdoor Recreation Acquisition Program that aimed to acquire one million acres of Wisconsin parkland, wetlands, and other open space with a penny-a-pack tax on cigarettes. In the U.S. Senate, he authored legislation to preserve the 2,100-mile Appalachian Trail corridor and to create a national hiking trails system. He also sponsored or cosponsored several conservation bills, including the Wilderness Act and the Alaska Lands Act. He became a counselor for the Wilderness Society in 1981 after he lost his seat in the Senate.

Gary Snyder, 1930–

Poet

Raised in Washington and Oregon, Snyder went to Reed College in 1947 where he published his first poems in a student journal. After graduating with a degree in anthropology and literature, Snyder worked as a timber-scaler on the Warm Springs Indian Reservation and gained experiences that inspired much of his early poetry. He later worked as a fire-lookout in a national park, converted to Buddhism, and adopted a more Eastern perspective on nature. After a semester of graduate study in anthropology at Indiana University, Snyder dropped out, began practicing self-taught Zen meditation, and moved to San Francisco to write poetry. In 1953 he enrolled at the University of California–Berkeley to study Asian culture and languages. During this time he became friends with Allen Ginsberg and Jack Kerouac, providing the inspiration for Kerouac's novel *The Dharma Bums*. Snyder published *Riprap,* a book about his experiences as a forest lookout and on a trail crew in Yosemite, in 1959. Snyder spent much of the 1960s in Japan studying Zen Buddhism. During this time, he published two collections of poetry: *Myths & Texts* (1960) and *Six Sections from Mountains and Rivers Without End* (1965). For some of this time he lived on Suwanose, a small Japanese island, with a group of Japanese naturalists. His collections of poetry, *The Back Country* (1968) and *Regarding Wave* (1969), published after his return to the San Francisco area, reflected the counterculture's emphasis on relationships and community. His work in the 1970s, particularly his Pulitzer Prize–winning *Turtle Island* (1974), cemented his reputation as a back-to-the-land environmentalist and icon of the 1960s and 1970s burgeoning environmental movement.

REFERENCES AND FURTHER READINGS

Baldwin, Malcolm Forbes. 1989. "The Federal Government's Role in the Management of Private Rural Land." In *Governmental and Environmental Politics: Essays on Historical Developments Since World War II*. Baltimore: Johns Hopkins University Press.

Bosso, Christopher. 2005. *Environment, Inc.: From Grassroots to Beltway*. Lawrence: University Press of Kansas.

Brower, David. 1990. "The Meaning of Wilderness in Science." In *For Earth's Sake,* 271–272. Salt Lake City: Peregrine Smith.

Caldwell, Lynton K. 1997. "Implementing NEPA: A Non-Technical Political Task." In *Environmental Policy and NEPA: Past, Present, and Future*. Boca Raton: St. Lucie Press.

Chafe, William H. 2003. *The Unfinished Journey: America since World War II*. 5th ed. New York: Oxford University Press.

Clark, Ray. 1997. "NEPA: The Rational Approach to Change." In *Environmental Policy and NEPA: Past, Present, and Future*. Boca Raton: St. Lucie Press.

Dewey, Scott Hamilton. 2000. *Don't Breathe the Air: Air Pollution and U.S. Environmental Politics, 1945–1970*. College Station: Texas A&M University Press.

Dunlap, Thomas R. 1978. "Science as a Guide in Regulating Technology: The Case of DDT in the United States." *Social Studies of Science* 8, no. 3: 265–285.

Ehrlich, Paul R. 1968. *The Population Bomb*. New York: Ballantine Books.

Farber, David, and Beth Bailey. 2001. *The Columbia Guide to America in the 1960s*. New York: Columbia University Press.

Gottlieb, Robert. 1993. *Forcing the Spring: The Transformation of the American Environmental Movement*. Washington, DC: Island Press.

Gregg, Frank. 1989. "Public Land Policy: Controversial Beginnings for the Third Century." In *Governmental and Environmental Politics: Essays on Historical Developments Since World War II*. Baltimore: Johns Hopkins University Press.

Hays, Samuel P. 2000. *A History of Environmental Politics since 1945*. Pittsburgh: University of Pittsburgh Press.

Jamison, Andrew. 2001. *The Making of Green Knowledge: Environmental Politics and Cultural Transformation*. New York: Cambridge University Press.

McCormick, John. 1989. *Reclaiming Paradise: The Global Environmental Movement*. Bloomington: Indiana University Press.

Mitchell, Robert Cameron. 1989. "From Conservation to Environmental Politics: The Historical Context." In *Governmental and Environmental Politics: Essays on Historical Developments Since World War II*. Baltimore: Johns Hopkins University Press.

Nash, Roderick Frazier. 1990. *American Environmentalism: Readings in Conservation History*. 3rd ed. New York: McGraw-Hill.

Nash, Roderick Frazier. 1989. *The Rights of Nature: A History of Environmental Ethics*. Madison, WI: The University of Wisconsin Press.

National Environmental Policy Act, 1969.

Neimark, Peninah, and Peter Rhoades Mott, eds. 1999. *The Environmental Debate: A Documentary History*. Westport, CT: Greenwood Press.

Reich, Charles A. 1970. *The Greening of America*. New York: Random House.

Sanders, Jeff. 2001. "Environmentalism." In *The Columbia Guide to America in the 1960s*. New York: Columbia University Press.

Sax, Joseph L. 1989. "Parks, Wilderness, and Recreation." In *Governmental and Environmental Politics: Essays on Historical Developments Since World War II*. Baltimore: Johns Hopkins University Press.

Scheffer, Victor B. 1991. *The Shaping of Environmentalism in America*. Seattle: University of Washington Press.

Schroeder, Christopher. 1989. "The Evolution of Federal Regulation of Toxic Substances." In *Governmental and Environmental Politics: Essays on Historical Developments Since World War II*. Baltimore: Johns Hopkins University Press.

Smythe, Robert B. 1997. "The Historical Roots of NEPA." In *Environmental Policy and NEPA: Past, Present, and Future*. Boca Raton: St. Lucie Press.

Snyder, Gary. 1969. *Earth House Hold*. New York: New Directions Publishing Company.

Switzer, Jacqueline Vaughn. 2001. *Environmental Politics: Domestic and Global Dimensions*. Belmont, CA: Bedford/St. Martin's.

Weiner, Kenneth S. 1997. "Basic Purposes and Policies of the NEPA Regulations." In *Environmental Policy and NEPA: Past, Present, and Future*. Boca Raton: St. Lucie Press.

People and Events in the 20th Century

THE 1900s

THE 1910s

THE 1920s

The 1930s

THE 1940s

THE 1950S

THE 1960s

THE 1970s

THE 1980s

THE 1990s

1960s Index

About the Author

Troy D. Paino earned his JD from Indiana University School of Law—Indianapolis and his PhD in American Studies from Michigan State University. He has written primarily on the 20th century social and cultural history of American sport. He is currently the provost, vice president of academic affairs, and professor of history at Truman State University.